BAKA

CRAZY FOR DOGS

14

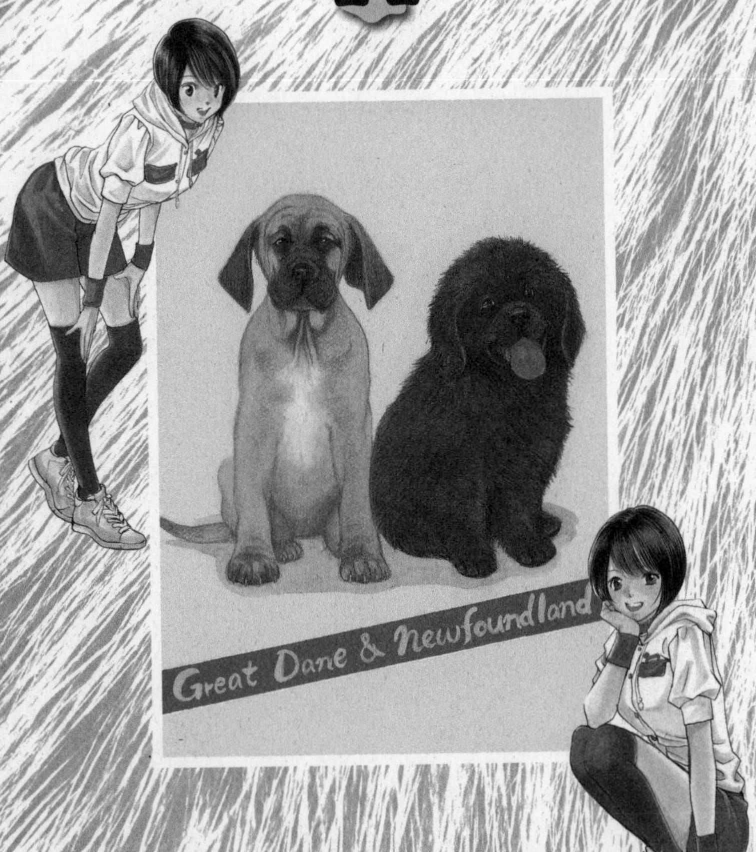
Great Dane & Newfoundland

YUKIYA SAKURAGI

Contents

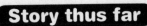

Teppei is the manager of the recently opened pet shop Woofles. He intended to breed his black Labrador Noa with a champion dog, but instead Noa was "taken advantage of" by an unknown and unfixed male dog!

The unknown dog's owner was Suguri Miyauchi, and her dog was a mutt named Lupin. Suguri is now working at Woofles to make up for her dog's actions.

Suguri's enthusiasm is more than a little unique. She has eaten dog food (and said it was tasty), caught dog poop with her bare hands, and caused dogs to have "happy pee" in her presence. Teppei is starting to realize that Suguri is indeed a very special girl.

The first generation of Woofles puppies had their first birthdays and graduated from the puppy-training class! By now they should have mastered basic behavior techniques. To test them, Suguri and her friends plan a trip to a cottage that welcomes pets. Though Suguri is initially worried that Teppei might not approve of her missing work, he is all for the idea. So Suguri and Woofles regulars Chizuru, Akiba and Kim head with their dogs to the Wink Dog Pension. Its wide-open spaces surpass everyone's expectations. Suguri and her friends are on cloud nine when four enormous dogs suddenly appear, blocking their path. Their sheer size is intimidating, but are they as scary as they look?

CHARACTERS

Suguri Miyauchi

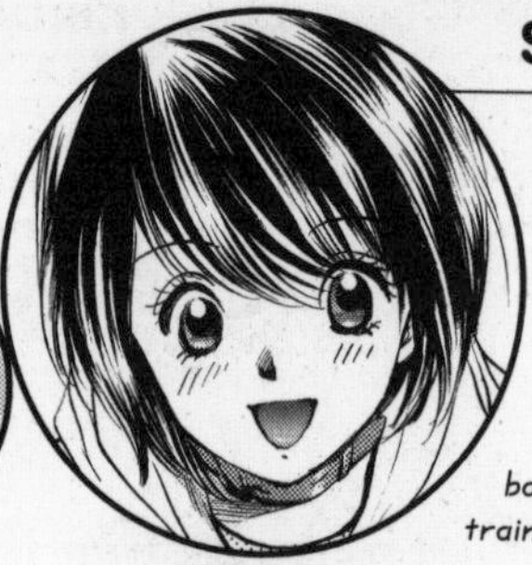

She seems to possess an almost supernatural connection with dogs. When she approaches them they often urinate with great excitement! She is crazy for dogs and can catch their droppings with her bare hands. She is currently a trainee at the Woofles Pet Shop.

Lupin

♂ Mutt (mongrel)

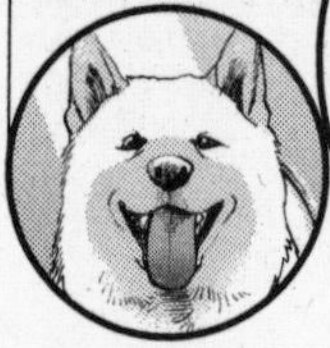

Teppei Iida

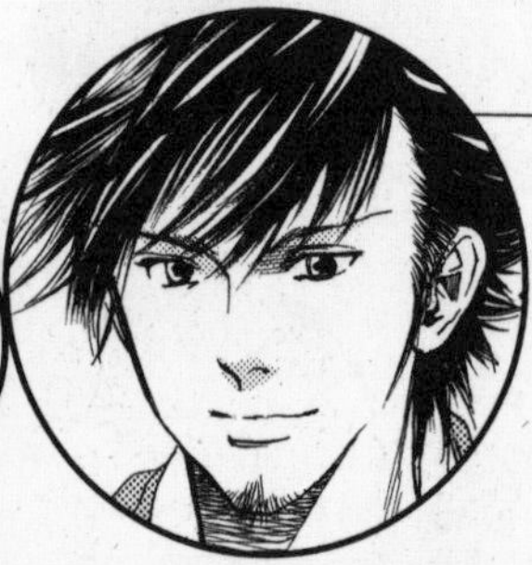

Manager of the recently opened pet shop Woofles. He is aware of Suguri's special ability and has hired her to work in his shop.

Noa

♀ Labrador retriever

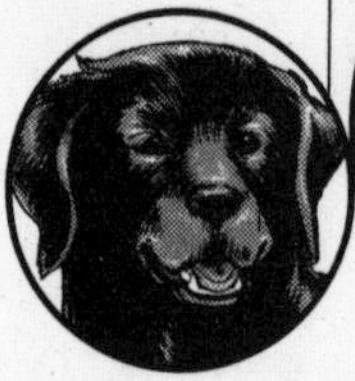

Momoko Takeuchi

The Woofles Pet Shop (second location) pet groomer. At first she had many problems and rarely smiled. But after meeting Suguri she's changed, and the two are now best friends.

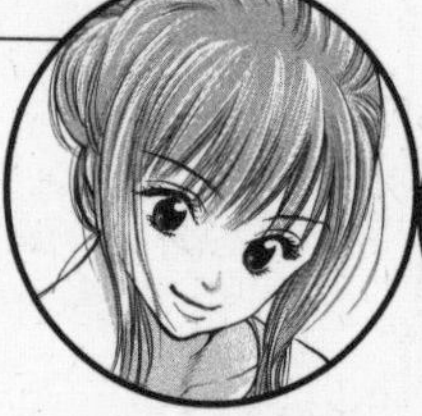

Mel

♀ Toy poodle

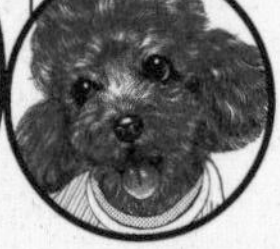

Show Kaneko

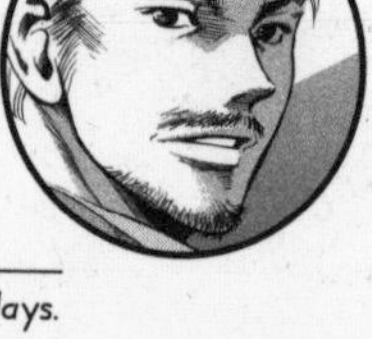

He is the manager of the main Woofles store and is Teppei's boss. He is very passionate about the business and makes TV appearances from time to time.

Kentaro Osada

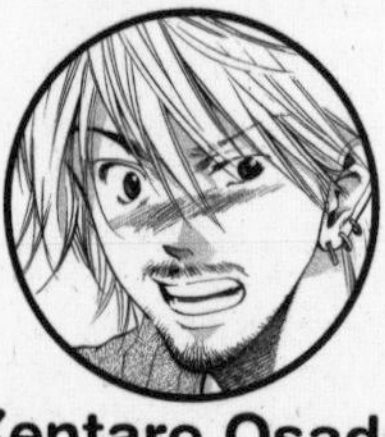

Teppei's buddy from their high school days. He's on the staff at Woofles' second store.

Chizuru Sawamura

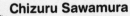

Adopted a Chihuahua, Melon, after her longtime pet golden retriever, Ricky, alerted her that Melon was ill. She works at a hostess bar to repay Melon's medical fees.

Melon

♂ *Chihuahua*

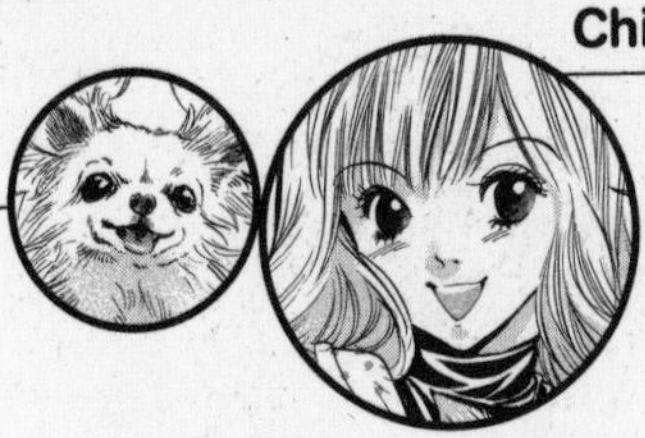

Kanako Mori

Teaches piano on the second floor of the same building as Woofles. She was depressed over the loss of her beloved dog Czerny, but meeting her new dog brought a smile to her face.

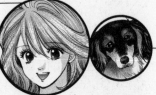

Sonata

♂ *Miniature dachshund*

Hiroshi Akiba

Pop-idol otaku turned dog otaku. His dream is to publish a photo collection of his dog, Zidane. He is a government employee.

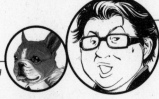

Zidane

♂ *French bulldog*

Mari Yamashita

A model whose nickname is Yamarin. She decided to keep an unsold papillon, Lucky, which was her costar in a bread commercial.

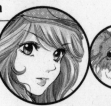

Lucky

♂ *Papillon*

Kim Hyeon-Jun

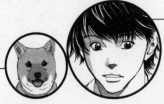

An international student who had a phobia of dogs. He has been working hard to get over it in order to get close to Suguri, whom he has a crush on.

Chanta

♀ *Shiba*

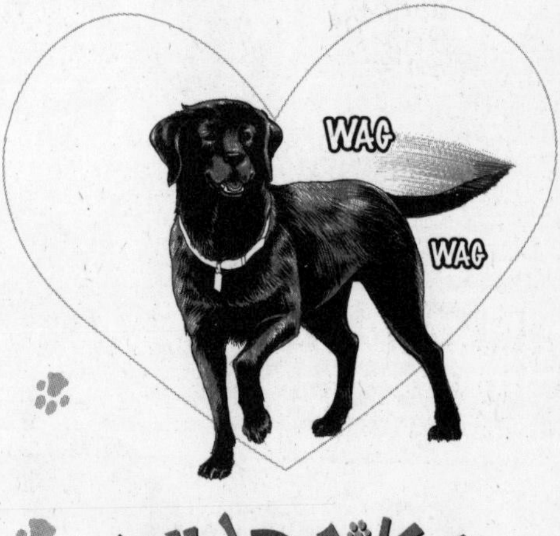
WAG
WAG

INUBAKA

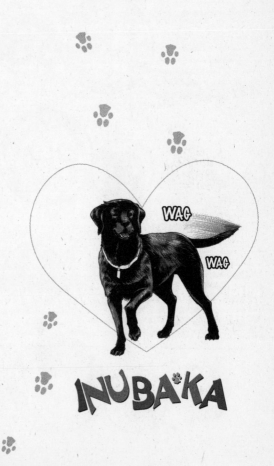

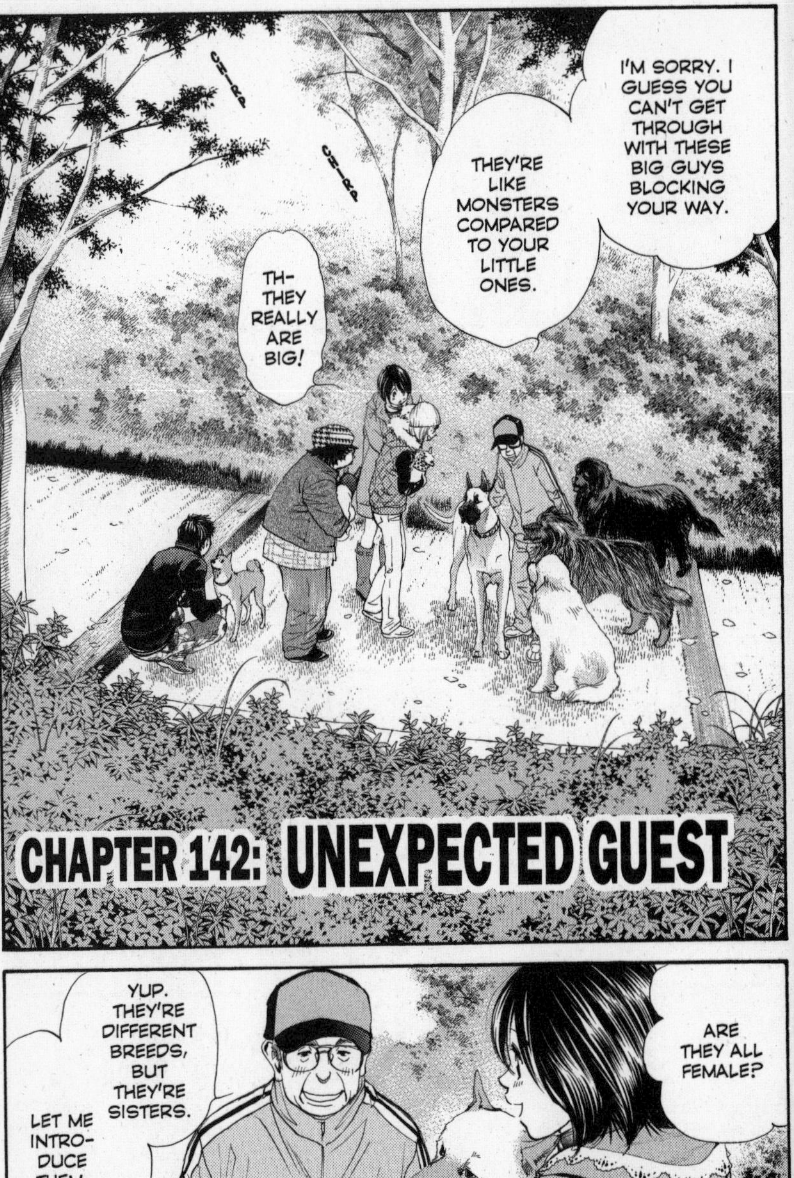
I'M SORRY. I GUESS YOU CAN'T GET THROUGH WITH THESE BIG GUYS BLOCKING YOUR WAY.
THEY'RE LIKE MONSTERS COMPARED TO YOUR LITTLE ONES.
CHIRP
CHIRP
TH- THEY REALLY ARE BIG!
CHAPTER 142: UNEXPECTED GUEST
ARE THEY ALL FEMALE?
YUP. THEY'RE DIFFERENT BREEDS, BUT THEY'RE SISTERS.
LET ME INTRO-DUCE THEM.

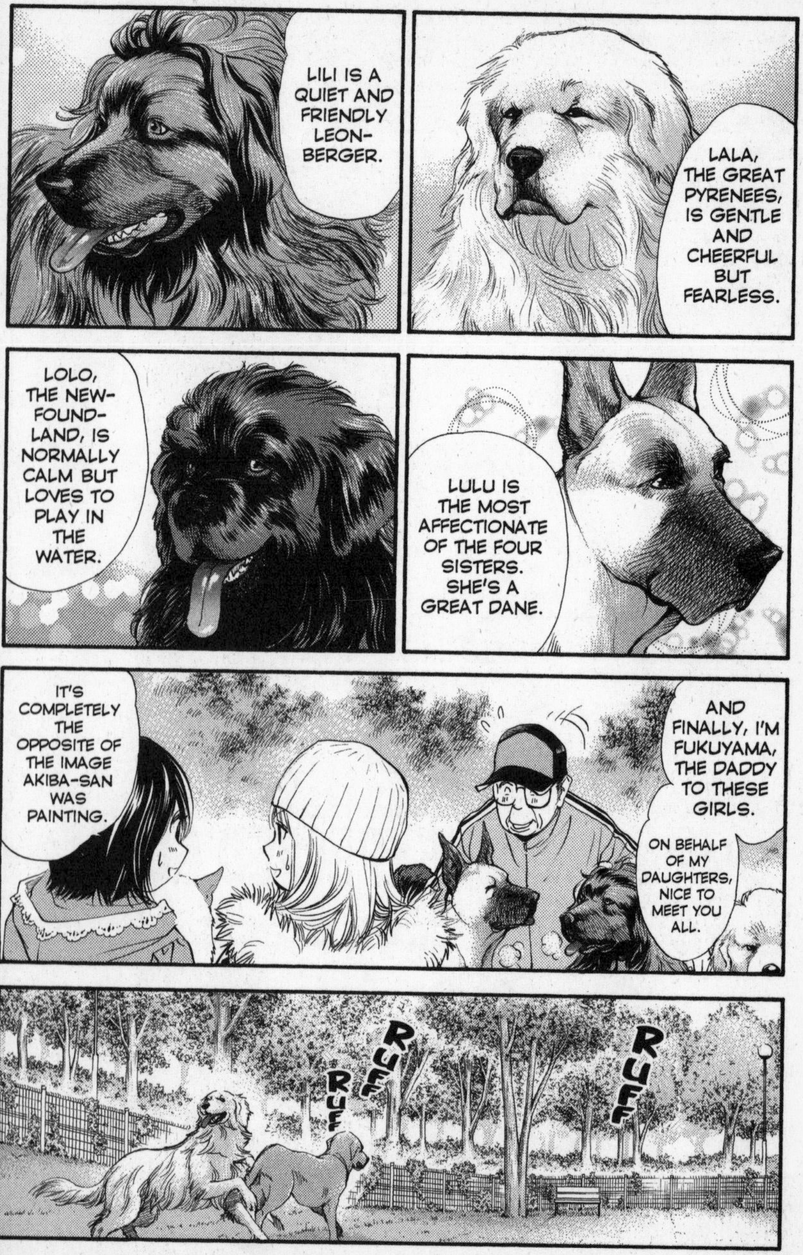
LALA, THE GREAT PYRENEES, IS GENTLE AND CHEERFUL BUT FEARLESS.
LILI IS A QUIET AND FRIENDLY LEON-BERGER.
LULU IS THE MOST AFFECTIONATE OF THE FOUR SISTERS. SHE'S A GREAT DANE.
LOLO, THE NEW-FOUND-LAND, IS NORMALLY CALM BUT LOVES TO PLAY IN THE WATER.
AND FINALLY, I'M FUKUYAMA, THE DADDY TO THESE GIRLS.
ON BEHALF OF MY DAUGHTERS, NICE TO MEET YOU ALL.
IT'S COMPLETELY THE OPPOSITE OF THE IMAGE AKIBA-SAN WAS PAINTING.
RUFF
RUFF
RUFF

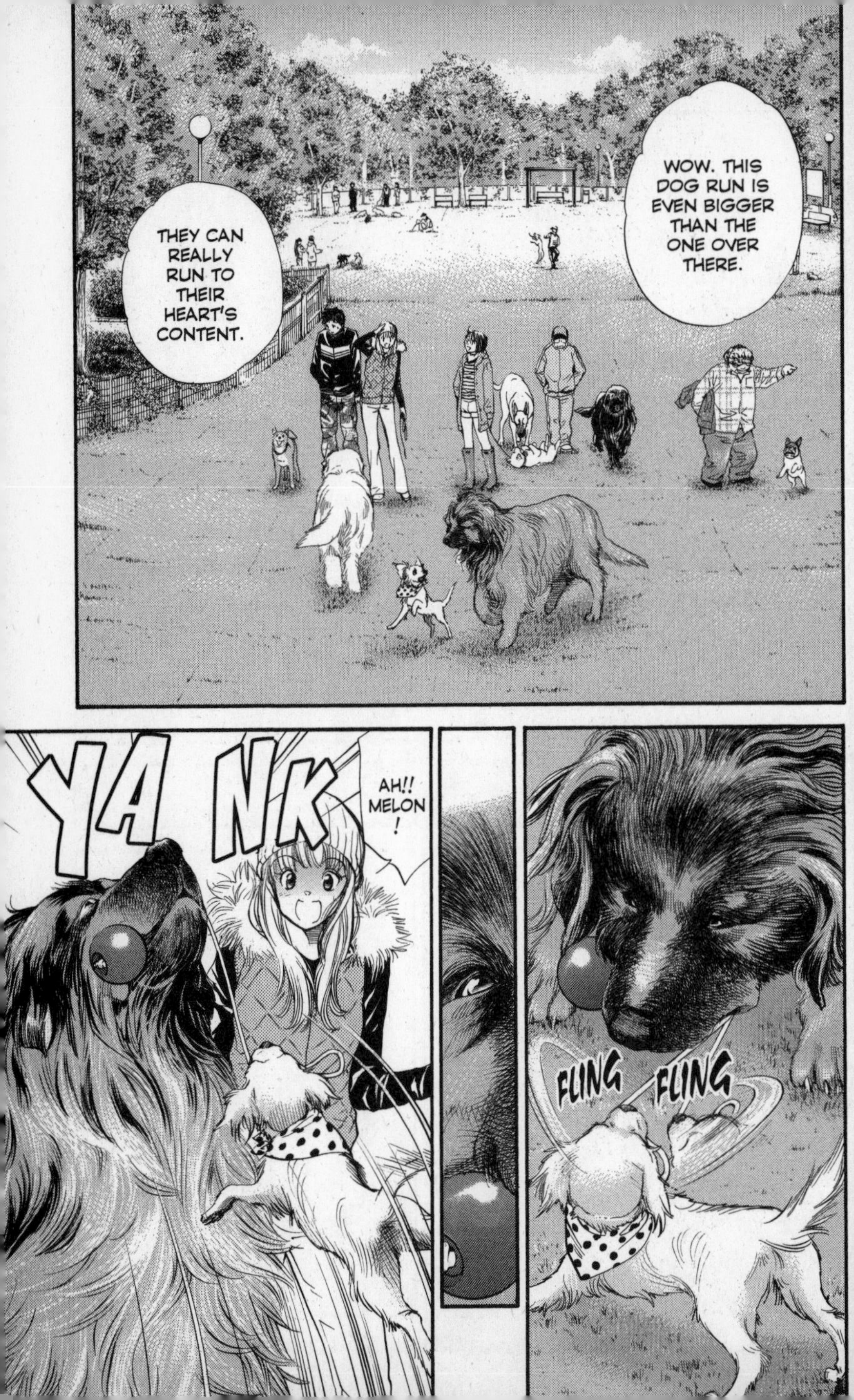
WOW. THIS DOG RUN IS EVEN BIGGER THAN THE ONE OVER THERE.
THEY CAN REALLY RUN TO THEIR HEART'S CONTENT.
FLING FLING
AH!! MELON!
YANK

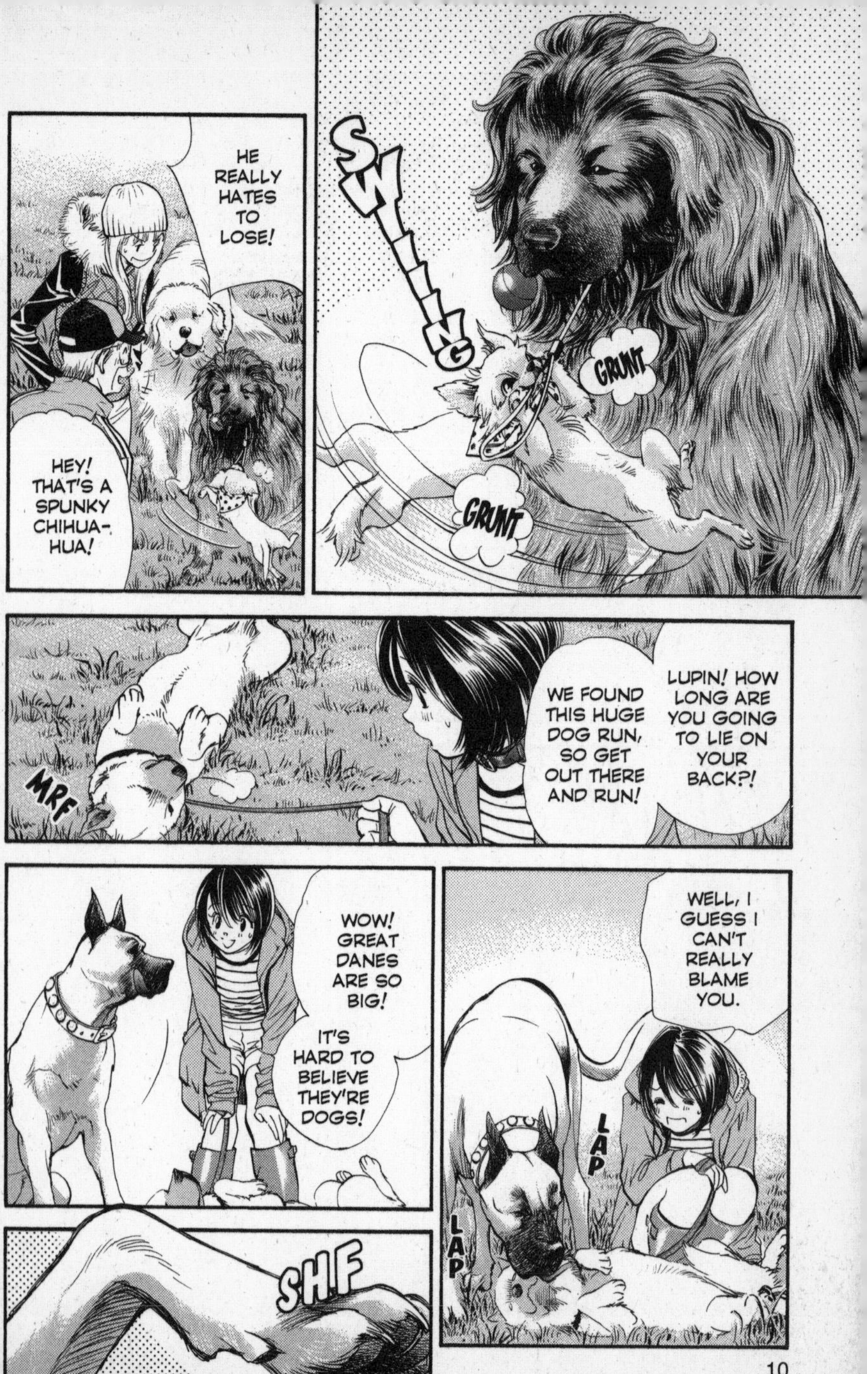
SWING
GRUNT
GRUNT
HE REALLY HATES TO LOSE!
HEY! THAT'S A SPUNKY CHIHUA-HUA!
LUPIN! HOW LONG ARE YOU GOING TO LIE ON YOUR BACK?!
WE FOUND THIS HUGE DOG RUN, SO GET OUT THERE AND RUN!
MRF
WELL, I GUESS I CAN'T REALLY BLAME YOU.
LAP
LAP
WOW! GREAT DANES ARE SO BIG!
IT'S HARD TO BELIEVE THEY'RE DOGS!
SHF

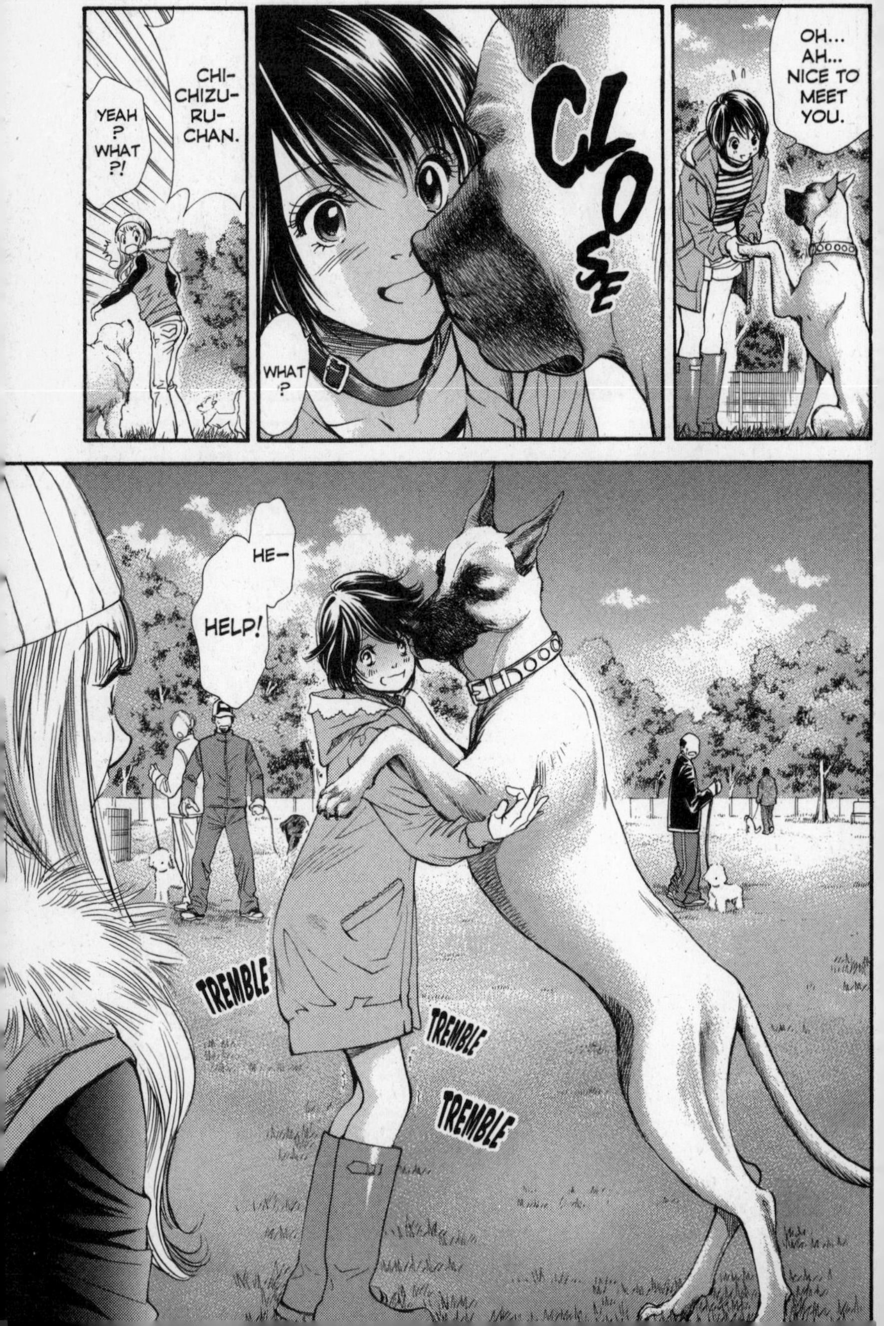
OH... AH... NICE TO MEET YOU.
CLOSE
WHAT?
CHI-CHIZU-RU-CHAN.
YEAH? WHAT?!
HE-
HELP!
TREMBLE
TREMBLE
TREMBLE

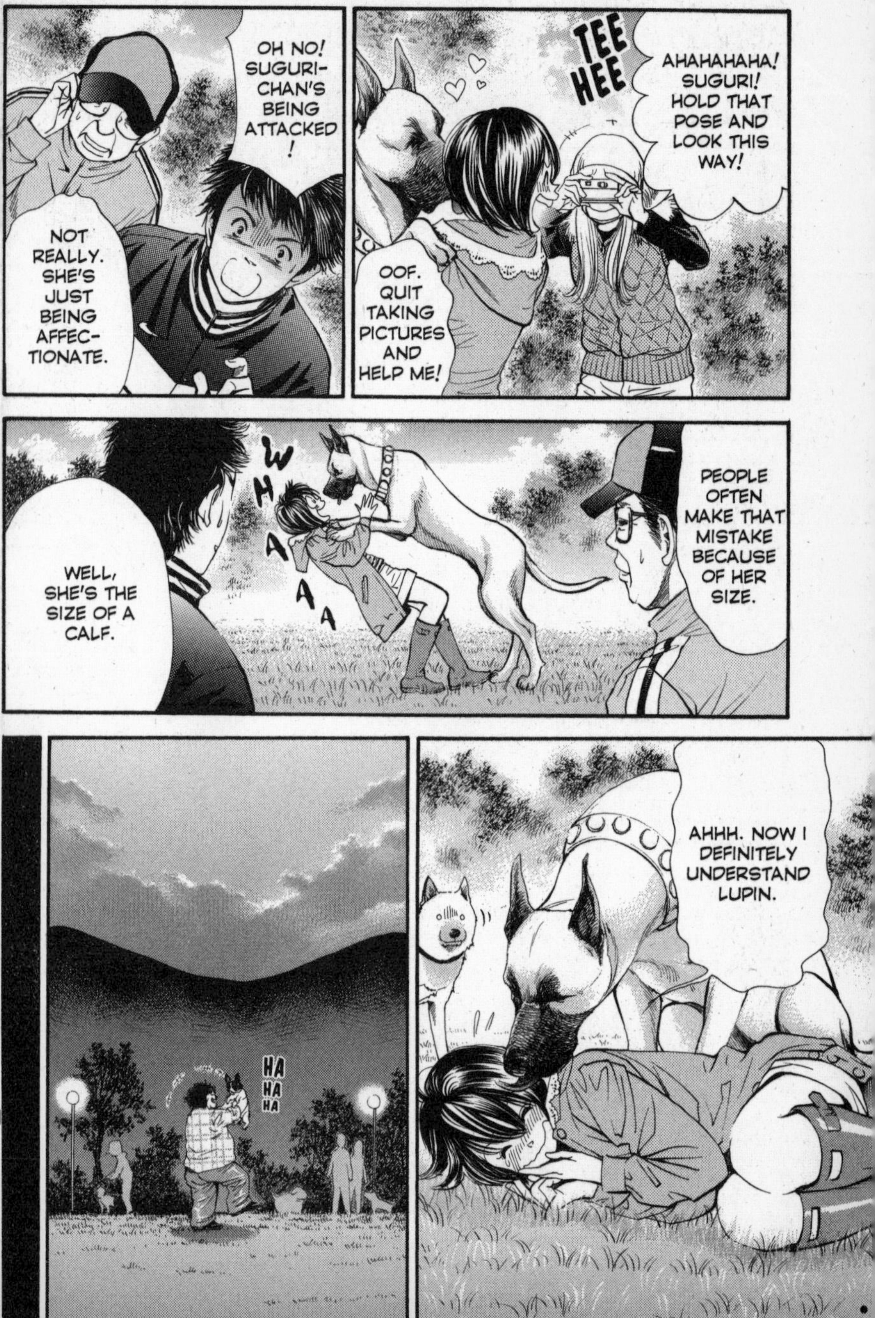
TEE HEE
AHAHAHAHA! SUGURI! HOLD THAT POSE AND LOOK THIS WAY!
OOF. QUIT TAKING PICTURES AND HELP ME!
OH NO! SUGURI-CHAN'S BEING ATTACKED!
NOT REALLY. SHE'S JUST BEING AFFECTIONATE.
PEOPLE OFTEN MAKE THAT MISTAKE BECAUSE OF HER SIZE.
WHAAAA
WELL, SHE'S THE SIZE OF A CALF.
AHHH. NOW I DEFINITELY UNDERSTAND LUPIN.
HA HA HA

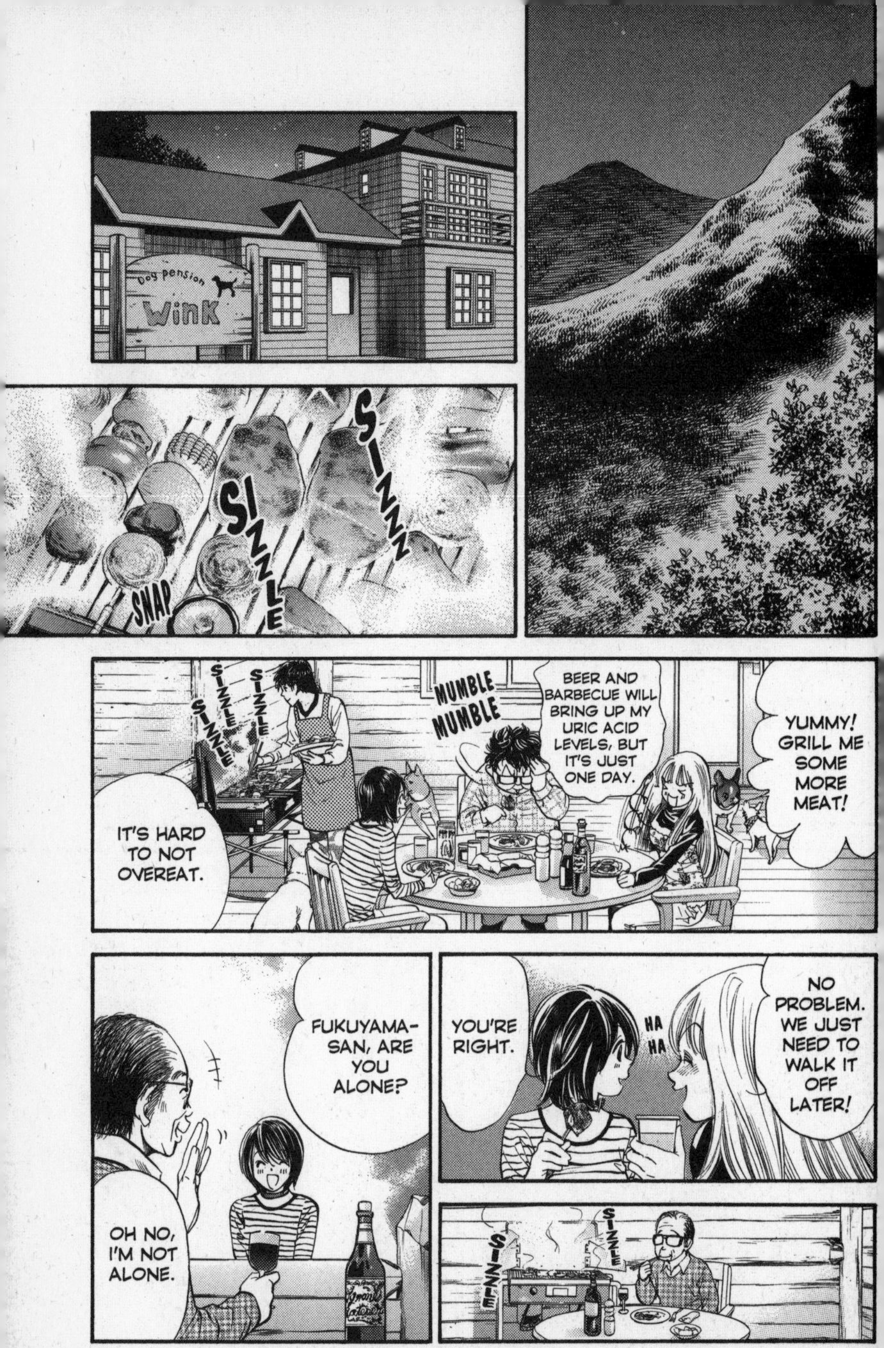
Dog pension
Wink
SIZZZZ
SIZZLE
SNAP
YUMMY! GRILL ME SOME MORE MEAT!
BEER AND BARBECUE WILL BRING UP MY URIC ACID LEVELS, BUT IT'S JUST ONE DAY.
MUMBLE MUMBLE
SIZZLE
SIZZLE
IT'S HARD TO NOT OVEREAT.
NO PROBLEM. WE JUST NEED TO WALK IT OFF LATER!
HA HA
YOU'RE RIGHT.
SIZZLE
SIZZLE
FUKUYAMA-SAN, ARE YOU ALONE?
OH NO, I'M NOT ALONE.

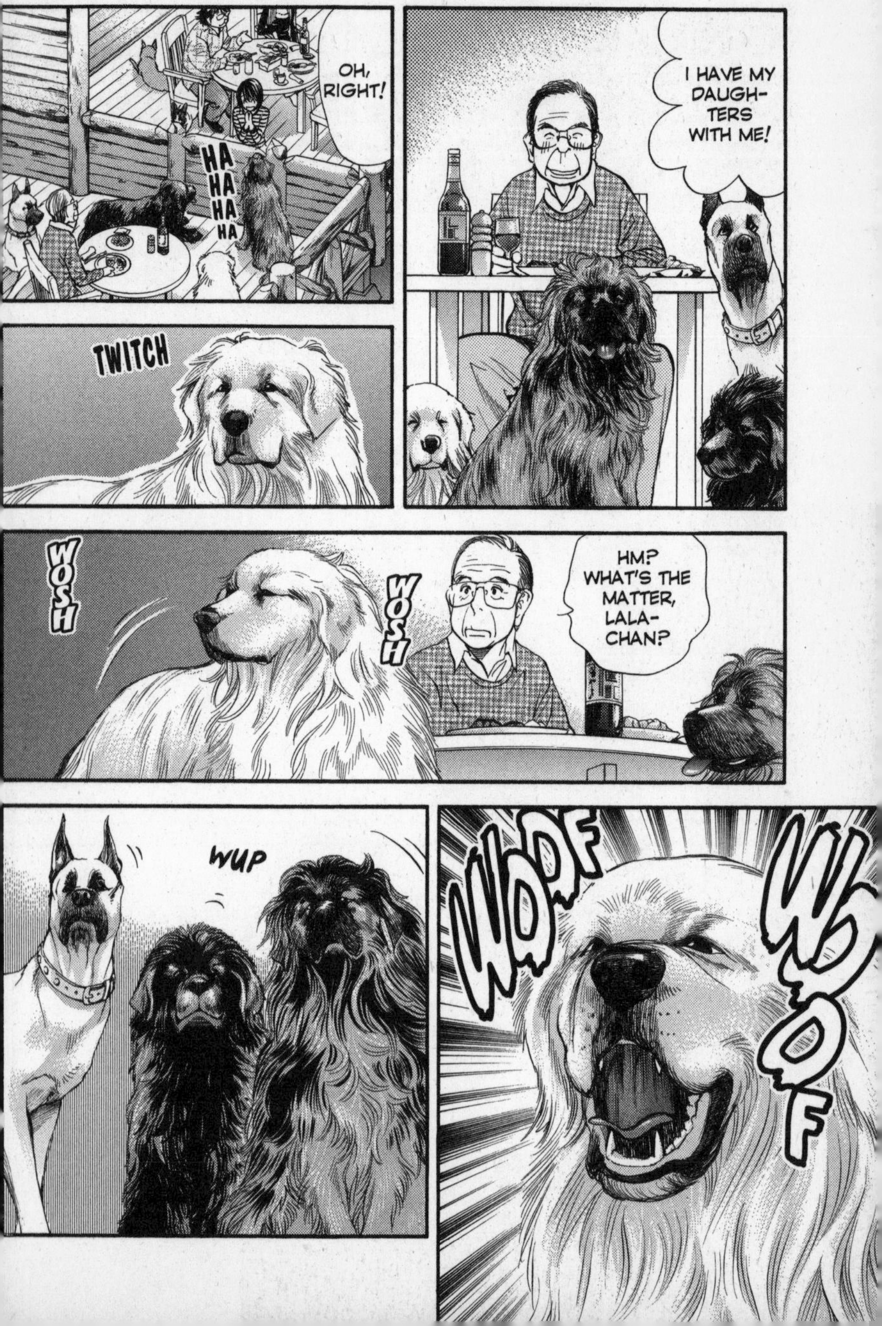
I HAVE MY DAUGH-TERS WITH ME!
OH, RIGHT!
HA HA HA HA HA
TWITCH
WOSH
HM? WHAT'S THE MATTER, LALA-CHAN?
WOSH
WOOF
WOOF
WUP

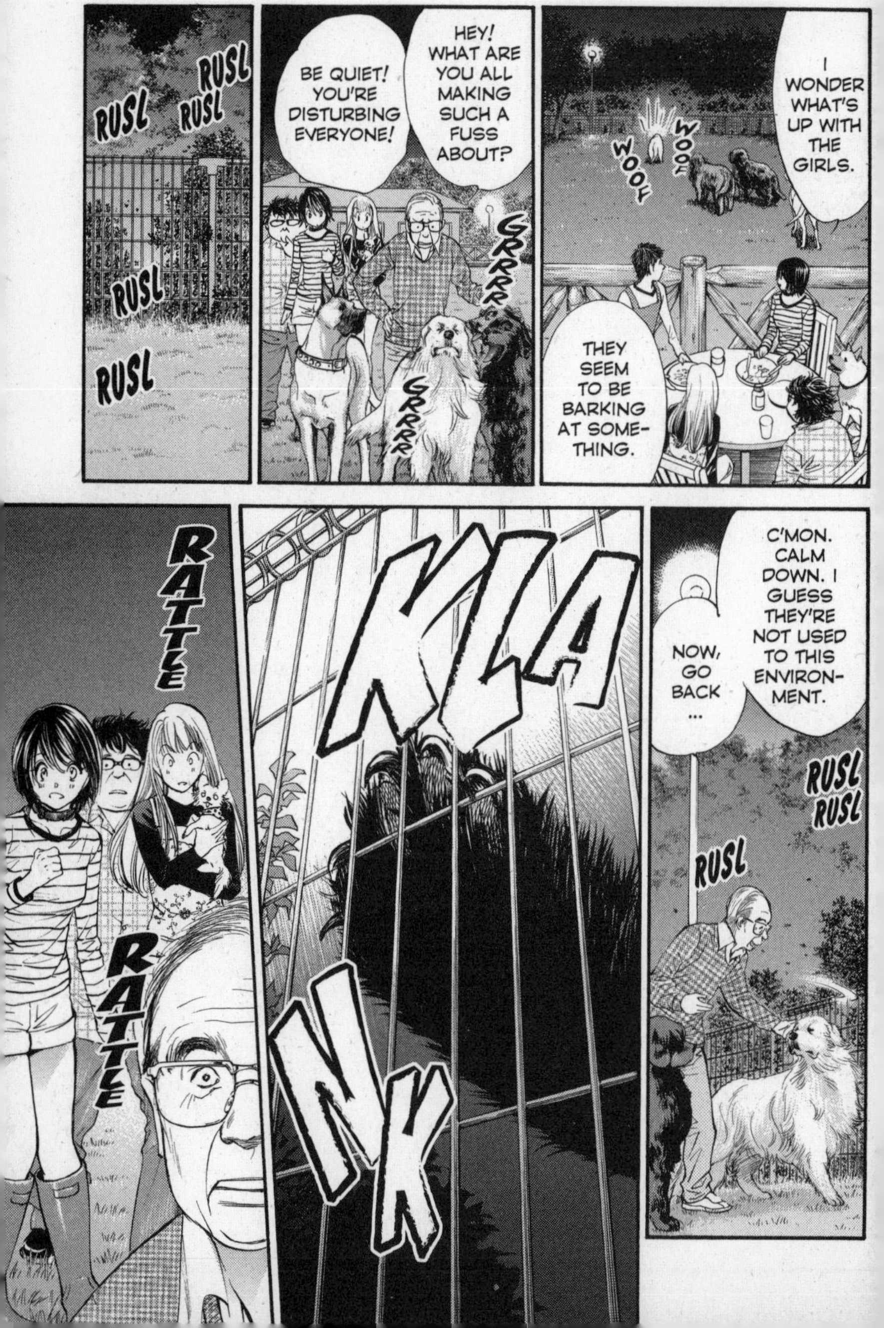
I WONDER WHAT'S UP WITH THE GIRLS.
WOOF WOOF
THEY SEEM TO BE BARKING AT SOMETHING.
HEY! WHAT ARE YOU ALL MAKING SUCH A FUSS ABOUT?
BE QUIET! YOU'RE DISTURBING EVERYONE!
GRRRR
GRRRR
RUSL RUSL
RUSL
RUSL
RUSL
C'MON. CALM DOWN. I GUESS THEY'RE NOT USED TO THIS ENVIRONMENT.
NOW, GO BACK...
RUSL RUSL
RUSL
KLANK
RATTLE
RATTLE

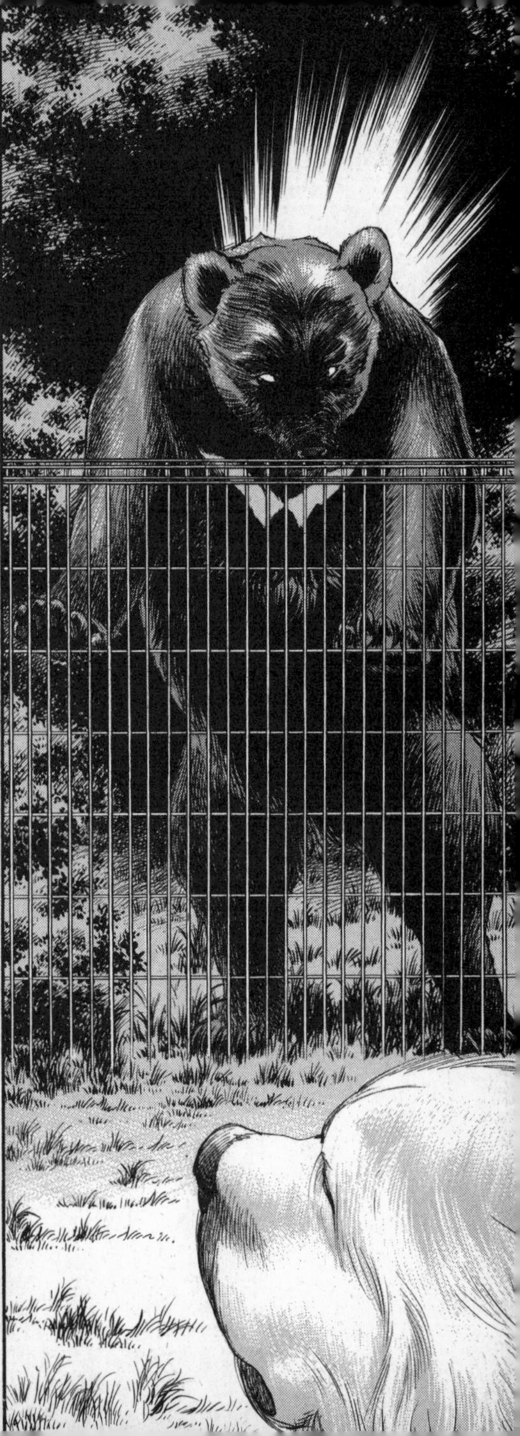

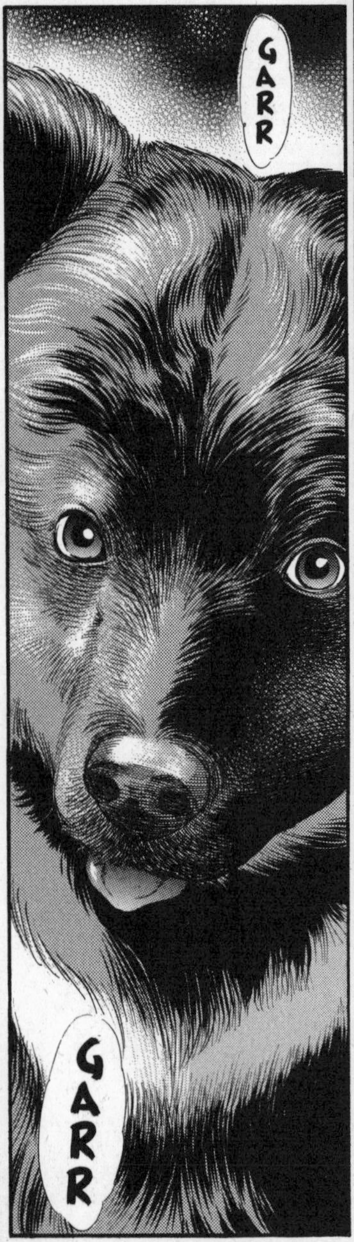
GARR
GARR

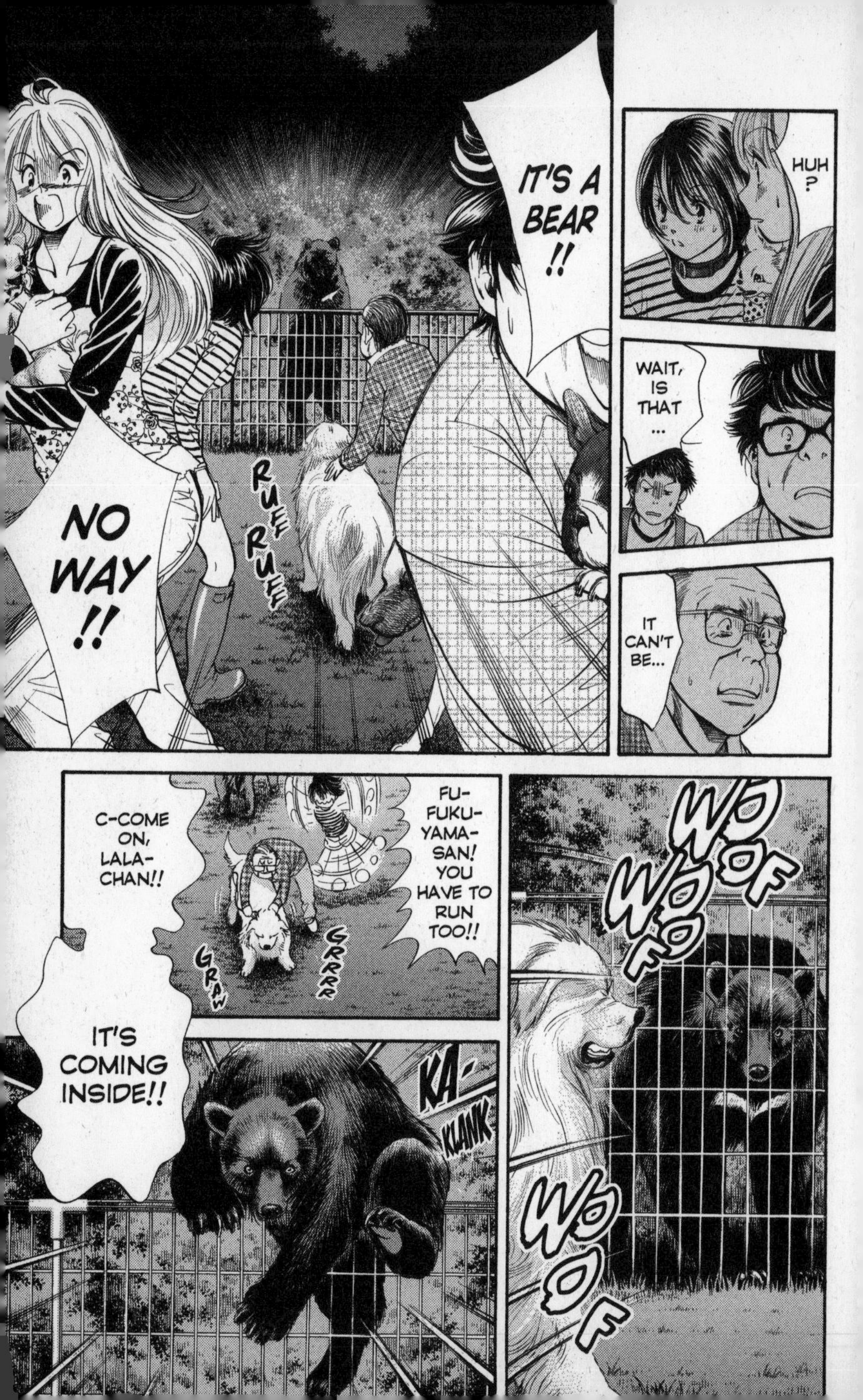
HUH?
WAIT, IS THAT...
IT CAN'T BE...
IT'S A BEAR!!
RUFF RUFF
NO WAY!!
WOOF WOOF WOOF
WOOF
FU-FUKUYAMA-SAN! YOU HAVE TO RUN TOO!!
C-COME ON, LALA-CHAN!!
GRRRR
GRAW
IT'S COMING INSIDE!!
KA-KLANK

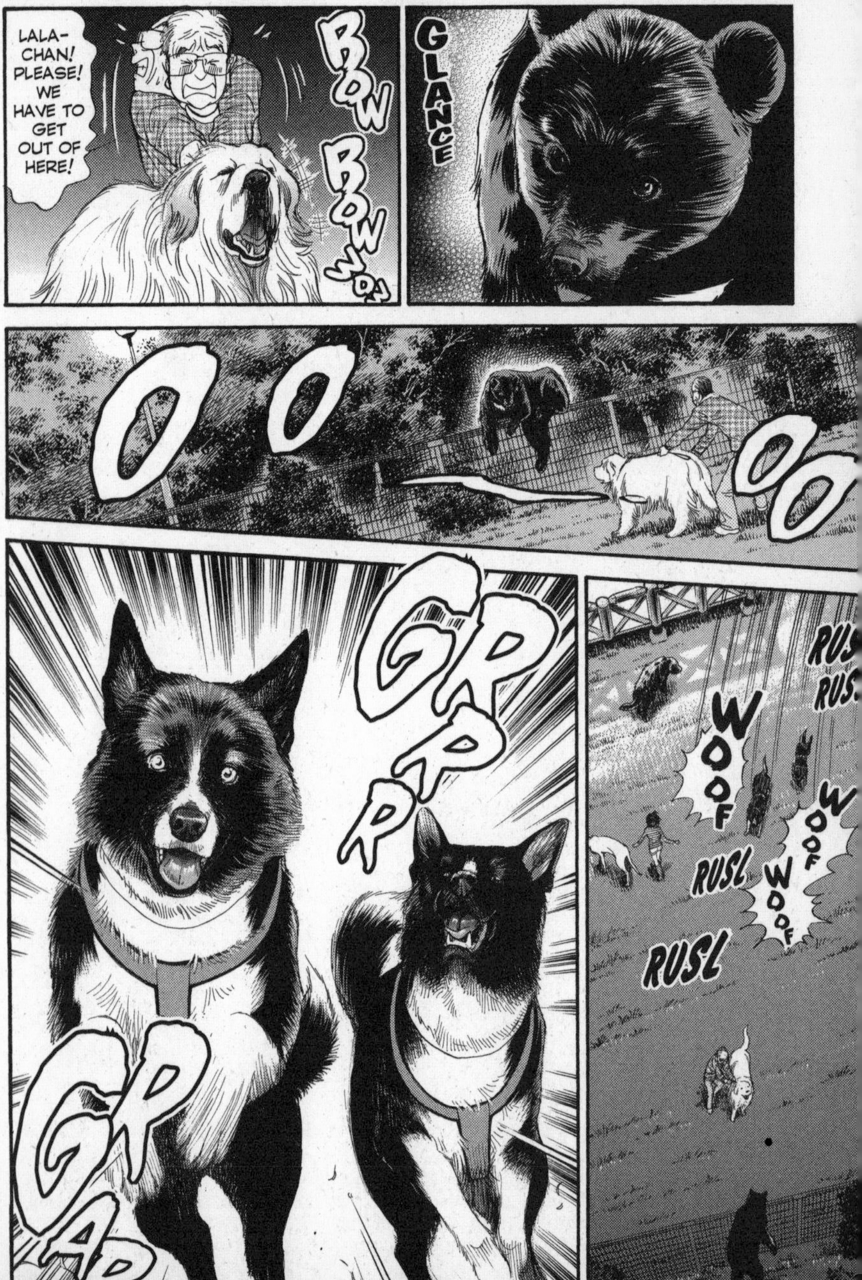
GLANCE
LALA-CHAN! PLEASE! WE HAVE TO GET OUT OF HERE!
BOW BOW WO
OOOO
RUS
RUS
WOOF
WOOF
WOOF
RUSL
WOOF
RUSL
GRRR
GRARR

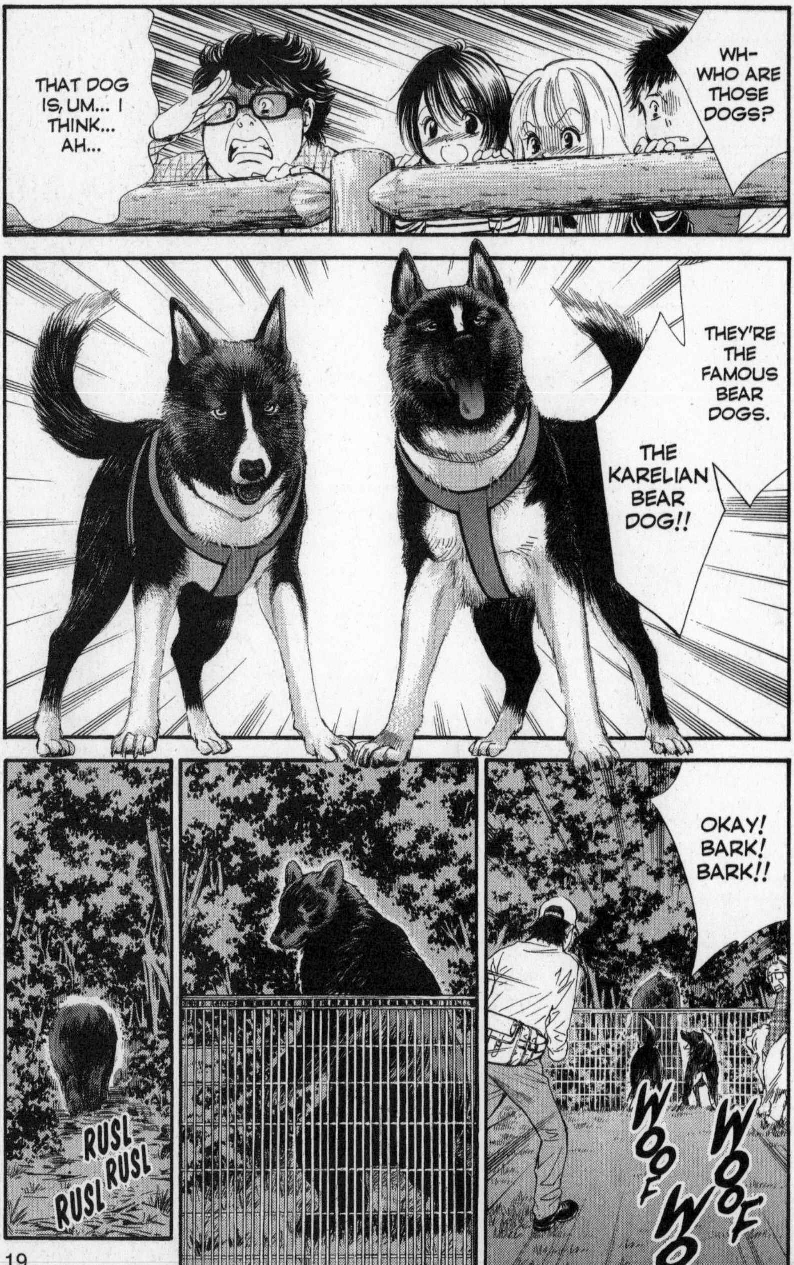
WH- WHO ARE THOSE DOGS?
THAT DOG IS, UM... I THINK... AH...
THEY'RE THE FAMOUS BEAR DOGS.
THE KARELIAN BEAR DOG!!
OKAY! BARK! BARK!!
WOOF WOOF
WOOF WOOF
RUSL RUSL RUSL

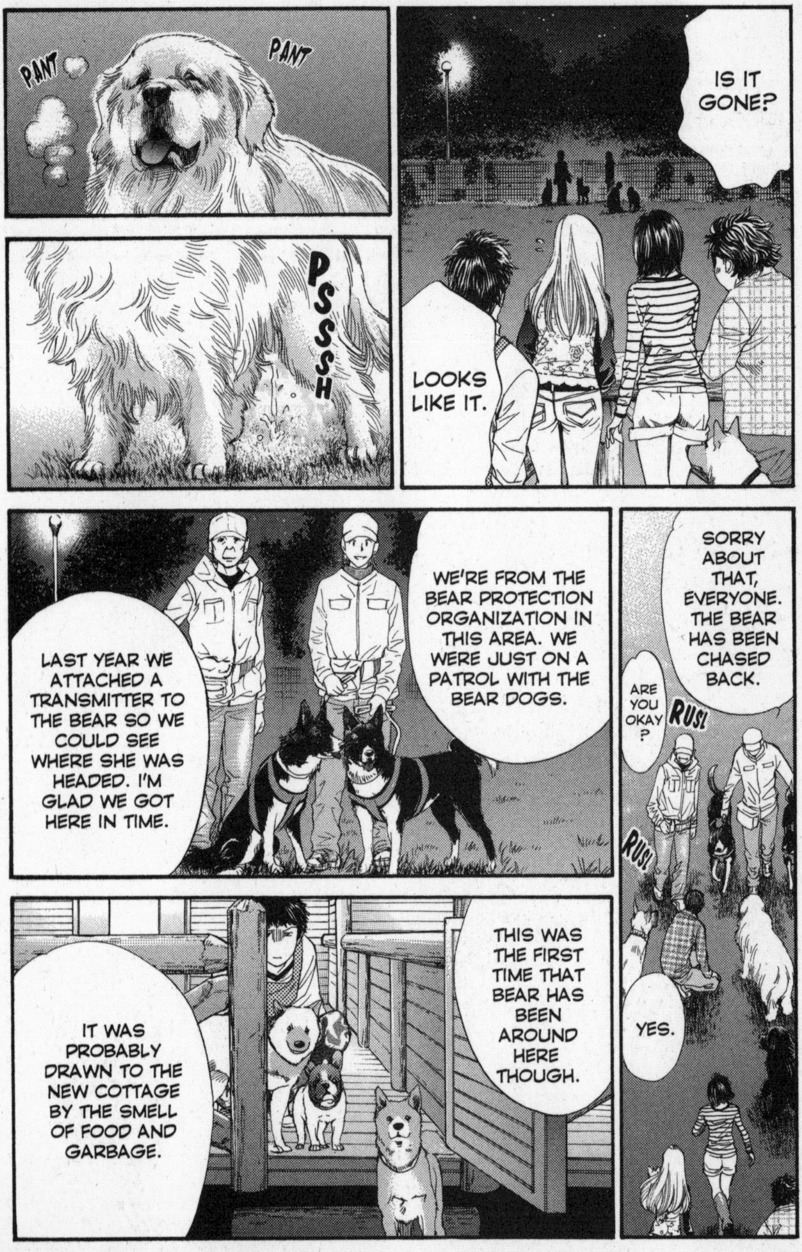
IS IT GONE?
LOOKS LIKE IT.
PANT
PANT
PSSSH
SORRY ABOUT THAT, EVERYONE. THE BEAR HAS BEEN CHASED BACK.
ARE YOU OKAY?
RUSL
RUSL
YES.
WE'RE FROM THE BEAR PROTECTION ORGANIZATION IN THIS AREA. WE WERE JUST ON A PATROL WITH THE BEAR DOGS.
LAST YEAR WE ATTACHED A TRANSMITTER TO THE BEAR SO WE COULD SEE WHERE SHE WAS HEADED. I'M GLAD WE GOT HERE IN TIME.
THIS WAS THE FIRST TIME THAT BEAR HAS BEEN AROUND HERE THOUGH.
IT WAS PROBABLY DRAWN TO THE NEW COTTAGE BY THE SMELL OF FOOD AND GARBAGE.

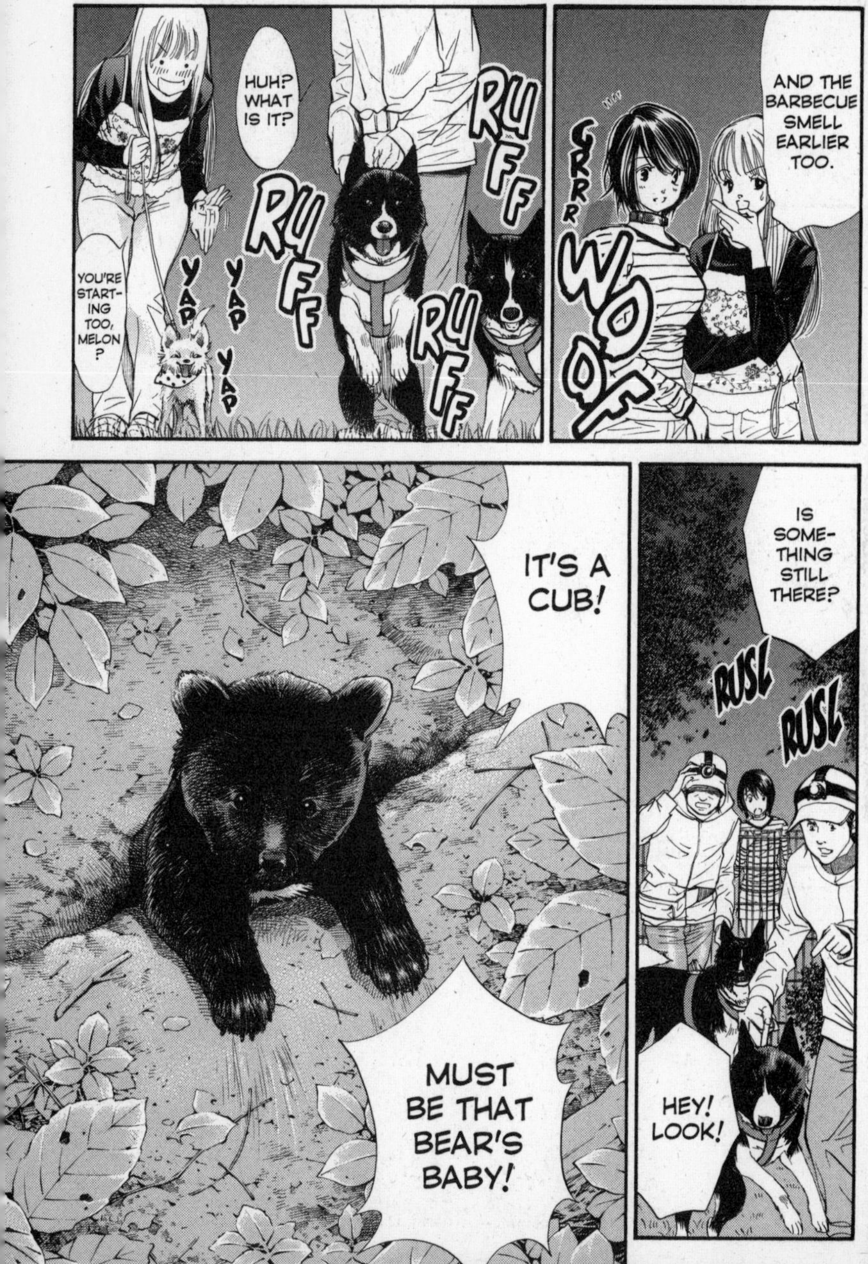
AND THE BARBECUE SMELL EARLIER TOO.
GRRR
WOOF
HUH? WHAT IS IT?
RUFF
RUFF
RUFF
YOU'RE STARTING TOO, MELON?
YAP
YAP
YAP
IS SOMETHING STILL THERE?
RUSL
RUSL
HEY! LOOK!
IT'S A CUB!
MUST BE THAT BEAR'S BABY!

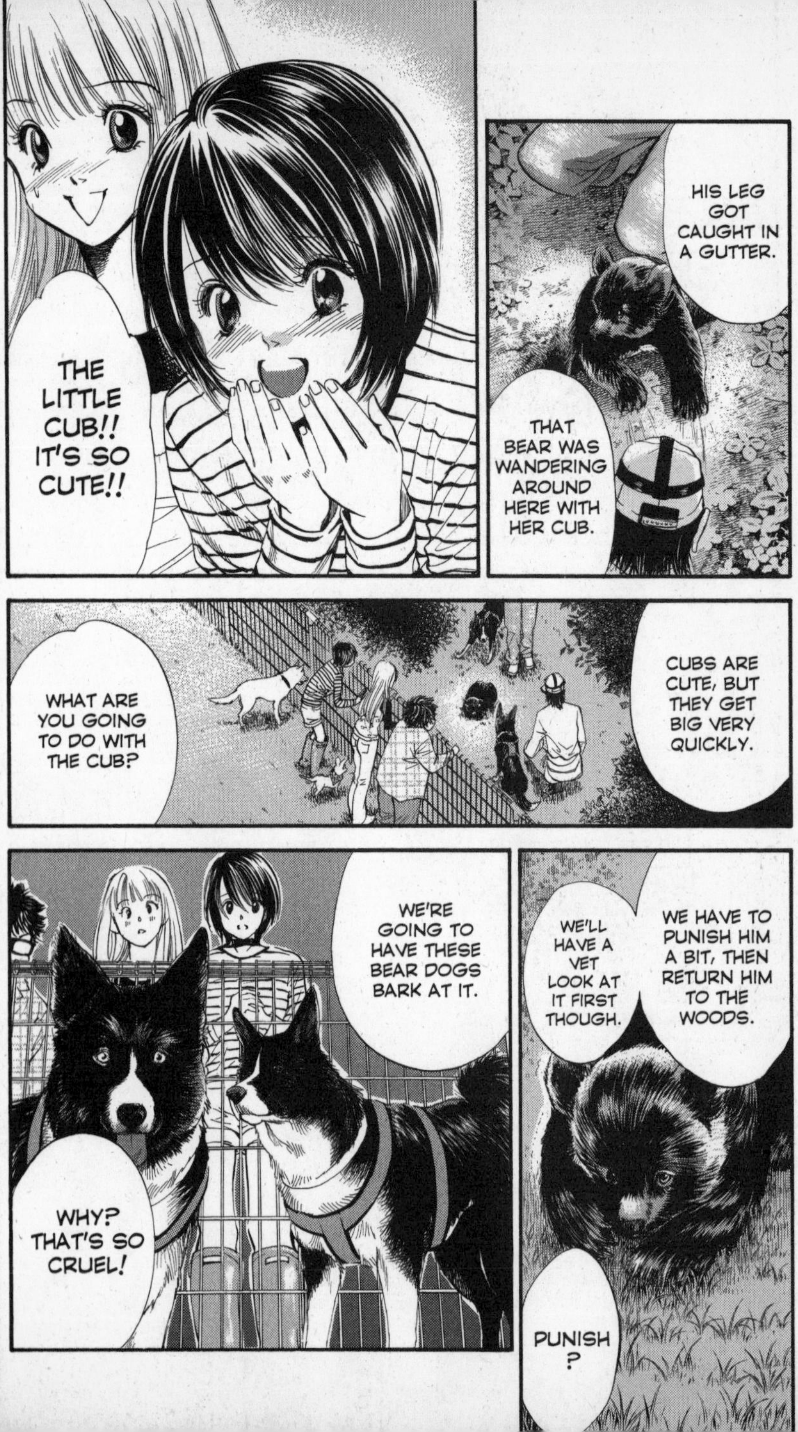
HIS LEG GOT CAUGHT IN A GUTTER.
THAT BEAR WAS WANDERING AROUND HERE WITH HER CUB.
THE LITTLE CUB!! IT'S SO CUTE!!
CUBS ARE CUTE, BUT THEY GET BIG VERY QUICKLY.
WHAT ARE YOU GOING TO DO WITH THE CUB?
WE HAVE TO PUNISH HIM A BIT, THEN RETURN HIM TO THE WOODS.
WE'LL HAVE A VET LOOK AT IT FIRST THOUGH.
PUNISH?
WE'RE GOING TO HAVE THESE BEAR DOGS BARK AT IT.
WHY? THAT'S SO CRUEL!

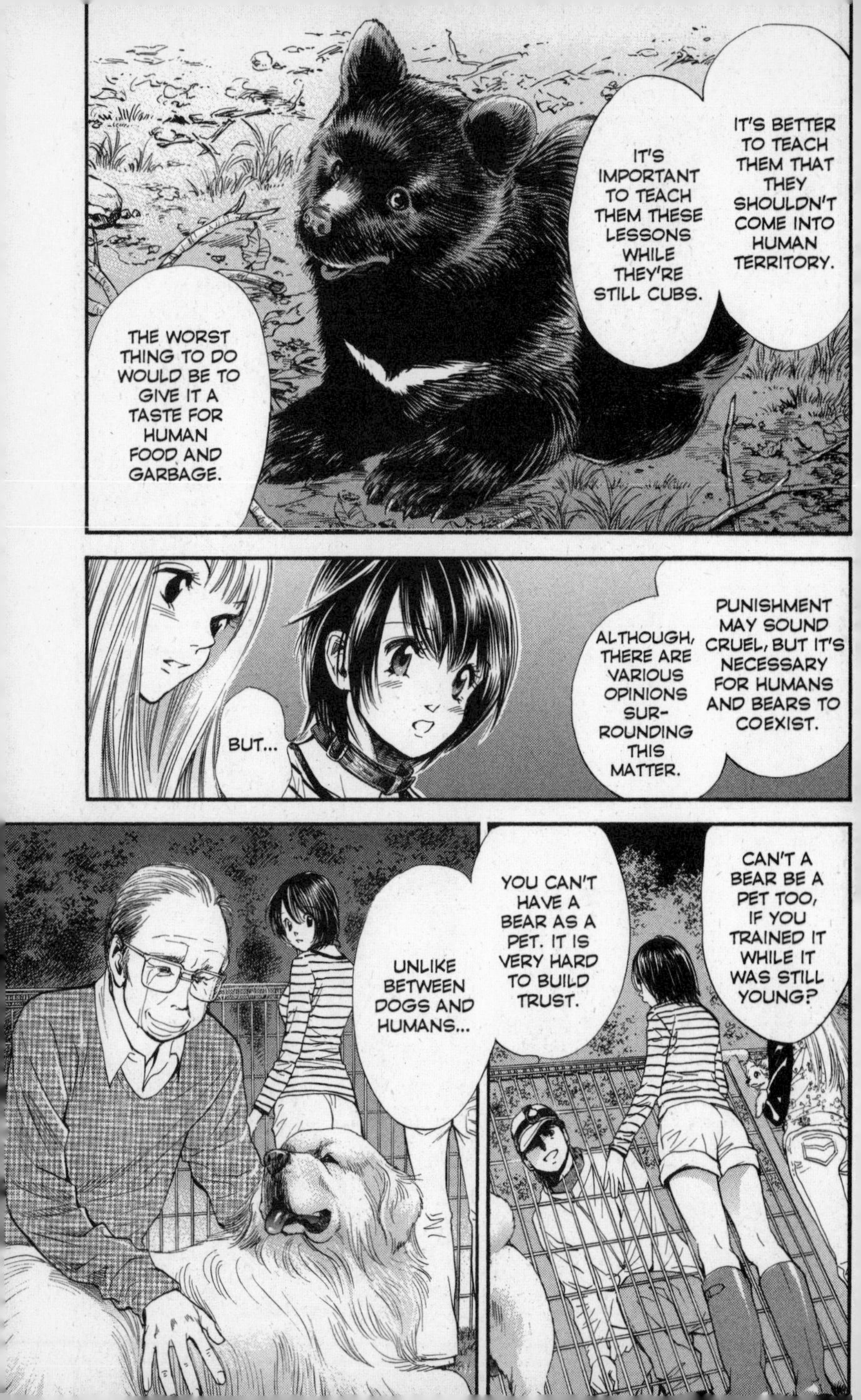
IT'S BETTER TO TEACH THEM THAT THEY SHOULDN'T COME INTO HUMAN TERRITORY.
IT'S IMPORTANT TO TEACH THEM THESE LESSONS WHILE THEY'RE STILL CUBS.
THE WORST THING TO DO WOULD BE TO GIVE IT A TASTE FOR HUMAN FOOD AND GARBAGE.
PUNISHMENT MAY SOUND CRUEL, BUT IT'S NECESSARY FOR HUMANS AND BEARS TO COEXIST.
ALTHOUGH, THERE ARE VARIOUS OPINIONS SUR-ROUNDING THIS MATTER.
BUT...
CAN'T A BEAR BE A PET TOO, IF YOU TRAINED IT WHILE IT WAS STILL YOUNG?
YOU CAN'T HAVE A BEAR AS A PET. IT IS VERY HARD TO BUILD TRUST.
UNLIKE BETWEEN DOGS AND HUMANS...

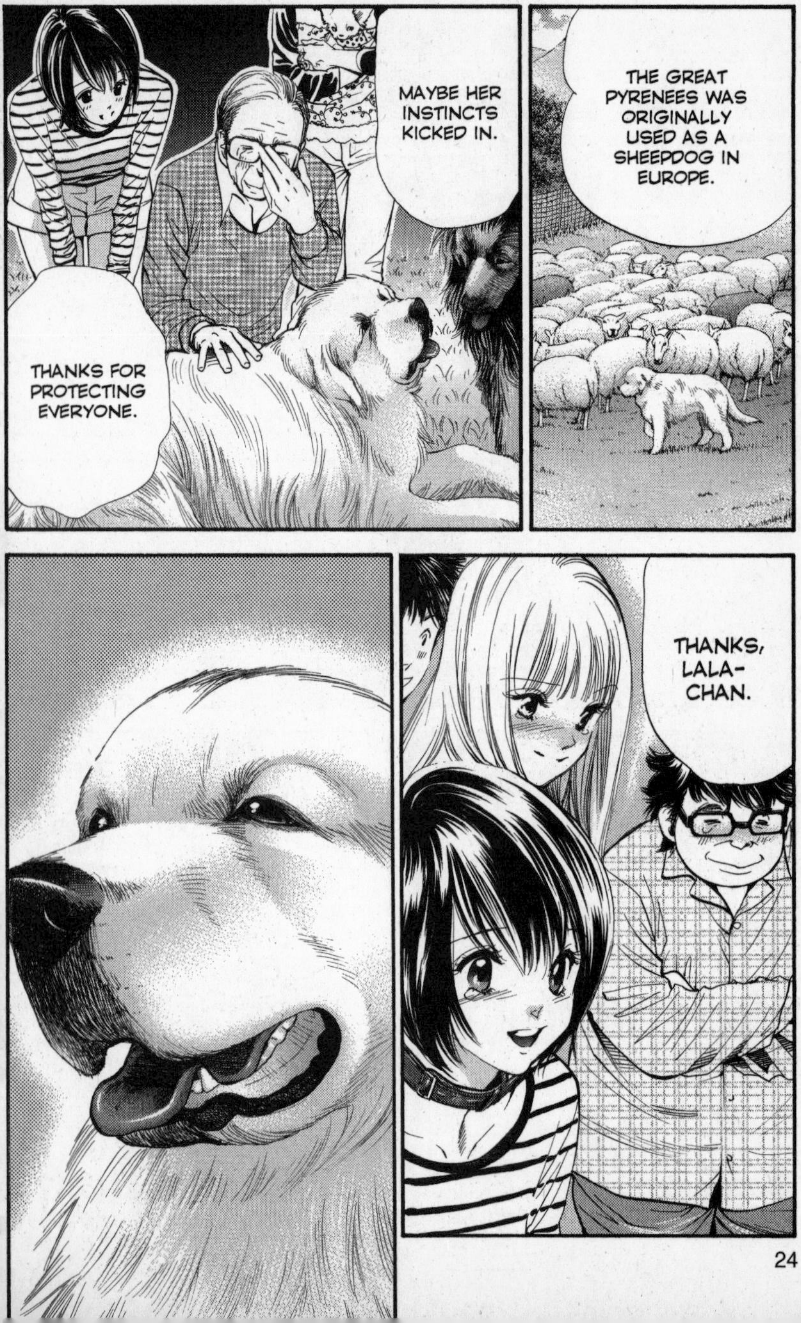
THE GREAT PYRENEES WAS ORIGINALLY USED AS A SHEEPDOG IN EUROPE.
MAYBE HER INSTINCTS KICKED IN.
THANKS FOR PROTECTING EVERYONE.
THANKS, LALA-CHAN.

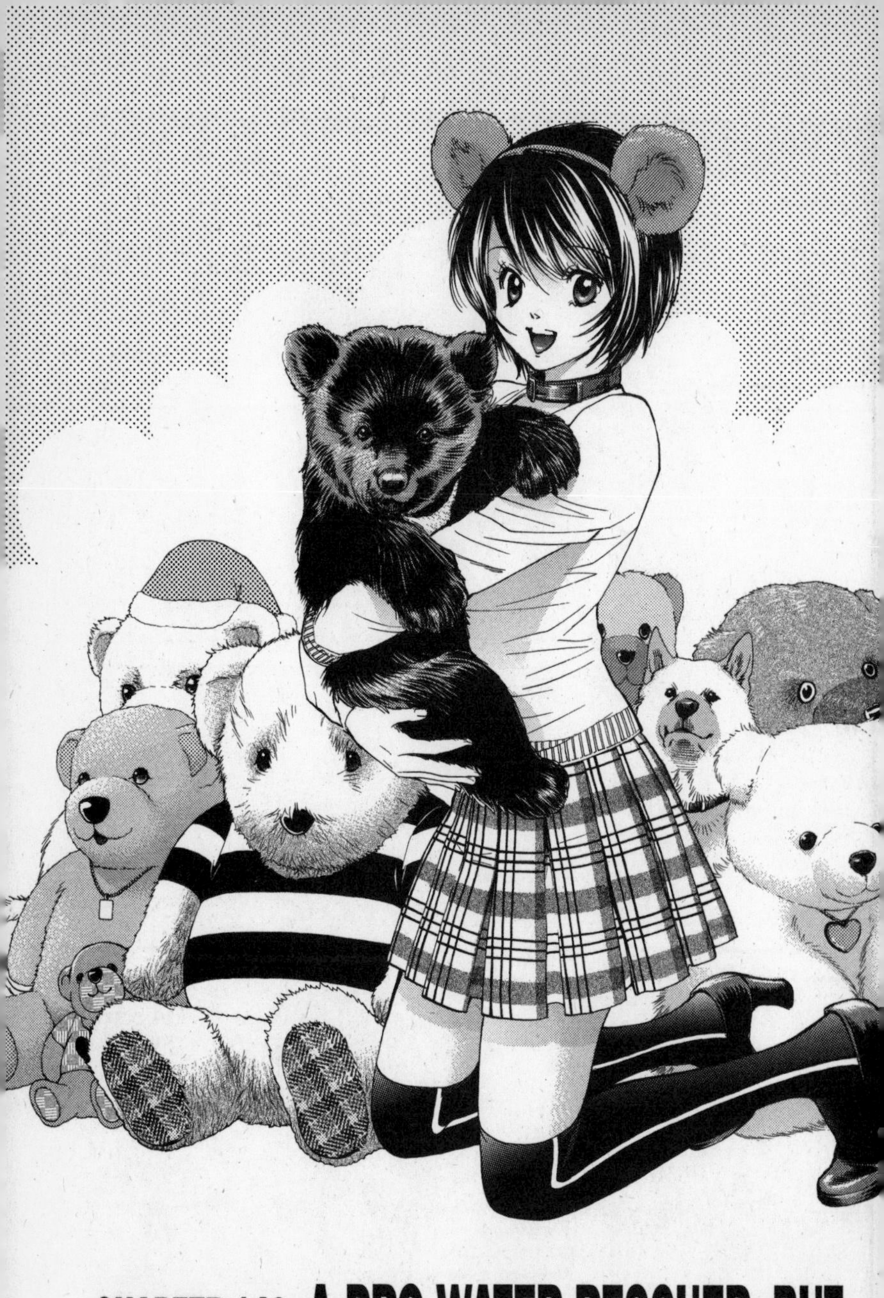

CHAPTER 143: A PRO WATER RESCUER, BUT...

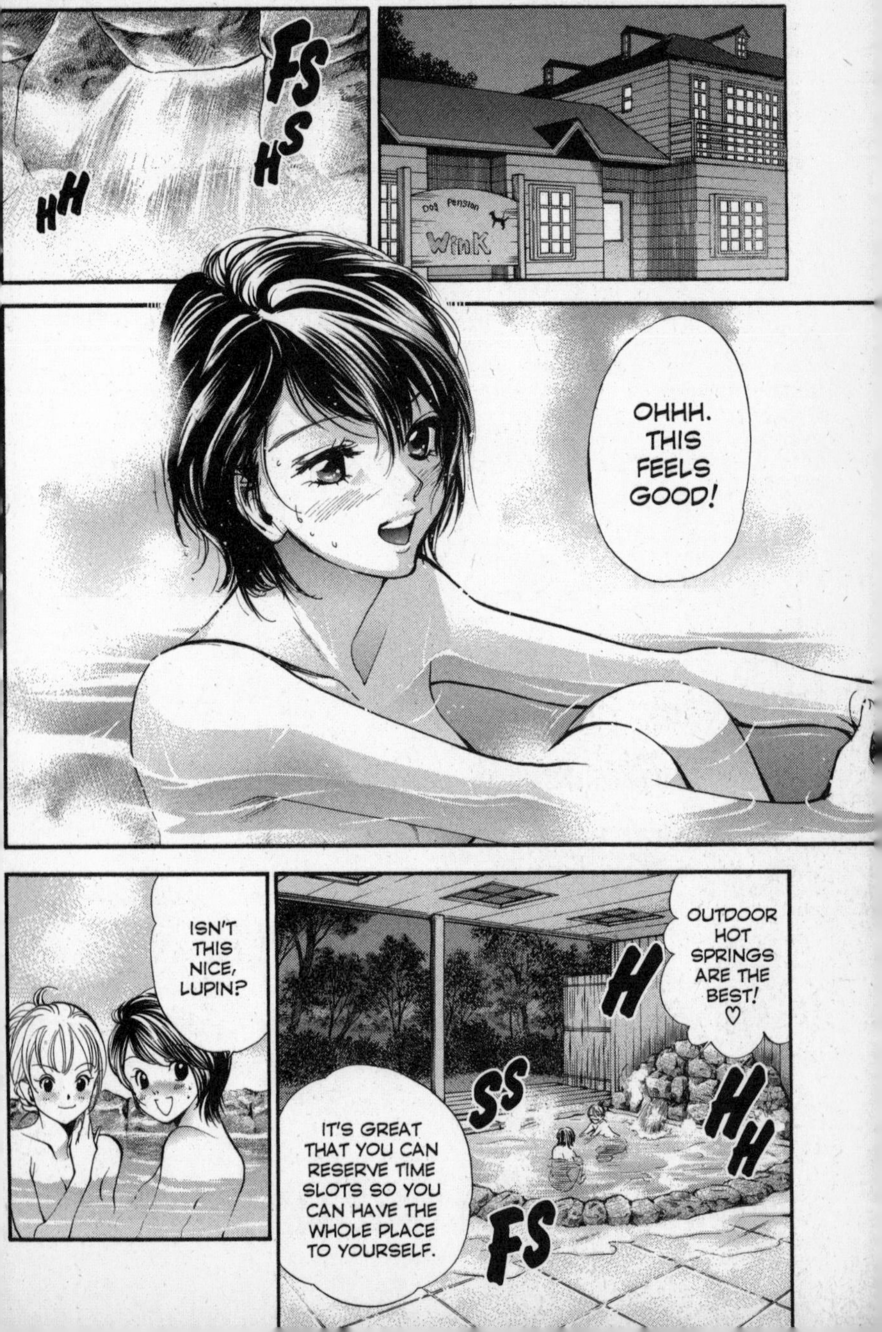
Dog Pension
WinK
FSSHHH
OHHH. THIS FEELS GOOD!
OUTDOOR HOT SPRINGS ARE THE BEST! ♡
HHHH
SS
IT'S GREAT THAT YOU CAN RESERVE TIME SLOTS SO YOU CAN HAVE THE WHOLE PLACE TO YOURSELF.
FS
ISN'T THIS NICE, LUPIN?

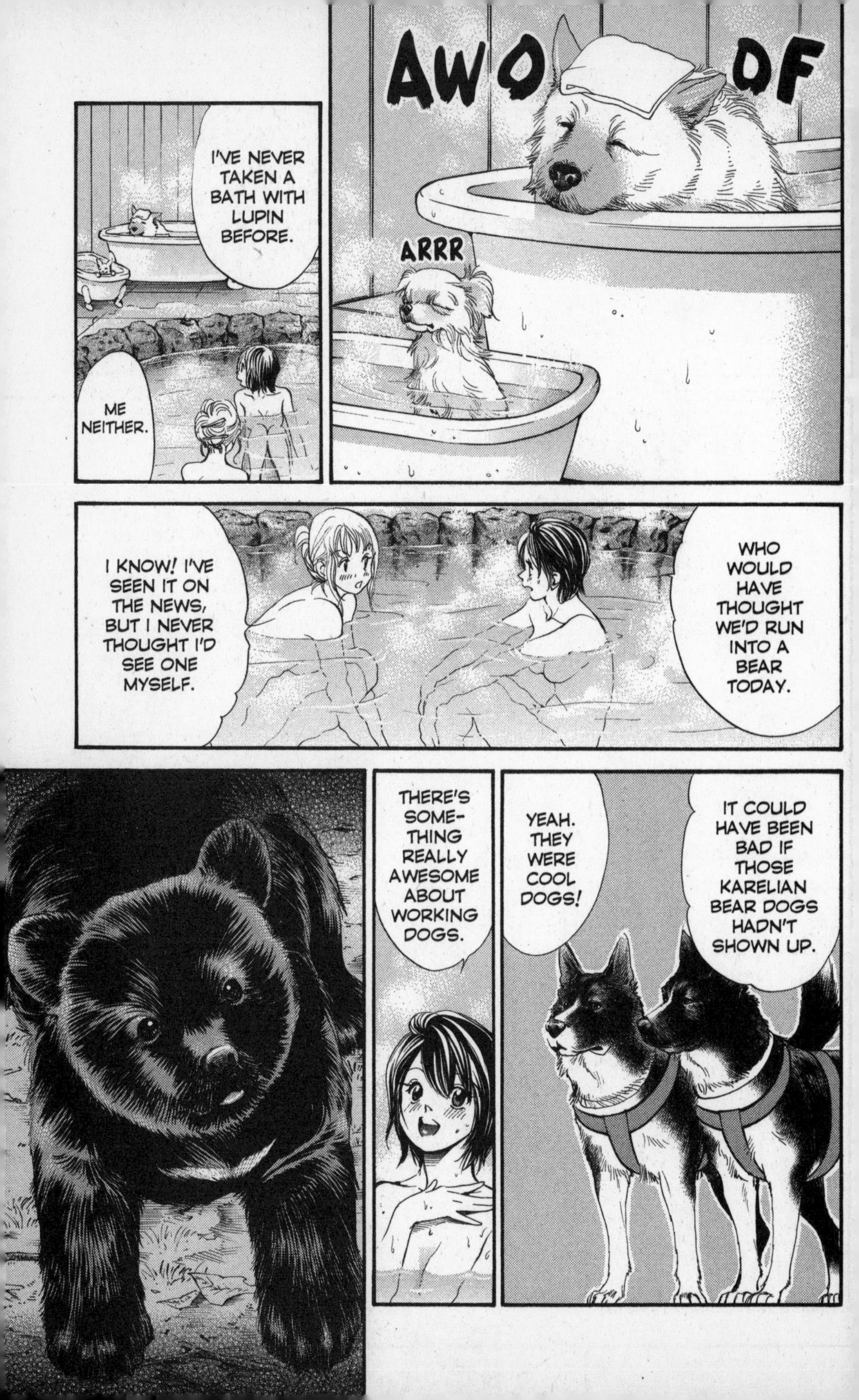
AWO OF
ARRR
I'VE NEVER TAKEN A BATH WITH LUPIN BEFORE.
ME NEITHER.
WHO WOULD HAVE THOUGHT WE'D RUN INTO A BEAR TODAY.
I KNOW! I'VE SEEN IT ON THE NEWS, BUT I NEVER THOUGHT I'D SEE ONE MYSELF.
IT COULD HAVE BEEN BAD IF THOSE KARELIAN BEAR DOGS HADN'T SHOWN UP.
YEAH. THEY WERE COOL DOGS!
THERE'S SOME-THING REALLY AWESOME ABOUT WORKING DOGS.

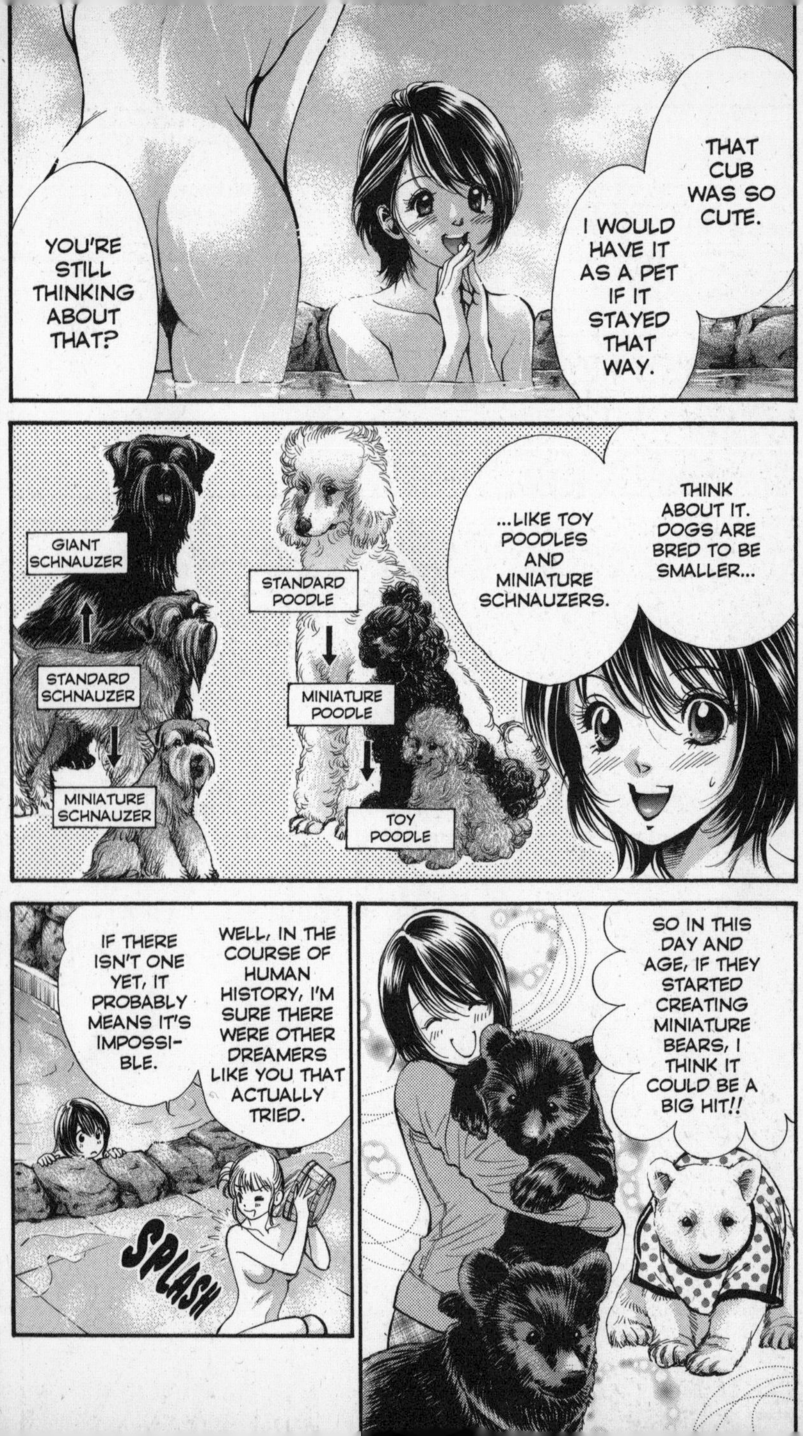
THAT CUB WAS SO CUTE.
I WOULD HAVE IT AS A PET IF IT STAYED THAT WAY.
YOU'RE STILL THINKING ABOUT THAT?
THINK ABOUT IT. DOGS ARE BRED TO BE SMALLER...
...LIKE TOY POODLES AND MINIATURE SCHNAUZERS.
STANDARD POODLE
MINIATURE POODLE
TOY POODLE
GIANT SCHNAUZER
STANDARD SCHNAUZER
MINIATURE SCHNAUZER
SO IN THIS DAY AND AGE, IF THEY STARTED CREATING MINIATURE BEARS, I THINK IT COULD BE A BIG HIT!!
WELL, IN THE COURSE OF HUMAN HISTORY, I'M SURE THERE WERE OTHER DREAMERS LIKE YOU THAT ACTUALLY TRIED.
IF THERE ISN'T ONE YET, IT PROBABLY MEANS IT'S IMPOSSI- BLE.
SPLASH

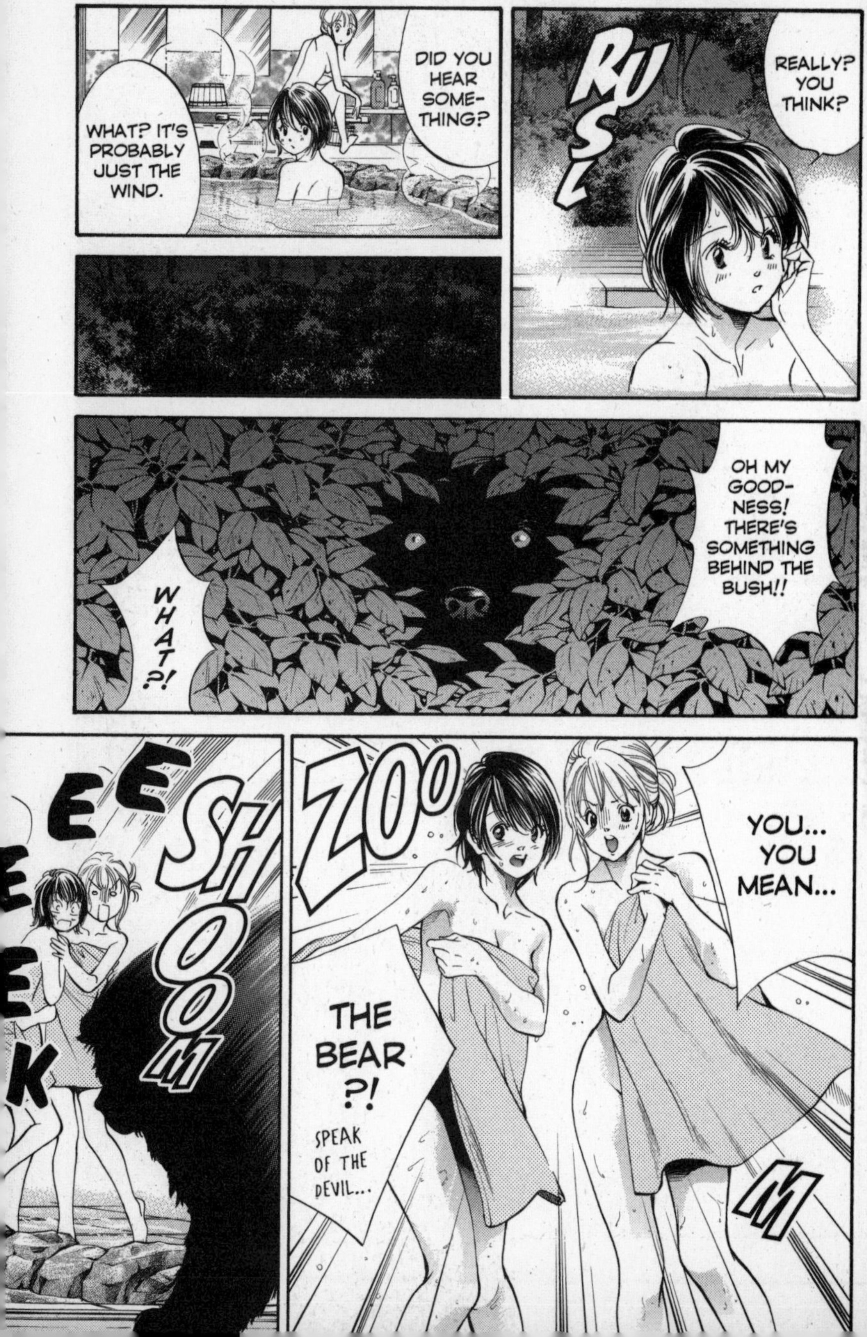
DID YOU HEAR SOMETHING?
WHAT? IT'S PROBABLY JUST THE WIND.
RUSL
REALLY? YOU THINK?
OH MY GOODNESS! THERE'S SOMETHING BEHIND THE BUSH!!
WHAT?!
ZOO
YOU... YOU MEAN...
THE BEAR?!
SPEAK OF THE DEVIL...
M
SHOOOM
EEEEK

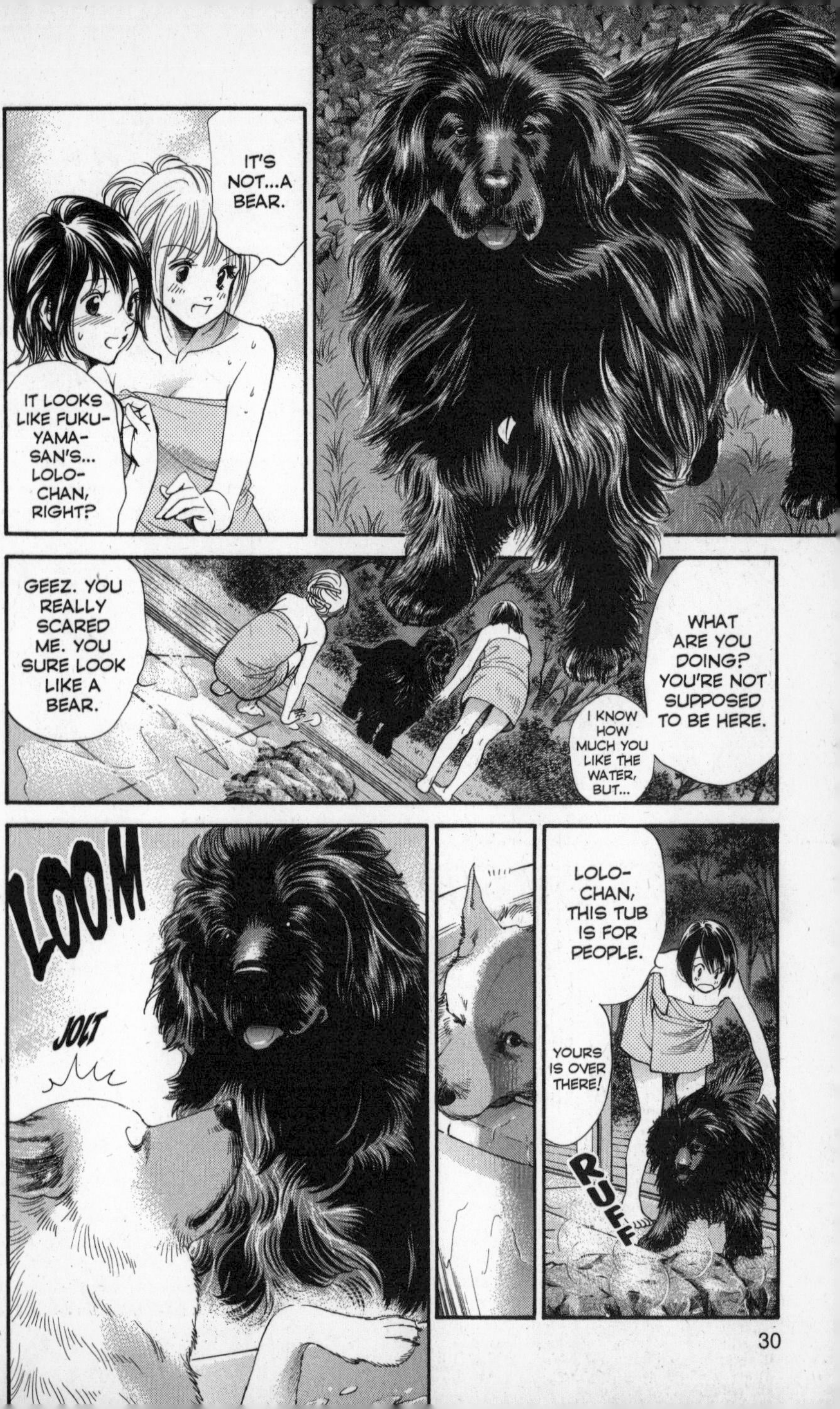
IT'S NOT...A BEAR.
IT LOOKS LIKE FUKUYAMA-SAN'S... LOLO-CHAN, RIGHT?
WHAT ARE YOU DOING? YOU'RE NOT SUPPOSED TO BE HERE.
I KNOW HOW MUCH YOU LIKE THE WATER, BUT...
GEEZ. YOU REALLY SCARED ME. YOU SURE LOOK LIKE A BEAR.
LOLO-CHAN, THIS TUB IS FOR PEOPLE.
YOURS IS OVER THERE!
RUFF
LOOM
JOLT

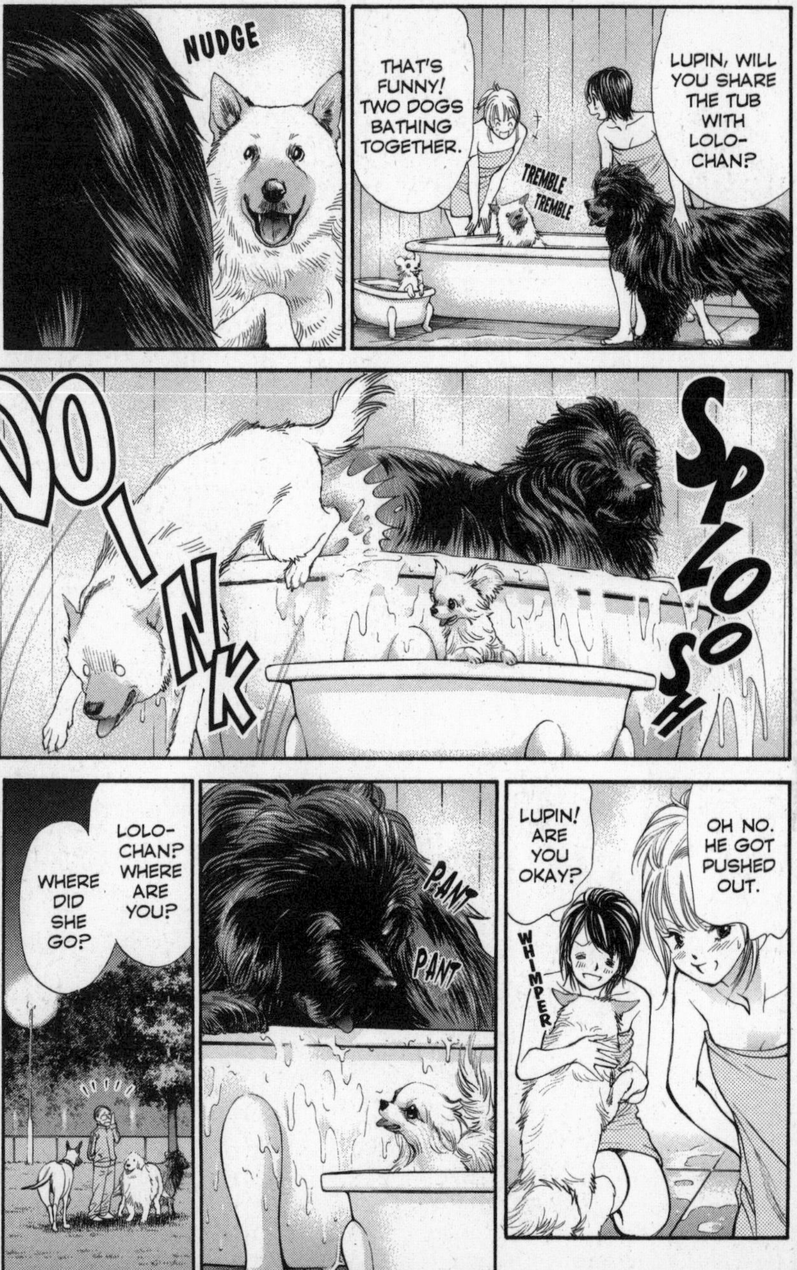

LUPIN, WILL YOU SHARE THE TUB WITH LOLO-CHAN?
THAT'S FUNNY! TWO DOGS BATHING TOGETHER.
TREMBLE TREMBLE
NUDGE
SPLOOSH
DOINK
OH NO. HE GOT PUSHED OUT.
LUPIN! ARE YOU OKAY?
WHIMPER
PANT
PANT
LOLO-CHAN? WHERE ARE YOU?
WHERE DID SHE GO?

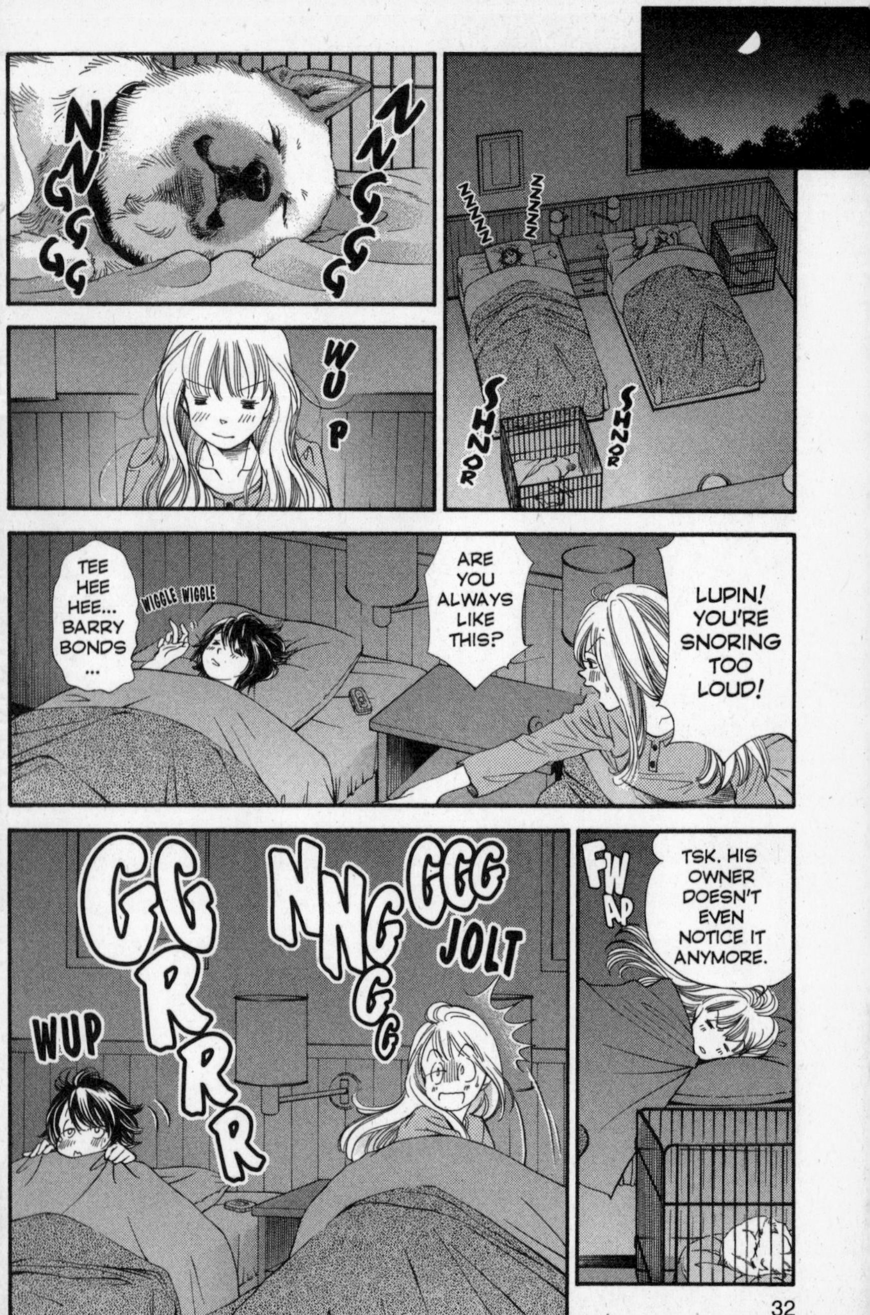

ZZZZZ
ZZZZZ
SHNOR
SHNOR
NNGGGG
NNGGGG
WUP
LUPIN! YOU'RE SNORING TOO LOUD!
ARE YOU ALWAYS LIKE THIS?
WIGGLE WIGGLE
TEE HEE HEE... BARRY BONDS ...
FWAP
TSK. HIS OWNER DOESN'T EVEN NOTICE IT ANYMORE.
GGNNGGGGNNGGG
JOLT
GGRRRR
WUP

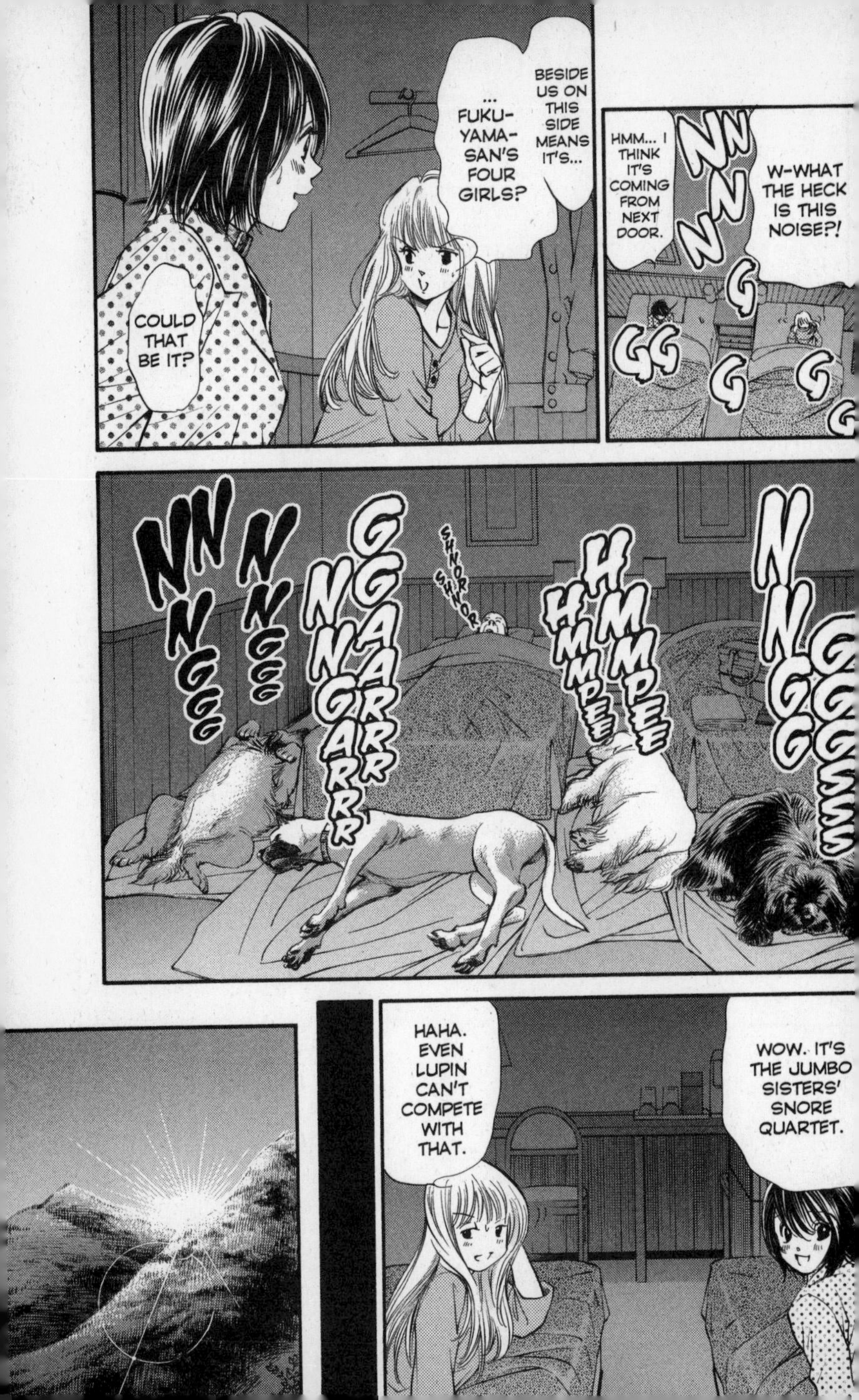

W-WHAT THE HECK IS THIS NOISE?!
HMM... I THINK IT'S COMING FROM NEXT DOOR.
NNNNGGGGG
BESIDE US ON THIS SIDE MEANS IT'S...
... FUKUYAMA-SAN'S FOUR GIRLS?
COULD THAT BE IT?
NNGGG
GGGSSS
HMMMPEE
HMMMPEE
SHNOR SHNOR
GGAARRR
NNGARRR
NNNGGG
NNNNGGG
WOW. IT'S THE JUMBO SISTERS' SNORE QUARTET.
HAHA. EVEN LUPIN CAN'T COMPETE WITH THAT.

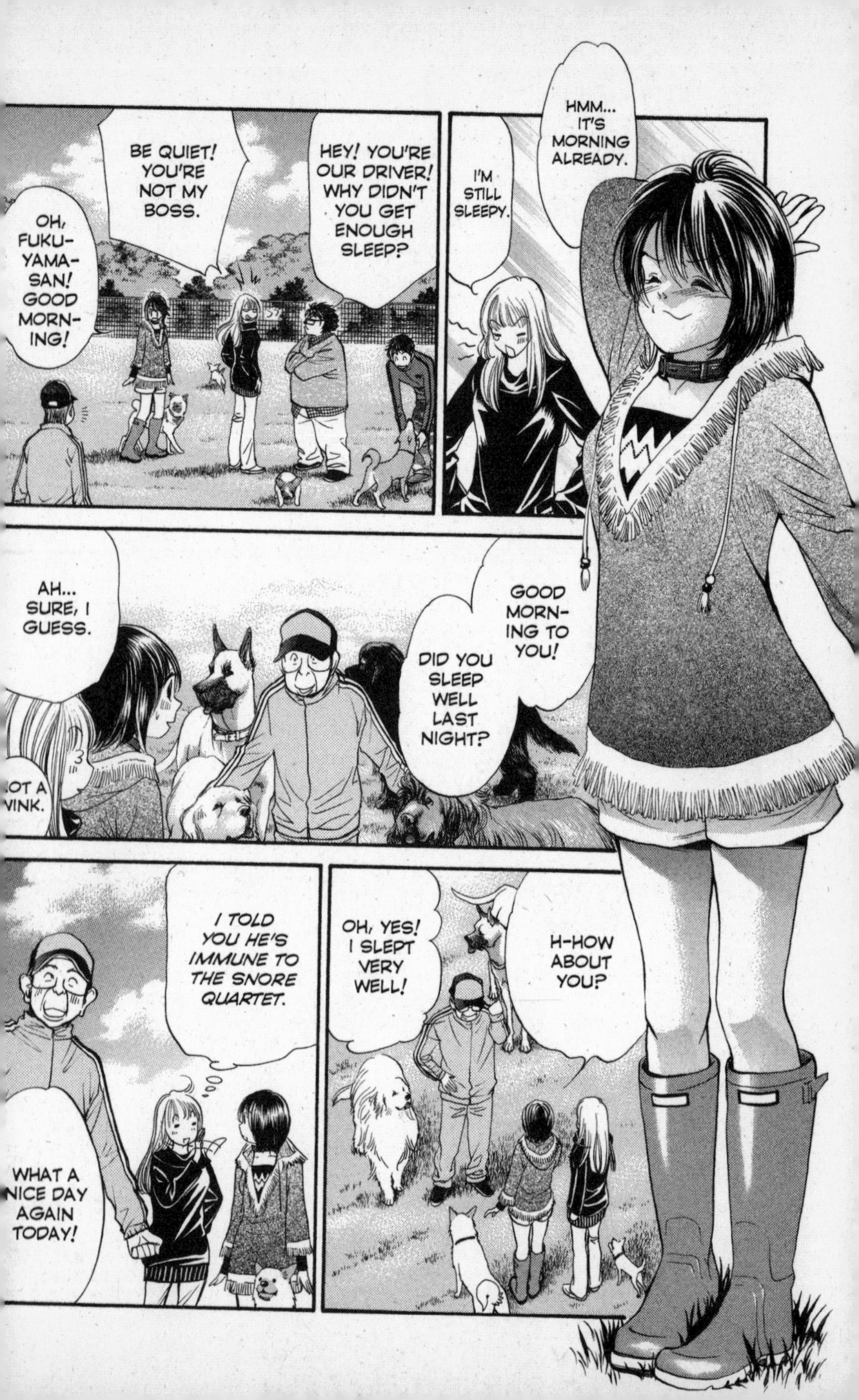
HMM... IT'S MORNING ALREADY.
I'M STILL SLEEPY.
HEY! YOU'RE OUR DRIVER! WHY DIDN'T YOU GET ENOUGH SLEEP?
BE QUIET! YOU'RE NOT MY BOSS.
OH, FUKU-YAMA-SAN! GOOD MORN-ING!
GOOD MORN-ING TO YOU!
DID YOU SLEEP WELL LAST NIGHT?
AH... SURE, I GUESS.
OT A VINK.
H-HOW ABOUT YOU?
OH, YES! I SLEPT VERY WELL!
I TOLD YOU HE'S IMMUNE TO THE SNORE QUARTET.
WHAT A NICE DAY AGAIN TODAY!

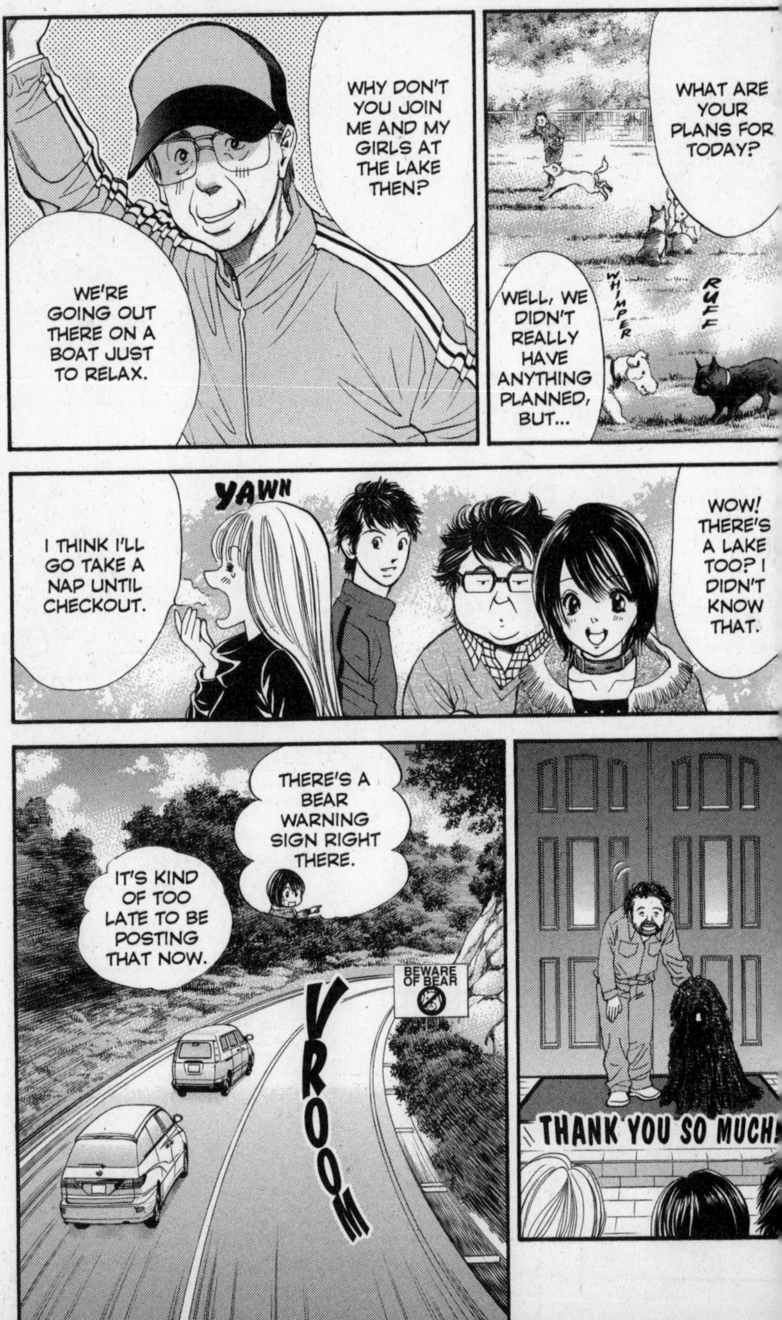
WHAT ARE YOUR PLANS FOR TODAY?
RUFF
WHIMPER
WELL, WE DIDN'T REALLY HAVE ANYTHING PLANNED, BUT...
WHY DON'T YOU JOIN ME AND MY GIRLS AT THE LAKE THEN?
WE'RE GOING OUT THERE ON A BOAT JUST TO RELAX.
WOW! THERE'S A LAKE TOO? I DIDN'T KNOW THAT.
YAWN
I THINK I'LL GO TAKE A NAP UNTIL CHECKOUT.
THANK YOU SO MUCH!
THERE'S A BEAR WARNING SIGN RIGHT THERE.
IT'S KIND OF TOO LATE TO BE POSTING THAT NOW.
BEWARE OF BEAR
VROOM

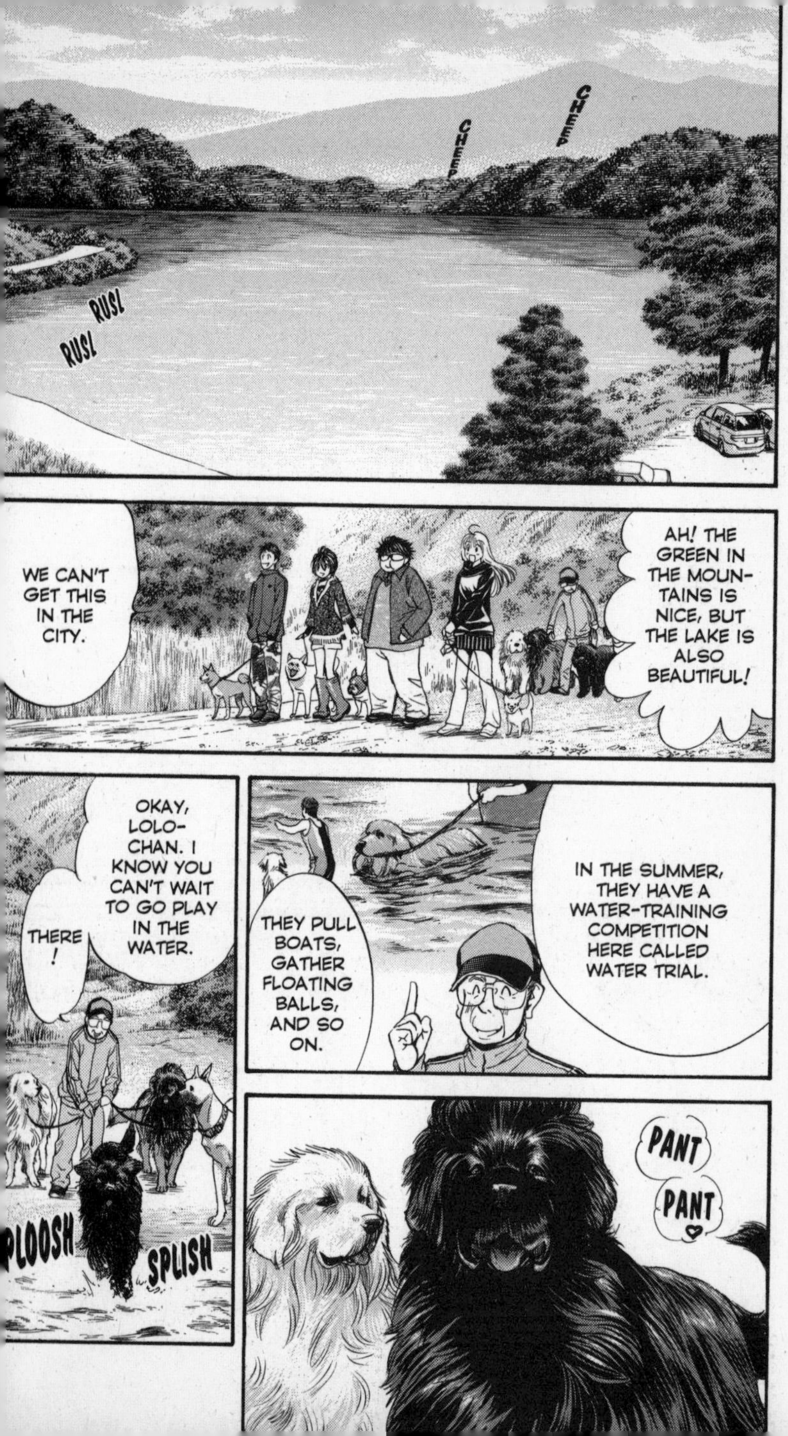
CHEEP
CHEEP
RUSL
RUSL
AH! THE GREEN IN THE MOUNTAINS IS NICE, BUT THE LAKE IS ALSO BEAUTIFUL!
WE CAN'T GET THIS IN THE CITY.
IN THE SUMMER, THEY HAVE A WATER-TRAINING COMPETITION HERE CALLED WATER TRIAL.
THEY PULL BOATS, GATHER FLOATING BALLS, AND SO ON.
PANT
PANT
OKAY, LOLO-CHAN. I KNOW YOU CAN'T WAIT TO GO PLAY IN THE WATER.
THERE!
PLOOSH
SPLISH

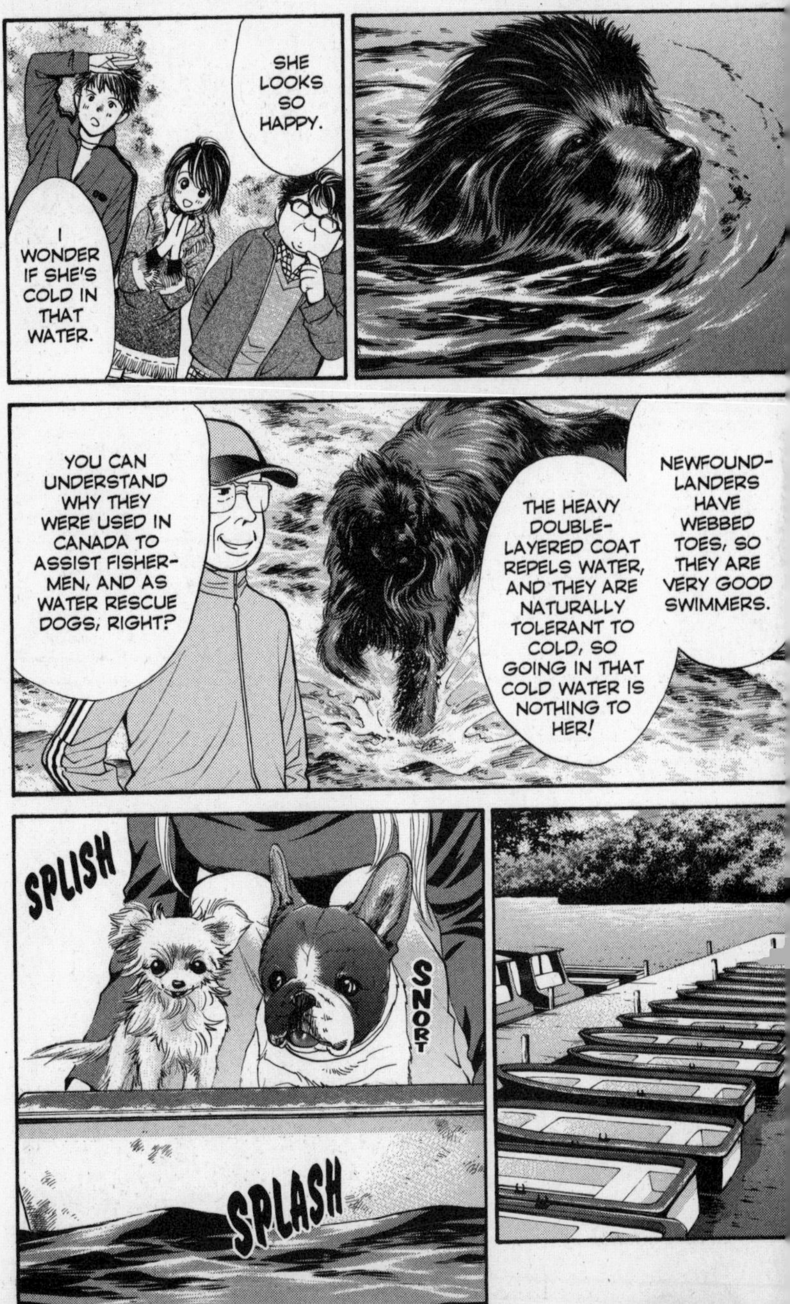
SHE LOOKS SO HAPPY.
I WONDER IF SHE'S COLD IN THAT WATER.
NEWFOUND-LANDERS HAVE WEBBED TOES, SO THEY ARE VERY GOOD SWIMMERS.
THE HEAVY DOUBLE-LAYERED COAT REPELS WATER, AND THEY ARE NATURALLY TOLERANT TO COLD, SO GOING IN THAT COLD WATER IS NOTHING TO HER!
YOU CAN UNDERSTAND WHY THEY WERE USED IN CANADA TO ASSIST FISHER-MEN, AND AS WATER RESCUE DOGS, RIGHT?
SNORT
SPLISH
SPLASH

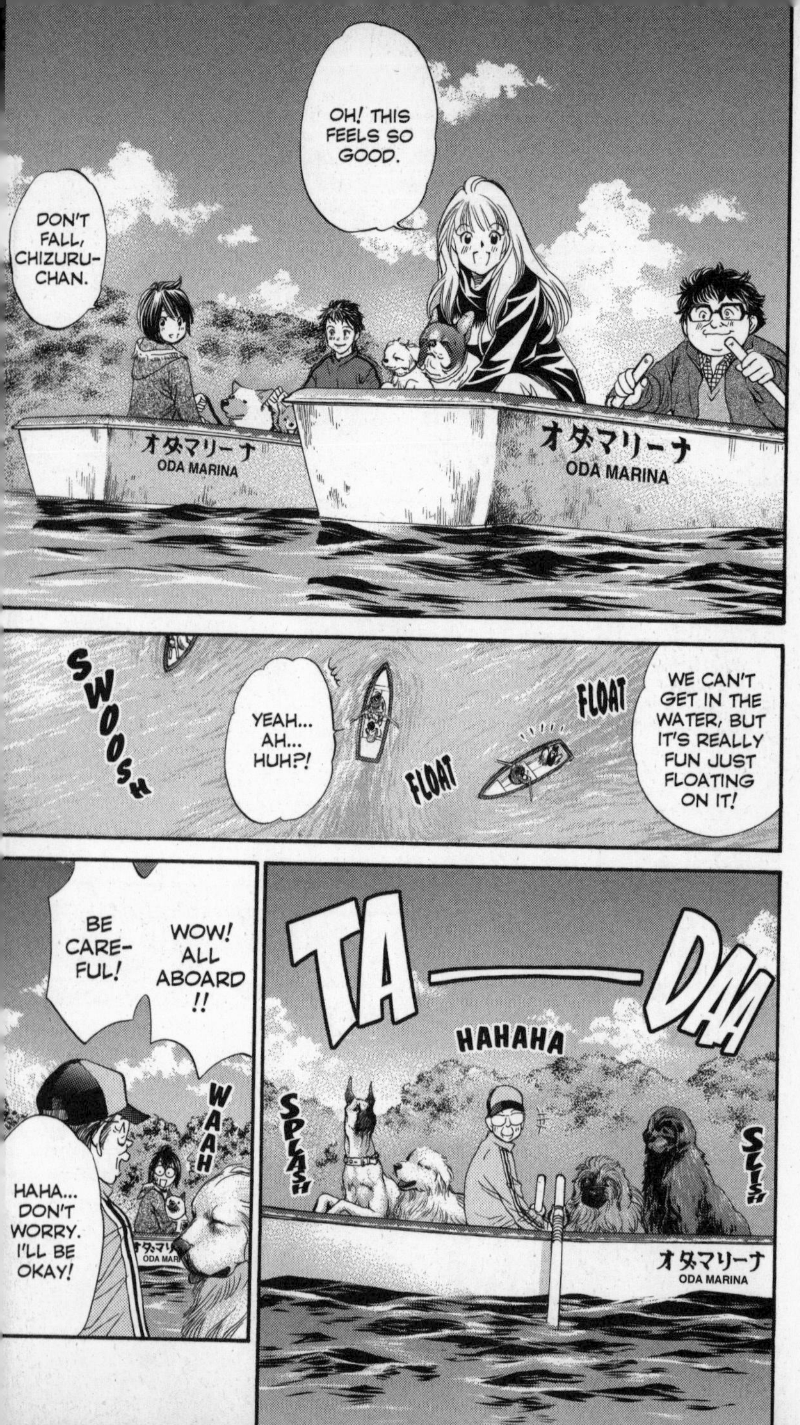
OH! THIS FEELS SO GOOD.
DON'T FALL, CHIZURU-CHAN.
オダマリーナ
ODA MARINA
オダマリーナ
ODA MARINA
WE CAN'T GET IN THE WATER, BUT IT'S REALLY FUN JUST FLOATING ON IT!
FLOAT
FLOAT
YEAH... AH... HUH?!
SWOOSH
TA——DAA
HAHAHA
SLISH
SPLASH
オダマリーナ
ODA MARINA
WOW! ALL ABOARD!!
BE CAREFUL!
WAAAH
HAHA... DON'T WORRY. I'LL BE OKAY!

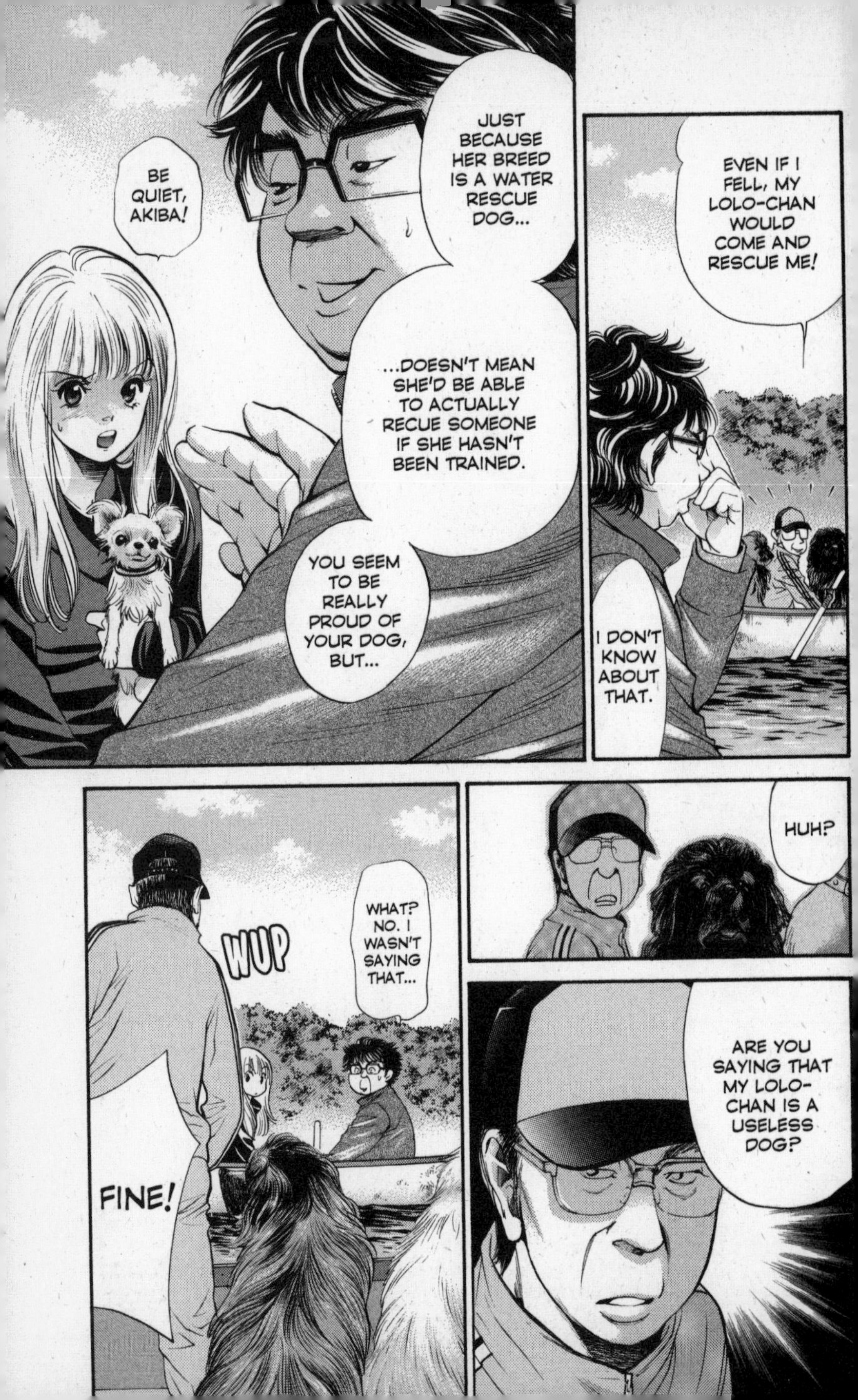
EVEN IF I FELL, MY LOLO-CHAN WOULD COME AND RESCUE ME!
I DON'T KNOW ABOUT THAT.
JUST BECAUSE HER BREED IS A WATER RESCUE DOG...
...DOESN'T MEAN SHE'D BE ABLE TO ACTUALLY RECUE SOMEONE IF SHE HASN'T BEEN TRAINED.
BE QUIET, AKIBA!
YOU SEEM TO BE REALLY PROUD OF YOUR DOG, BUT...
HUH?
ARE YOU SAYING THAT MY LOLO-CHAN IS A USELESS DOG?
WHAT? NO. I WASN'T SAYING THAT...
WUP
FINE!

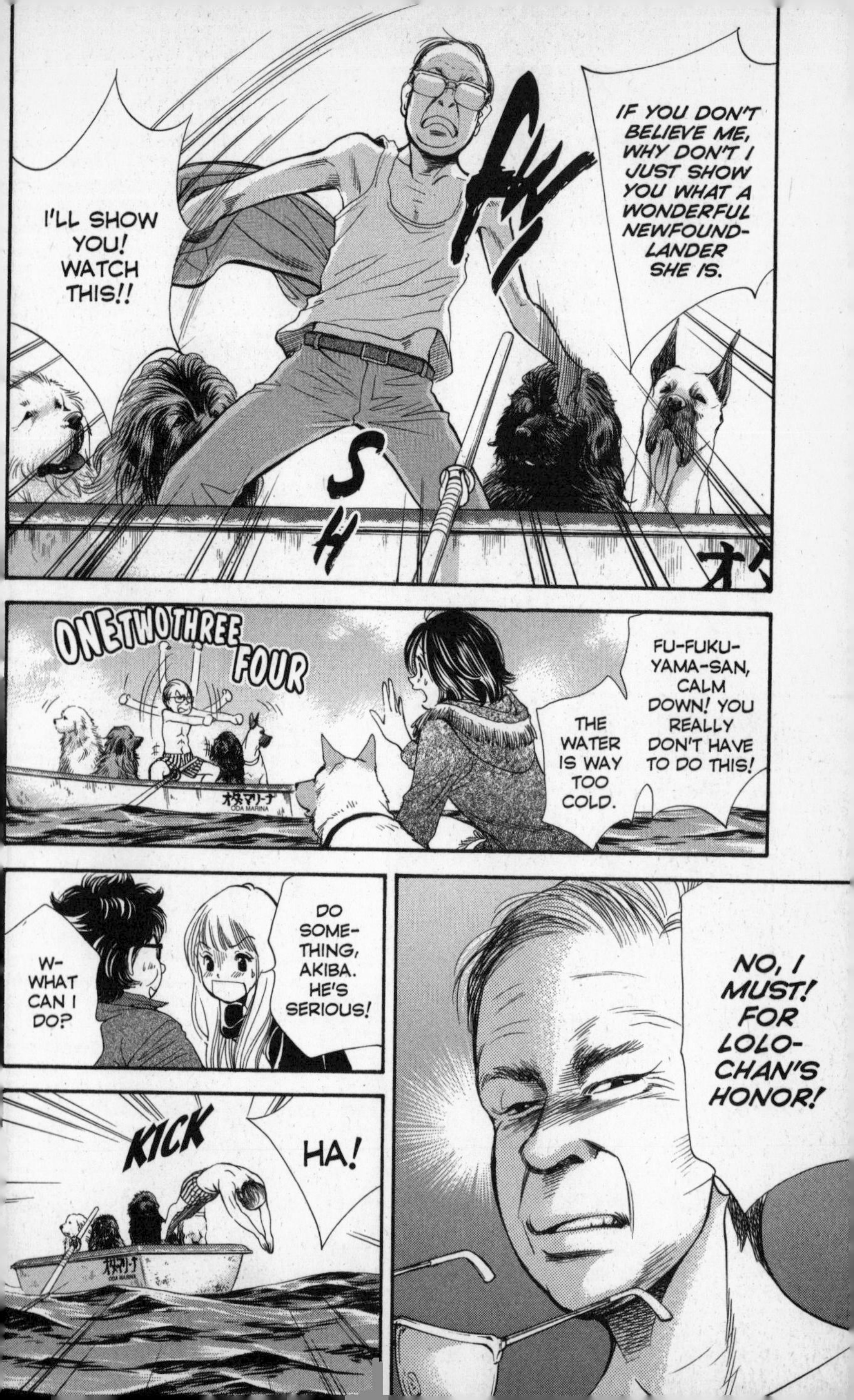
IF YOU DON'T BELIEVE ME, WHY DON'T I JUST SHOW YOU WHAT A WONDERFUL NEWFOUND-LANDER SHE IS.
I'LL SHOW YOU! WATCH THIS!!
FU-FUKU-YAMA-SAN, CALM DOWN! YOU REALLY DON'T HAVE TO DO THIS!
THE WATER IS WAY TOO COLD.
ONE TWO THREE FOUR
オダマリーナ
ODA MARINA
NO, I MUST! FOR LOLO-CHAN'S HONOR!
DO SOME-THING, AKIBA. HE'S SERIOUS!
W-WHAT CAN I DO?
HA!
KICK

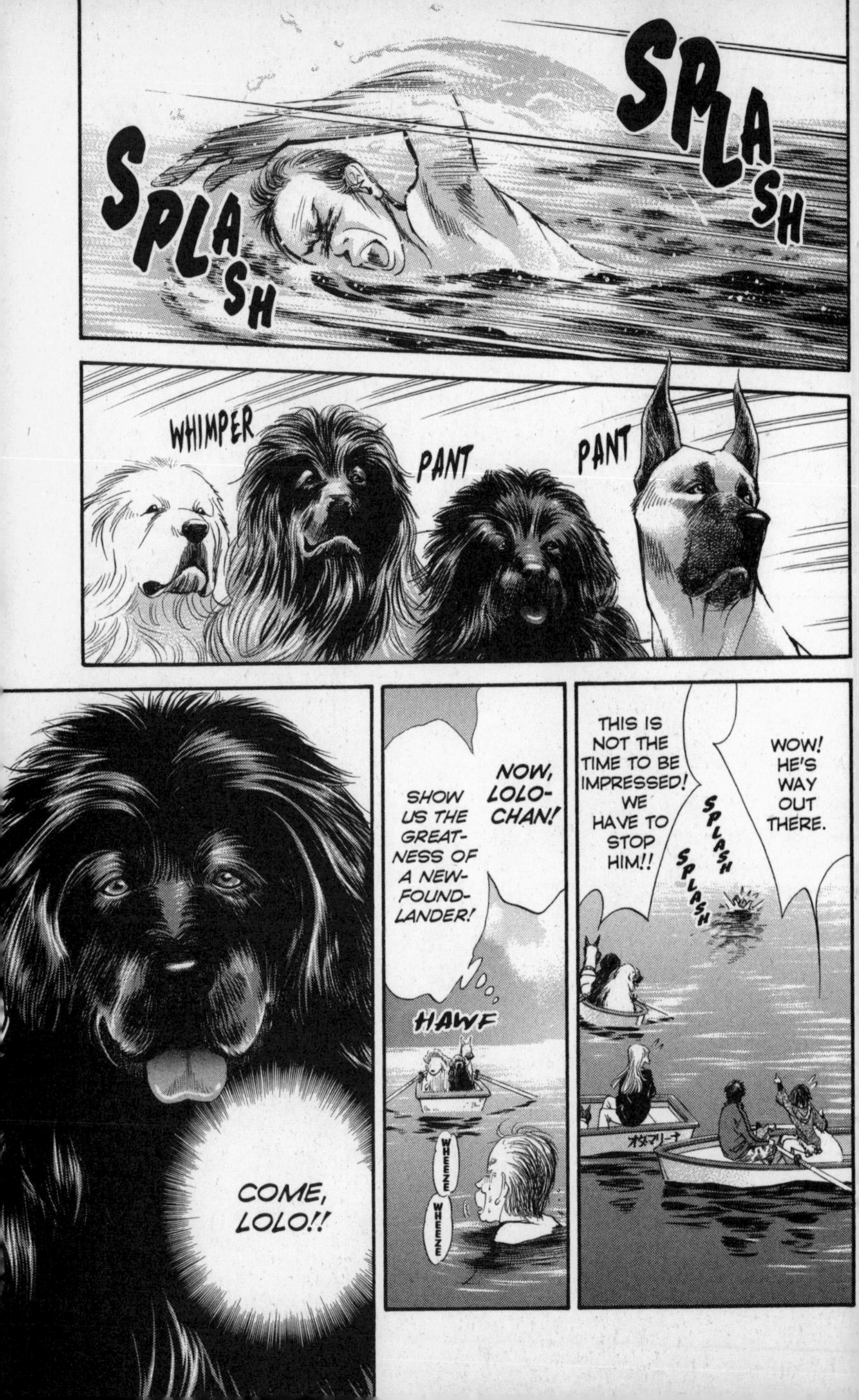
SPLASH
SPLASH
PANT
PANT
WHIMPER
WOW! HE'S WAY OUT THERE.
THIS IS NOT THE TIME TO BE IMPRESSED! WE HAVE TO STOP HIM!!
SPLASH
SPLASH
NOW, LOLO-CHAN!
SHOW US THE GREAT-NESS OF A NEW-FOUND-LANDER!
HAWF
WHEEZE
WHEEZE
COME, LOLO!!

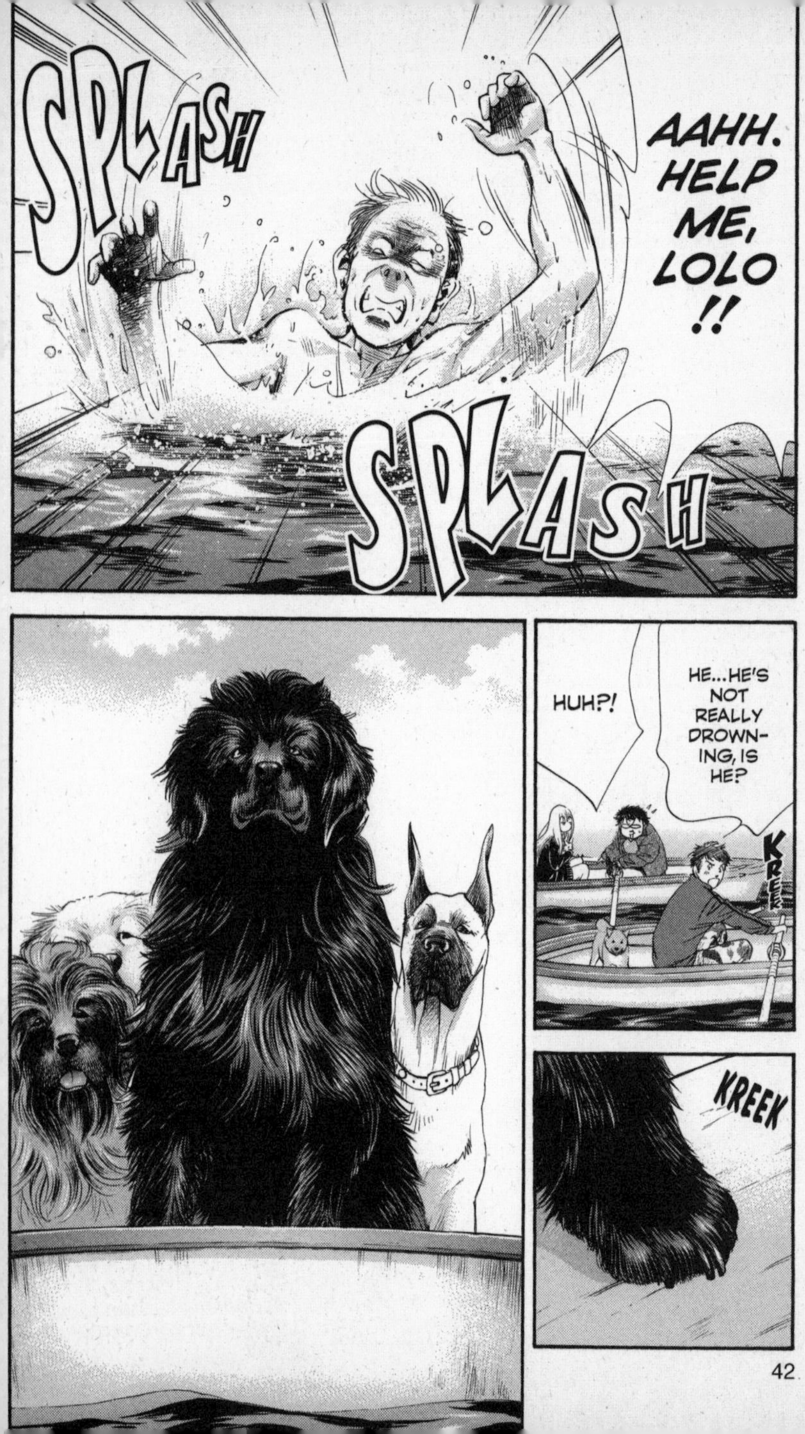
SPLASH
AAHH. HELP ME, LOLO!!
SPLASH
HE...HE'S NOT REALLY DROWNING, IS HE?
HUH?!
KREEK
KREEK

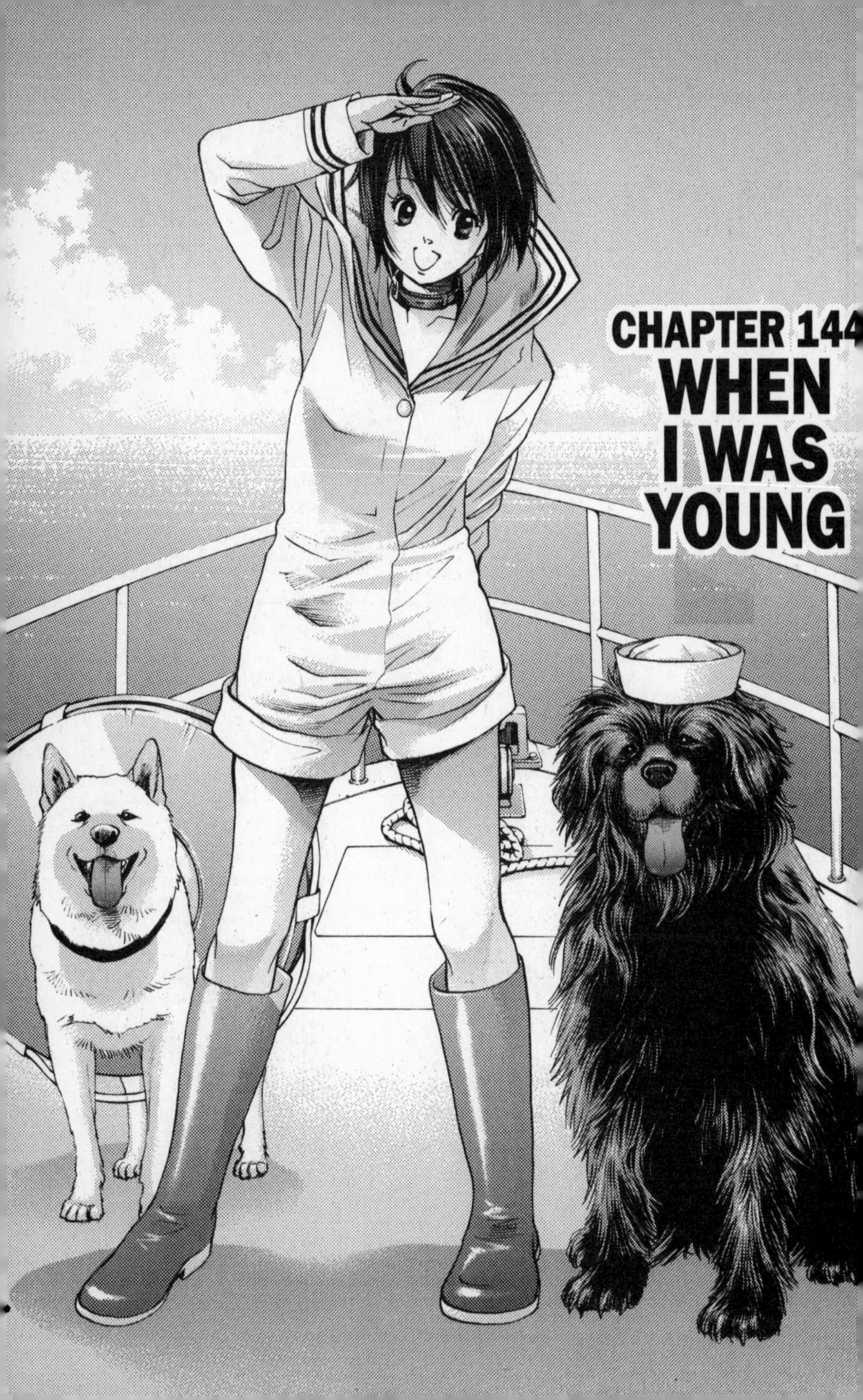
CHAPTER 144
WHEN I WAS YOUNG

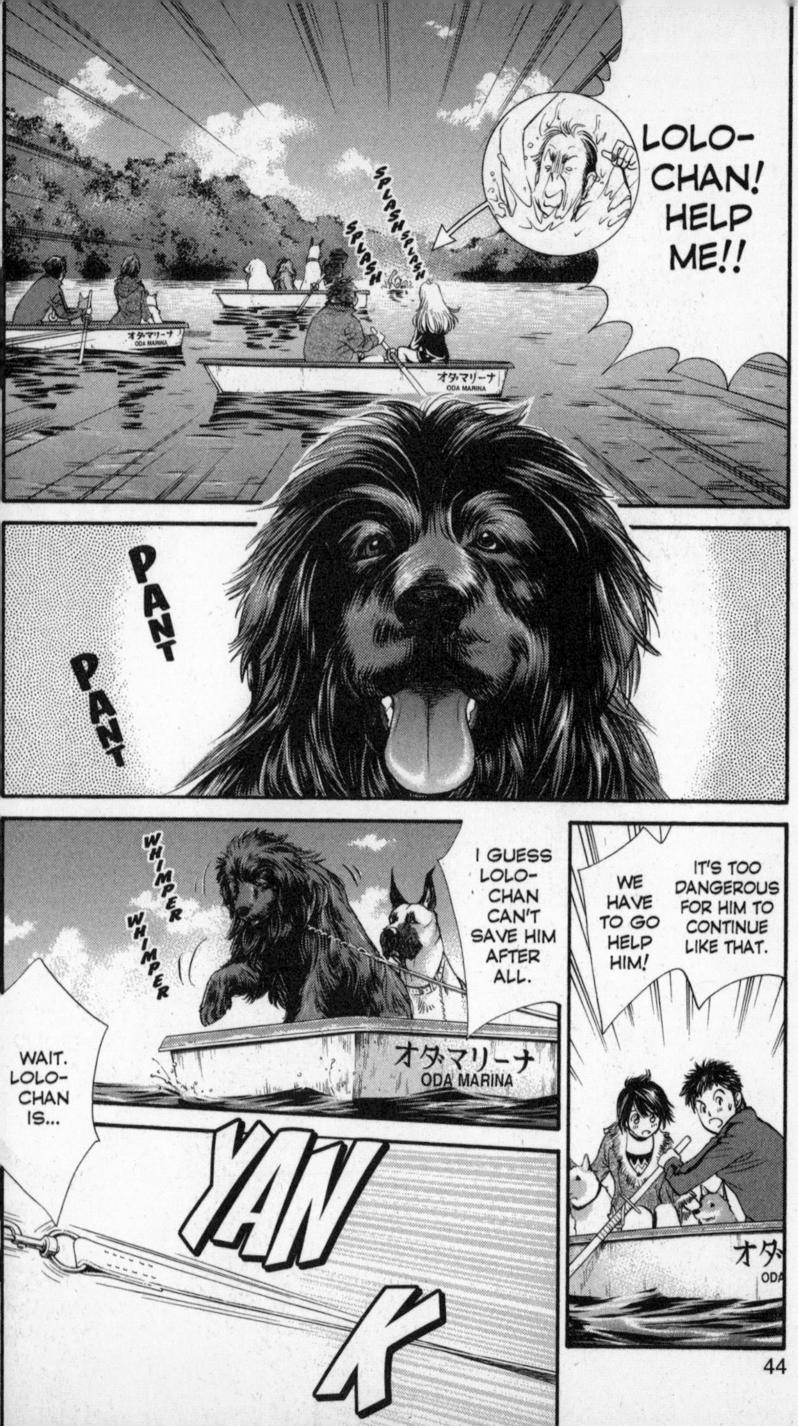
LOLO-CHAN! HELP ME!!
SPLASH SPLASH SPLASH
オダマリーナ
ODA MARINA
PANT PANT
IT'S TOO DANGEROUS FOR HIM TO CONTINUE LIKE THAT.
WE HAVE TO GO HELP HIM!
I GUESS LOLO-CHAN CAN'T SAVE HIM AFTER ALL.
WHIMPER WHIMPER
オダマリーナ
ODA MARINA
WAIT. LOLO-CHAN IS...
YANK

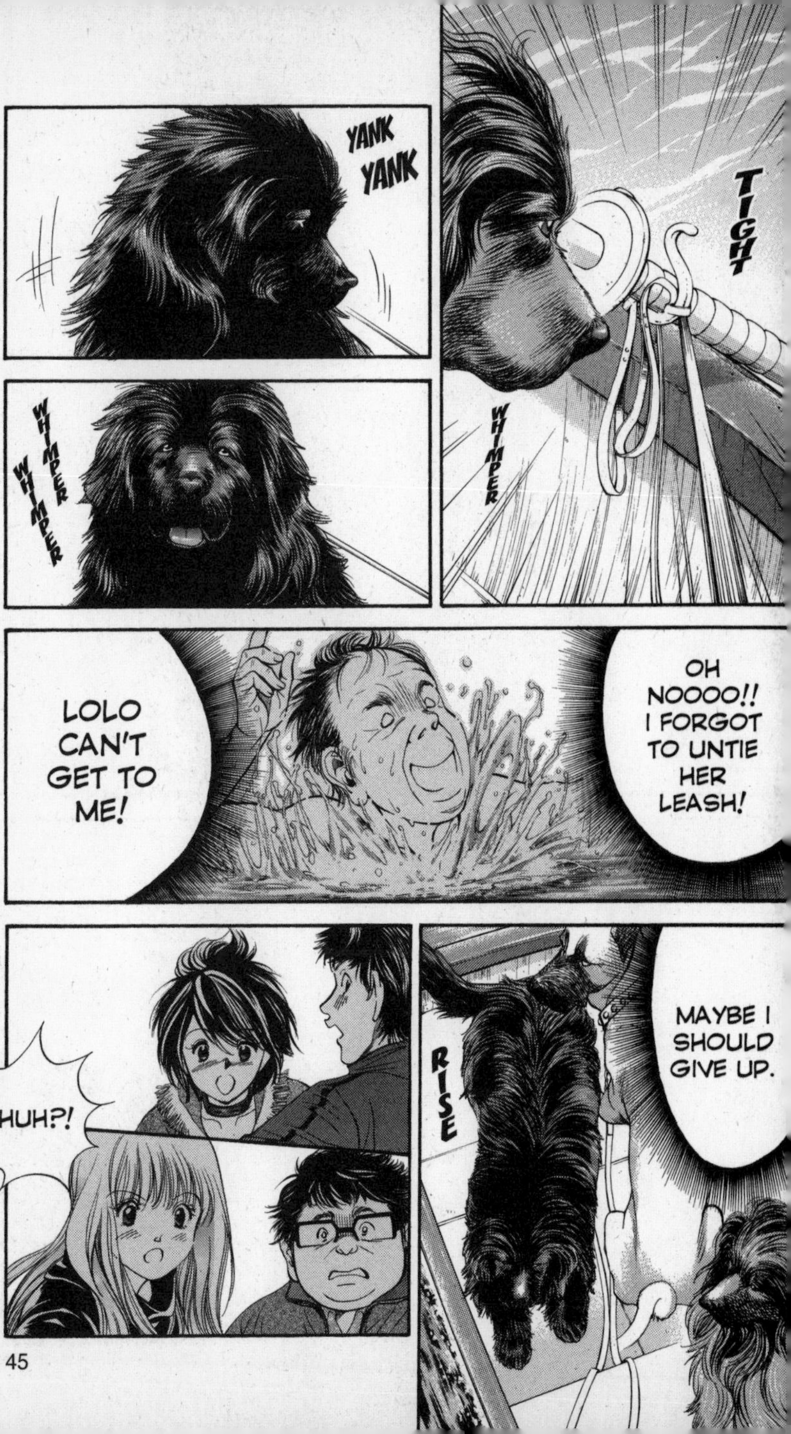
TIGHT
WHIMPER
YANK YANK
WHIMPER WHIMPER
OH NOOOO!! I FORGOT TO UNTIE HER LEASH!
LOLO CAN'T GET TO ME!
MAYBE I SHOULD GIVE UP.
RISE
HUH?!

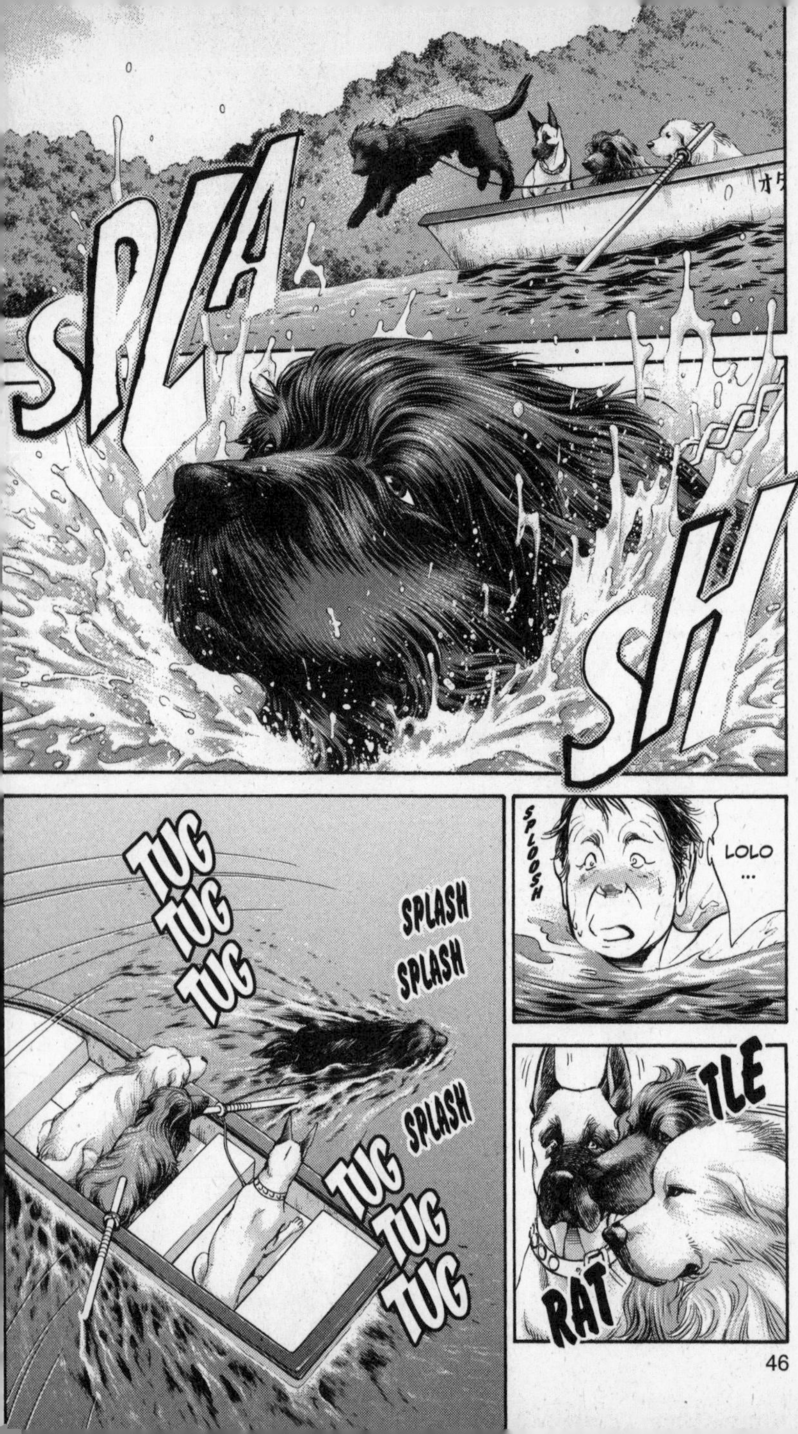
SPLASH
SPLOOSH
LOLO ...
RATTLE
TUG TUG TUG
SPLASH
SPLASH
SPLASH
TUG TUG TUG

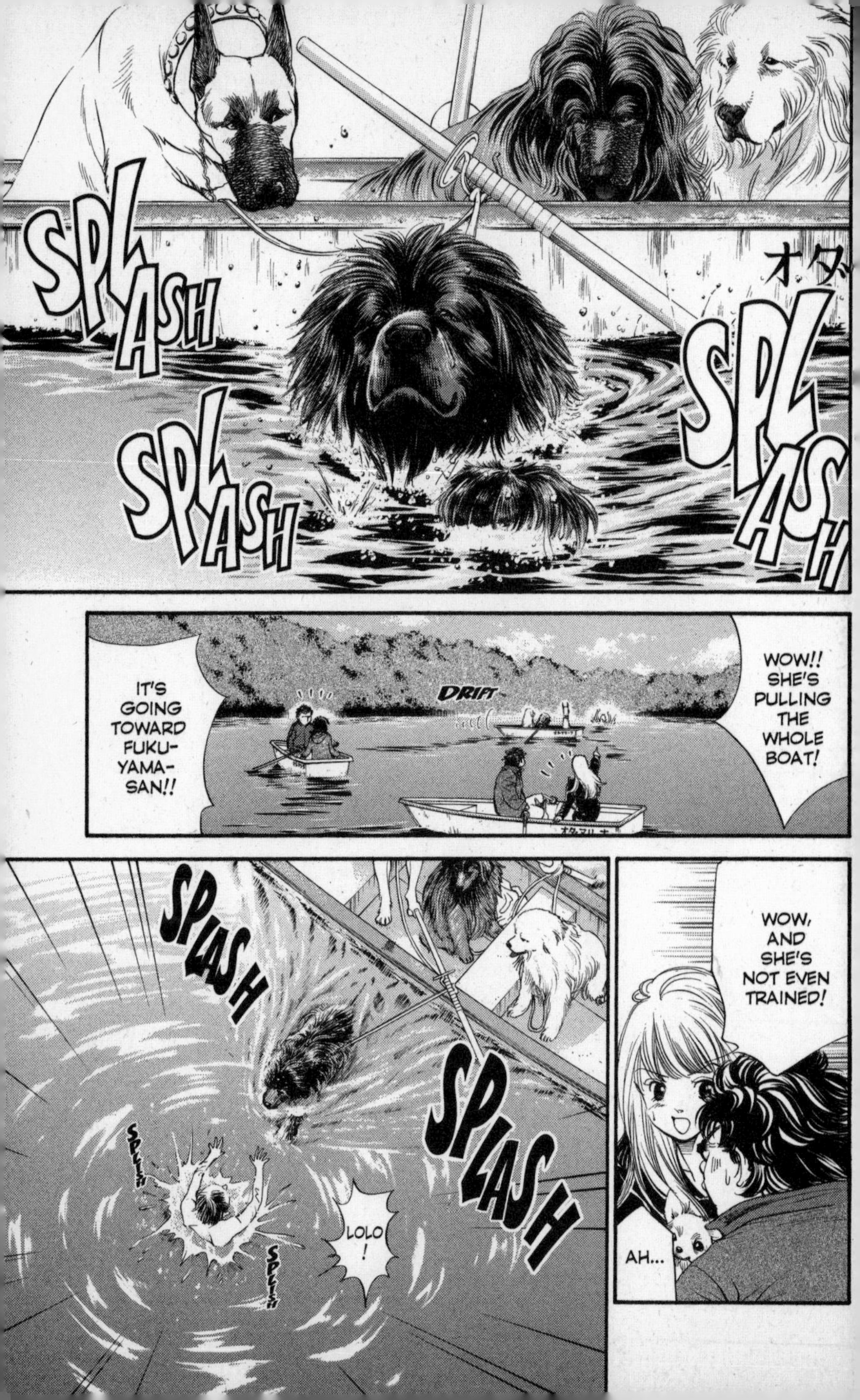
オダ
SPLASH
SPLASH
SPLASH
WOW!! SHE'S PULLING THE WHOLE BOAT!
DRIFT
IT'S GOING TOWARD FUKU-YAMA-SAN!!
WOW, AND SHE'S NOT EVEN TRAINED!
AH...
SPLASH
SPLASH
LOLO!
SPLISH
SPLISH

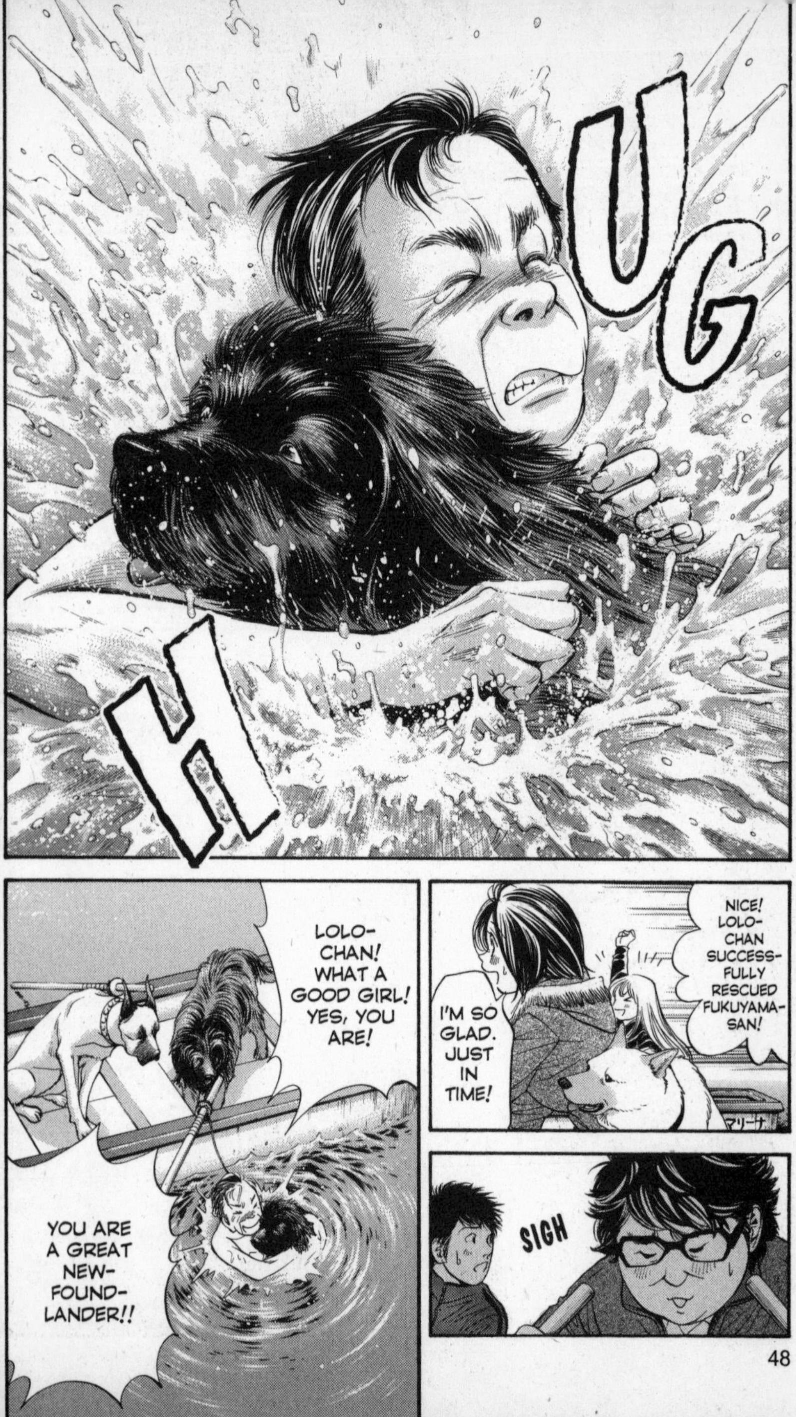
HUG
NICE! LOLO-CHAN SUCCESSFULLY RESCUED FUKUYAMA-SAN!
I'M SO GLAD. JUST IN TIME!
マリーナ
SIGH
LOLO-CHAN! WHAT A GOOD GIRL! YES, YOU ARE!
YOU ARE A GREAT NEW-FOUNDLANDER!!

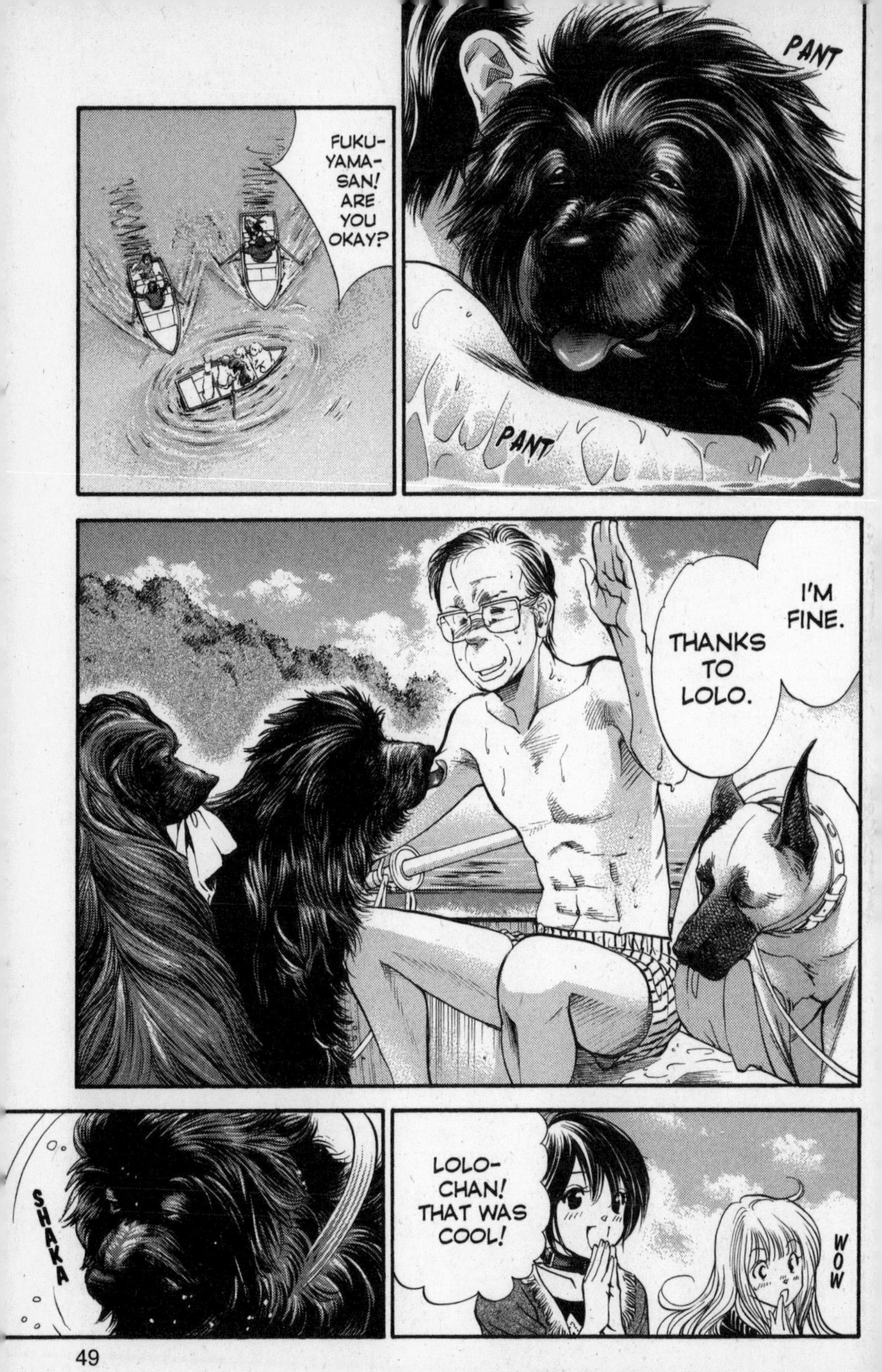
PANT
PANT
FUKU-YAMA-SAN! ARE YOU OKAY?
I'M FINE.
THANKS TO LOLO.
LOLO-CHAN! THAT WAS COOL!
WOW
SHAKA

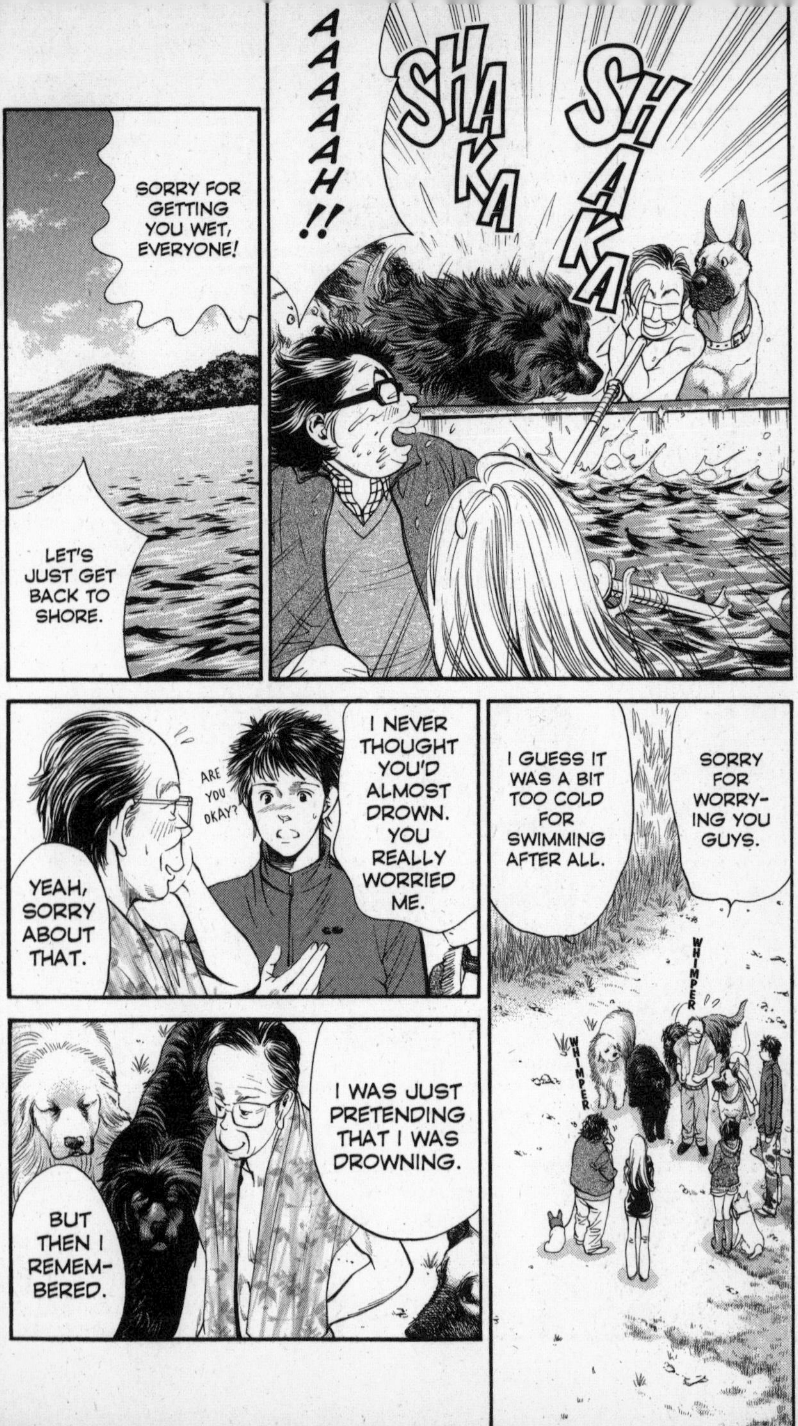
SHAKA
SHAKA
AAAAAAH!!
SORRY FOR GETTING YOU WET, EVERYONE!
LET'S JUST GET BACK TO SHORE.
SORRY FOR WORRYING YOU GUYS.
I GUESS IT WAS A BIT TOO COLD FOR SWIMMING AFTER ALL.
WHIMPER
WHIMPER
I NEVER THOUGHT YOU'D ALMOST DROWN. YOU REALLY WORRIED ME.
ARE YOU OKAY?
YEAH, SORRY ABOUT THAT.
I WAS JUST PRETENDING THAT I WAS DROWNING.
BUT THEN I REMEMBERED.

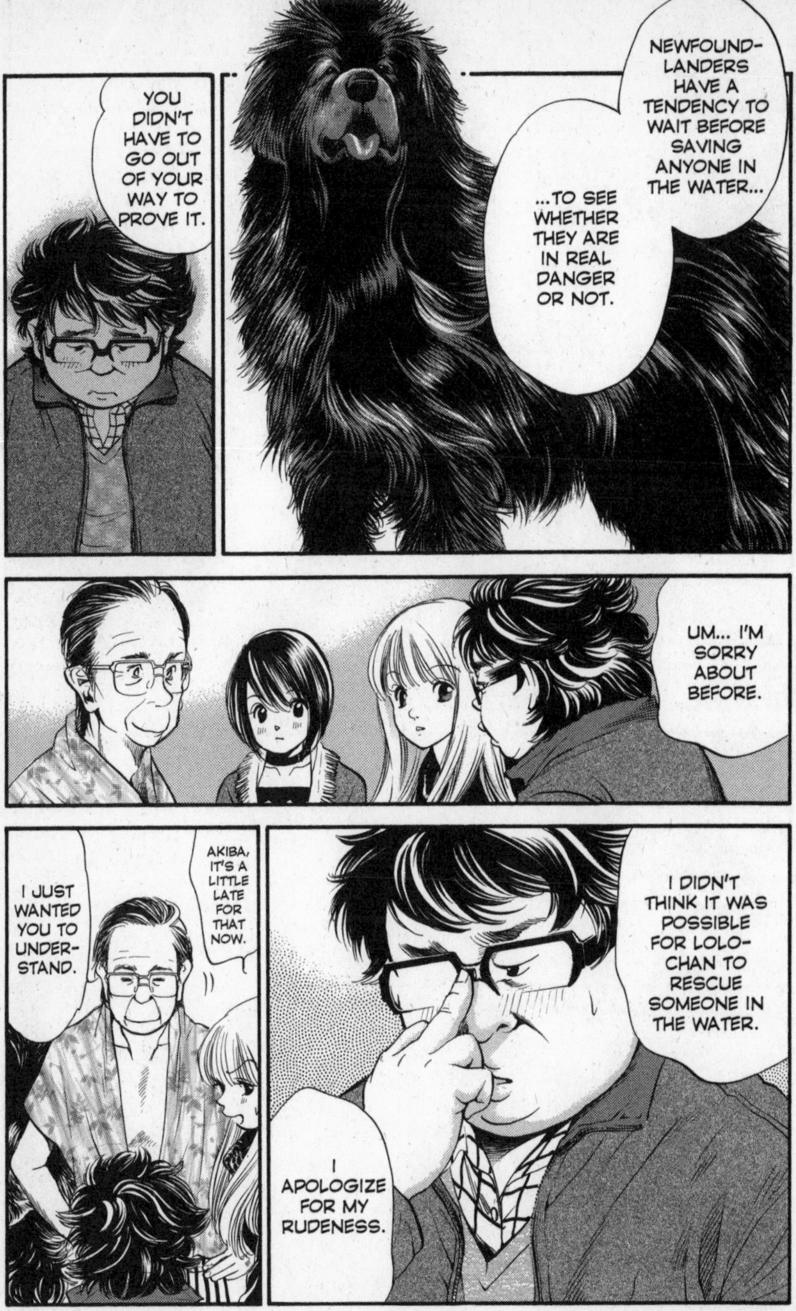
NEWFOUNDLANDERS HAVE A TENDENCY TO WAIT BEFORE SAVING ANYONE IN THE WATER...
...TO SEE WHETHER THEY ARE IN REAL DANGER OR NOT.
YOU DIDN'T HAVE TO GO OUT OF YOUR WAY TO PROVE IT.
UM... I'M SORRY ABOUT BEFORE.
I DIDN'T THINK IT WAS POSSIBLE FOR LOLO-CHAN TO RESCUE SOMEONE IN THE WATER.
I APOLOGIZE FOR MY RUDENESS.
AKIBA, IT'S A LITTLE LATE FOR THAT NOW.
I JUST WANTED YOU TO UNDERSTAND.

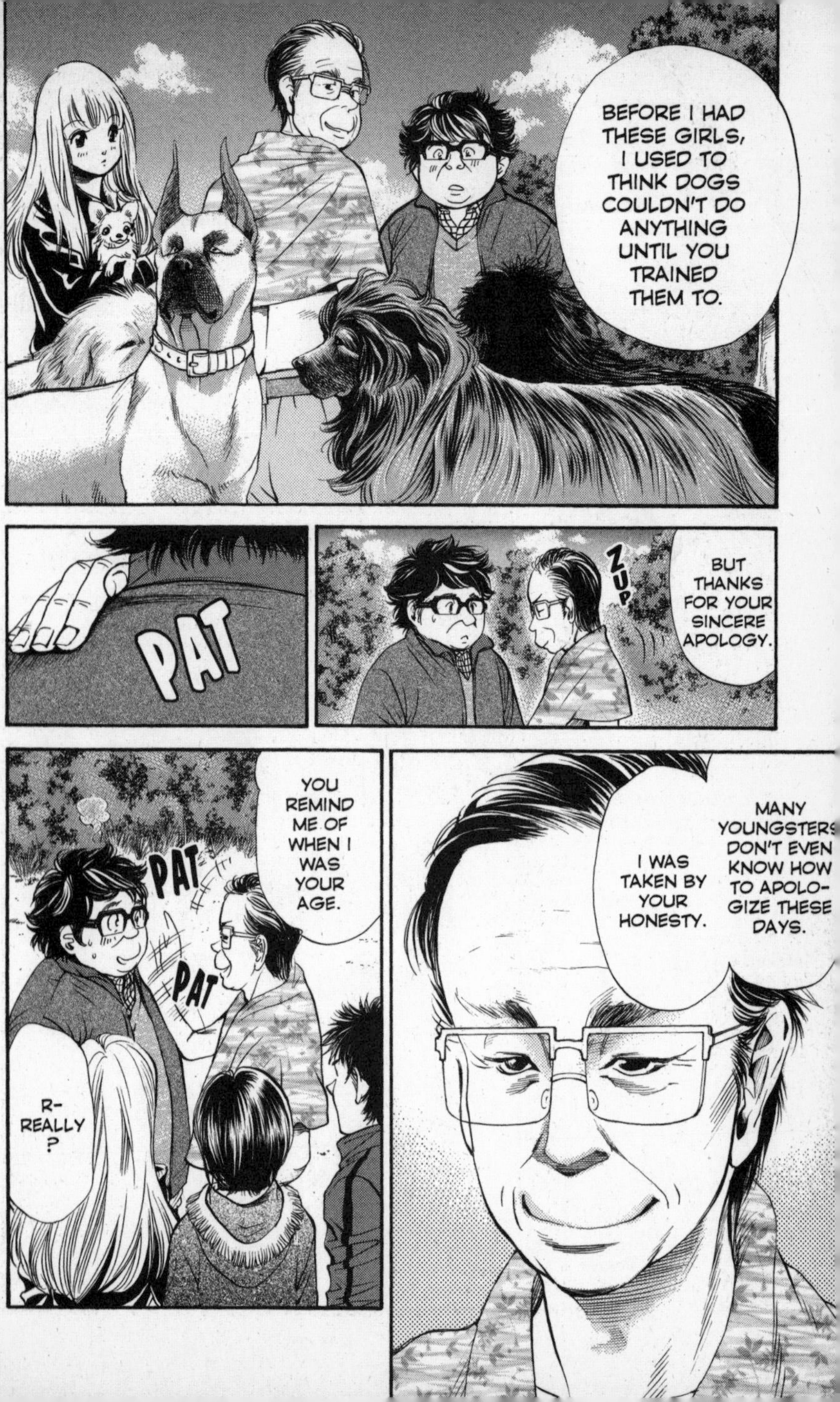
BEFORE I HAD THESE GIRLS, I USED TO THINK DOGS COULDN'T DO ANYTHING UNTIL YOU TRAINED THEM TO.
ZUP
BUT THANKS FOR YOUR SINCERE APOLOGY.
PAT
MANY YOUNGSTERS DON'T EVEN KNOW HOW TO APOLOGIZE THESE DAYS.
I WAS TAKEN BY YOUR HONESTY.
YOU REMIND ME OF WHEN I WAS YOUR AGE.
PAT
PAT
R-REALLY?

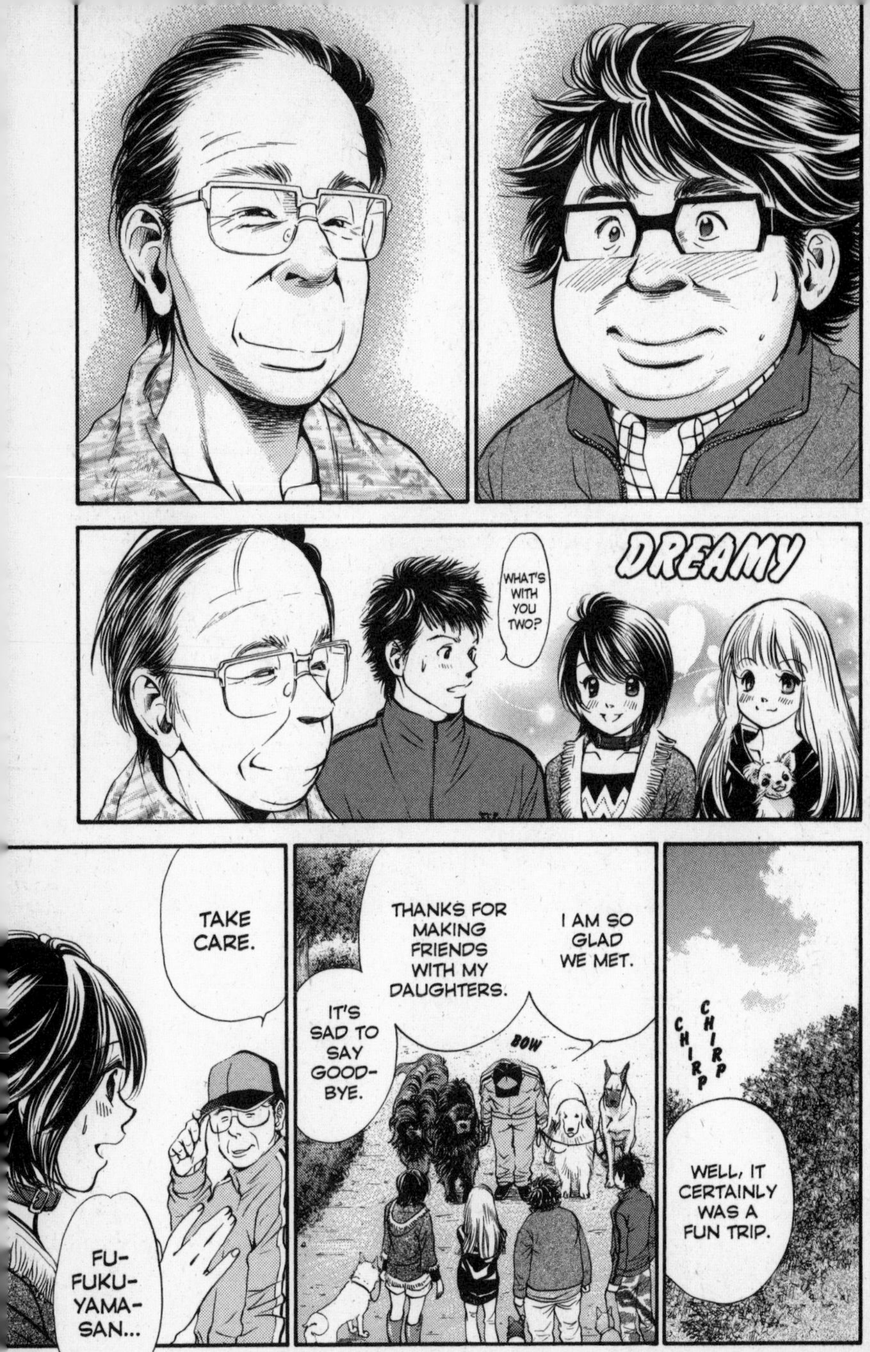
DREAMY
WHAT'S WITH YOU TWO?
CHIRP CHIRP
WELL, IT CERTAINLY WAS A FUN TRIP.
I AM SO GLAD WE MET.
THANKS FOR MAKING FRIENDS WITH MY DAUGHTERS.
BOW
IT'S SAD TO SAY GOOD-BYE.
TAKE CARE.
FU-FUKU-YAMA-SAN...

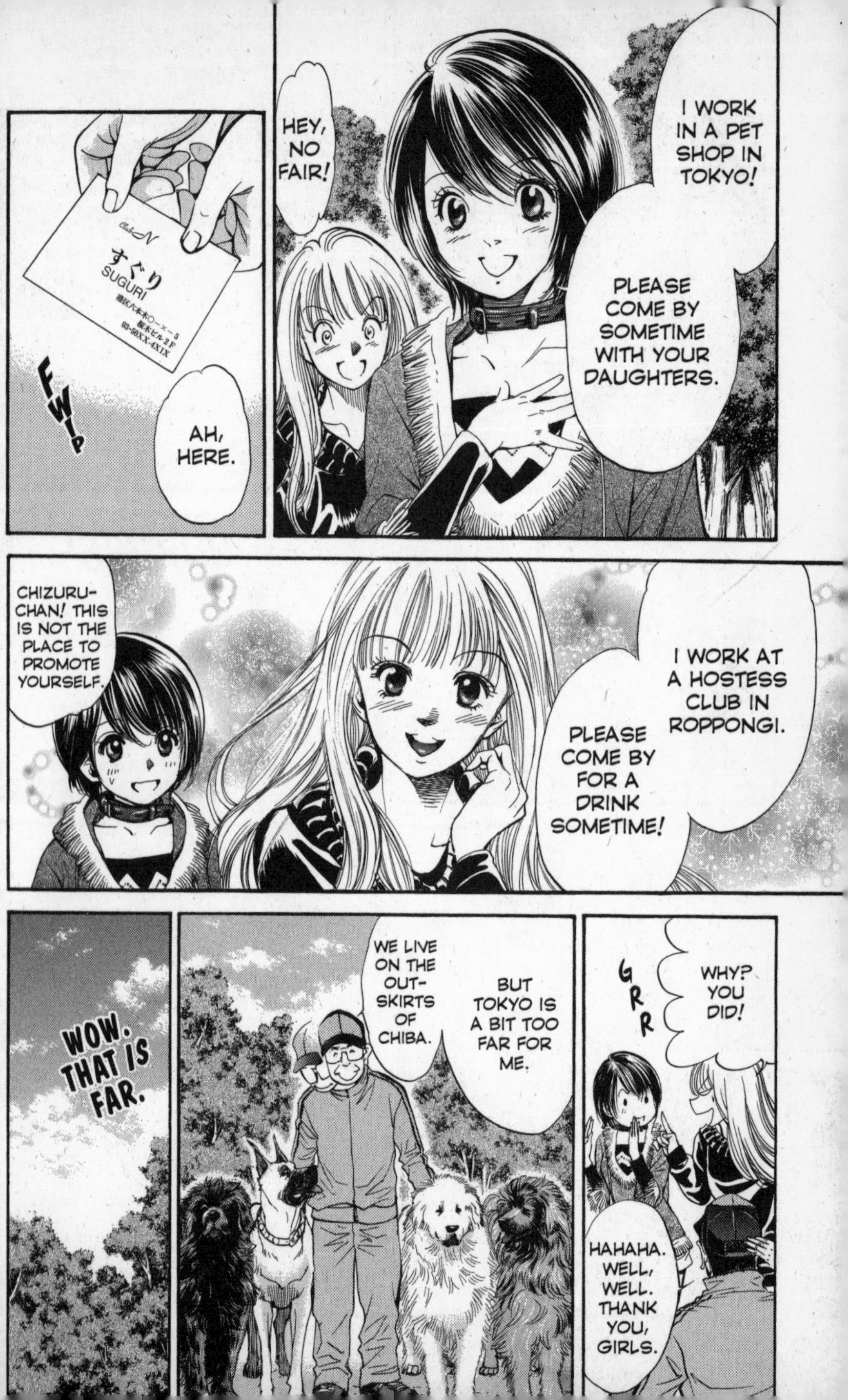
I WORK IN A PET SHOP IN TOKYO!
PLEASE COME BY SOMETIME WITH YOUR DAUGHTERS.
HEY, NO FAIR!
Club N
すぐり
SUGURI
FWIP
AH, HERE.
I WORK AT A HOSTESS CLUB IN ROPPONGI.
PLEASE COME BY FOR A DRINK SOMETIME!
CHIZURU-CHAN! THIS IS NOT THE PLACE TO PROMOTE YOURSELF.
WHY? YOU DID!
GRR
HAHAHA. WELL, WELL. THANK YOU, GIRLS.
BUT TOKYO IS A BIT TOO FAR FOR ME.
WE LIVE ON THE OUT-SKIRTS OF CHIBA.
WOW. THAT IS FAR.

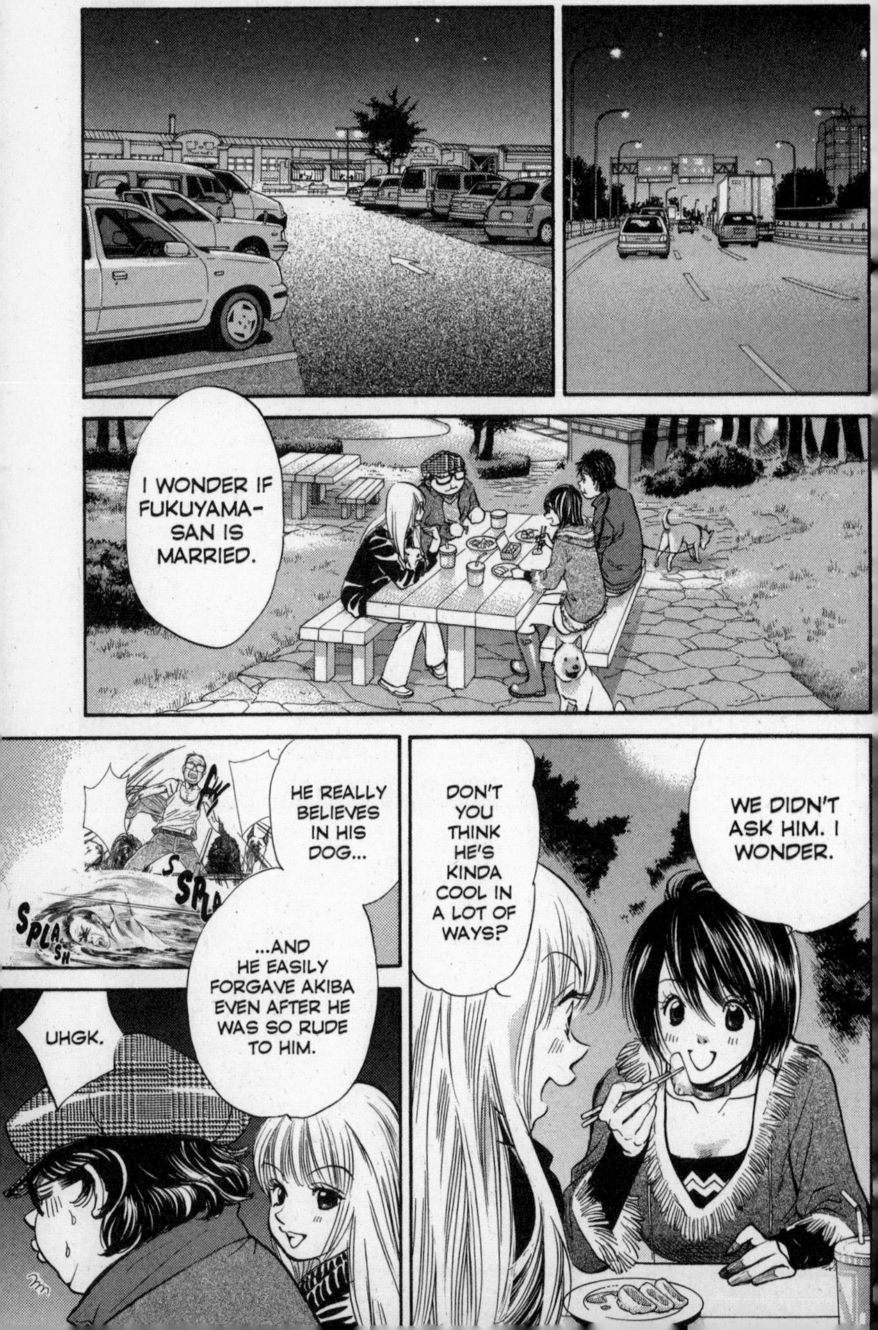
I WONDER IF FUKUYAMA-SAN IS MARRIED.
WE DIDN'T ASK HIM. I WONDER.
DON'T YOU THINK HE'S KINDA COOL IN A LOT OF WAYS?
HE REALLY BELIEVES IN HIS DOG...
SPLASH
...AND HE EASILY FORGAVE AKIBA EVEN AFTER HE WAS SO RUDE TO HIM.
UHGK.

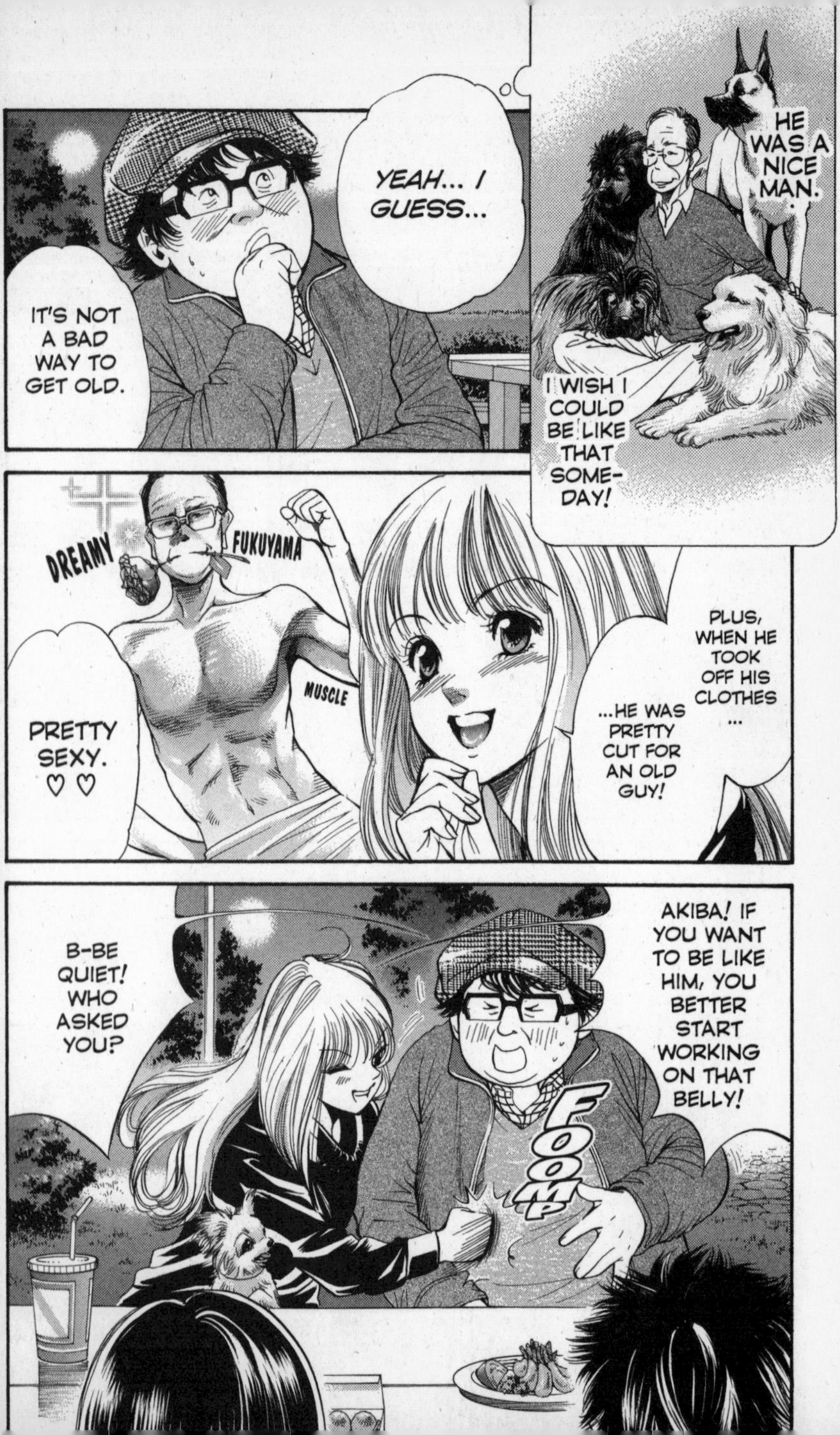
HE WAS A NICE MAN.
I WISH I COULD BE LIKE THAT SOME-DAY!
YEAH... I GUESS...
IT'S NOT A BAD WAY TO GET OLD.
PLUS, WHEN HE TOOK OFF HIS CLOTHES ...
...HE WAS PRETTY CUT FOR AN OLD GUY!
FUKUYAMA
DREAMY
MUSCLE
PRETTY SEXY. ♡ ♡
AKIBA! IF YOU WANT TO BE LIKE HIM, YOU BETTER START WORKING ON THAT BELLY!
FOOMP
B-BE QUIET! WHO ASKED YOU?

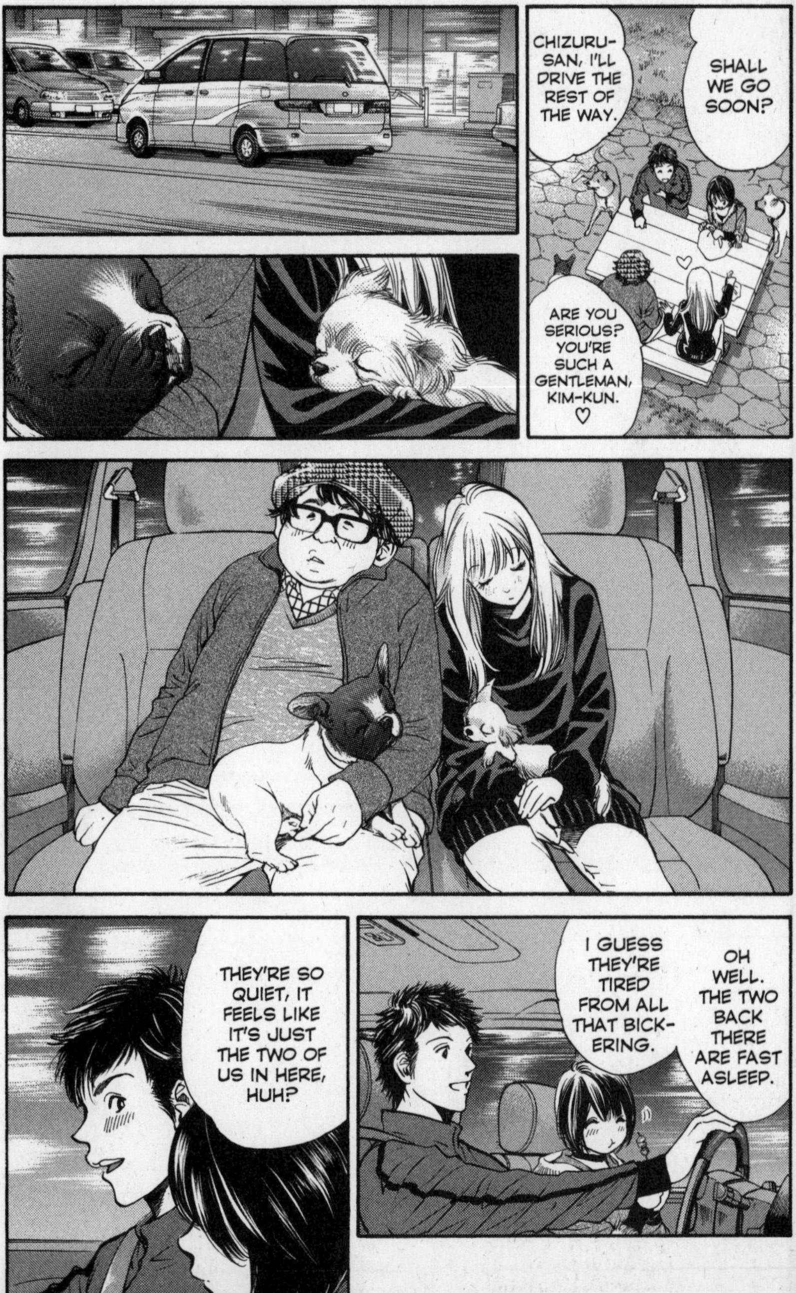
SHALL WE GO SOON?
CHIZURU-SAN, I'LL DRIVE THE REST OF THE WAY.
ARE YOU SERIOUS? YOU'RE SUCH A GENTLEMAN, KIM-KUN. ♡
OH WELL. THE TWO BACK THERE ARE FAST ASLEEP.
I GUESS THEY'RE TIRED FROM ALL THAT BICK-ERING.
THEY'RE SO QUIET, IT FEELS LIKE IT'S JUST THE TWO OF US IN HERE, HUH?

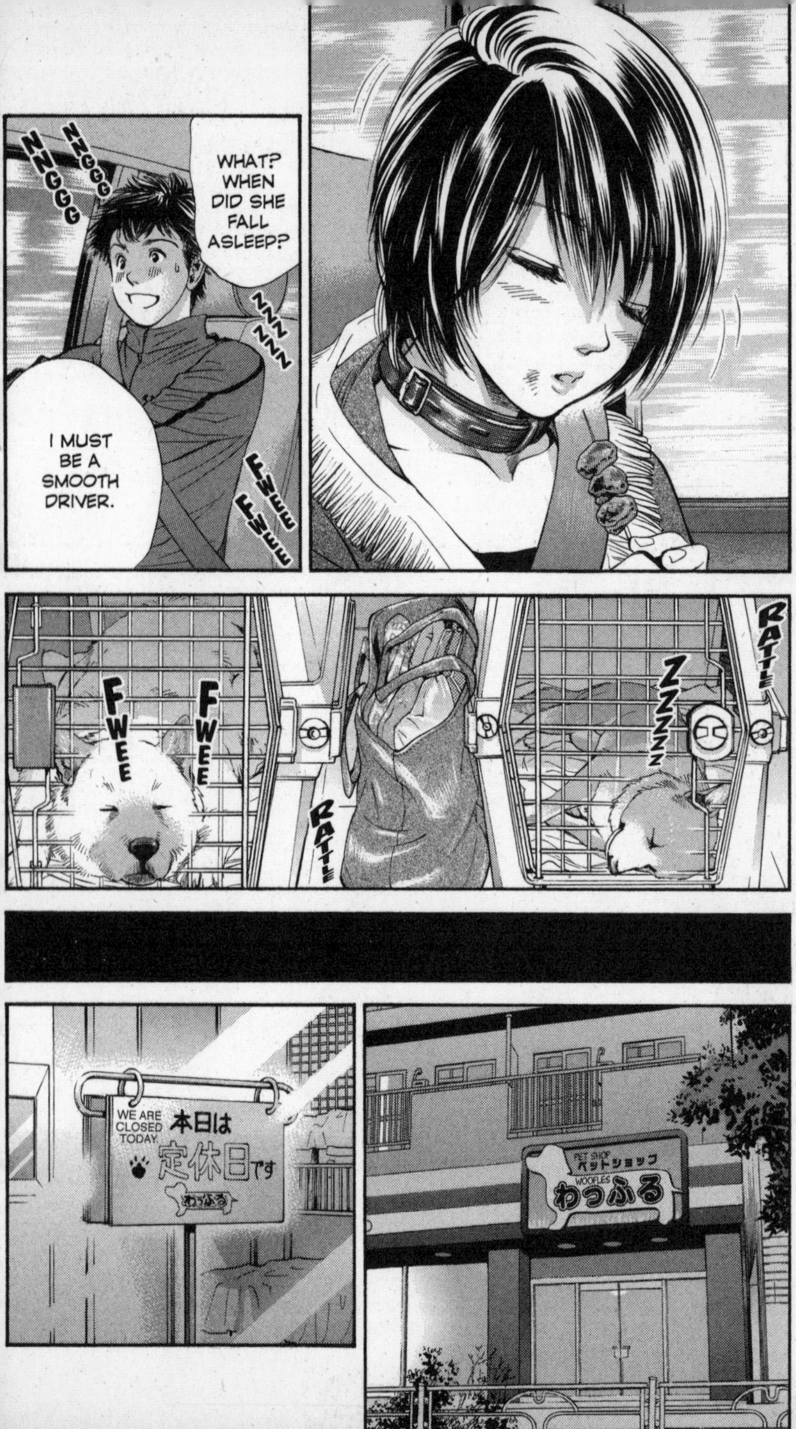
WHAT? WHEN DID SHE FALL ASLEEP?
NNGGG NNGGG
ZNNN ZNNN
I MUST BE A SMOOTH DRIVER.
FWEEE FWEEE
RATTLE
ZZZZZ
RATTLE
FWEE FWEE
PET SHOP ペットショップ
WOOFLES わっふる
WE ARE CLOSED TODAY
本日は定休日です
わっふる

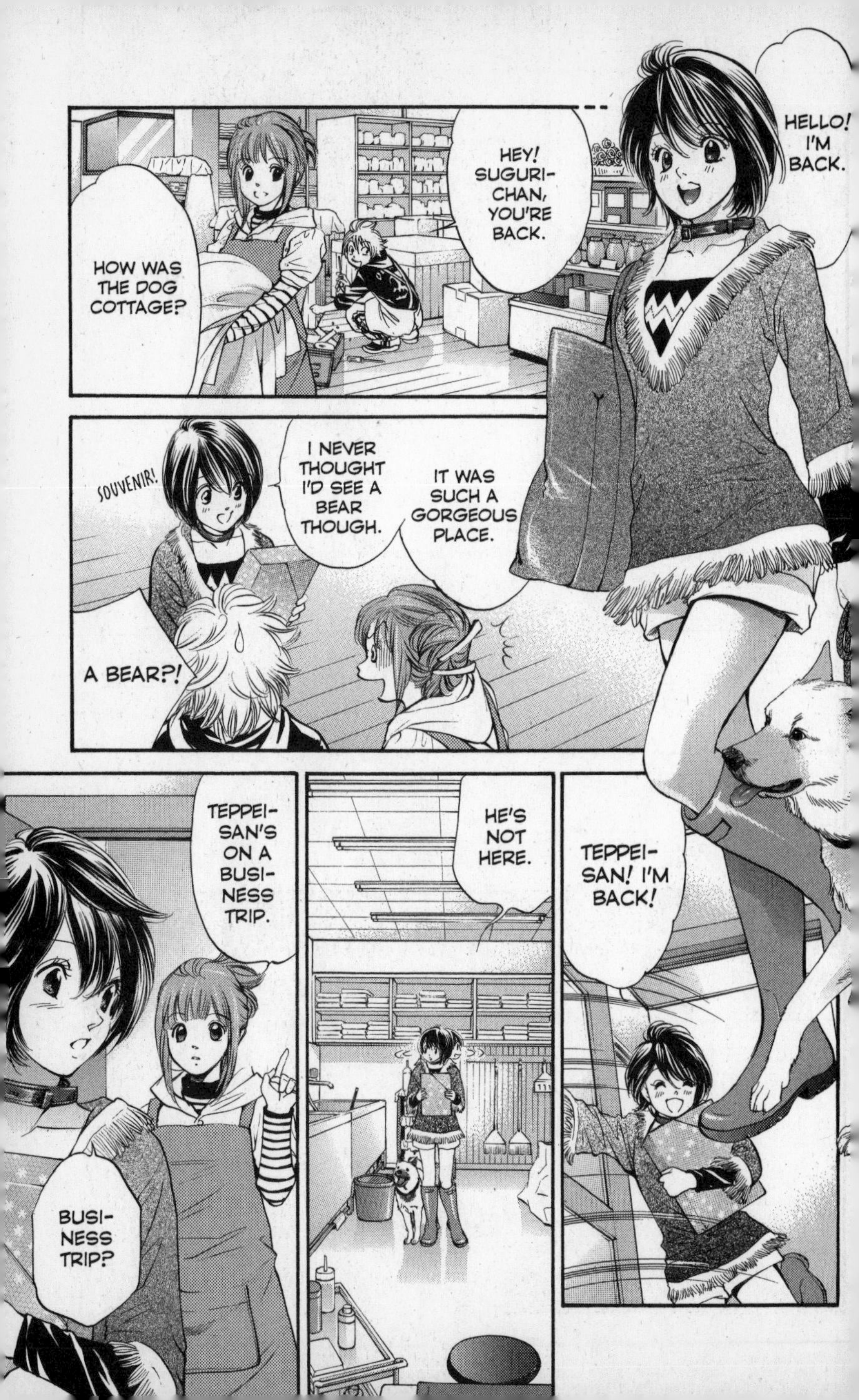
HELLO! I'M BACK.
HEY! SUGURI-CHAN, YOU'RE BACK.
HOW WAS THE DOG COTTAGE?
IT WAS SUCH A GORGEOUS PLACE.
I NEVER THOUGHT I'D SEE A BEAR THOUGH.
SOUVENIR!
A BEAR?!
TEPPEI-SAN! I'M BACK!
HE'S NOT HERE.
TEPPEI-SAN'S ON A BUSI-NESS TRIP.
BUSI-NESS TRIP?

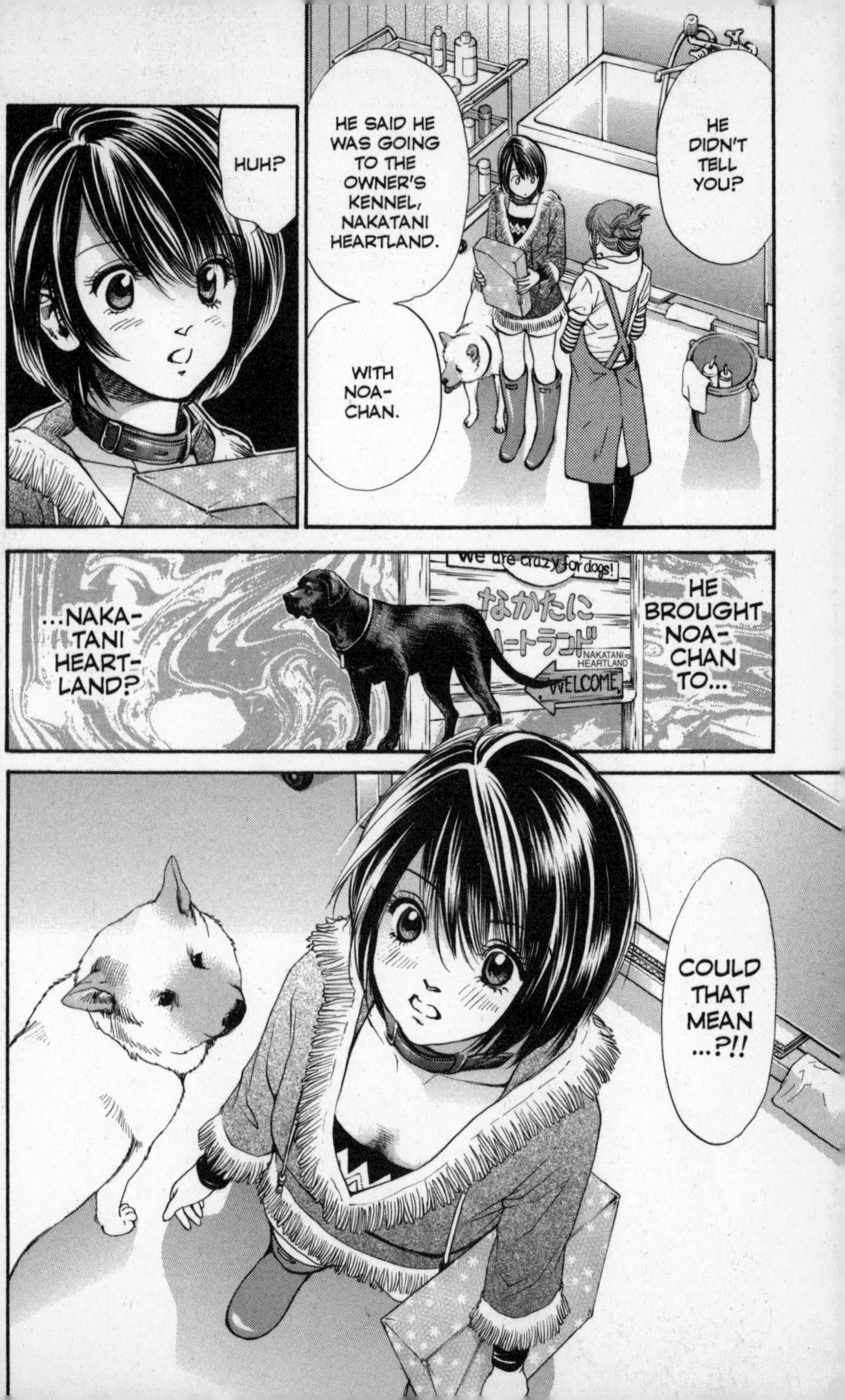
HE DIDN'T TELL YOU?
HE SAID HE WAS GOING TO THE OWNER'S KENNEL, NAKATANI HEARTLAND.
WITH NOA-CHAN.
HUH?
HE BROUGHT NOA-CHAN TO...
we are crazy for dogs!
なかたに
NAKATANI HEARTLAND
WELCOME
...NAKATANI HEARTLAND?
COULD THAT MEAN ...?!!

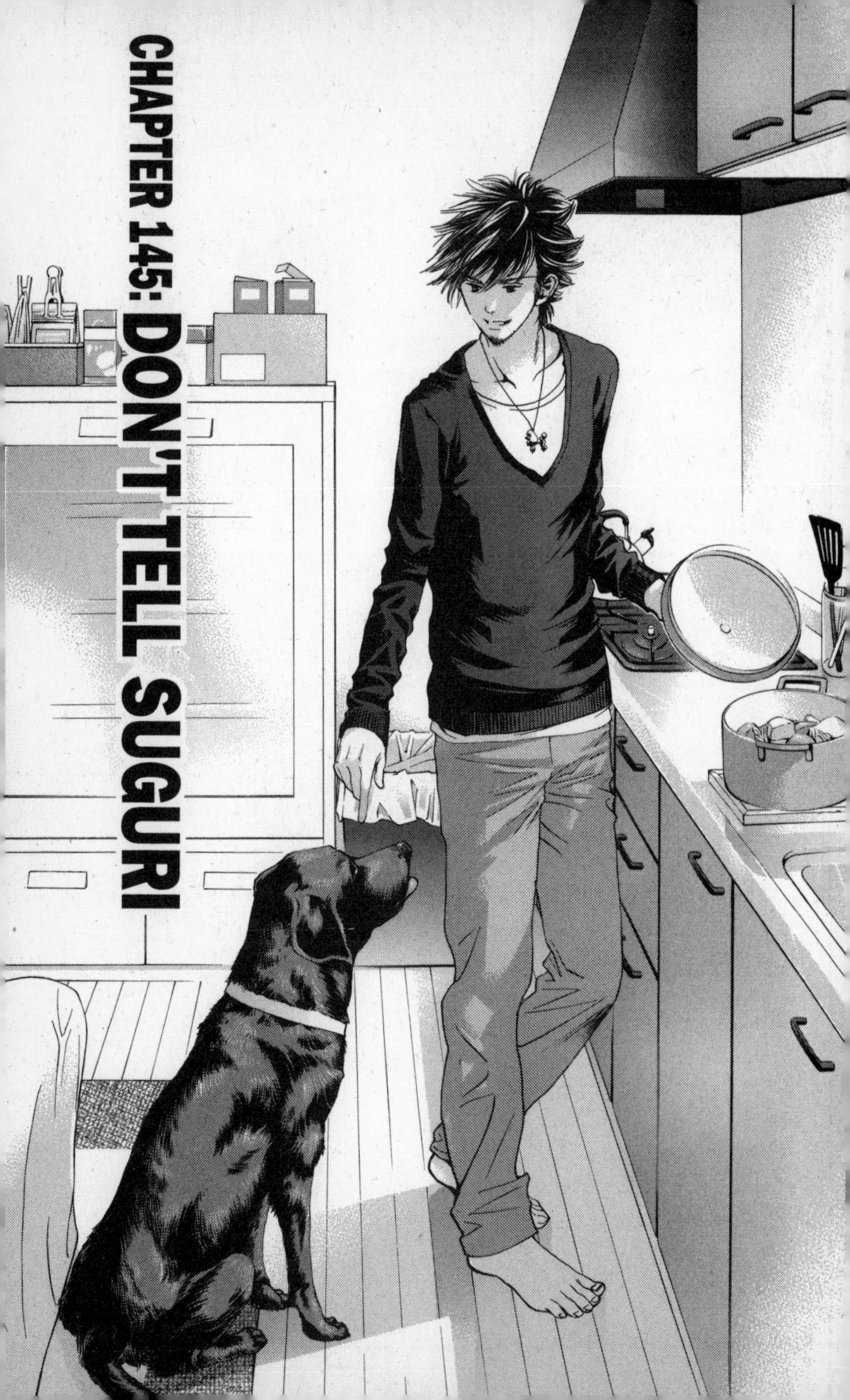
CHAPTER 145: DON'T TELL SUGURI

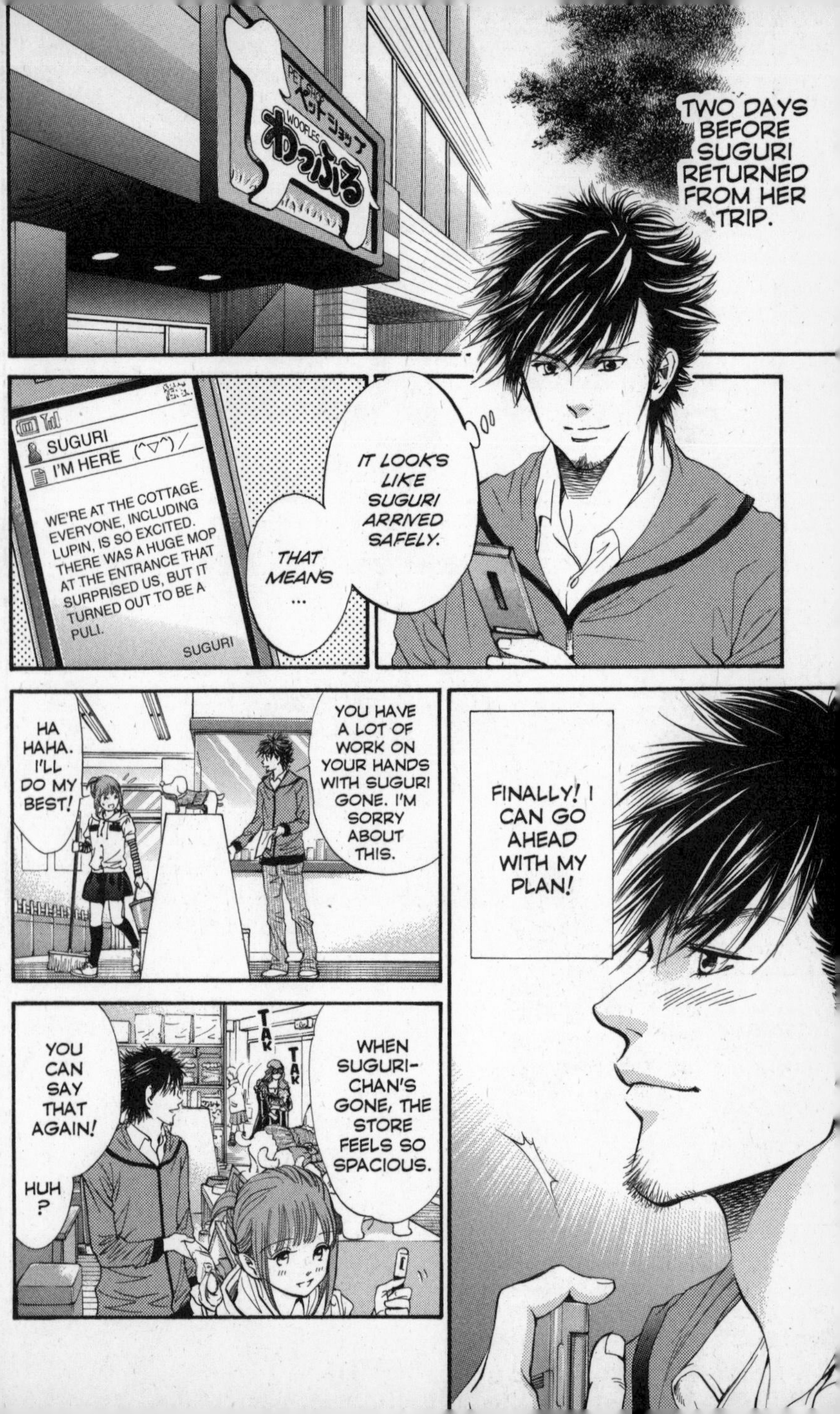
PET SHOP
WOOFLES
TWO DAYS BEFORE SUGURI RETURNED FROM HER TRIP.
IT LOOKS LIKE SUGURI ARRIVED SAFELY.
THAT MEANS...
SUGURI
I'M HERE (^▽^)/
WE'RE AT THE COTTAGE. EVERYONE, INCLUDING LUPIN, IS SO EXCITED. THERE WAS A HUGE MOP AT THE ENTRANCE THAT SURPRISED US, BUT IT TURNED OUT TO BE A PULI.
SUGURI
FINALLY! I CAN GO AHEAD WITH MY PLAN!
YOU HAVE A LOT OF WORK ON YOUR HANDS WITH SUGURI GONE. I'M SORRY ABOUT THIS.
HA HAHA. I'LL DO MY BEST!
TAK
TAK
WHEN SUGURI-CHAN'S GONE, THE STORE FEELS SO SPACIOUS.
YOU CAN SAY THAT AGAIN!
HUH?

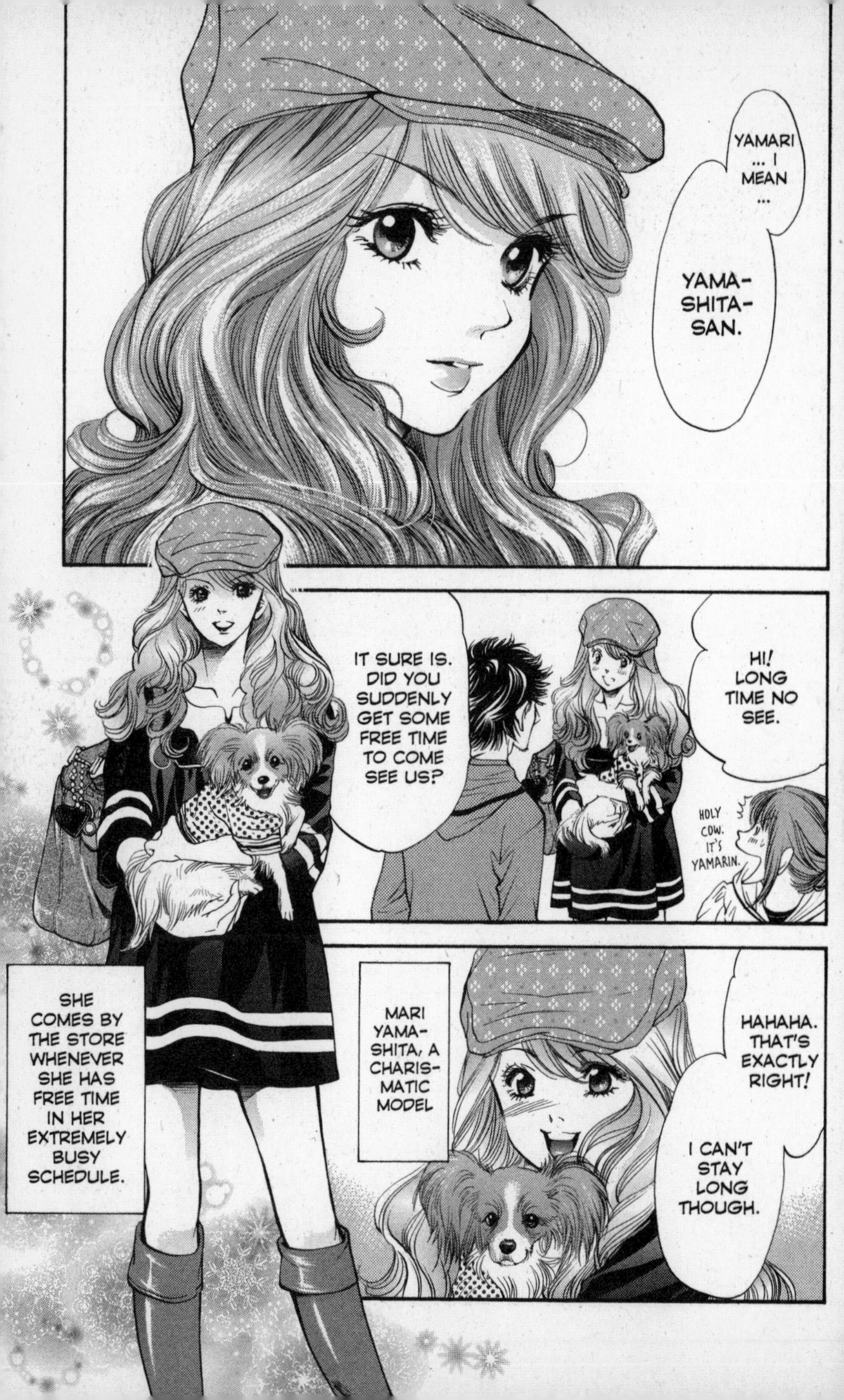
YAMARI ... I MEAN ...
YAMA-SHITA-SAN.
HI! LONG TIME NO SEE.
HOLY COW. IT'S YAMARIN.
IT SURE IS. DID YOU SUDDENLY GET SOME FREE TIME TO COME SEE US?
HAHAHA. THAT'S EXACTLY RIGHT!
I CAN'T STAY LONG THOUGH.
MARI YAMA-SHITA, A CHARIS-MATIC MODEL
SHE COMES BY THE STORE WHENEVER SHE HAS FREE TIME IN HER EXTREMELY BUSY SCHEDULE.

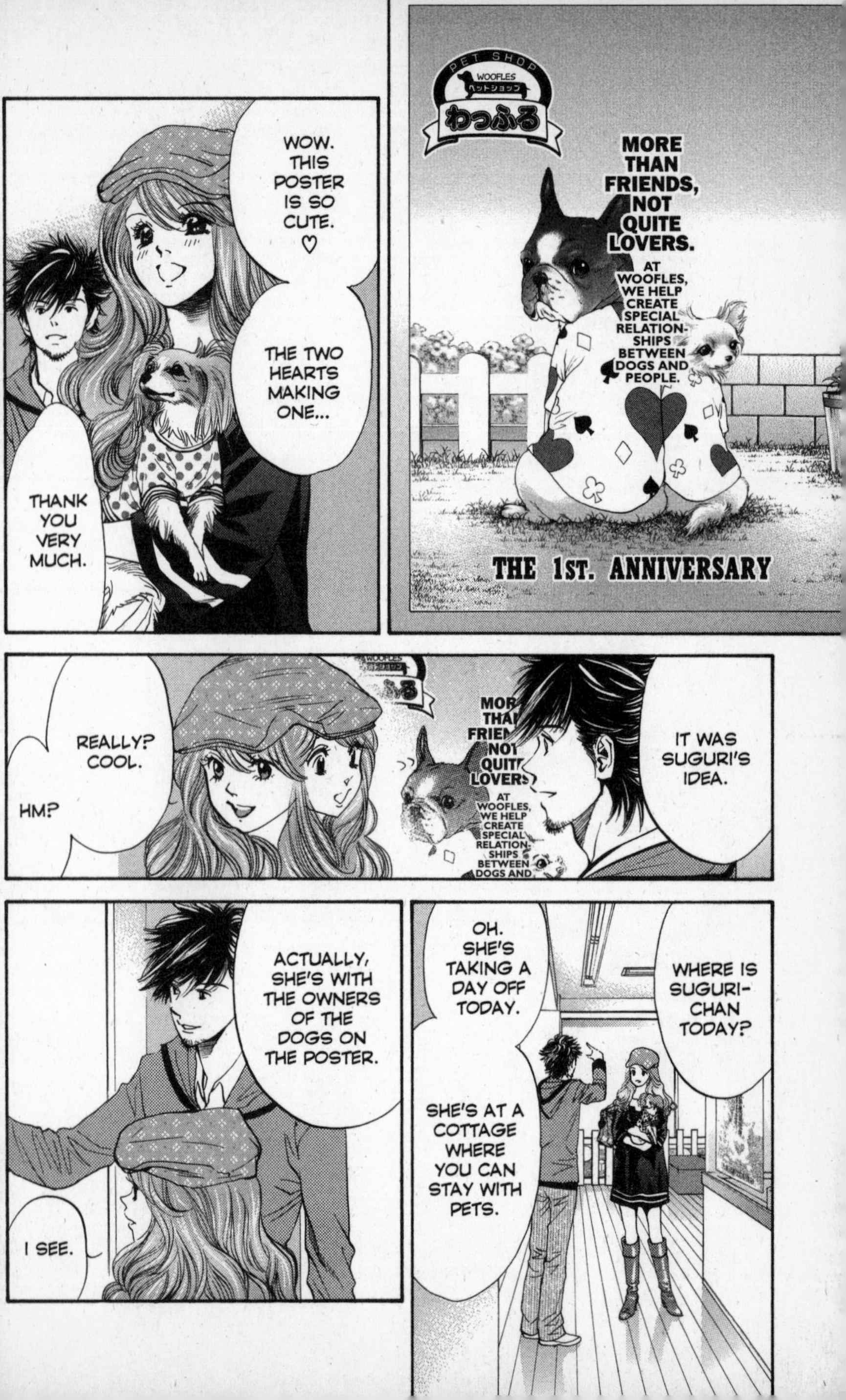
PET SHOP
WOOFLES
ペットショップ
わっふる
MORE THAN FRIENDS, NOT QUITE LOVERS.
AT WOOFLES, WE HELP CREATE SPECIAL RELATIONSHIPS BETWEEN DOGS AND PEOPLE.
THE 1ST. ANNIVERSARY
WOW. THIS POSTER IS SO CUTE. ♡
THE TWO HEARTS MAKING ONE...
THANK YOU VERY MUCH.
IT WAS SUGURI'S IDEA.
REALLY? COOL.
HM?
WHERE IS SUGURI-CHAN TODAY?
OH. SHE'S TAKING A DAY OFF TODAY.
SHE'S AT A COTTAGE WHERE YOU CAN STAY WITH PETS.
ACTUALLY, SHE'S WITH THE OWNERS OF THE DOGS ON THE POSTER.
I SEE.

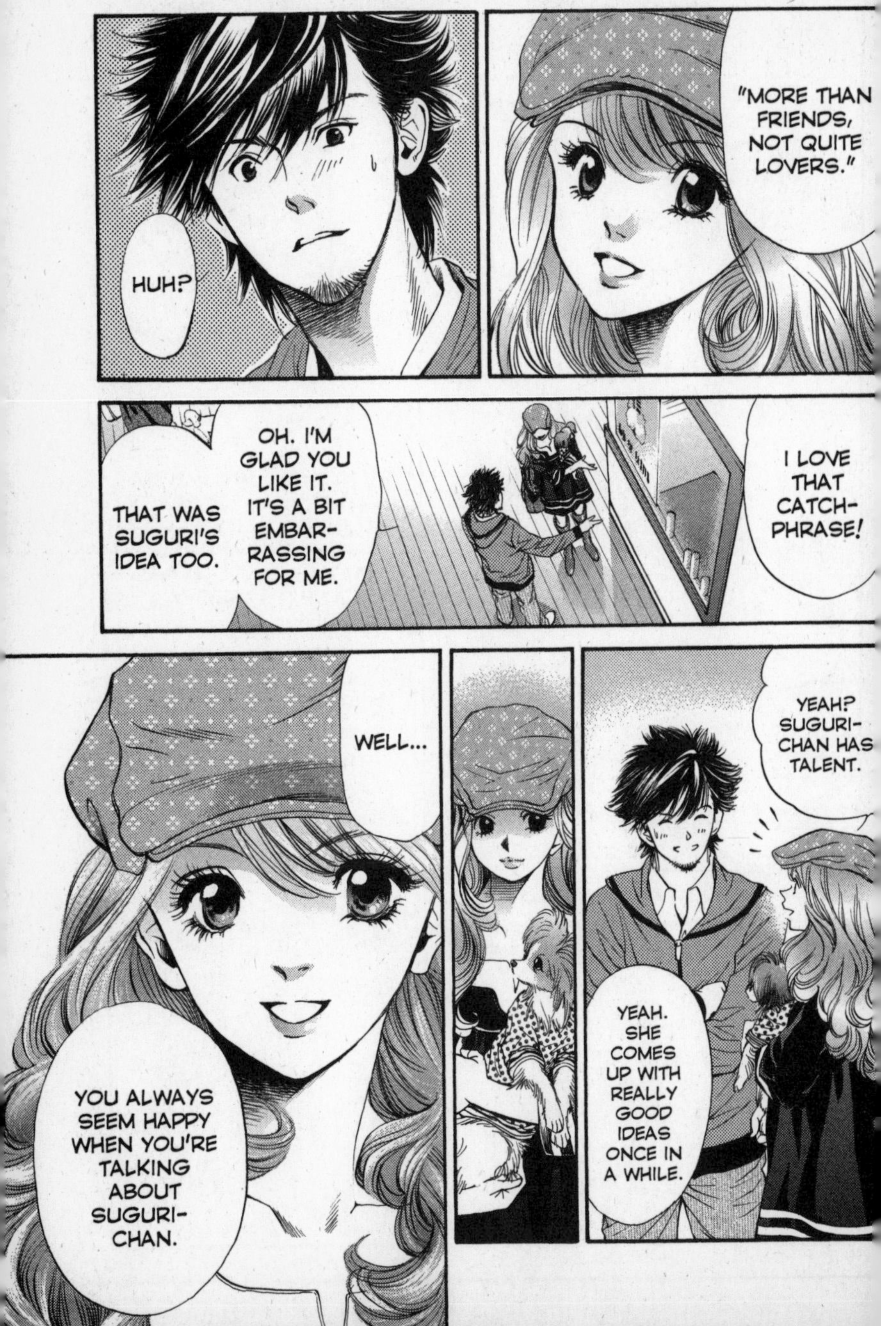
"MORE THAN FRIENDS, NOT QUITE LOVERS."
HUH?
I LOVE THAT CATCH-PHRASE!
OH. I'M GLAD YOU LIKE IT. IT'S A BIT EMBARRASSING FOR ME.
THAT WAS SUGURI'S IDEA TOO.
YEAH? SUGURI-CHAN HAS TALENT.
YEAH. SHE COMES UP WITH REALLY GOOD IDEAS ONCE IN A WHILE.
WELL...
YOU ALWAYS SEEM HAPPY WHEN YOU'RE TALKING ABOUT SUGURI-CHAN.

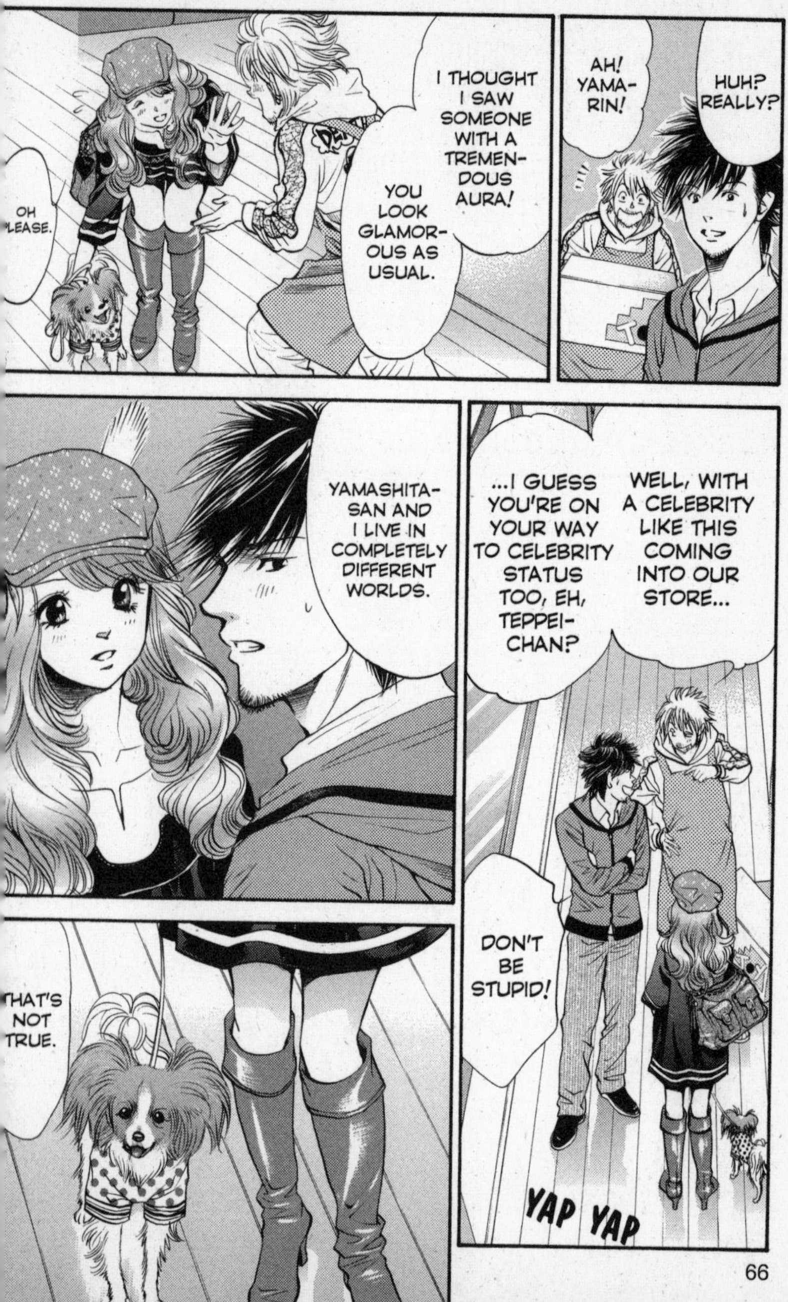
HUH? REALLY?
AH! YAMA-RIN!
I THOUGHT I SAW SOMEONE WITH A TREMEN-DOUS AURA!
YOU LOOK GLAMOR-OUS AS USUAL.
OH PLEASE.
WELL, WITH A CELEBRITY LIKE THIS COMING INTO OUR STORE...
...I GUESS YOU'RE ON YOUR WAY TO CELEBRITY STATUS TOO, EH, TEPPEI-CHAN?
DON'T BE STUPID!
YAP YAP
YAMASHITA-SAN AND I LIVE IN COMPLETELY DIFFERENT WORLDS.
THAT'S NOT TRUE.

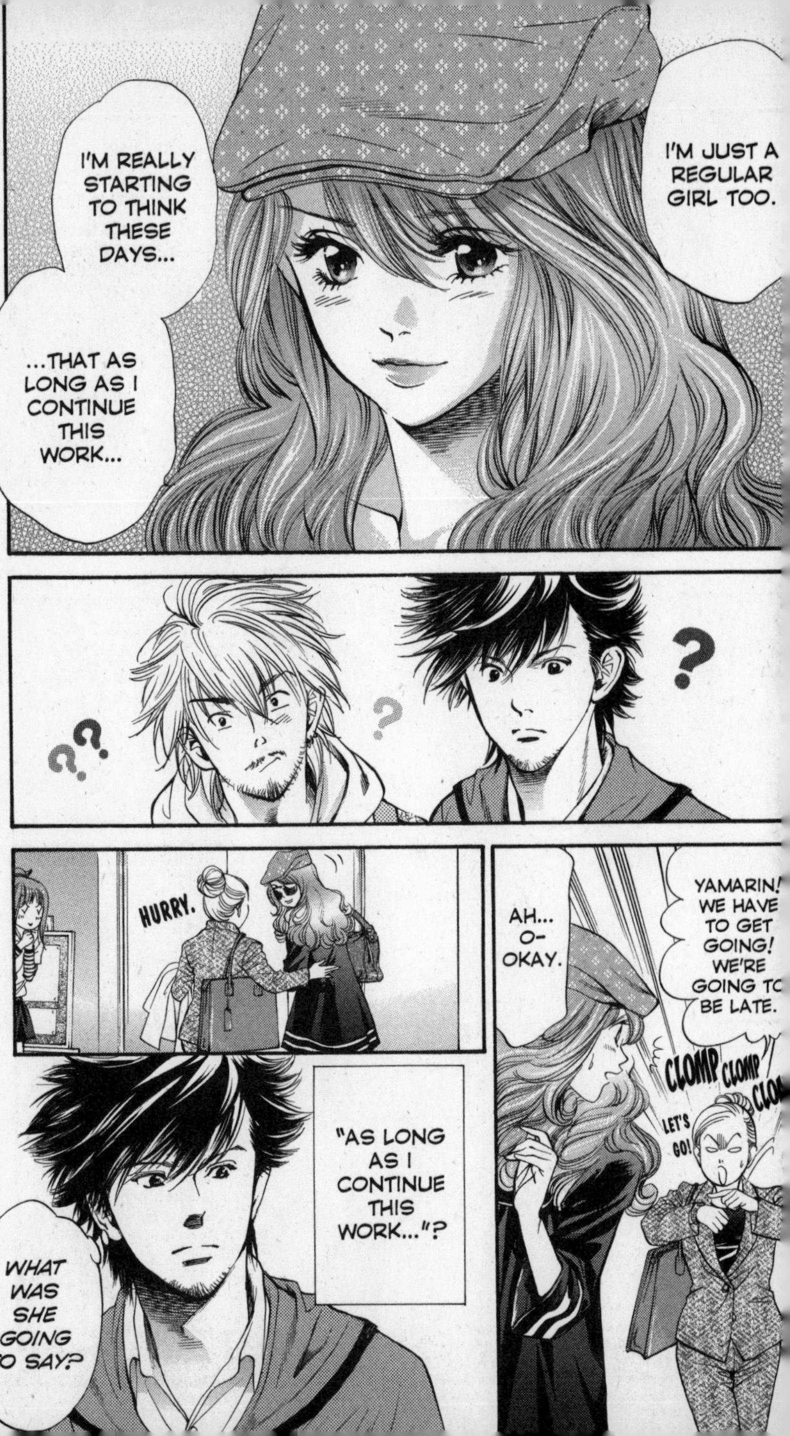
I'M JUST A REGULAR GIRL TOO.
I'M REALLY STARTING TO THINK THESE DAYS...
...THAT AS LONG AS I CONTINUE THIS WORK...
YAMARIN! WE HAVE TO GET GOING! WE'RE GOING TO BE LATE.
AH... O-OKAY.
CLOMP CLOMP CLO
LET'S GO!
HURRY.
"AS LONG AS I CONTINUE THIS WORK..."?
WHAT WAS SHE GOING TO SAY?

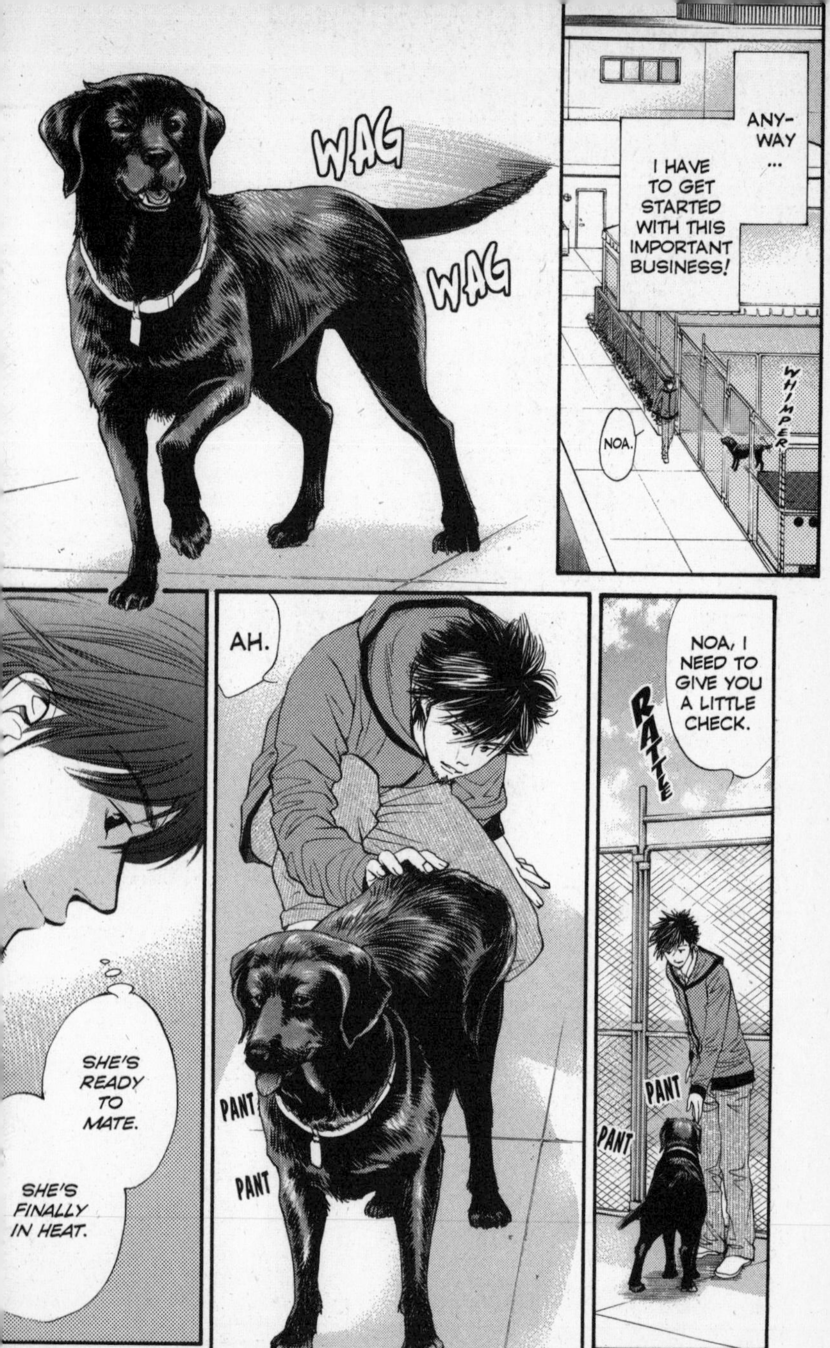
ANY-WAY ...
I HAVE TO GET STARTED WITH THIS IMPORTANT BUSINESS!
NOA.
WHIMPER
WAG
WAG
NOA, I NEED TO GIVE YOU A LITTLE CHECK.
RATTLE
PANT
PANT
AH.
PANT
PANT
SHE'S READY TO MATE.
SHE'S FINALLY IN HEAT.

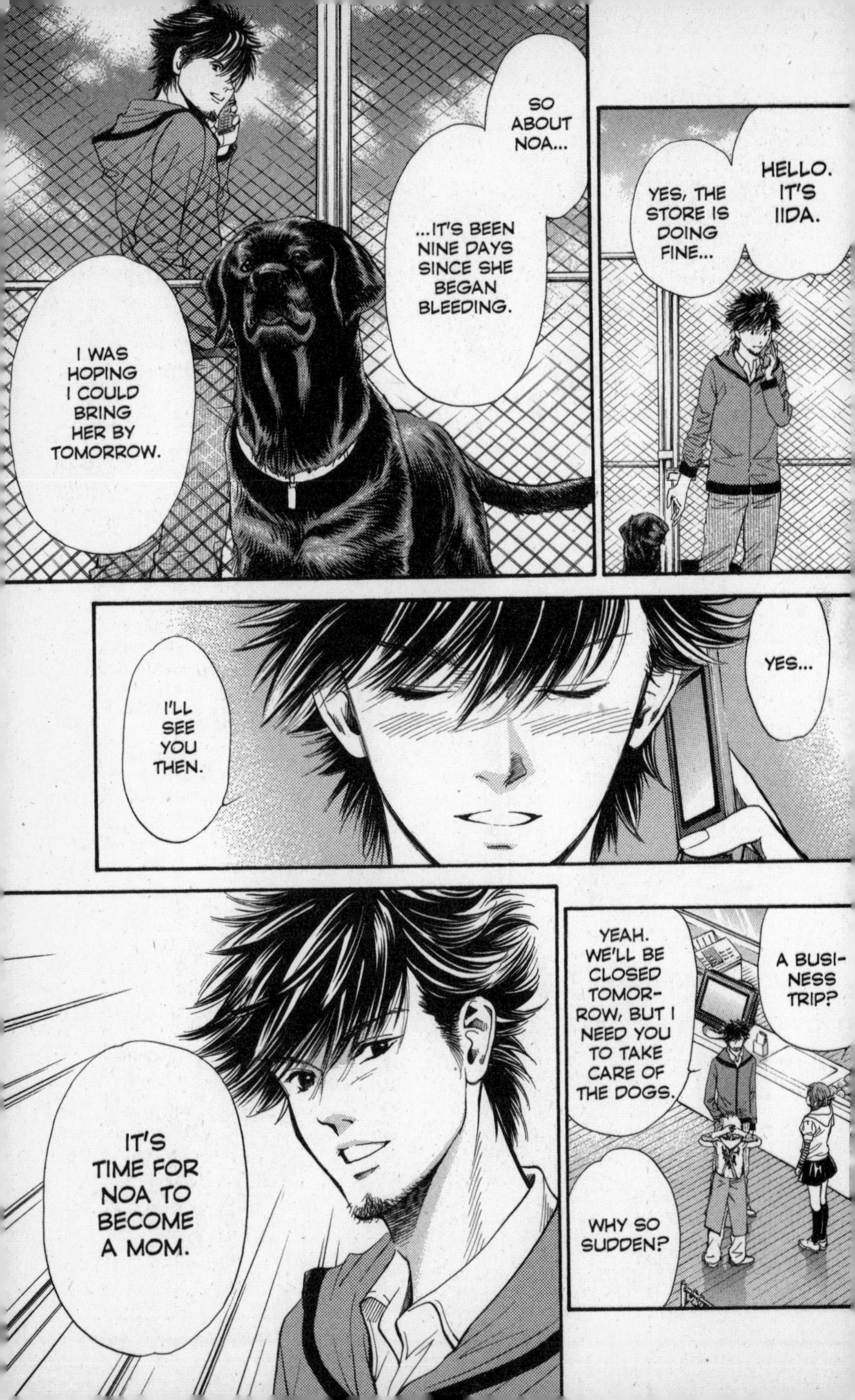
HELLO. IT'S IIDA.
YES, THE STORE IS DOING FINE...
SO ABOUT NOA...
...IT'S BEEN NINE DAYS SINCE SHE BEGAN BLEEDING.
I WAS HOPING I COULD BRING HER BY TOMORROW.
YES...
I'LL SEE YOU THEN.
A BUSINESS TRIP?
YEAH. WE'LL BE CLOSED TOMORROW, BUT I NEED YOU TO TAKE CARE OF THE DOGS.
WHY SO SUDDEN?
IT'S TIME FOR NOA TO BECOME A MOM.

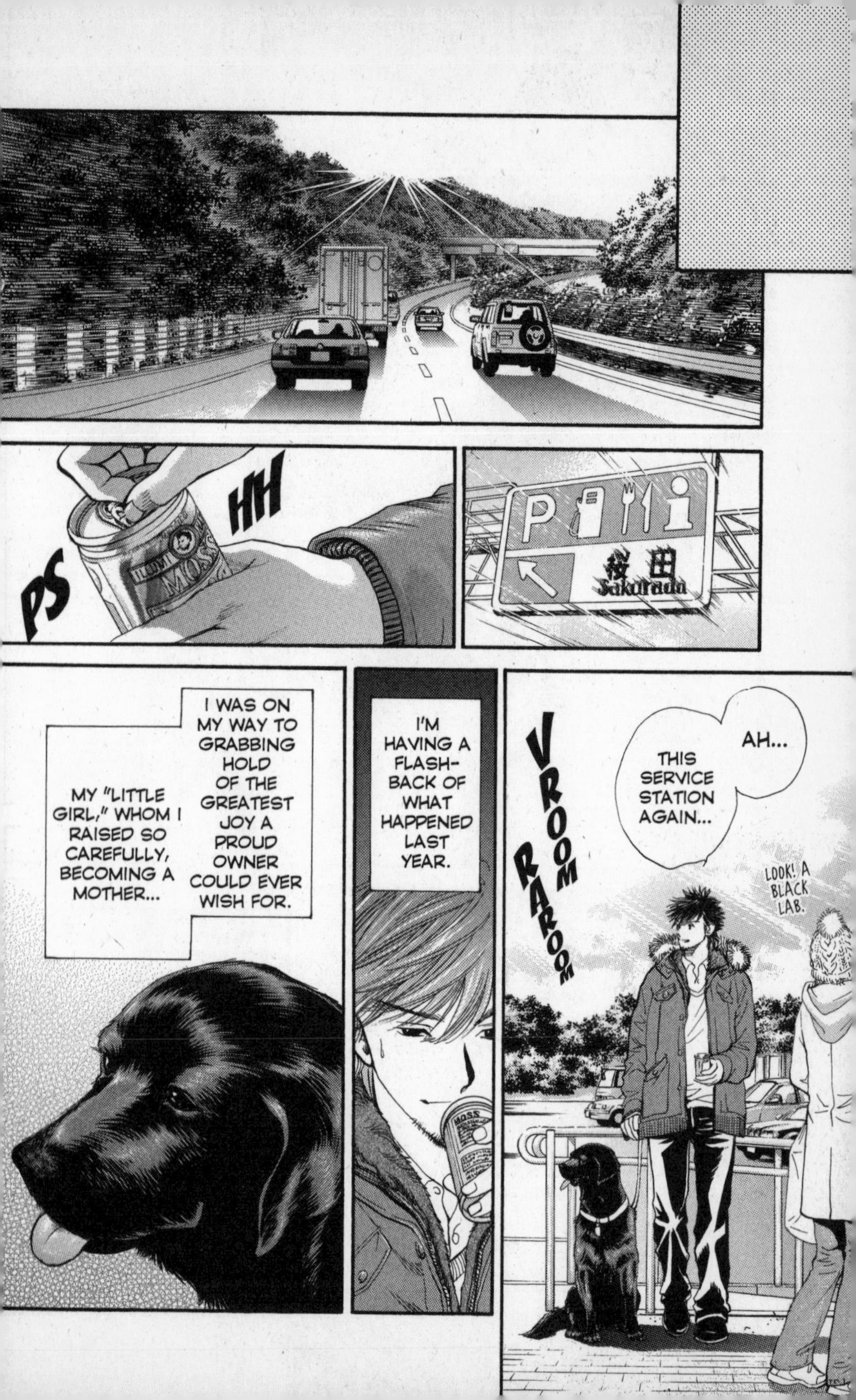

桜田
Sakurada
PSHH
MOSS
AH...
THIS SERVICE STATION AGAIN...
LOOK! A BLACK LAB.
VROOM
RAROOM
I'M HAVING A FLASH-BACK OF WHAT HAPPENED LAST YEAR.
I WAS ON MY WAY TO GRABBING HOLD OF THE GREATEST JOY A PROUD OWNER COULD EVER WISH FOR.
MY "LITTLE GIRL," WHOM I RAISED SO CAREFULLY, BECOMING A MOTHER...

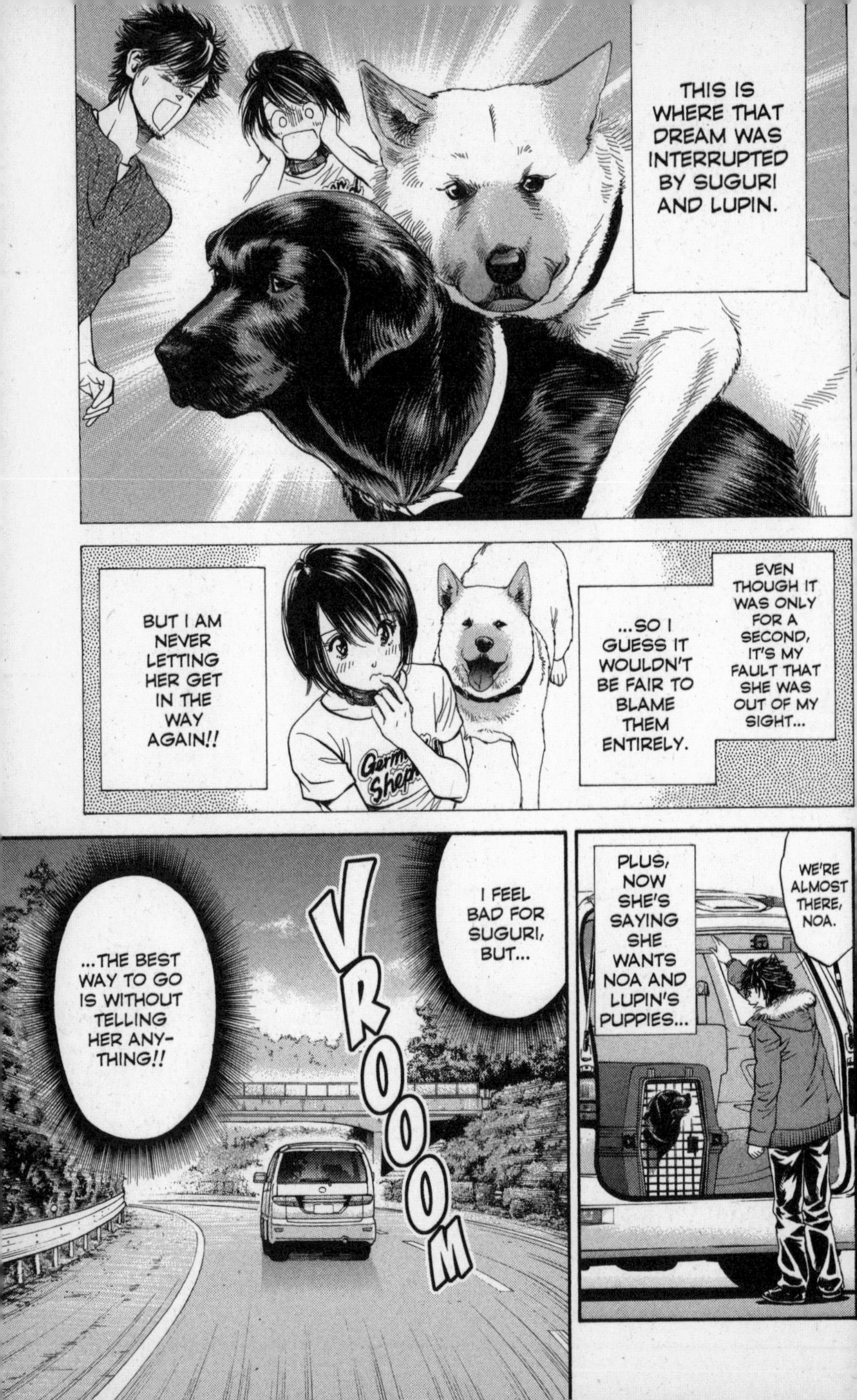
THIS IS WHERE THAT DREAM WAS INTERRUPTED BY SUGURI AND LUPIN.
EVEN THOUGH IT WAS ONLY FOR A SECOND, IT'S MY FAULT THAT SHE WAS OUT OF MY SIGHT...
...SO I GUESS IT WOULDN'T BE FAIR TO BLAME THEM ENTIRELY.
BUT I AM NEVER LETTING HER GET IN THE WAY AGAIN!!
WE'RE ALMOST THERE, NOA.
PLUS, NOW SHE'S SAYING SHE WANTS NOA AND LUPIN'S PUPPIES...
I FEEL BAD FOR SUGURI, BUT...
VROOOOM
...THE BEST WAY TO GO IS WITHOUT TELLING HER ANYTHING!!

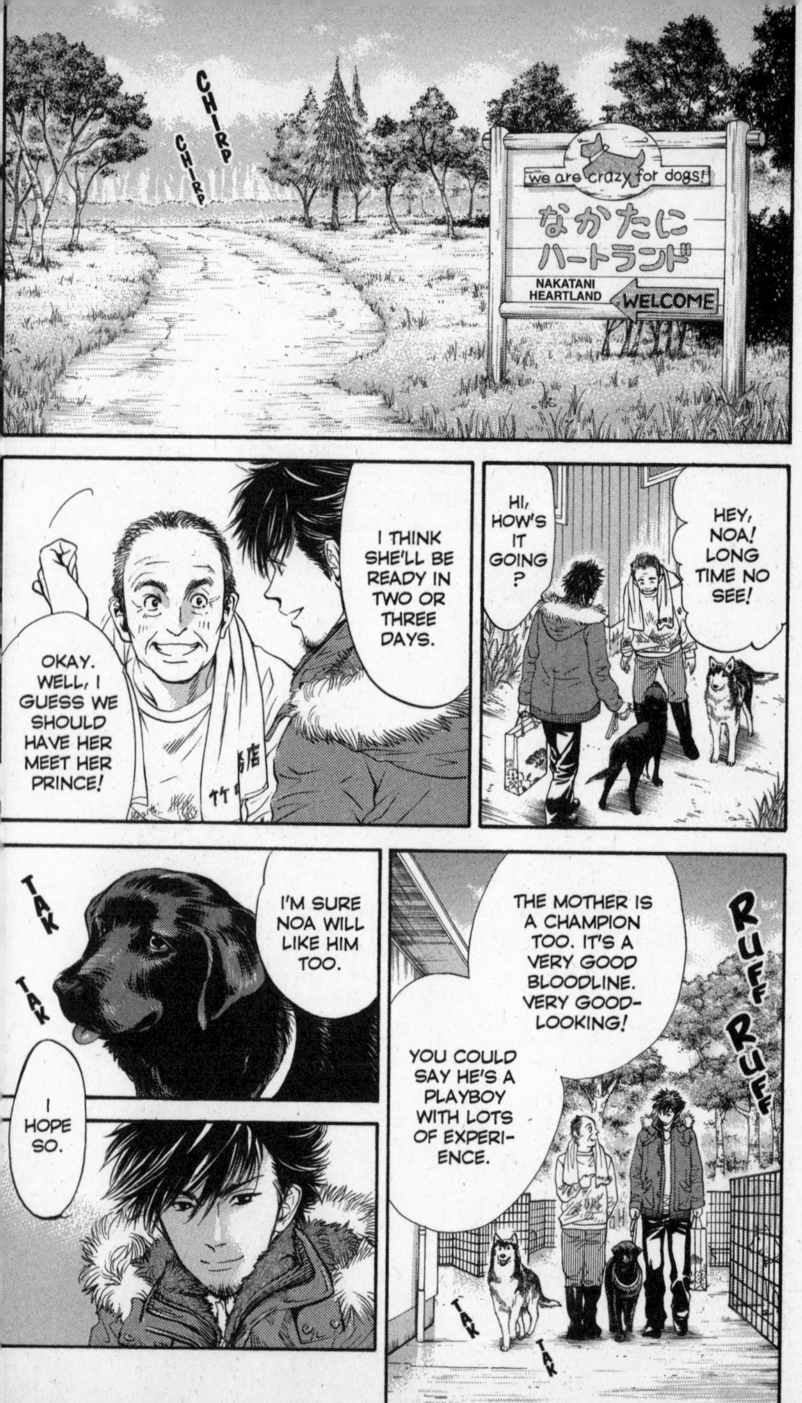

CHIRP
CHIRP
we are crazy for dogs!
なかたに
ハートランド
NAKATANI HEARTLAND
WELCOME
HEY, NOA! LONG TIME NO SEE!
HI, HOW'S IT GOING?
I THINK SHE'LL BE READY IN TWO OR THREE DAYS.
OKAY. WELL, I GUESS WE SHOULD HAVE HER MEET HER PRINCE!
RUFF RUFF
THE MOTHER IS A CHAMPION TOO. IT'S A VERY GOOD BLOODLINE. VERY GOOD-LOOKING!
YOU COULD SAY HE'S A PLAYBOY WITH LOTS OF EXPERIENCE.
TAK
TAK
I'M SURE NOA WILL LIKE HIM TOO.
TAK
TAK
I HOPE SO.

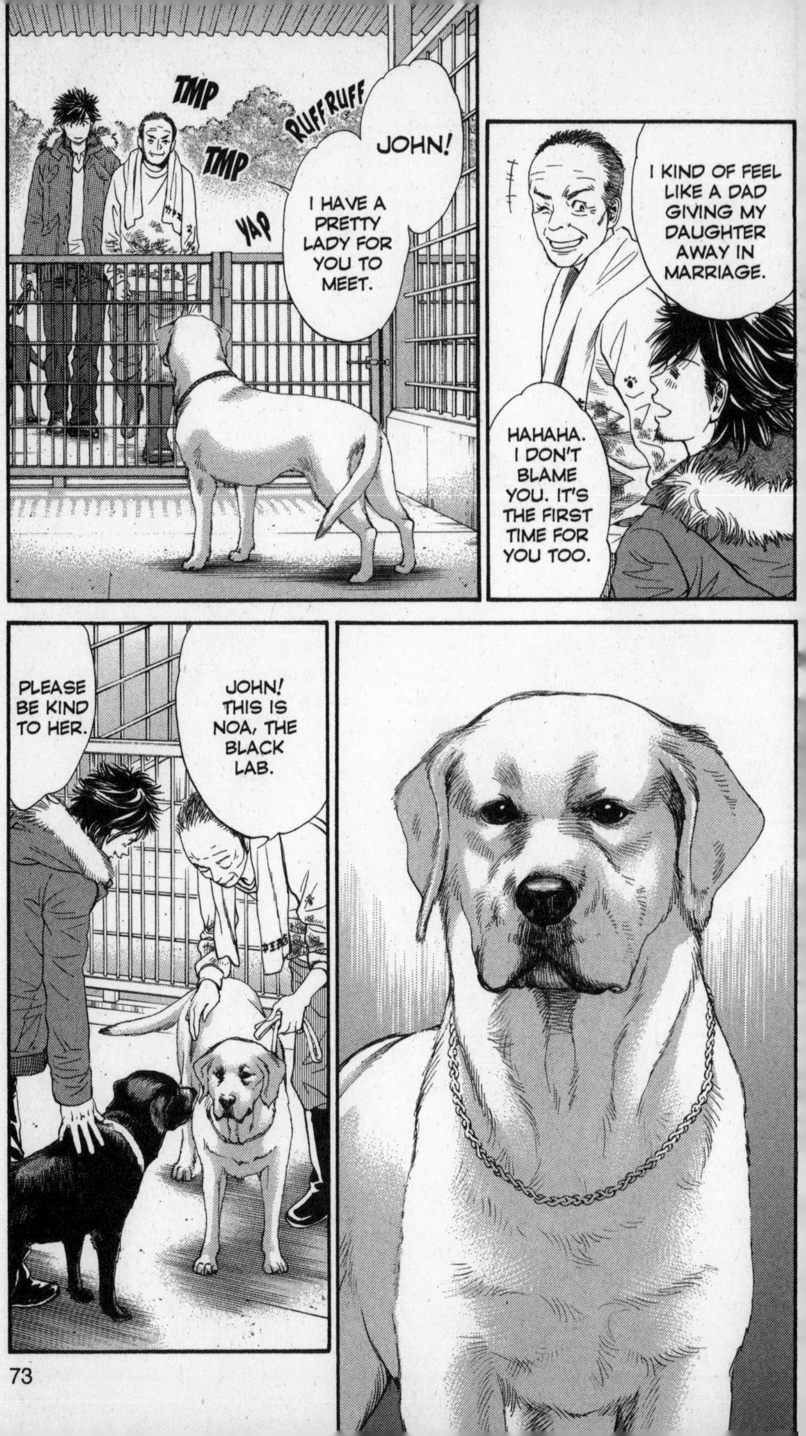
I KIND OF FEEL LIKE A DAD GIVING MY DAUGHTER AWAY IN MARRIAGE.
HAHAHA. I DON'T BLAME YOU. IT'S THE FIRST TIME FOR YOU TOO.
JOHN!
RUFF RUFF
TMP
I HAVE A PRETTY LADY FOR YOU TO MEET.
TMP
YAP
JOHN! THIS IS NOA, THE BLACK LAB.
PLEASE BE KIND TO HER.

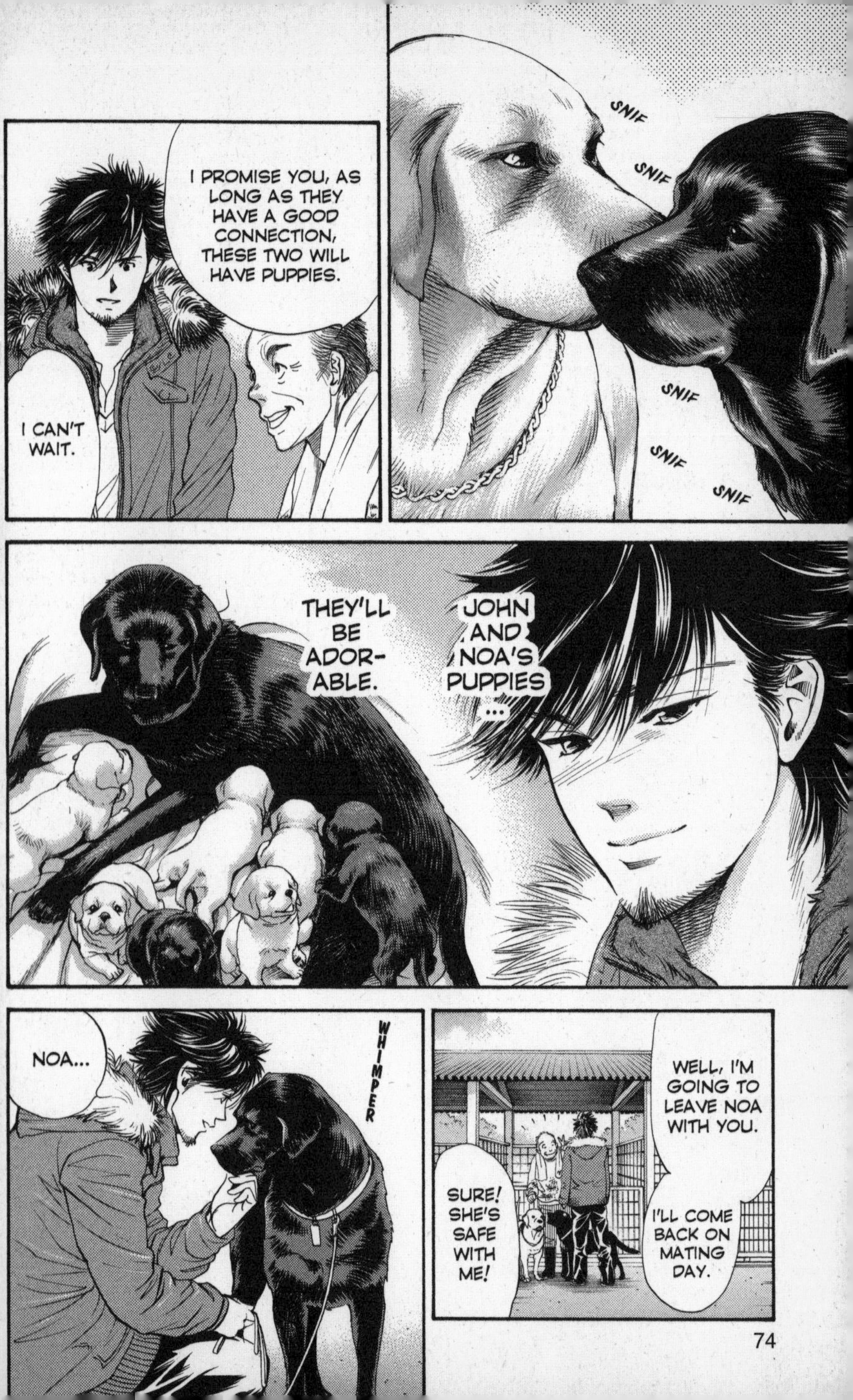
SNIF
SNIF
SNIF
SNIF
SNIF
I PROMISE YOU, AS LONG AS THEY HAVE A GOOD CONNECTION, THESE TWO WILL HAVE PUPPIES.
I CAN'T WAIT.
JOHN AND NOA'S PUPPIES...
THEY'LL BE ADOR-ABLE.
WELL, I'M GOING TO LEAVE NOA WITH YOU.
SURE! SHE'S SAFE WITH ME!
I'LL COME BACK ON MATING DAY.
WHIMPER
NOA...

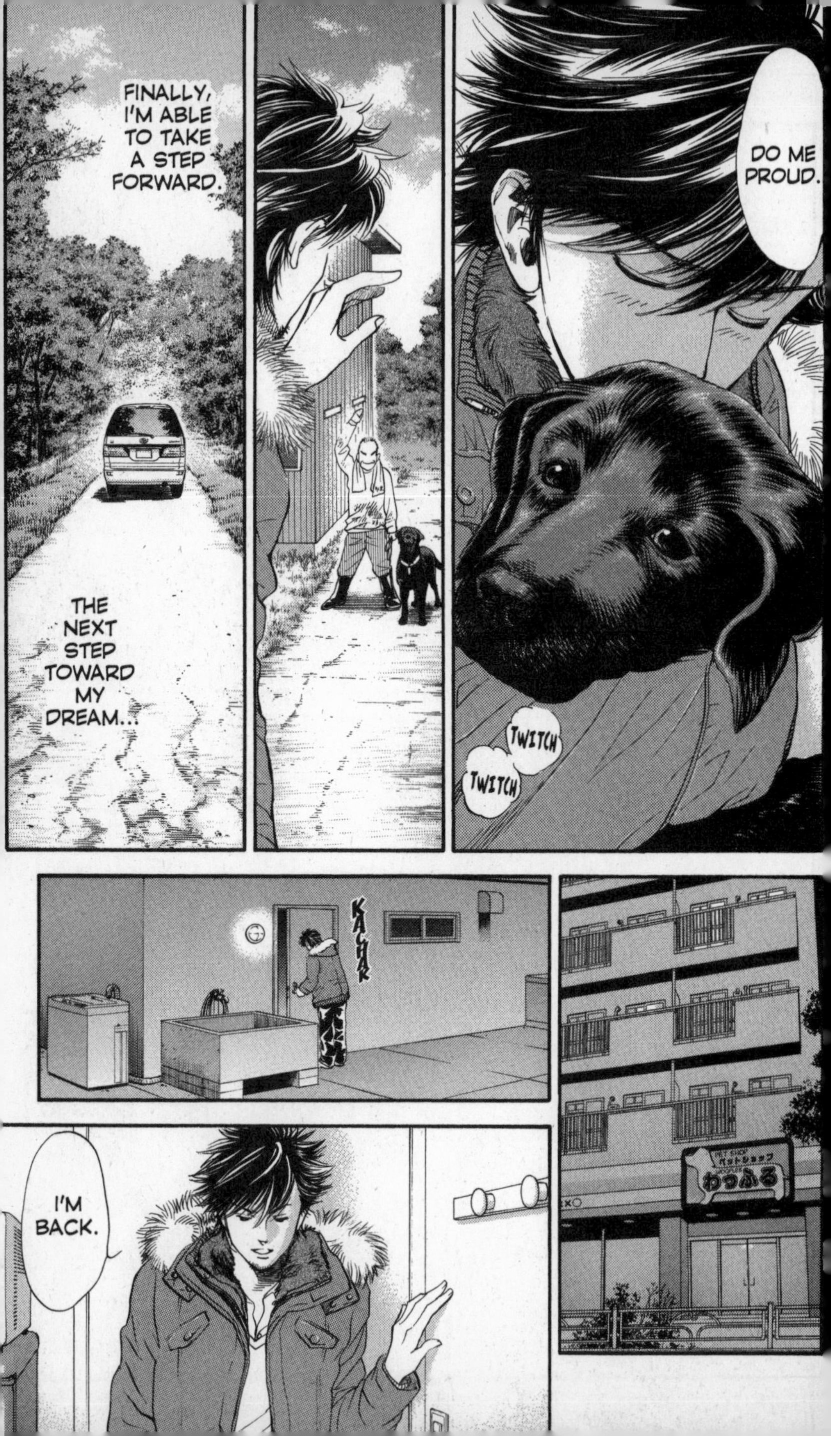
DO ME PROUD.
TWITCH
TWITCH
FINALLY, I'M ABLE TO TAKE A STEP FORWARD.
THE NEXT STEP TOWARD MY DREAM...
わっふる
KACHAR
I'M BACK.

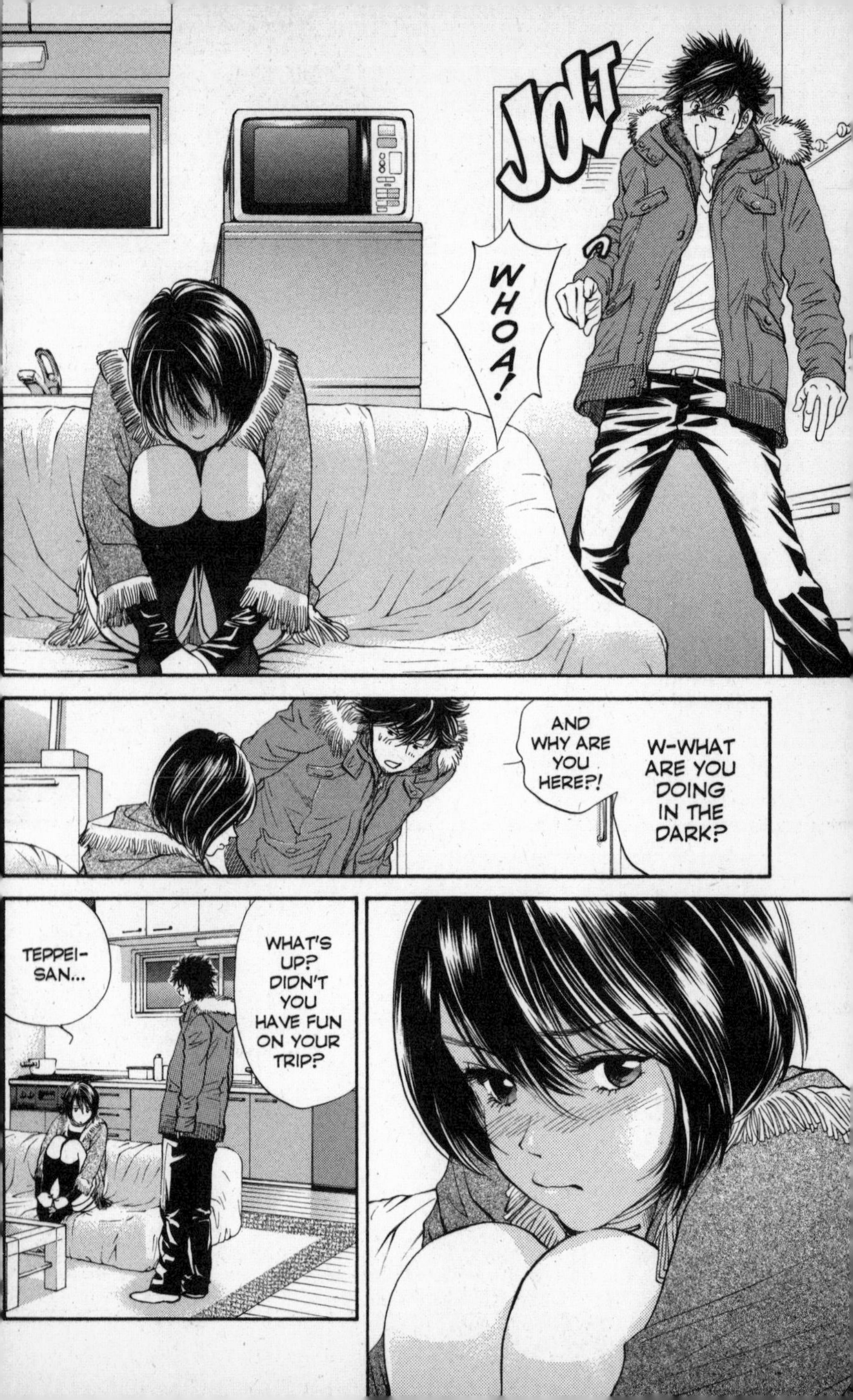
JOLT
WHOA!
W-WHAT ARE YOU DOING IN THE DARK?
AND WHY ARE YOU HERE?!
WHAT'S UP? DIDN'T YOU HAVE FUN ON YOUR TRIP?
TEPPEI-SAN...

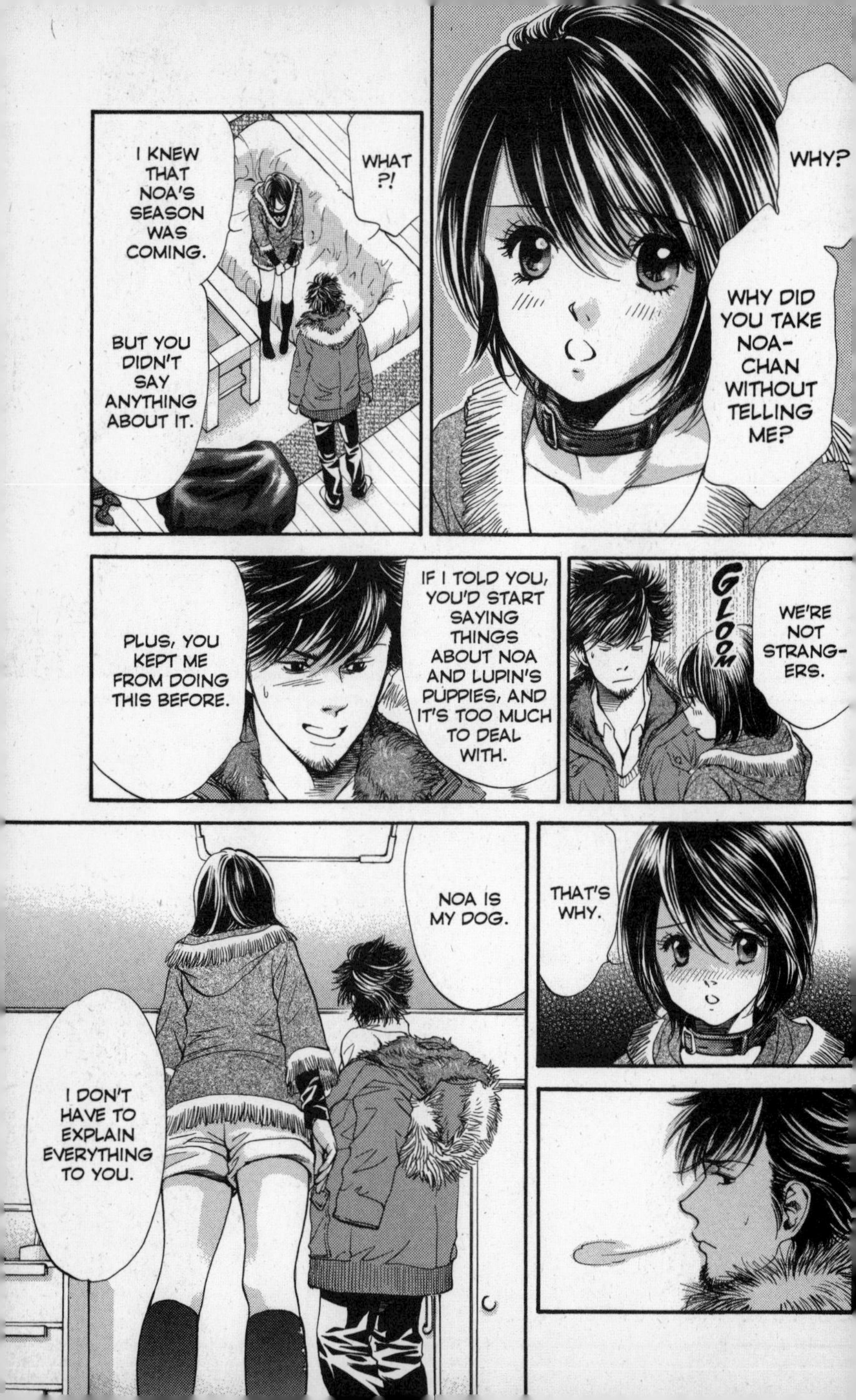
WHY?
WHY DID YOU TAKE NOA-CHAN WITHOUT TELLING ME?
WHAT?!
I KNEW THAT NOA'S SEASON WAS COMING.
BUT YOU DIDN'T SAY ANYTHING ABOUT IT.
GLOOM
WE'RE NOT STRANGERS.
IF I TOLD YOU, YOU'D START SAYING THINGS ABOUT NOA AND LUPIN'S PUPPIES, AND IT'S TOO MUCH TO DEAL WITH.
PLUS, YOU KEPT ME FROM DOING THIS BEFORE.
THAT'S WHY.
NOA IS MY DOG.
I DON'T HAVE TO EXPLAIN EVERYTHING TO YOU.

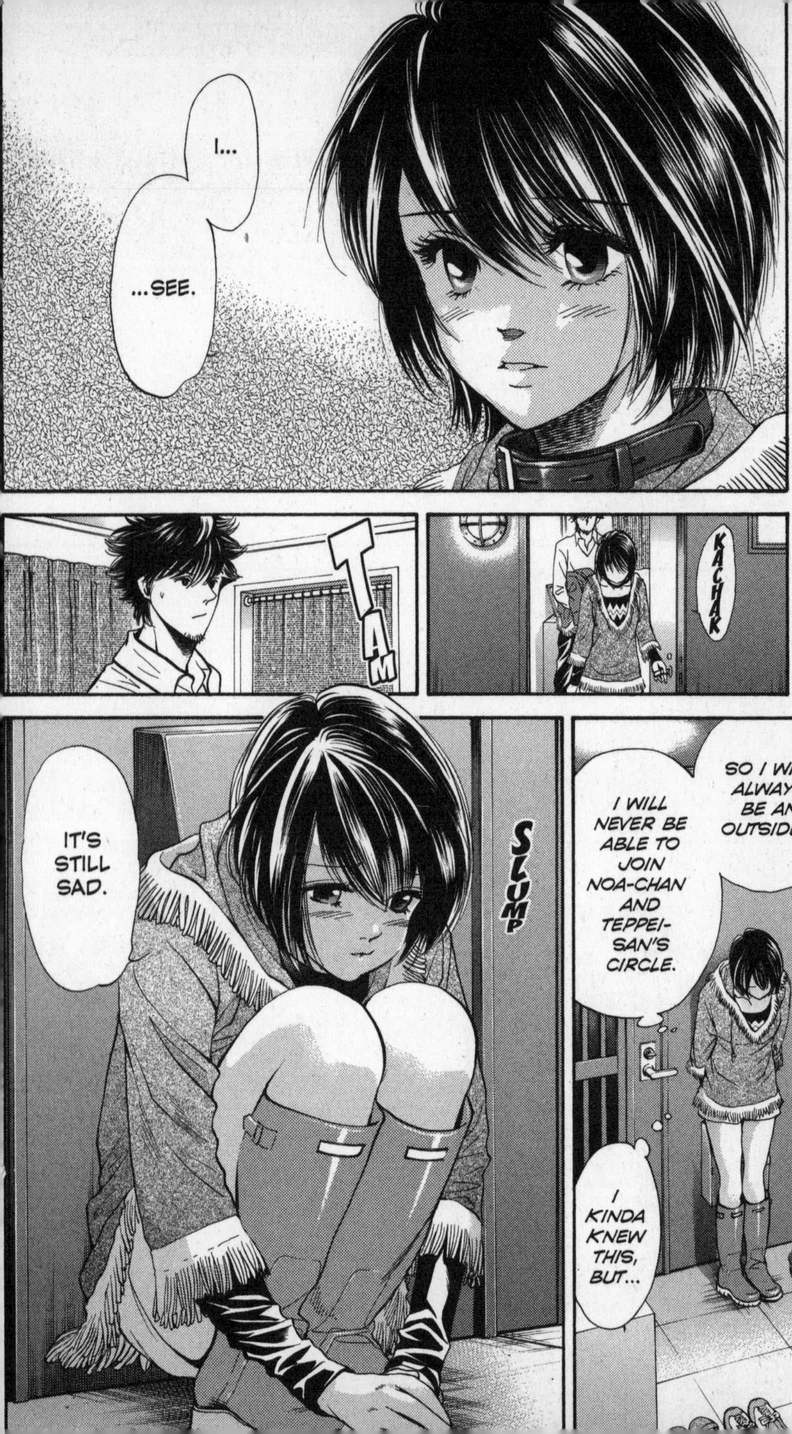
I...
...SEE.
KACHAK
TAM
SO I WILL ALWAYS BE AN OUTSIDER.
I WILL NEVER BE ABLE TO JOIN NOA-CHAN AND TEPPEI-SAN'S CIRCLE.
I KINDA KNEW THIS, BUT...
SLUMP
IT'S STILL SAD.

CHAPTER 146: I WANT BABIES!

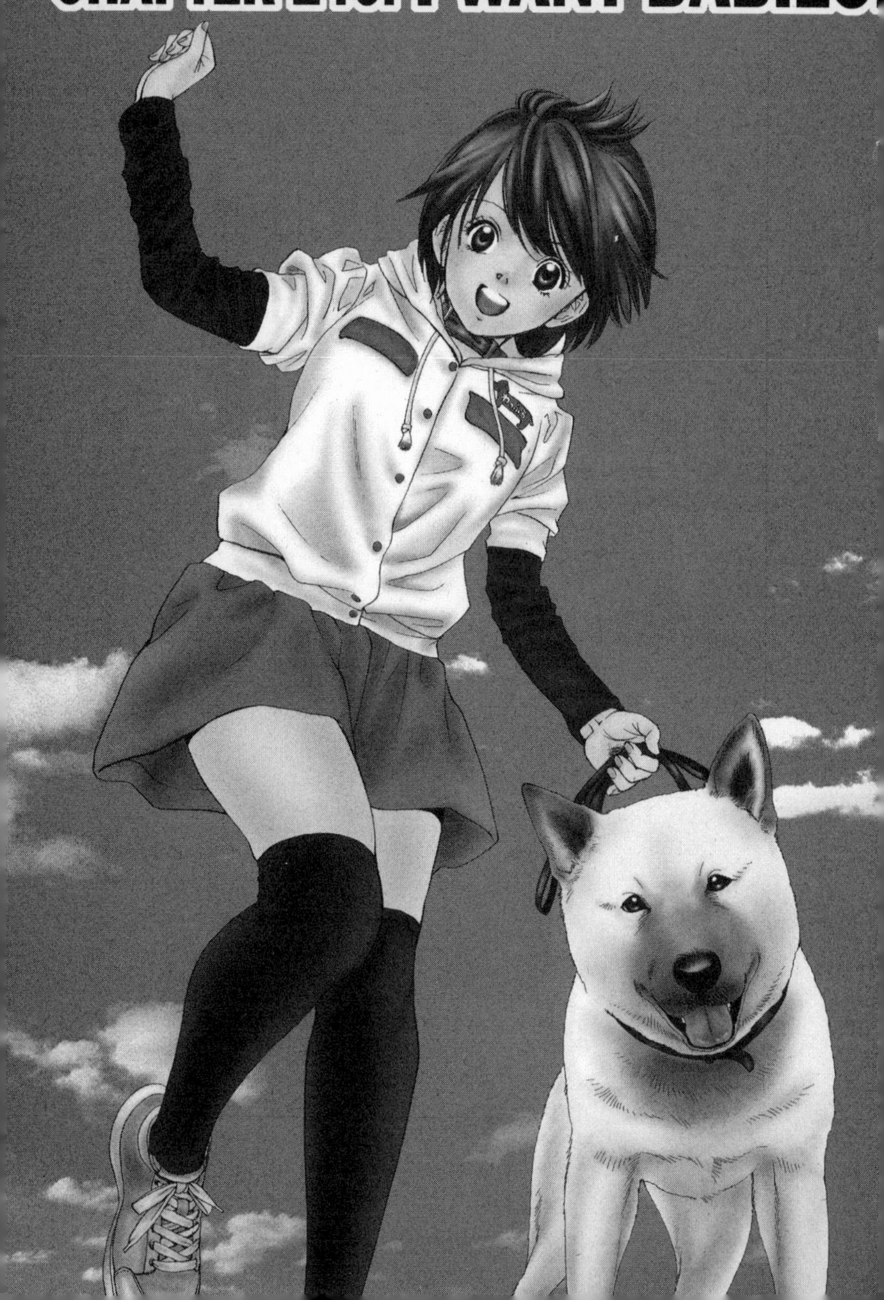

OH! INVESTIGATOR RICEBALL'S ADVENTURE!

FUN DRAFTS AND STORYBOARDS PART 1

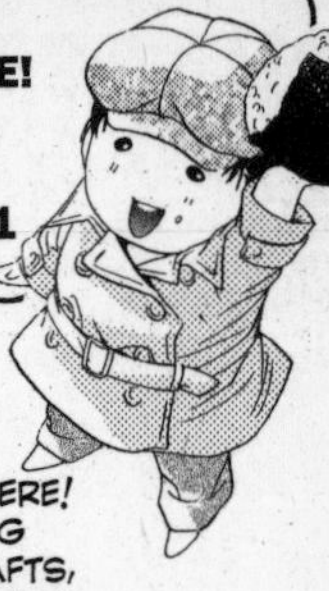

HEY, EVERYBODY! INVESTIGATOR RICEBALL HERE! THIS TIME, I'M INTRODUCING YOU TO SOME SECRET DRAFTS, STORYBOARDS AND SCRIBBLES BY YUKIYAN SENSEI! IF YOU CAN TELL RIGHT AWAY WHAT SCENE IT IS FROM THE DRAWINGS, YOU ARE AN *INUBAKA* MANIAC! ↓ SO GET READY! HERE'S LUPIN!

KIND OF LIKE A STORYBOARD BEFORE THE INITIAL DRAFT.

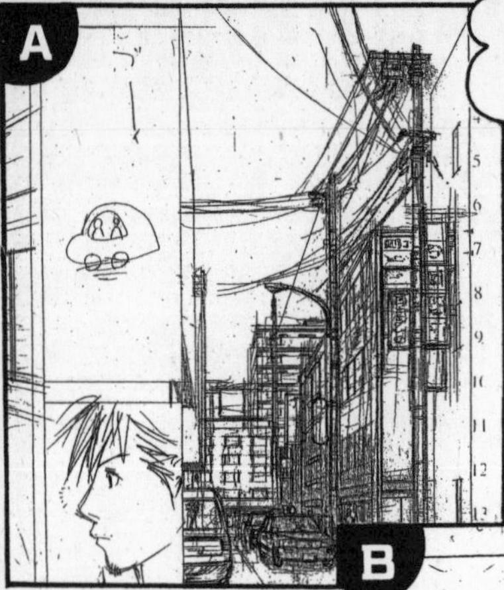

↑ CHECK OUT THE CAR. IT SEEMS THIS IS THE KIND OF LOOSE INSTRUCTIONS YUKIYAN SENSEI GIVES. (LAUGH)

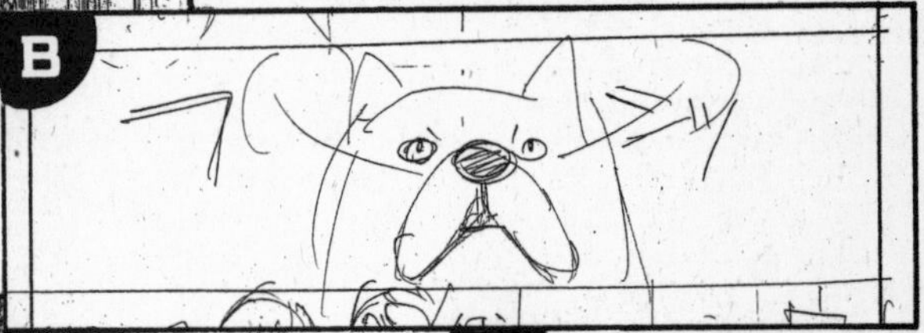

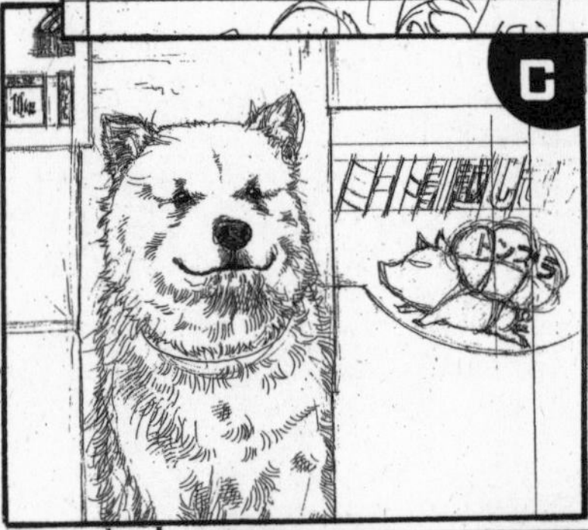

← LUPIN LOOKS SAD, BUT NEXT TO HIM IS A...FLYING PIG?

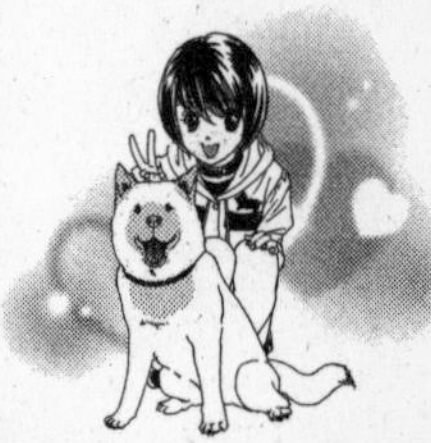

↓ SO THAT'S WHAT THE MOVIE POSTER ORIGINALLY LOOKED LIKE. (LAUGH)

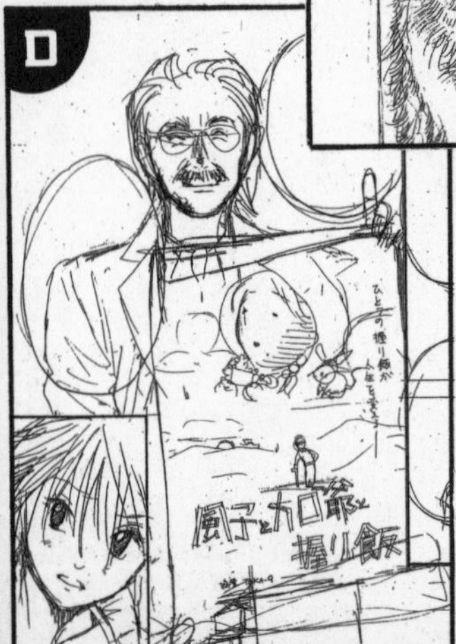

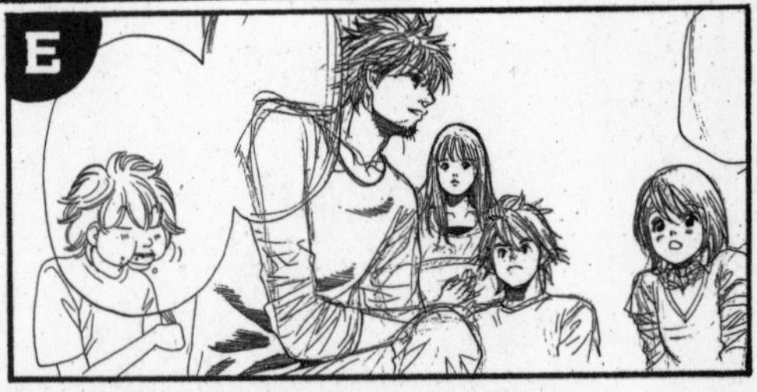

↑ LOOK WHAT WE FOUND THAT GOT BURIED BEHIND THE BALLOON.

CONTINUED ON PAGE 153

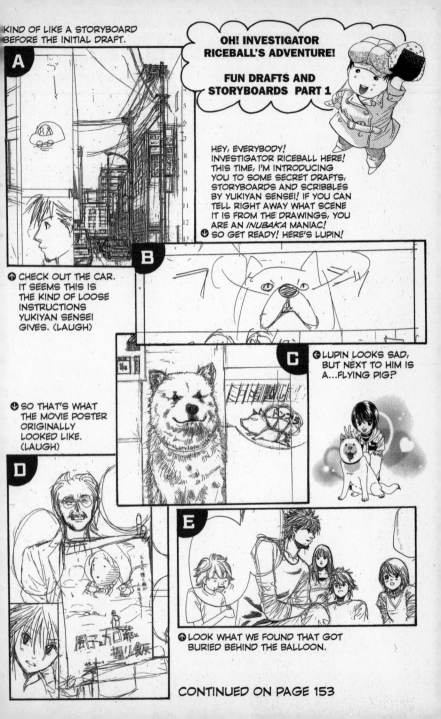

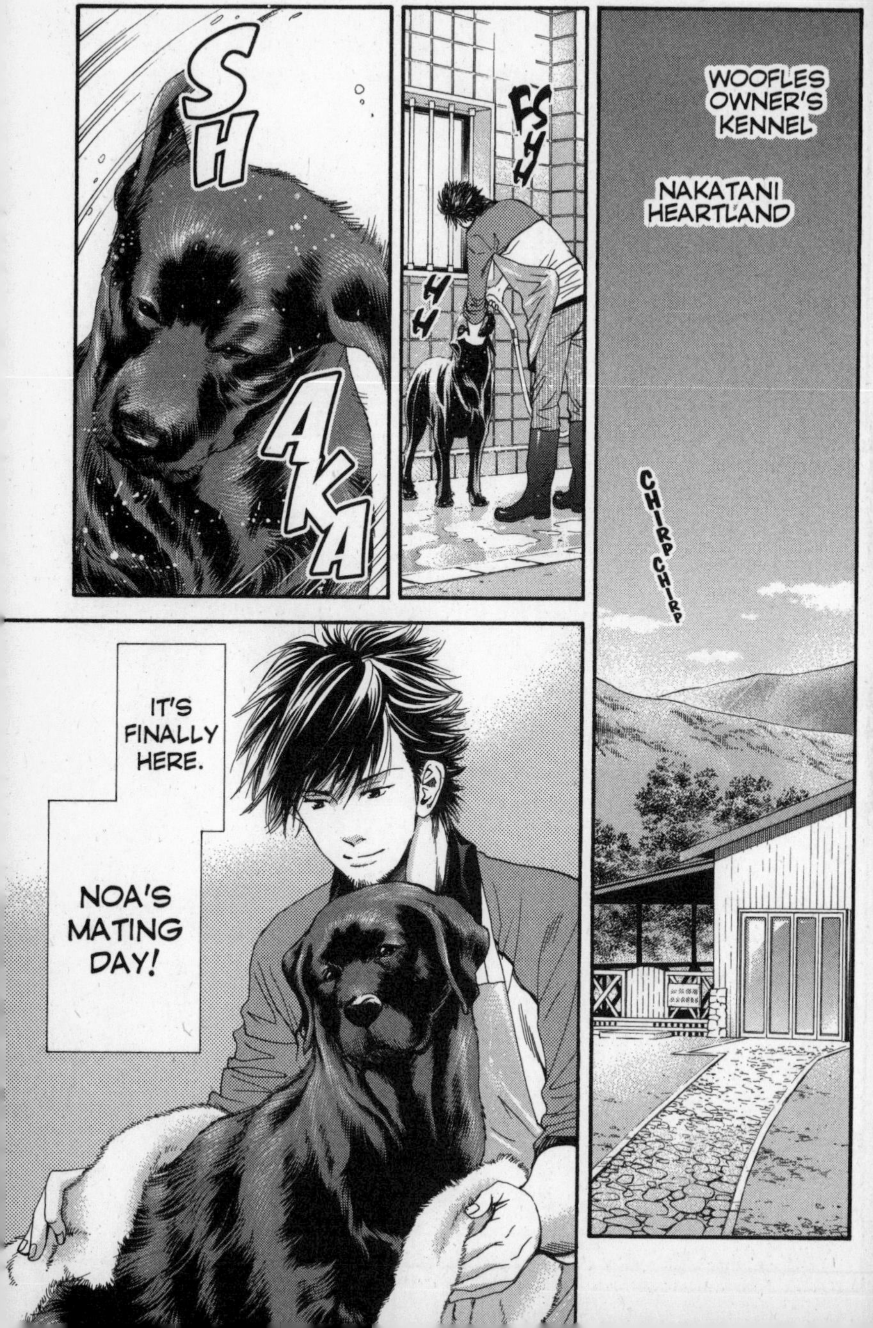
WOOFLES OWNER'S KENNEL
NAKATANI HEARTLAND
CHIRP CHIRP
FSHH
HHH
SHAKA
IT'S FINALLY HERE.
NOA'S MATING DAY!

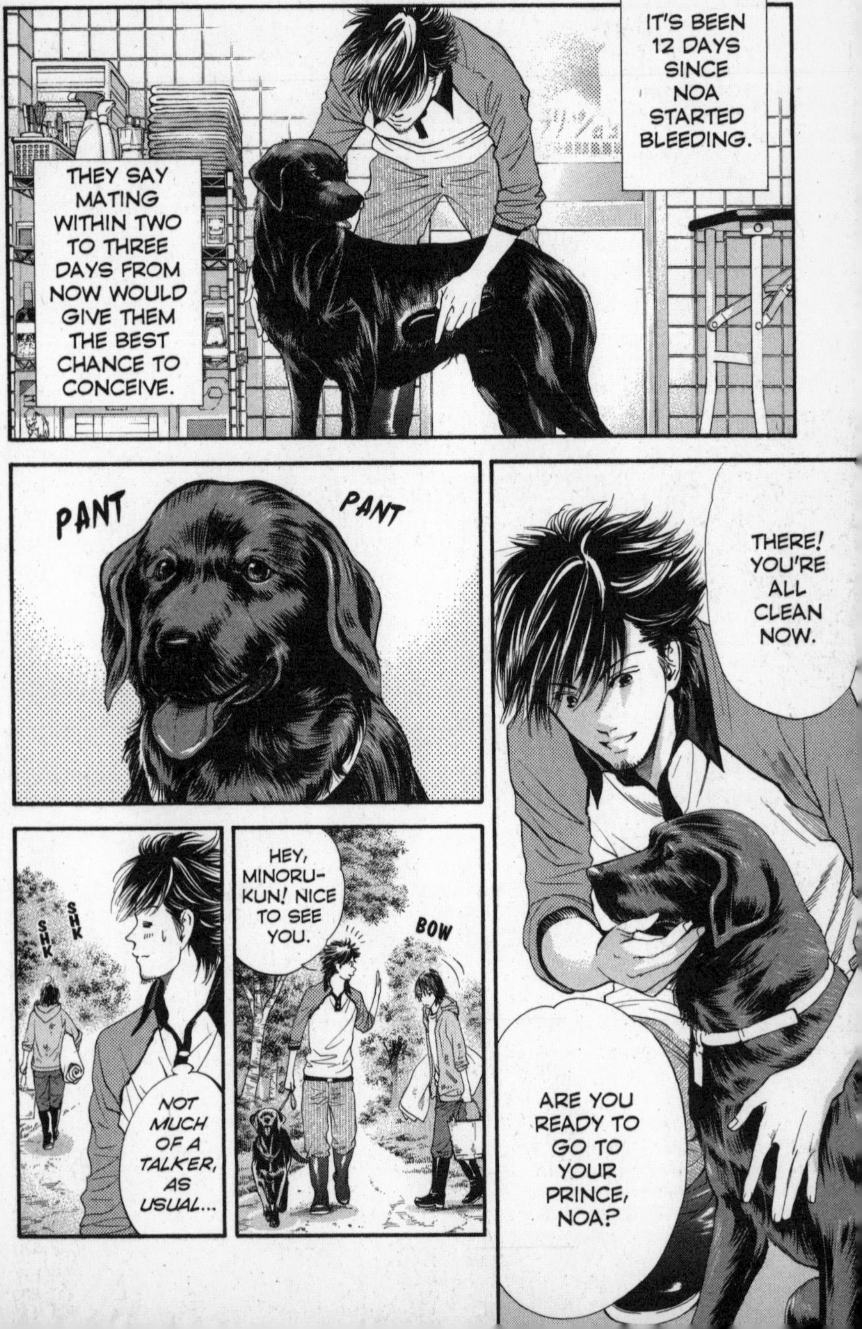
IT'S BEEN 12 DAYS SINCE NOA STARTED BLEEDING.
THEY SAY MATING WITHIN TWO TO THREE DAYS FROM NOW WOULD GIVE THEM THE BEST CHANCE TO CONCEIVE.
THERE! YOU'RE ALL CLEAN NOW.
ARE YOU READY TO GO TO YOUR PRINCE, NOA?
PANT
PANT
HEY, MINORU-KUN! NICE TO SEE YOU.
BOW
SHK
SHK
NOT MUCH OF A TALKER, AS USUAL...

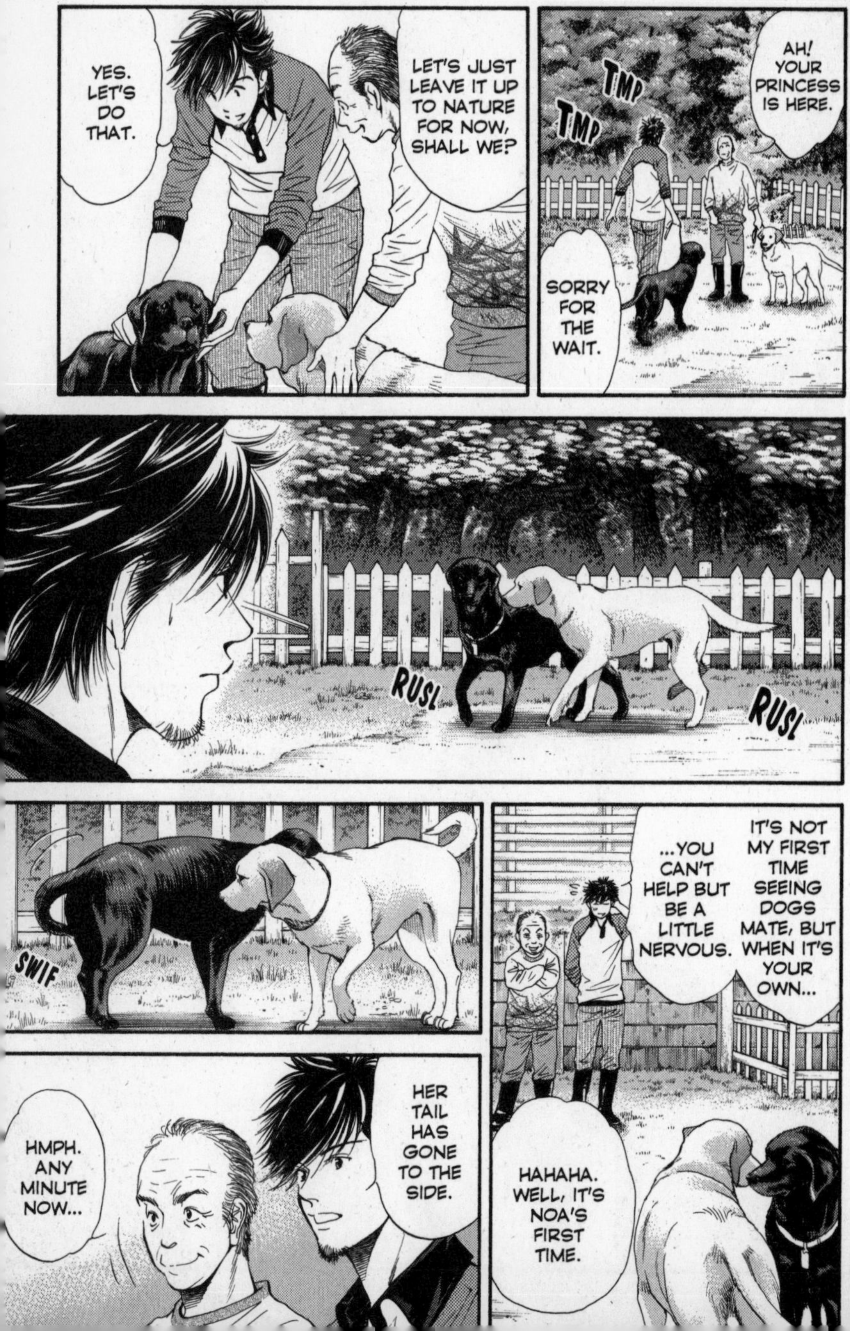
AH! YOUR PRINCESS IS HERE.
TMP
TMP
SORRY FOR THE WAIT.
LET'S JUST LEAVE IT UP TO NATURE FOR NOW, SHALL WE?
YES. LET'S DO THAT.
RUSL
RUSL
IT'S NOT MY FIRST TIME SEEING DOGS MATE, BUT WHEN IT'S YOUR OWN...
...YOU CAN'T HELP BUT BE A LITTLE NERVOUS.
HAHAHA. WELL, IT'S NOA'S FIRST TIME.
SWIF
HER TAIL HAS GONE TO THE SIDE.
HMPH. ANY MINUTE NOW...

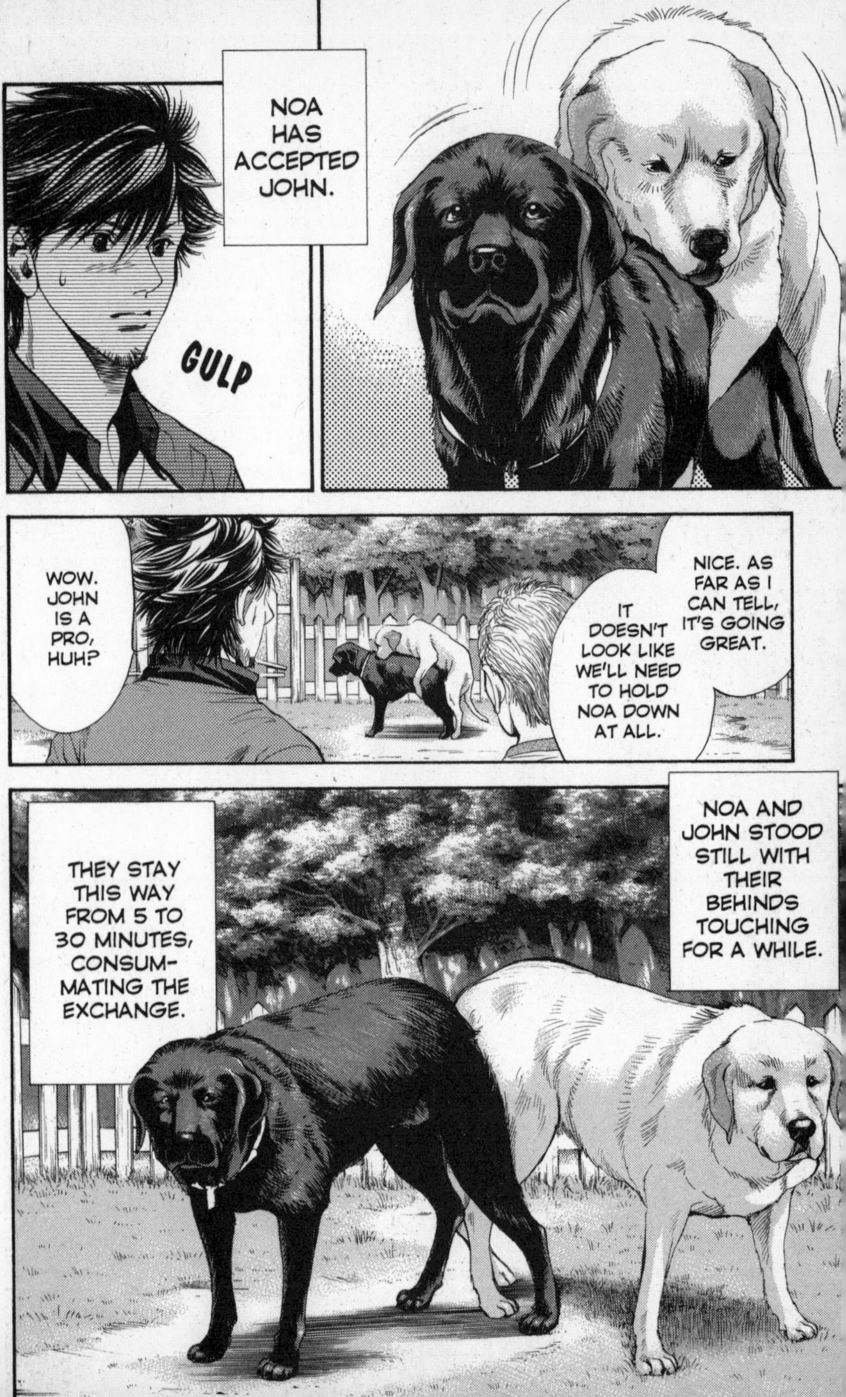
NOA HAS ACCEPTED JOHN.
GULP
NICE. AS FAR AS I CAN TELL, IT'S GOING GREAT.
IT DOESN'T LOOK LIKE WE'LL NEED TO HOLD NOA DOWN AT ALL.
WOW. JOHN IS A PRO, HUH?
NOA AND JOHN STOOD STILL WITH THEIR BEHINDS TOUCHING FOR A WHILE.
THEY STAY THIS WAY FROM 5 TO 30 MINUTES, CONSUMMATING THE EXCHANGE.

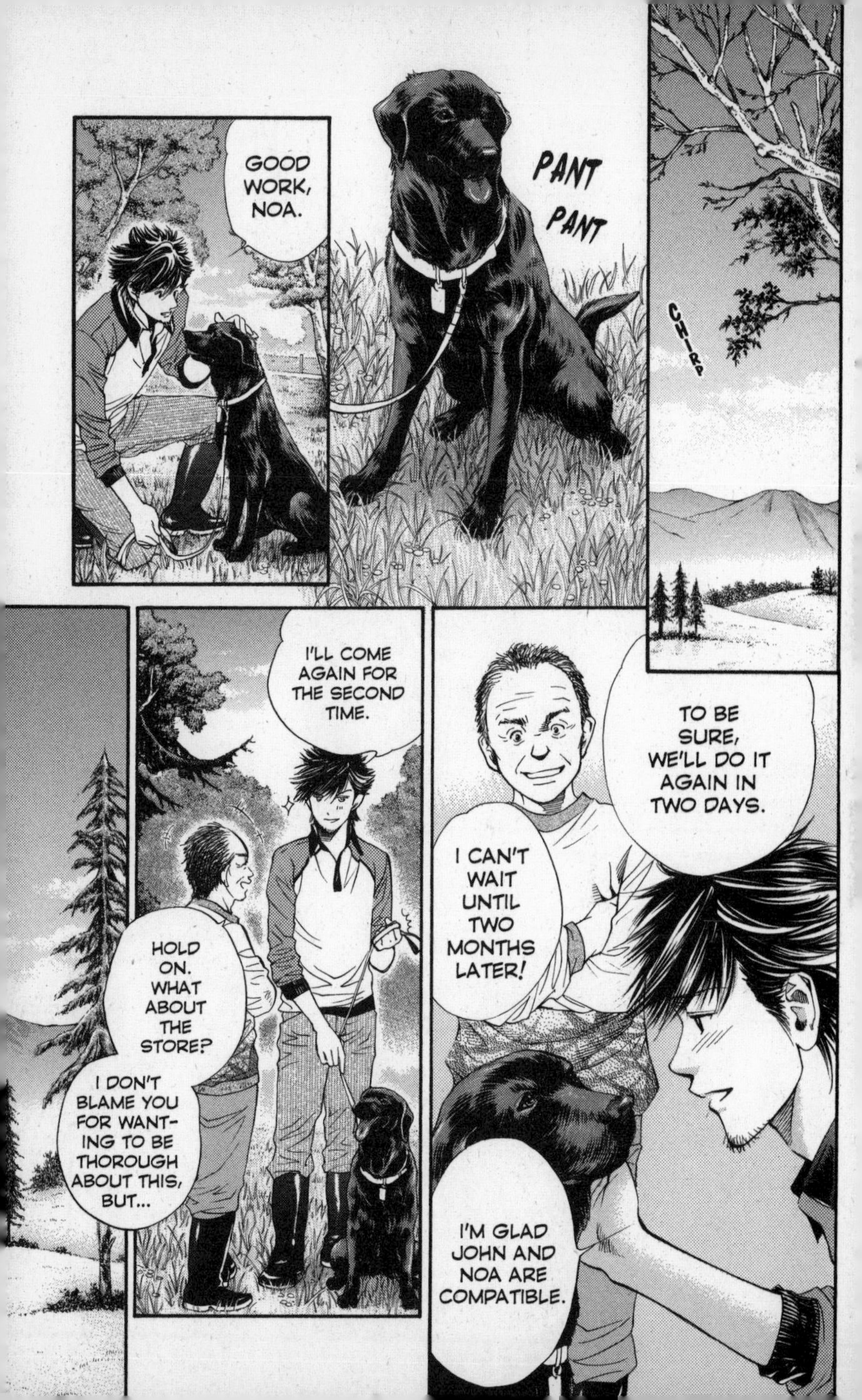
CHIRP
PANT
PANT
GOOD WORK, NOA.
TO BE SURE, WE'LL DO IT AGAIN IN TWO DAYS.
I CAN'T WAIT UNTIL TWO MONTHS LATER!
I'M GLAD JOHN AND NOA ARE COMPATIBLE.
I'LL COME AGAIN FOR THE SECOND TIME.
HOLD ON. WHAT ABOUT THE STORE?
I DON'T BLAME YOU FOR WANT-ING TO BE THOROUGH ABOUT THIS, BUT...

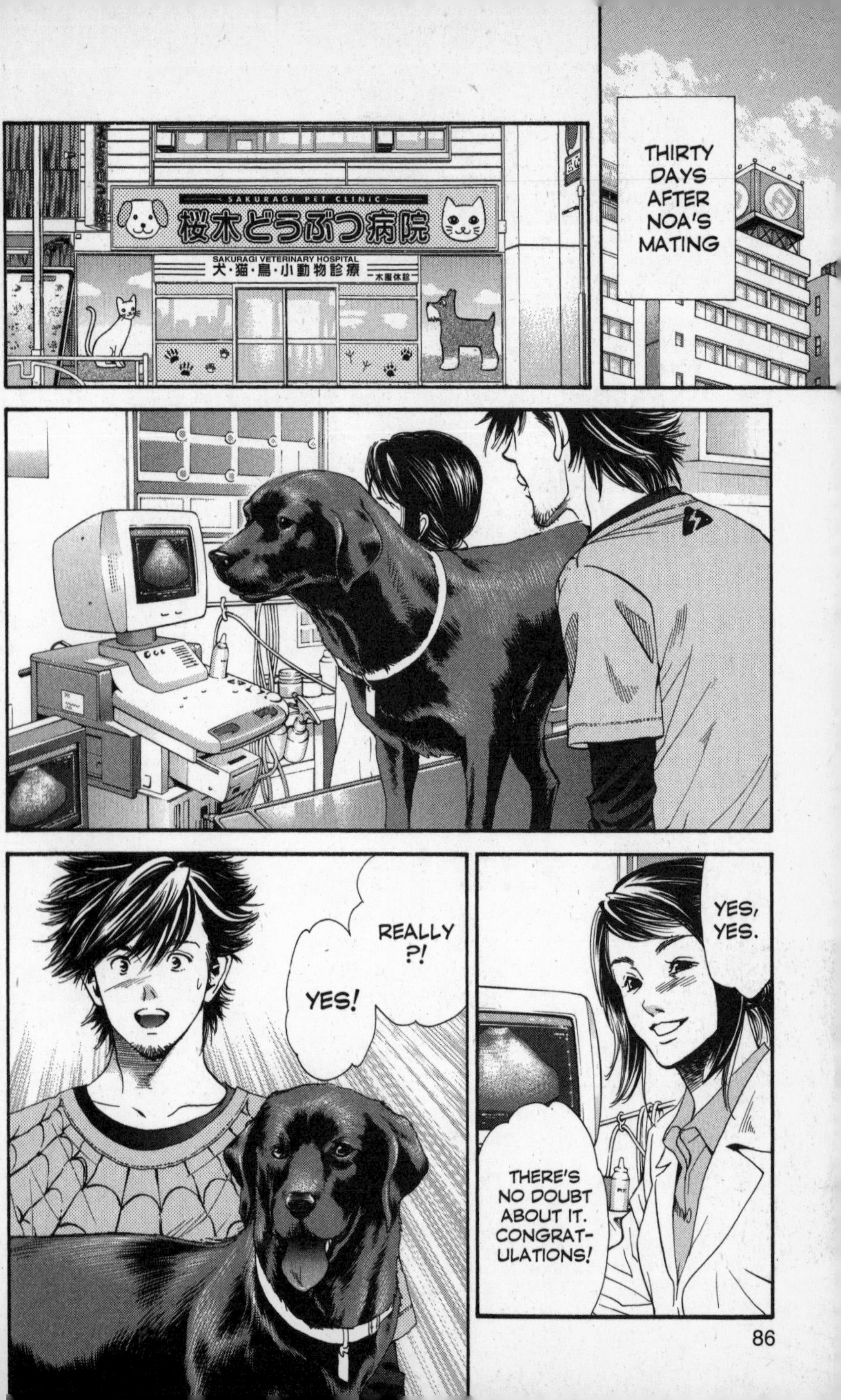
THIRTY DAYS AFTER NOA'S MATING
SAKURAGI PET CLINIC
桜木どうぶつ病院
SAKURAGI VETERINARY HOSPITAL
犬・猫・鳥・小動物診療
木曜休診
YES, YES.
THERE'S NO DOUBT ABOUT IT. CONGRAT-ULATIONS!
REALLY?!
YES!

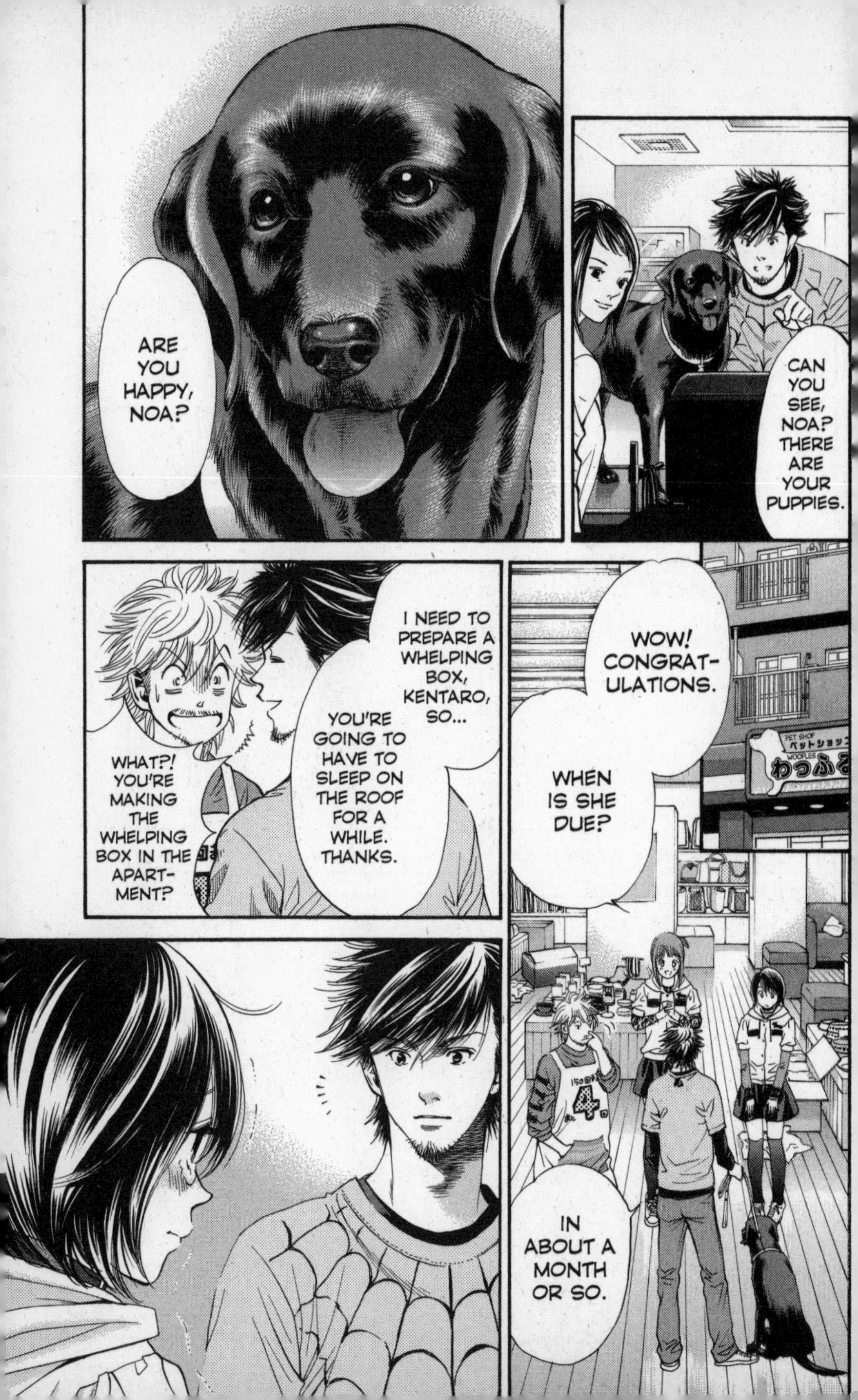
CAN YOU SEE, NOA? THERE ARE YOUR PUPPIES.
ARE YOU HAPPY, NOA?
WOW! CONGRAT-ULATIONS.
WHEN IS SHE DUE?
IN ABOUT A MONTH OR SO.
PET SHOP
WOOFLES
I NEED TO PREPARE A WHELPING BOX, KENTARO, SO...
YOU'RE GOING TO HAVE TO SLEEP ON THE ROOF FOR A WHILE. THANKS.
WHAT?! YOU'RE MAKING THE WHELPING BOX IN THE APART-MENT?

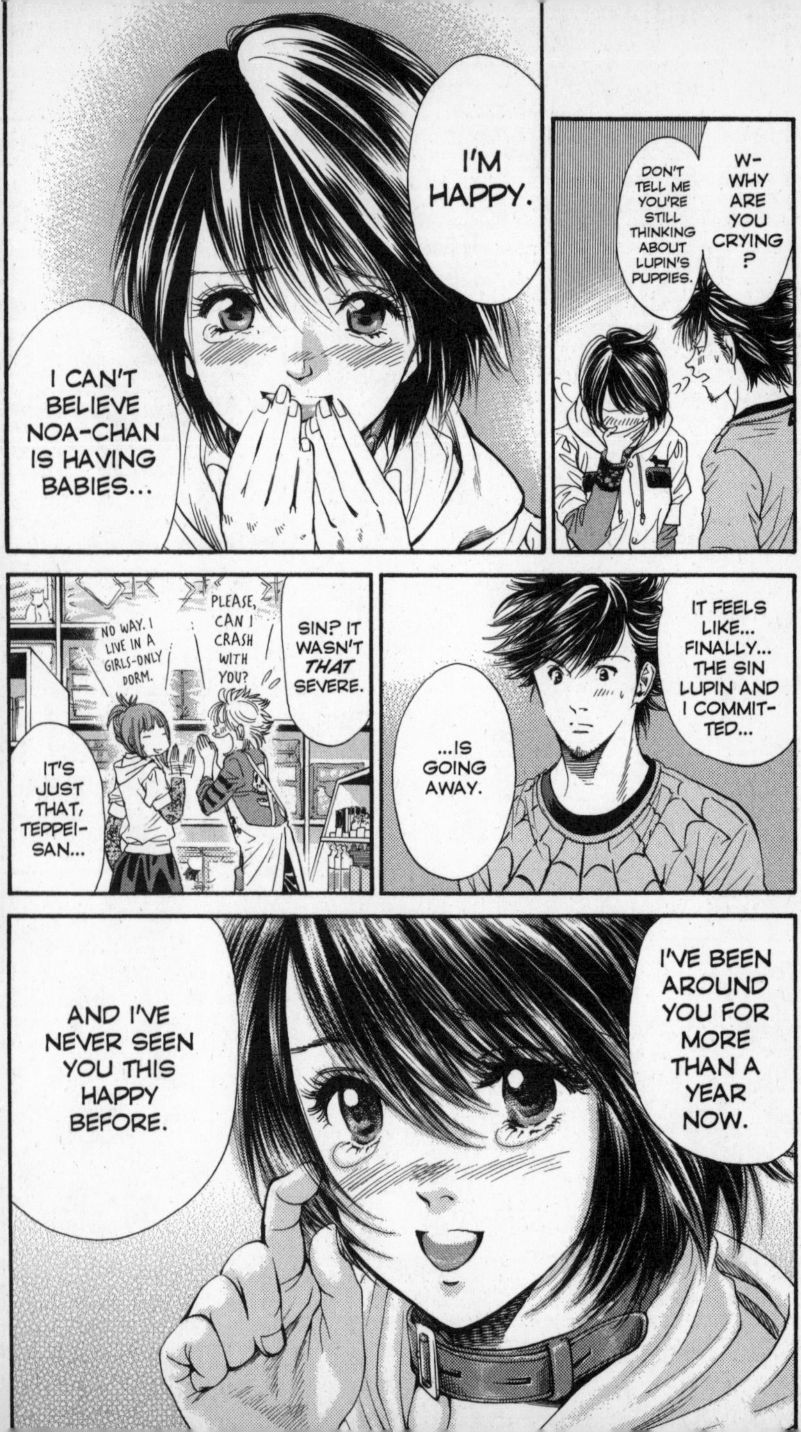
W-WHY ARE YOU CRYING?
DON'T TELL ME YOU'RE STILL THINKING ABOUT LUPIN'S PUPPIES.
I'M HAPPY.
I CAN'T BELIEVE NOA-CHAN IS HAVING BABIES...
IT FEELS LIKE... FINALLY... THE SIN LUPIN AND I COMMITTED...
...IS GOING AWAY.
SIN? IT WASN'T *THAT* SEVERE.
PLEASE, CAN I CRASH WITH YOU?
NO WAY. I LIVE IN A GIRLS-ONLY DORM.
IT'S JUST THAT, TEPPEI-SAN...
I'VE BEEN AROUND YOU FOR MORE THAN A YEAR NOW.
AND I'VE NEVER SEEN YOU THIS HAPPY BEFORE.

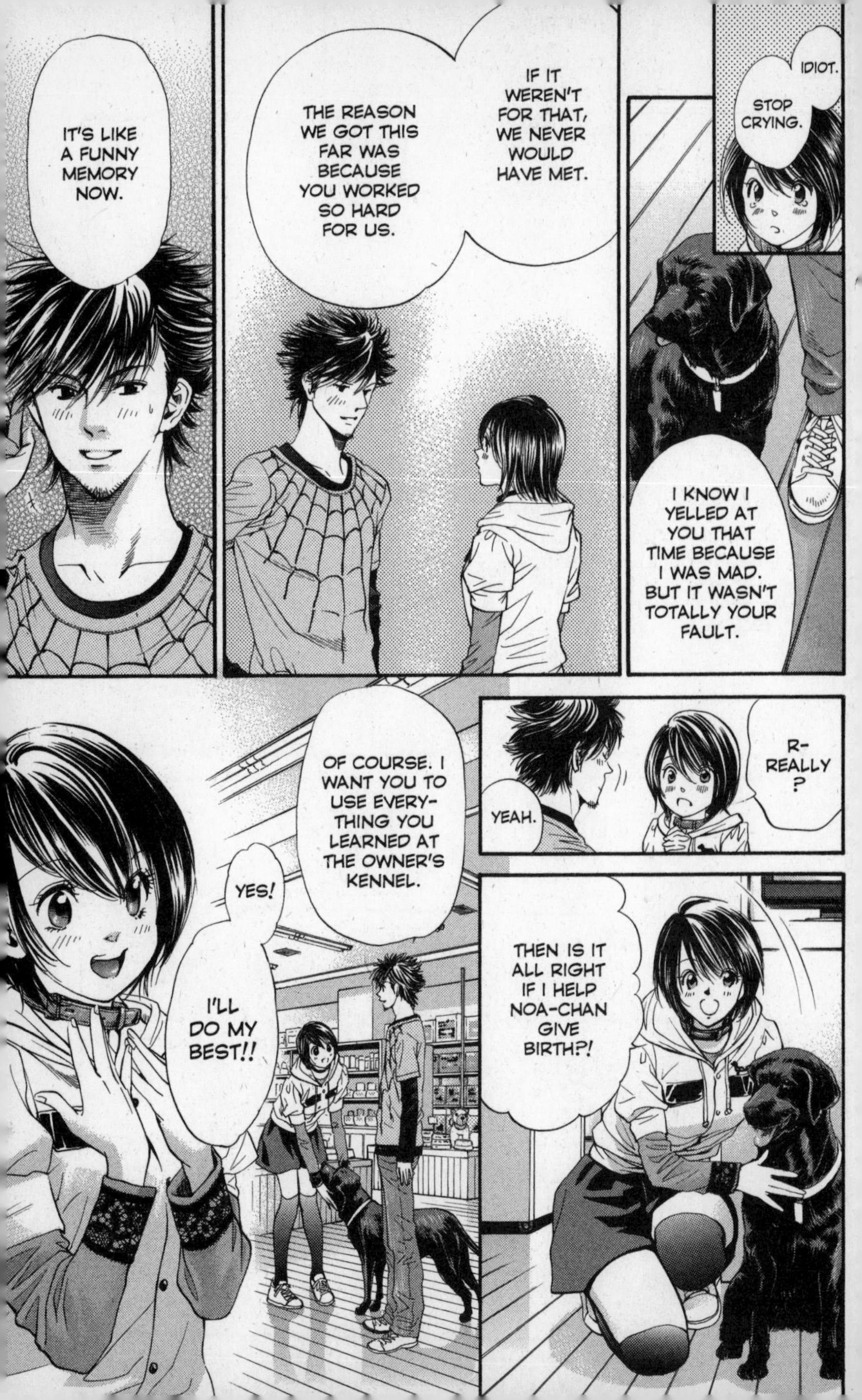

IDIOT.
STOP CRYING.
I KNOW I YELLED AT YOU THAT TIME BECAUSE I WAS MAD. BUT IT WASN'T TOTALLY YOUR FAULT.
IF IT WEREN'T FOR THAT, WE NEVER WOULD HAVE MET.
THE REASON WE GOT THIS FAR WAS BECAUSE YOU WORKED SO HARD FOR US.
IT'S LIKE A FUNNY MEMORY NOW.
R-REALLY?
YEAH.
THEN IS IT ALL RIGHT IF I HELP NOA-CHAN GIVE BIRTH?!
OF COURSE. I WANT YOU TO USE EVERY-THING YOU LEARNED AT THE OWNER'S KENNEL.
YES!
I'LL DO MY BEST!!

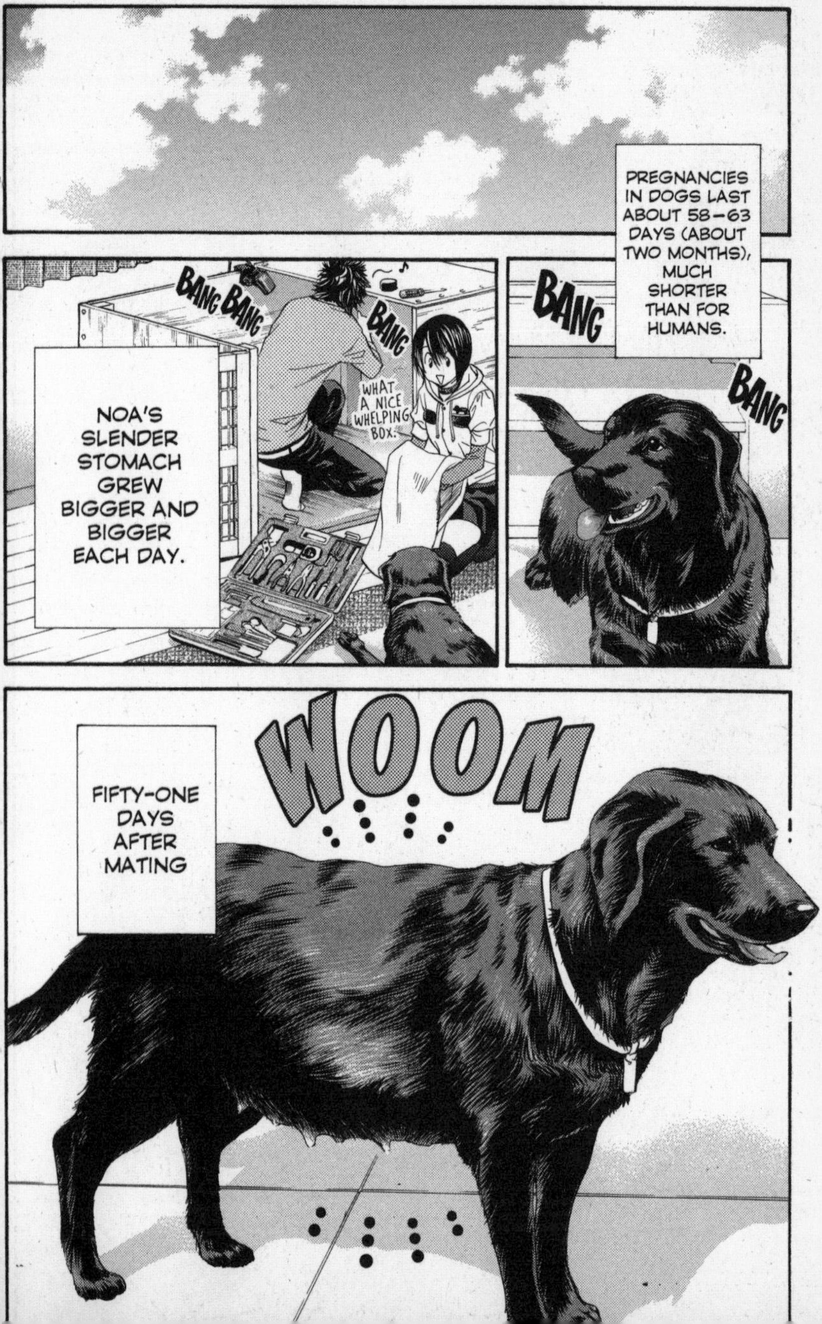
PREGNANCIES IN DOGS LAST ABOUT 58–63 DAYS (ABOUT TWO MONTHS), MUCH SHORTER THAN FOR HUMANS.
BANG
BANG
BANG BANG
BANG
NOA'S SLENDER STOMACH GREW BIGGER AND BIGGER EACH DAY.
WHAT A NICE WHELPING BOX.
FIFTY-ONE DAYS AFTER MATING
WOOM

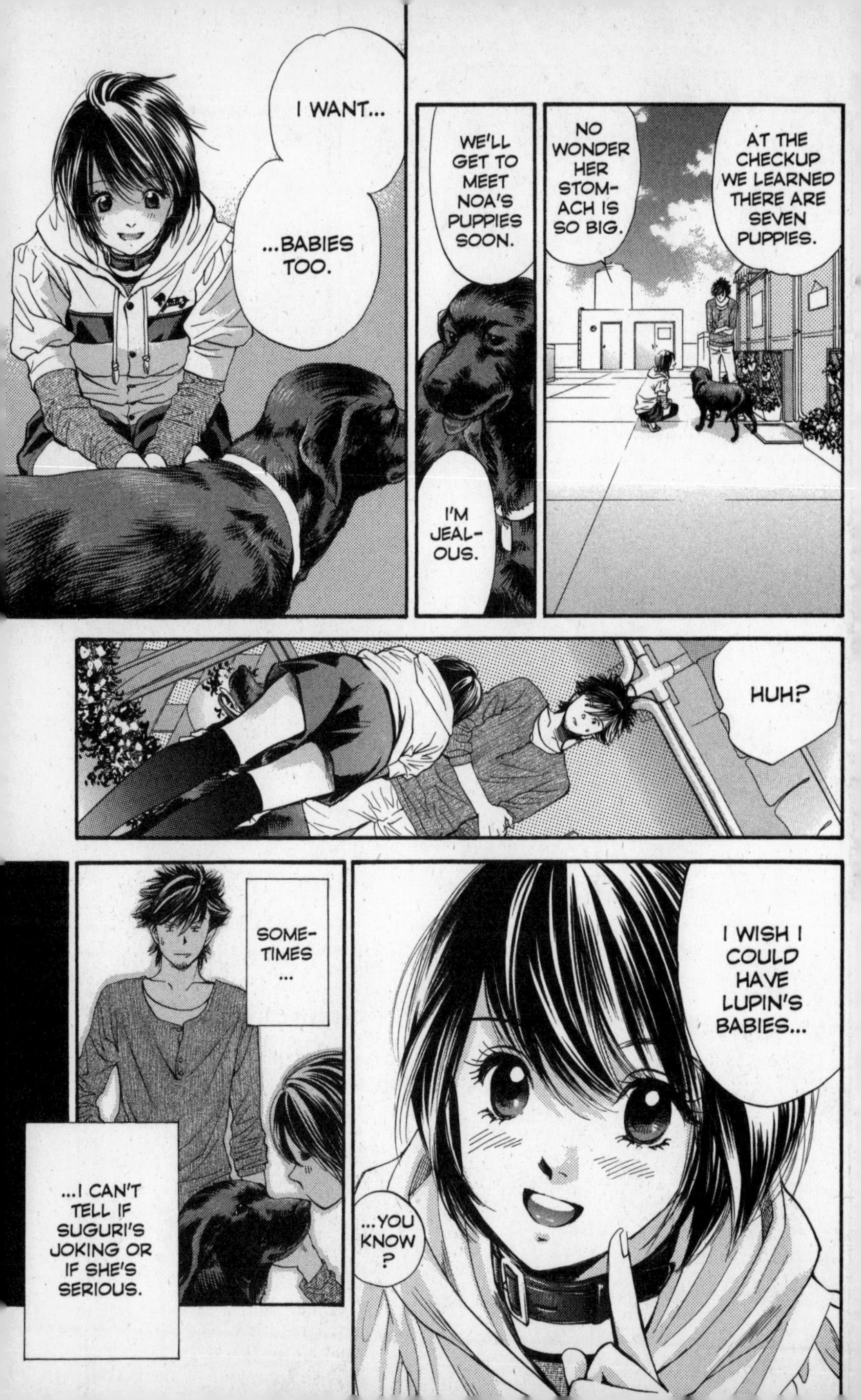
AT THE CHECKUP WE LEARNED THERE ARE SEVEN PUPPIES.
NO WONDER HER STOMACH IS SO BIG.
WE'LL GET TO MEET NOA'S PUPPIES SOON.
I'M JEALOUS.
I WANT...
...BABIES TOO.
HUH?
I WISH I COULD HAVE LUPIN'S BABIES...
...YOU KNOW?
SOMETIMES...
...I CAN'T TELL IF SUGURI'S JOKING OR IF SHE'S SERIOUS.

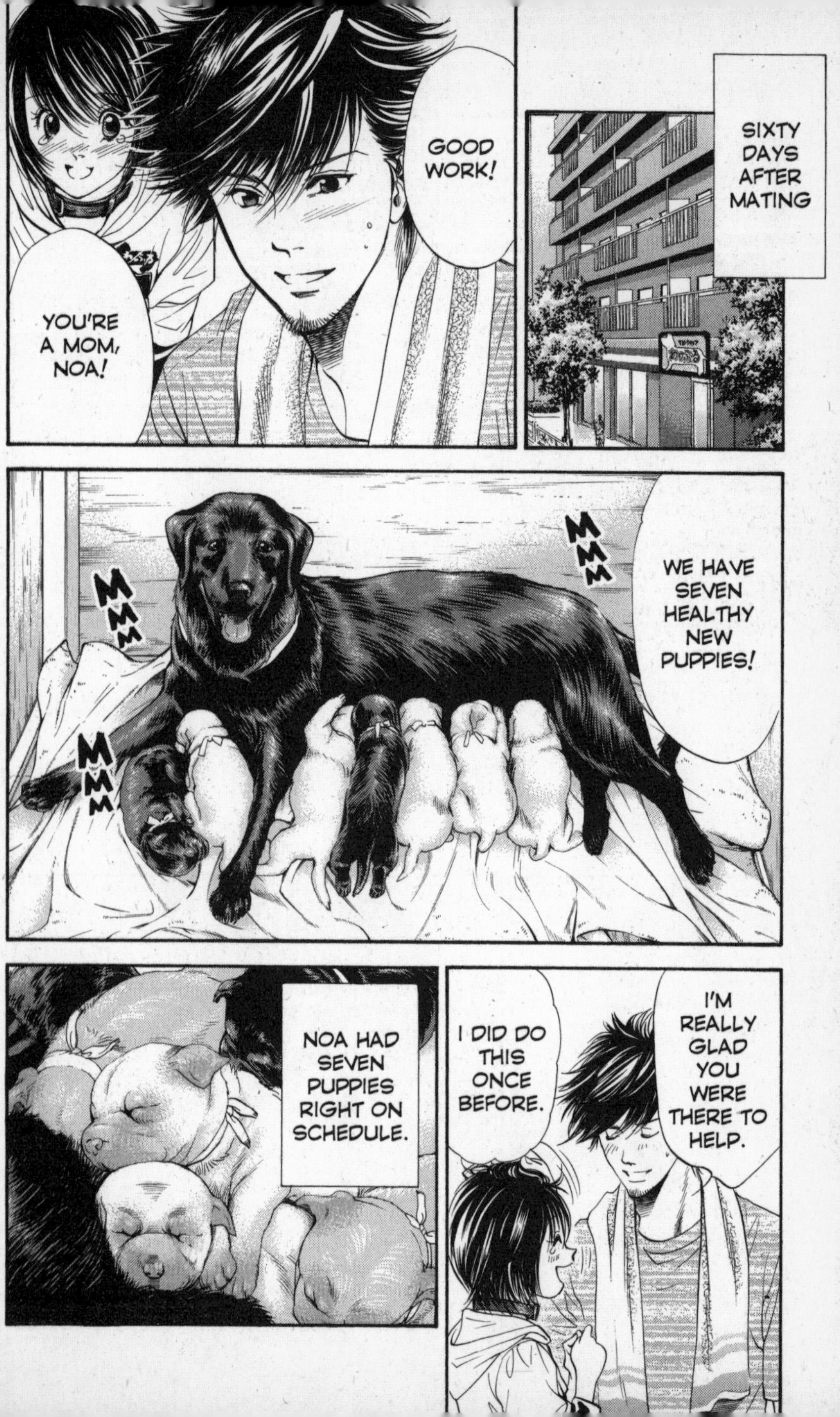
SIXTY DAYS AFTER MATING
GOOD WORK!
YOU'RE A MOM, NOA!
WE HAVE SEVEN HEALTHY NEW PUPPIES!
MMM
MMM
MMM
I'M REALLY GLAD YOU WERE THERE TO HELP.
I DID DO THIS ONCE BEFORE.
NOA HAD SEVEN PUPPIES RIGHT ON SCHEDULE.

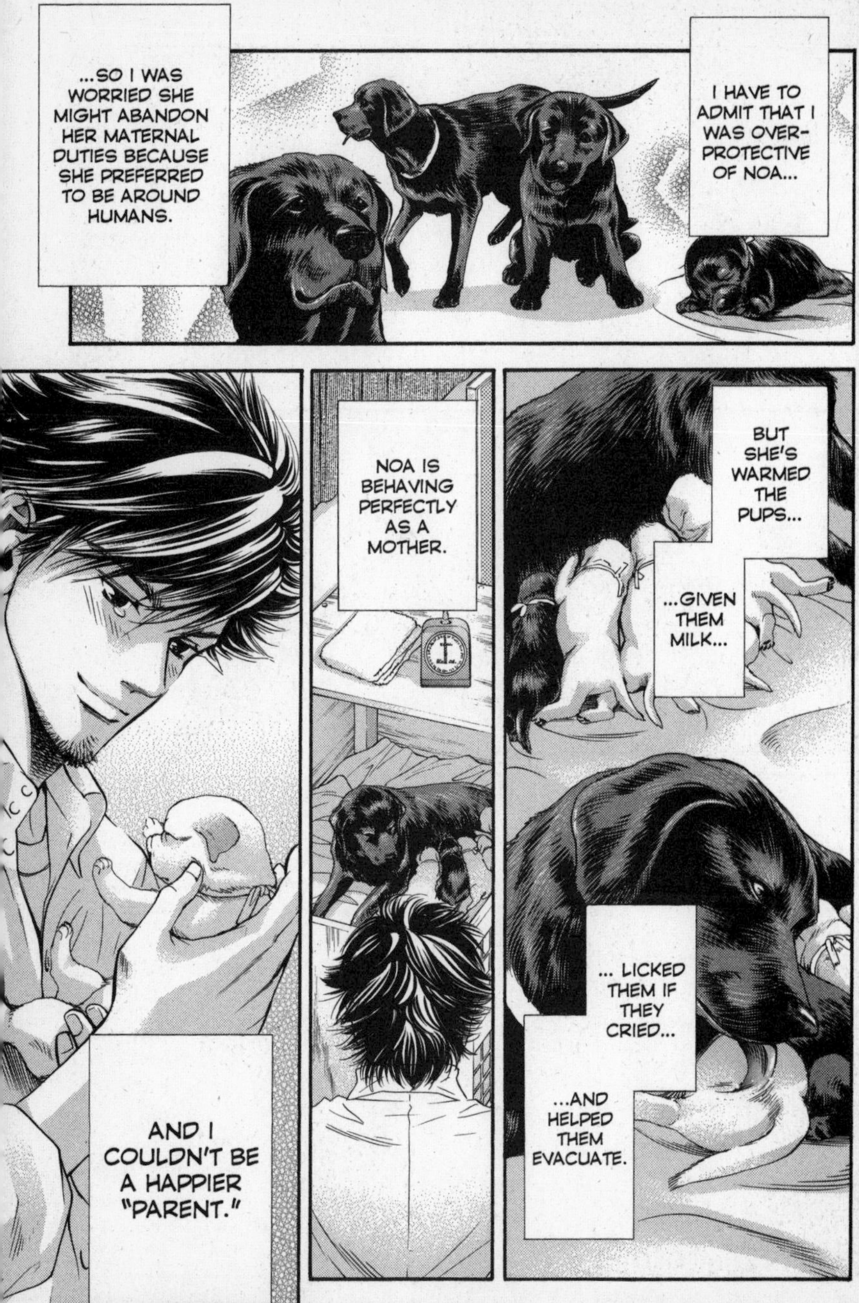
I HAVE TO ADMIT THAT I WAS OVER-PROTECTIVE OF NOA...
...SO I WAS WORRIED SHE MIGHT ABANDON HER MATERNAL DUTIES BECAUSE SHE PREFERRED TO BE AROUND HUMANS.
BUT SHE'S WARMED THE PUPS...
...GIVEN THEM MILK...
... LICKED THEM IF THEY CRIED...
...AND HELPED THEM EVACUATE.
NOA IS BEHAVING PERFECTLY AS A MOTHER.
AND I COULDN'T BE A HAPPIER "PARENT."

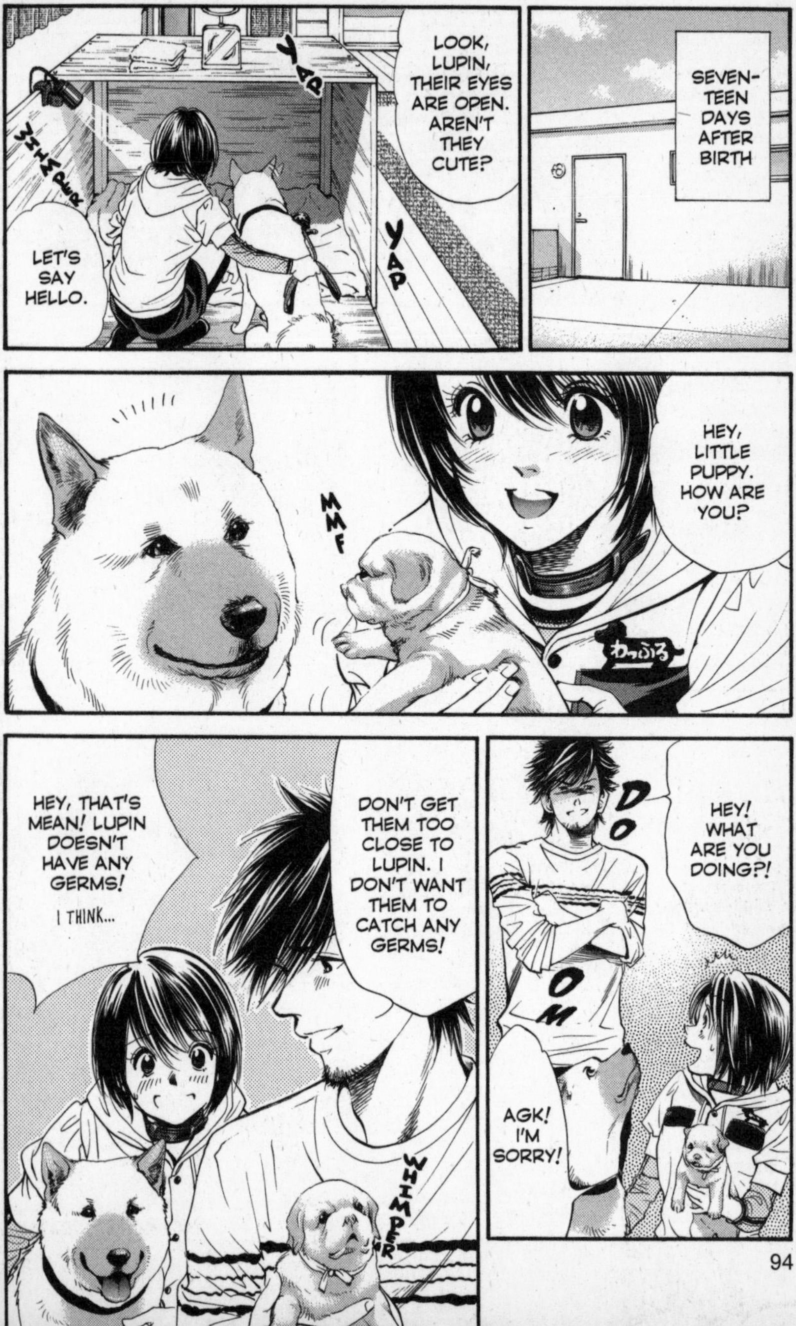
SEVENTEEN DAYS AFTER BIRTH
LOOK, LUPIN, THEIR EYES ARE OPEN. AREN'T THEY CUTE?
YAP
YAP
LET'S SAY HELLO.
HEY, LITTLE PUPPY. HOW ARE YOU?
MMF
わっふる
HEY! WHAT ARE YOU DOING?!
DOOM
AGK! I'M SORRY!
DON'T GET THEM TOO CLOSE TO LUPIN. I DON'T WANT THEM TO CATCH ANY GERMS!
HEY, THAT'S MEAN! LUPIN DOESN'T HAVE ANY GERMS!
I THINK...
WHIMPER

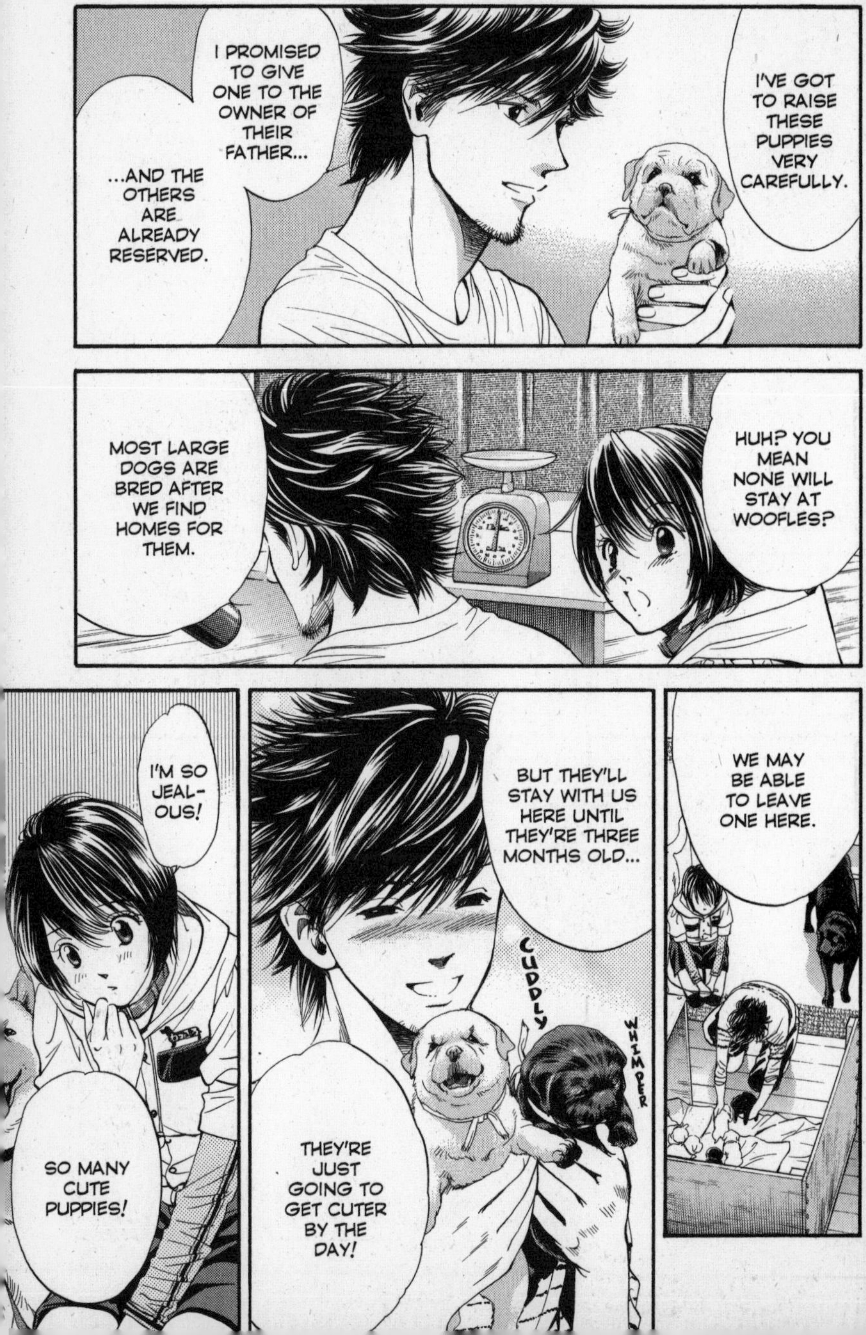
I'VE GOT TO RAISE THESE PUPPIES VERY CAREFULLY.
I PROMISED TO GIVE ONE TO THE OWNER OF THEIR FATHER...
...AND THE OTHERS ARE ALREADY RESERVED.
HUH? YOU MEAN NONE WILL STAY AT WOOFLES?
MOST LARGE DOGS ARE BRED AFTER WE FIND HOMES FOR THEM.
WE MAY BE ABLE TO LEAVE ONE HERE.
BUT THEY'LL STAY WITH US HERE UNTIL THEY'RE THREE MONTHS OLD...
WHIMPER
CUDDLY
THEY'RE JUST GOING TO GET CUTER BY THE DAY!
I'M SO JEAL-OUS!
SO MANY CUTE PUPPIES!

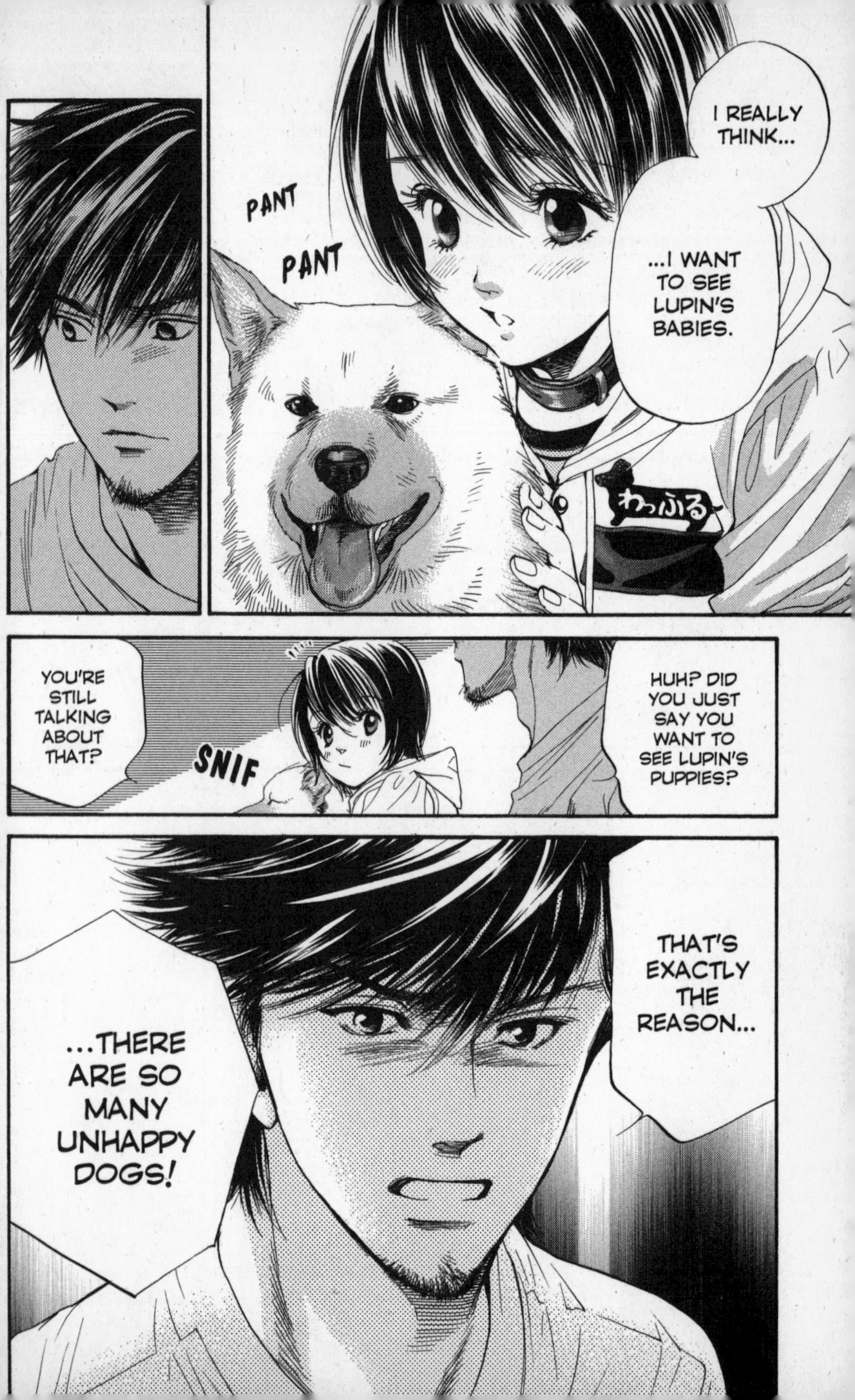
I REALLY THINK...
...I WANT TO SEE LUPIN'S BABIES.
PANT
PANT
わっふる
HUH? DID YOU JUST SAY YOU WANT TO SEE LUPIN'S PUPPIES?
SNIF
YOU'RE STILL TALKING ABOUT THAT?
THAT'S EXACTLY THE REASON...
...THERE ARE SO MANY UNHAPPY DOGS!

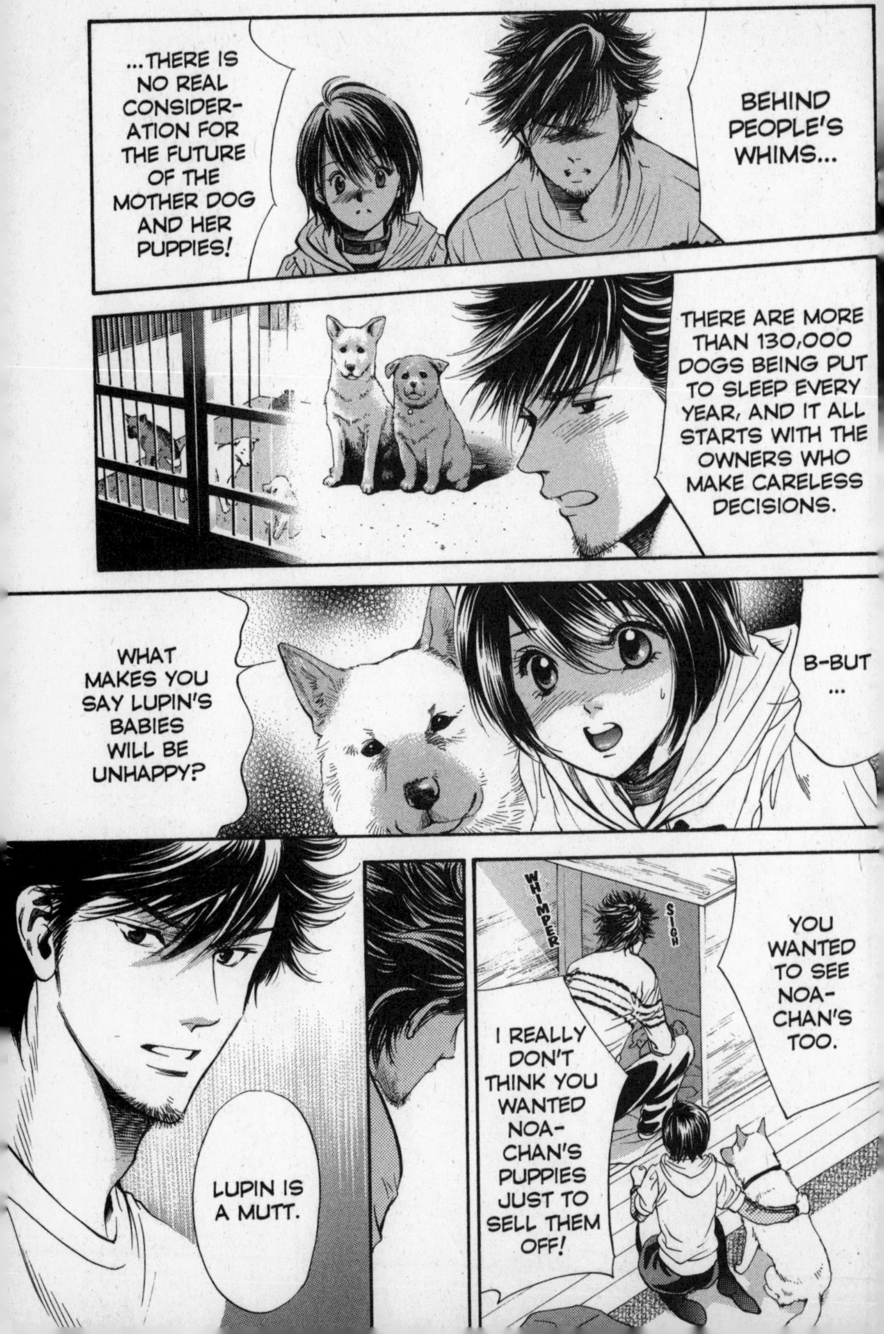
BEHIND PEOPLE'S WHIMS...
...THERE IS NO REAL CONSIDER-ATION FOR THE FUTURE OF THE MOTHER DOG AND HER PUPPIES!
THERE ARE MORE THAN 130,000 DOGS BEING PUT TO SLEEP EVERY YEAR, AND IT ALL STARTS WITH THE OWNERS WHO MAKE CARELESS DECISIONS.
B-BUT ...
WHAT MAKES YOU SAY LUPIN'S BABIES WILL BE UNHAPPY?
YOU WANTED TO SEE NOA-CHAN'S TOO.
SIGH
WHIMPER
I REALLY DON'T THINK YOU WANTED NOA-CHAN'S PUPPIES JUST TO SELL THEM OFF!
LUPIN IS A MUTT.

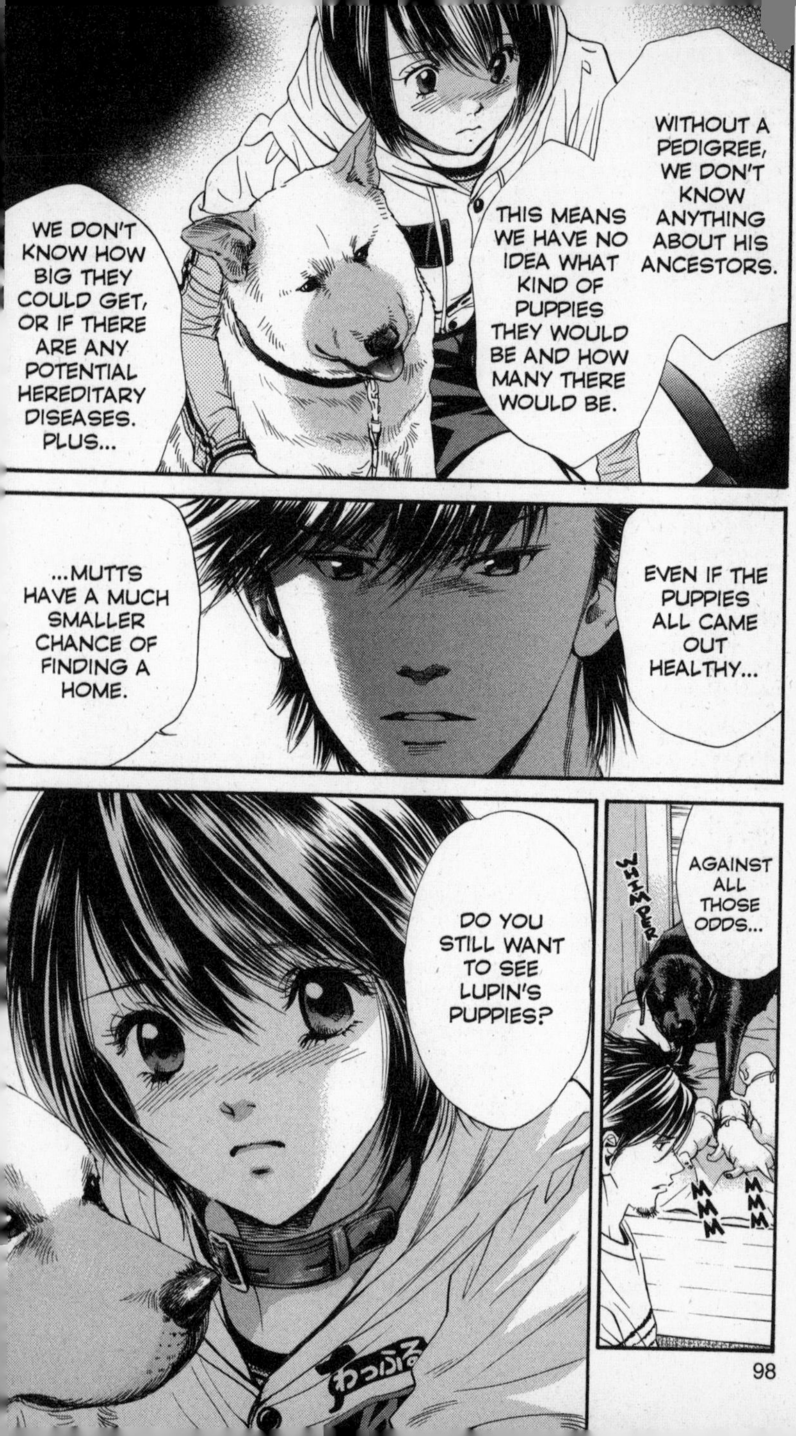
WITHOUT A PEDIGREE, WE DON'T KNOW ANYTHING ABOUT HIS ANCESTORS.
THIS MEANS WE HAVE NO IDEA WHAT KIND OF PUPPIES THEY WOULD BE AND HOW MANY THERE WOULD BE.
WE DON'T KNOW HOW BIG THEY COULD GET, OR IF THERE ARE ANY POTENTIAL HEREDITARY DISEASES. PLUS...
EVEN IF THE PUPPIES ALL CAME OUT HEALTHY...
...MUTTS HAVE A MUCH SMALLER CHANCE OF FINDING A HOME.
WHIMPER
AGAINST ALL THOSE ODDS...
MMM
MMM
DO YOU STILL WANT TO SEE LUPIN'S PUPPIES?

CHAPTER 147: LUPIN'S BRIDE?!

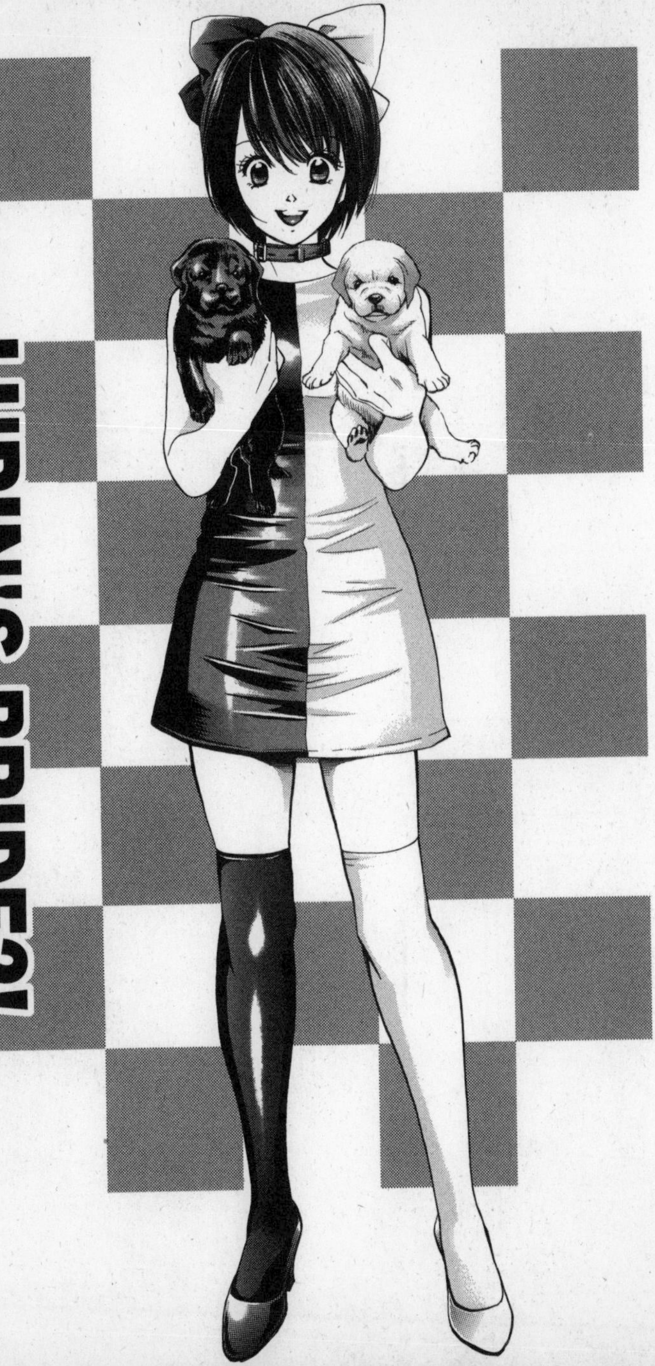

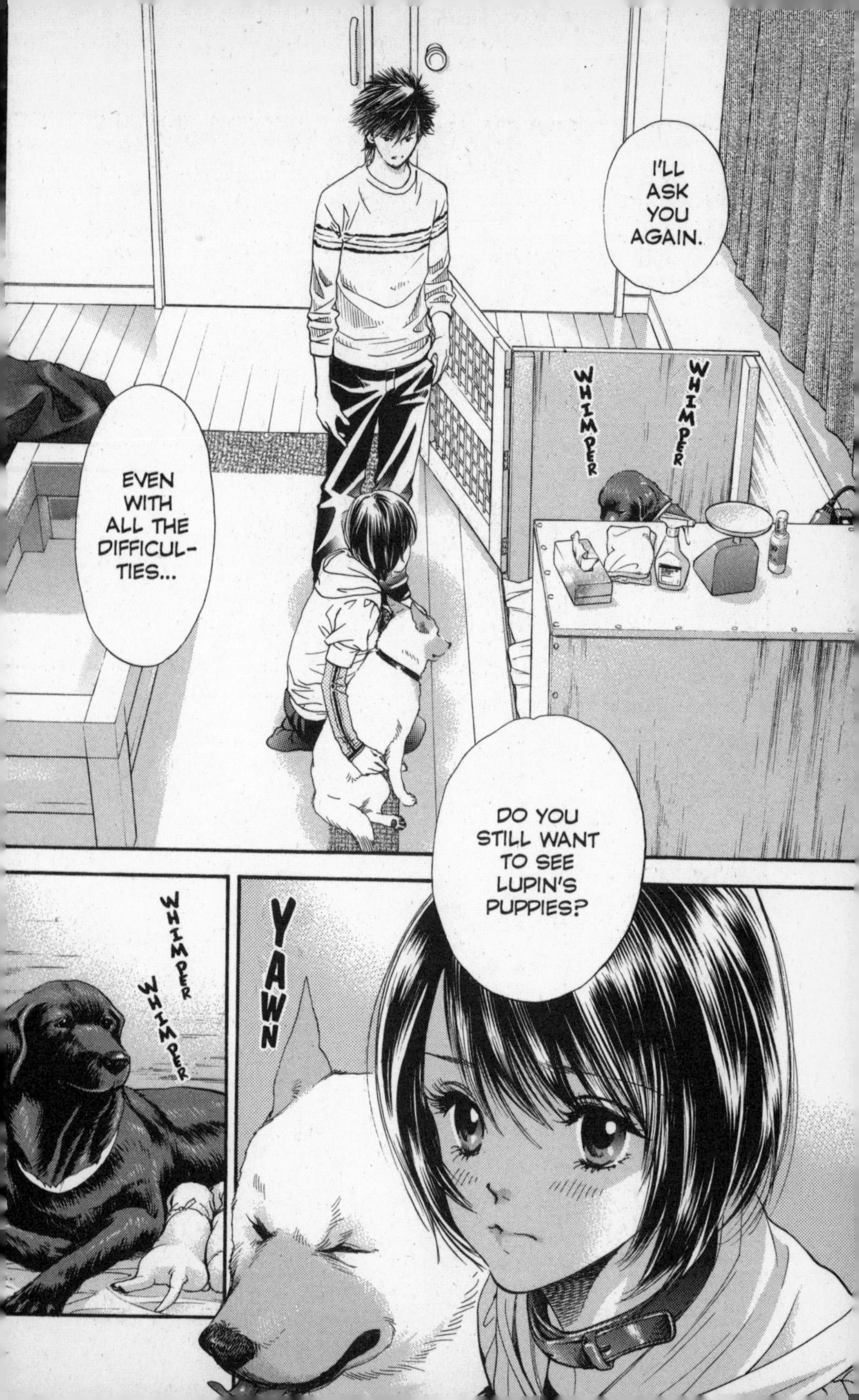
I'LL ASK YOU AGAIN.
WHIMPER
WHIMPER
EVEN WITH ALL THE DIFFICUL-TIES...
DO YOU STILL WANT TO SEE LUPIN'S PUPPIES?
YAWN
WHIMPER
WHIMPER

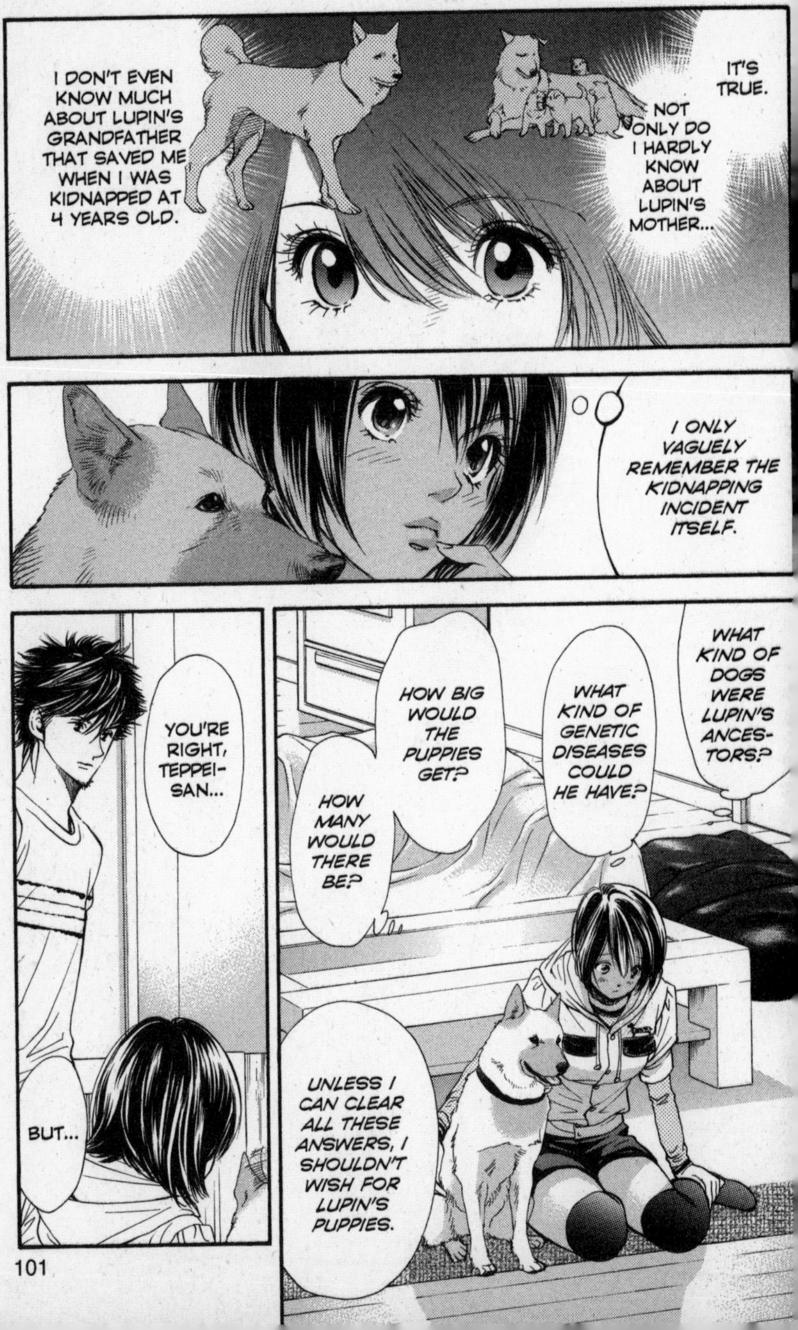
IT'S TRUE.
NOT ONLY DO I HARDLY KNOW ABOUT LUPIN'S MOTHER...
I DON'T EVEN KNOW MUCH ABOUT LUPIN'S GRANDFATHER THAT SAVED ME WHEN I WAS KIDNAPPED AT 4 YEARS OLD.
I ONLY VAGUELY REMEMBER THE KIDNAPPING INCIDENT ITSELF.
WHAT KIND OF DOGS WERE LUPIN'S ANCES-TORS?
WHAT KIND OF GENETIC DISEASES COULD HE HAVE?
HOW BIG WOULD THE PUPPIES GET?
HOW MANY WOULD THERE BE?
UNLESS I CAN CLEAR ALL THESE ANSWERS, I SHOULDN'T WISH FOR LUPIN'S PUPPIES.
YOU'RE RIGHT, TEPPEI-SAN...
BUT...

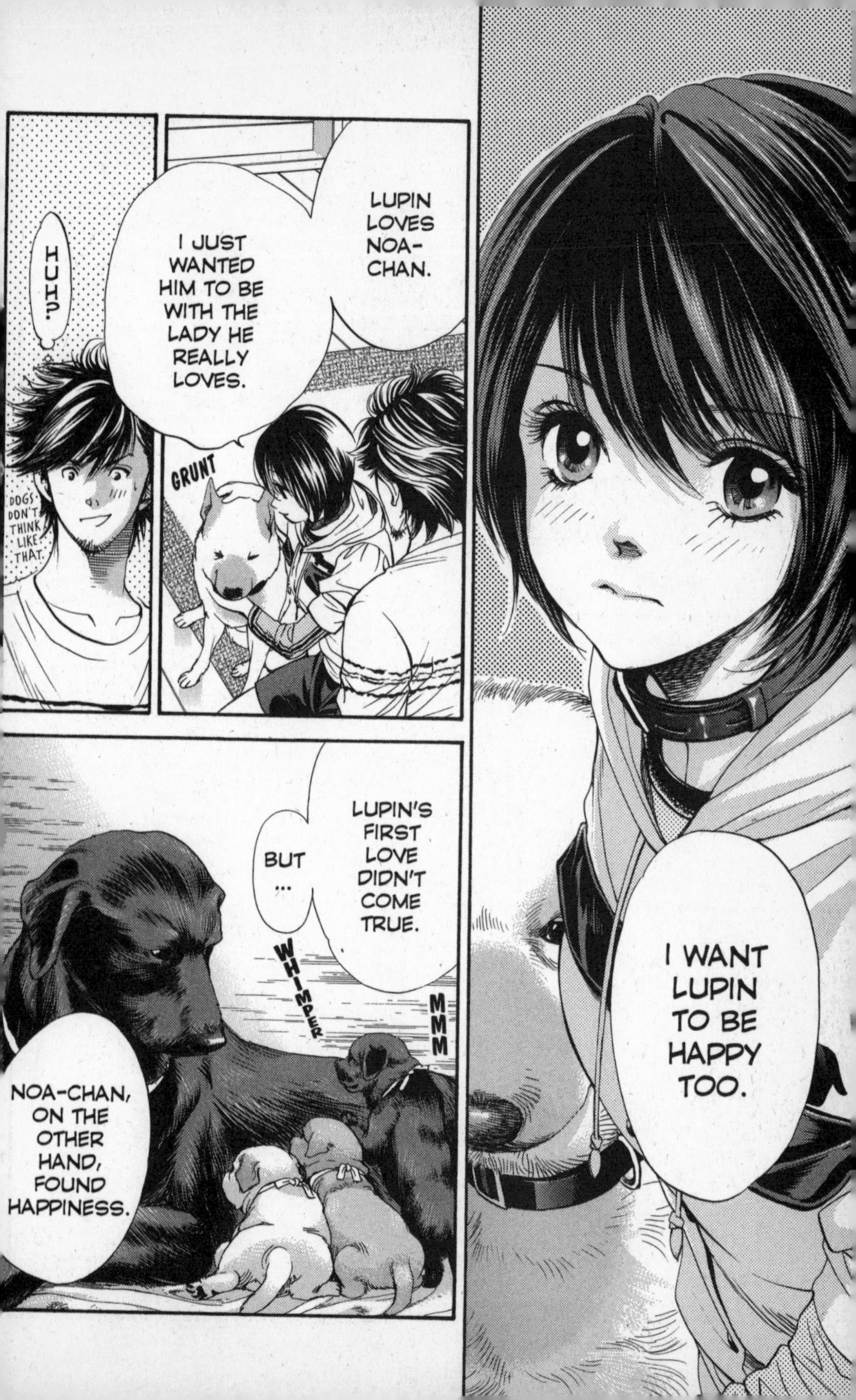

I WANT LUPIN TO BE HAPPY TOO.
LUPIN LOVES NOA-CHAN.
I JUST WANTED HIM TO BE WITH THE LADY HE REALLY LOVES.
GRUNT
HUH?
DOGS DON'T THINK LIKE THAT.
LUPIN'S FIRST LOVE DIDN'T COME TRUE.
BUT ...
WHIMPER
MMM
NOA-CHAN, ON THE OTHER HAND, FOUND HAPPINESS.

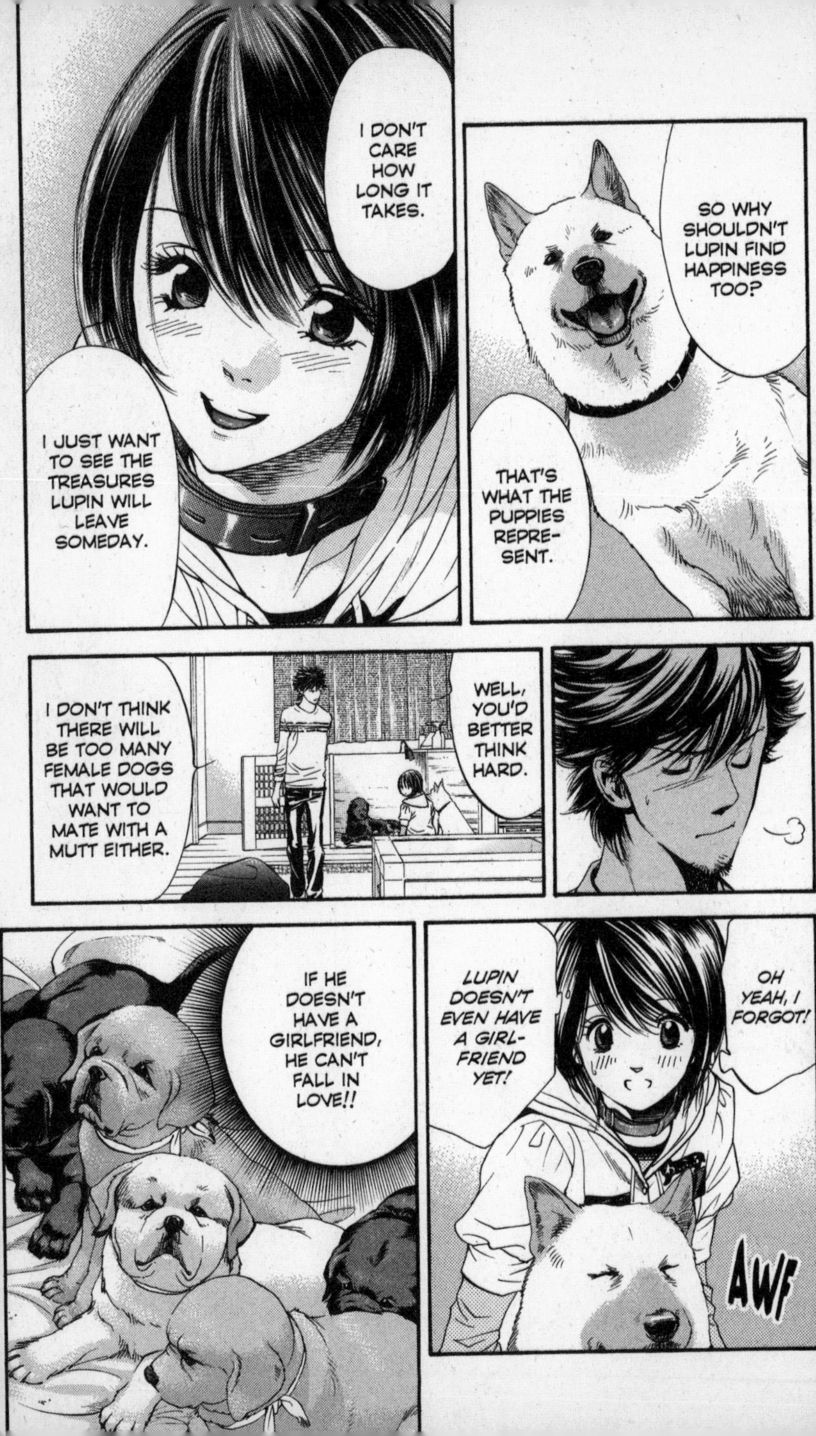
SO WHY SHOULDN'T LUPIN FIND HAPPINESS TOO?
THAT'S WHAT THE PUPPIES REPRE-SENT.
I DON'T CARE HOW LONG IT TAKES.
I JUST WANT TO SEE THE TREASURES LUPIN WILL LEAVE SOMEDAY.
WELL, YOU'D BETTER THINK HARD.
I DON'T THINK THERE WILL BE TOO MANY FEMALE DOGS THAT WOULD WANT TO MATE WITH A MUTT EITHER.
OH YEAH, I FORGOT!
LUPIN DOESN'T EVEN HAVE A GIRL-FRIEND YET!
AWF
IF HE DOESN'T HAVE A GIRLFRIEND, HE CAN'T FALL IN LOVE!!

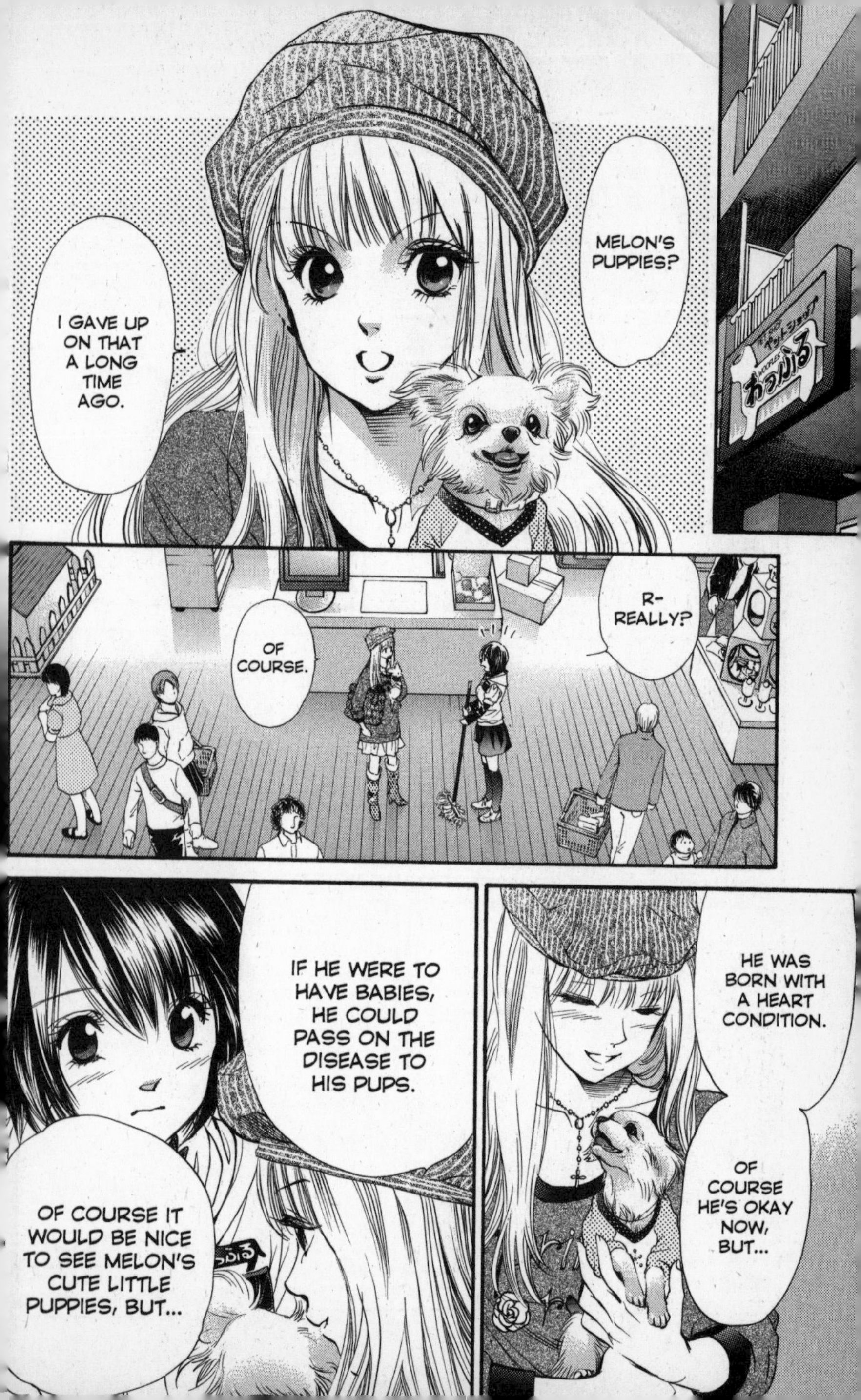
MELON'S PUPPIES?
I GAVE UP ON THAT A LONG TIME AGO.
R-REALLY?
OF COURSE.
HE WAS BORN WITH A HEART CONDITION.
OF COURSE HE'S OKAY NOW, BUT...
IF HE WERE TO HAVE BABIES, HE COULD PASS ON THE DISEASE TO HIS PUPS.
OF COURSE IT WOULD BE NICE TO SEE MELON'S CUTE LITTLE PUPPIES, BUT...

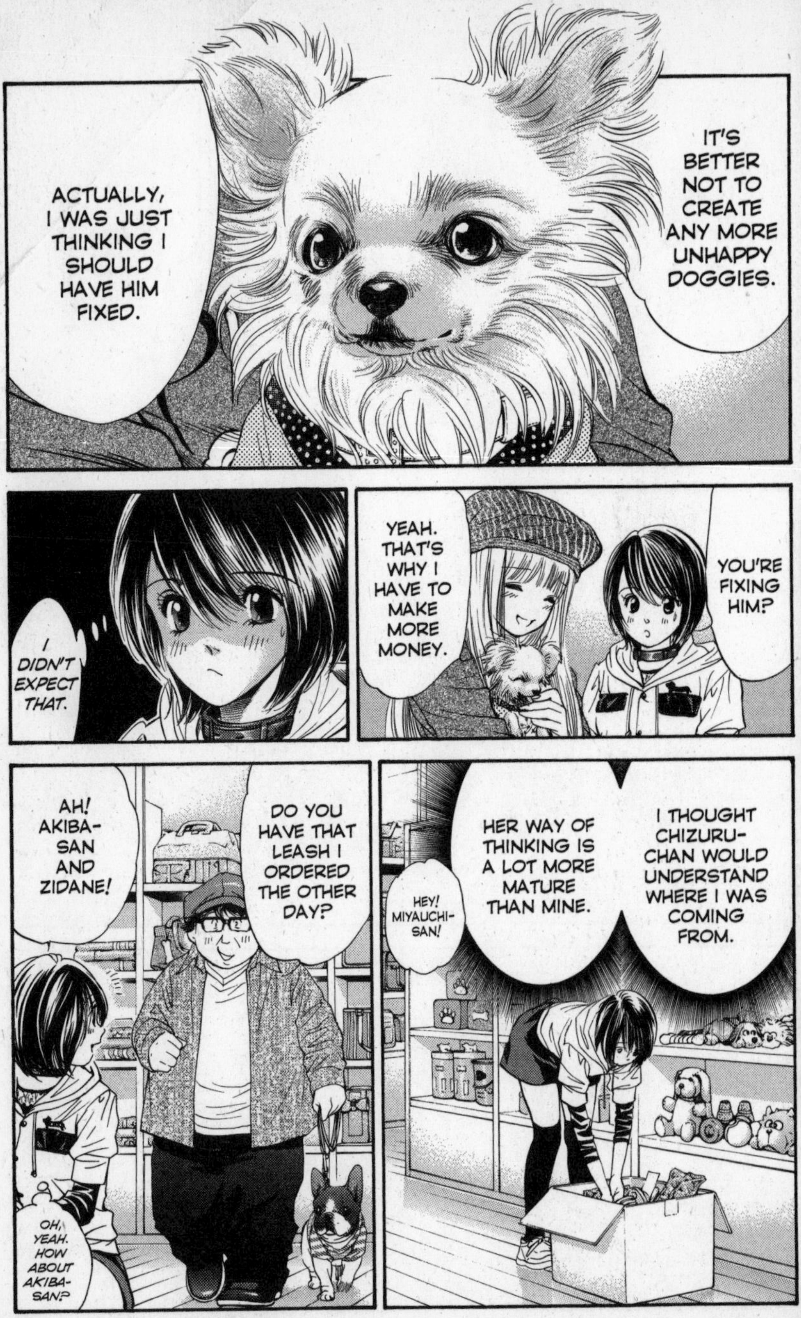
IT'S BETTER NOT TO CREATE ANY MORE UNHAPPY DOGGIES.
ACTUALLY, I WAS JUST THINKING I SHOULD HAVE HIM FIXED.
YOU'RE FIXING HIM?
YEAH. THAT'S WHY I HAVE TO MAKE MORE MONEY.
I DIDN'T EXPECT THAT.
I THOUGHT CHIZURU-CHAN WOULD UNDERSTAND WHERE I WAS COMING FROM.
HER WAY OF THINKING IS A LOT MORE MATURE THAN MINE.
HEY! MIYAUCHI-SAN!
DO YOU HAVE THAT LEASH I ORDERED THE OTHER DAY?
AH! AKIBA-SAN AND ZIDANE!
OH, YEAH. HOW ABOUT AKIBA-SAN?

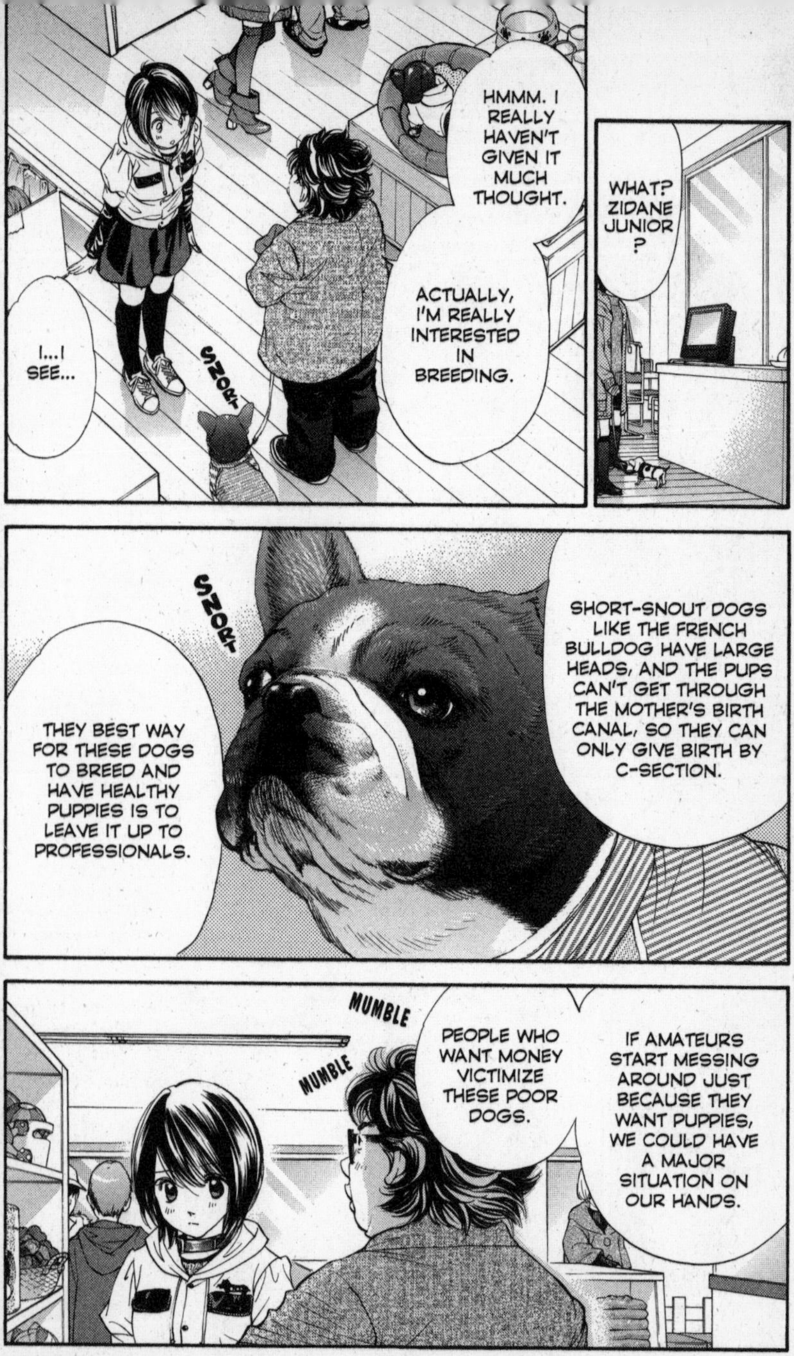
WHAT? ZIDANE JUNIOR?
HMMM. I REALLY HAVEN'T GIVEN IT MUCH THOUGHT.
ACTUALLY, I'M REALLY INTERESTED IN BREEDING.
SNORT
I...I SEE...
SHORT-SNOUT DOGS LIKE THE FRENCH BULLDOG HAVE LARGE HEADS, AND THE PUPS CAN'T GET THROUGH THE MOTHER'S BIRTH CANAL, SO THEY CAN ONLY GIVE BIRTH BY C-SECTION.
SNORT
THEY BEST WAY FOR THESE DOGS TO BREED AND HAVE HEALTHY PUPPIES IS TO LEAVE IT UP TO PROFESSIONALS.
IF AMATEURS START MESSING AROUND JUST BECAUSE THEY WANT PUPPIES, WE COULD HAVE A MAJOR SITUATION ON OUR HANDS.
PEOPLE WHO WANT MONEY VICTIMIZE THESE POOR DOGS.
MUMBLE
MUMBLE

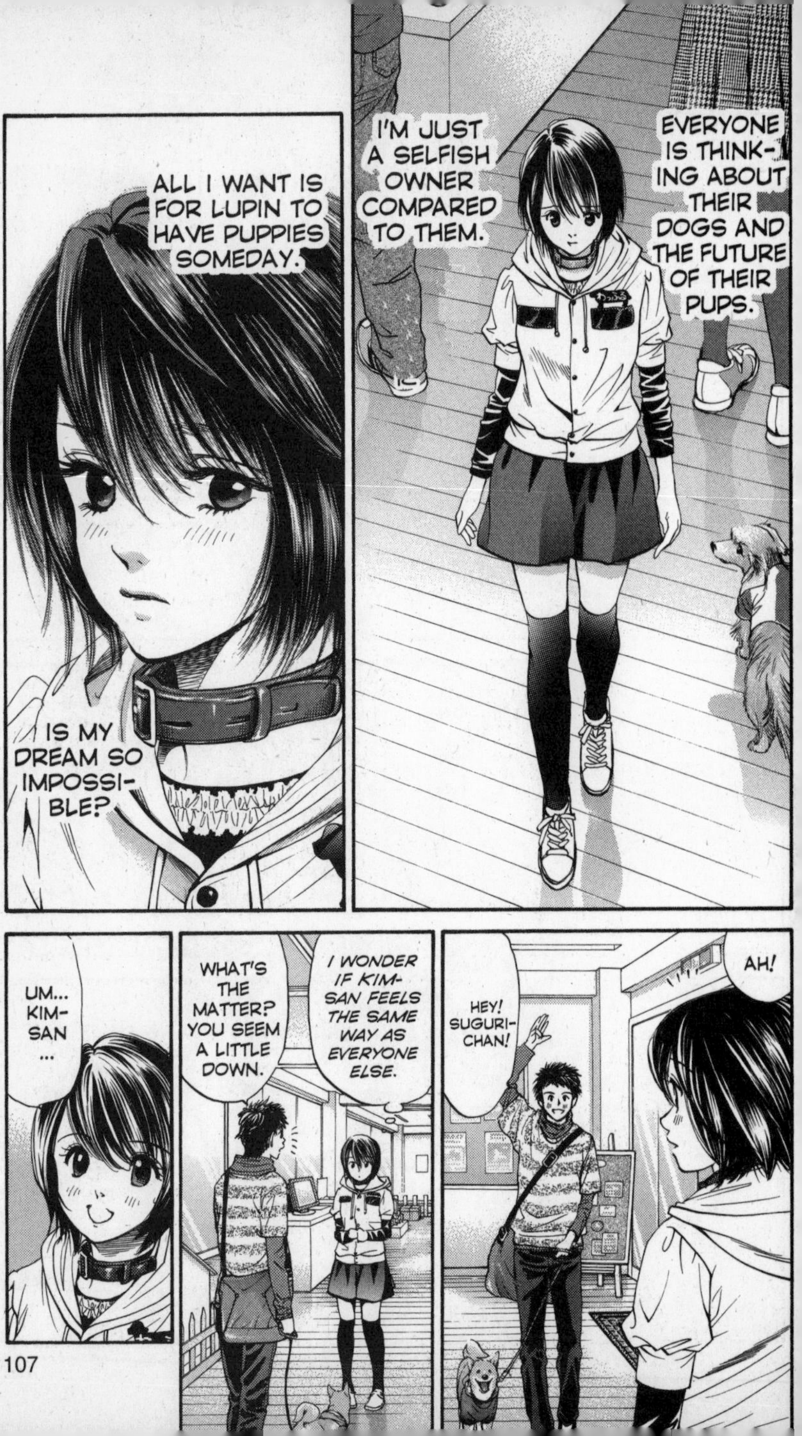
EVERYONE IS THINK-ING ABOUT THEIR DOGS AND THE FUTURE OF THEIR PUPS.
I'M JUST A SELFISH OWNER COMPARED TO THEM.
ALL I WANT IS FOR LUPIN TO HAVE PUPPIES SOMEDAY.
IS MY DREAM SO IMPOSSI-BLE?
AH!
HEY! SUGURI-CHAN!
I WONDER IF KIM-SAN FEELS THE SAME WAY AS EVERYONE ELSE.
WHAT'S THE MATTER? YOU SEEM A LITTLE DOWN.
UM... KIM-SAN ...

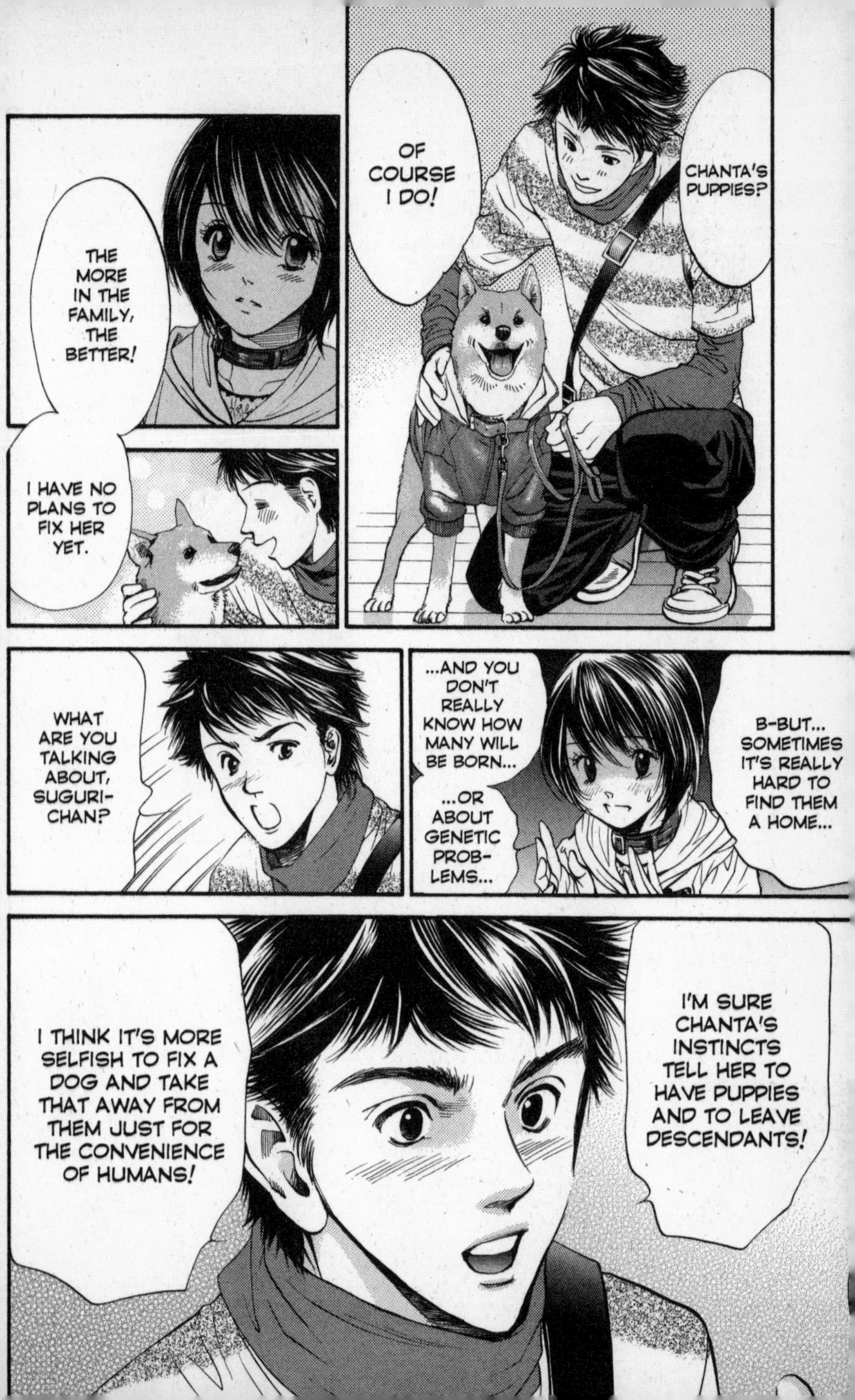
CHANTA'S PUPPIES?
OF COURSE I DO!
THE MORE IN THE FAMILY, THE BETTER!
I HAVE NO PLANS TO FIX HER YET.
B-BUT... SOMETIMES IT'S REALLY HARD TO FIND THEM A HOME...
...AND YOU DON'T REALLY KNOW HOW MANY WILL BE BORN...
...OR ABOUT GENETIC PROB-LEMS...
WHAT ARE YOU TALKING ABOUT, SUGURI-CHAN?
I'M SURE CHANTA'S INSTINCTS TELL HER TO HAVE PUPPIES AND TO LEAVE DESCENDANTS!
I THINK IT'S MORE SELFISH TO FIX A DOG AND TAKE THAT AWAY FROM THEM JUST FOR THE CONVENIENCE OF HUMANS!

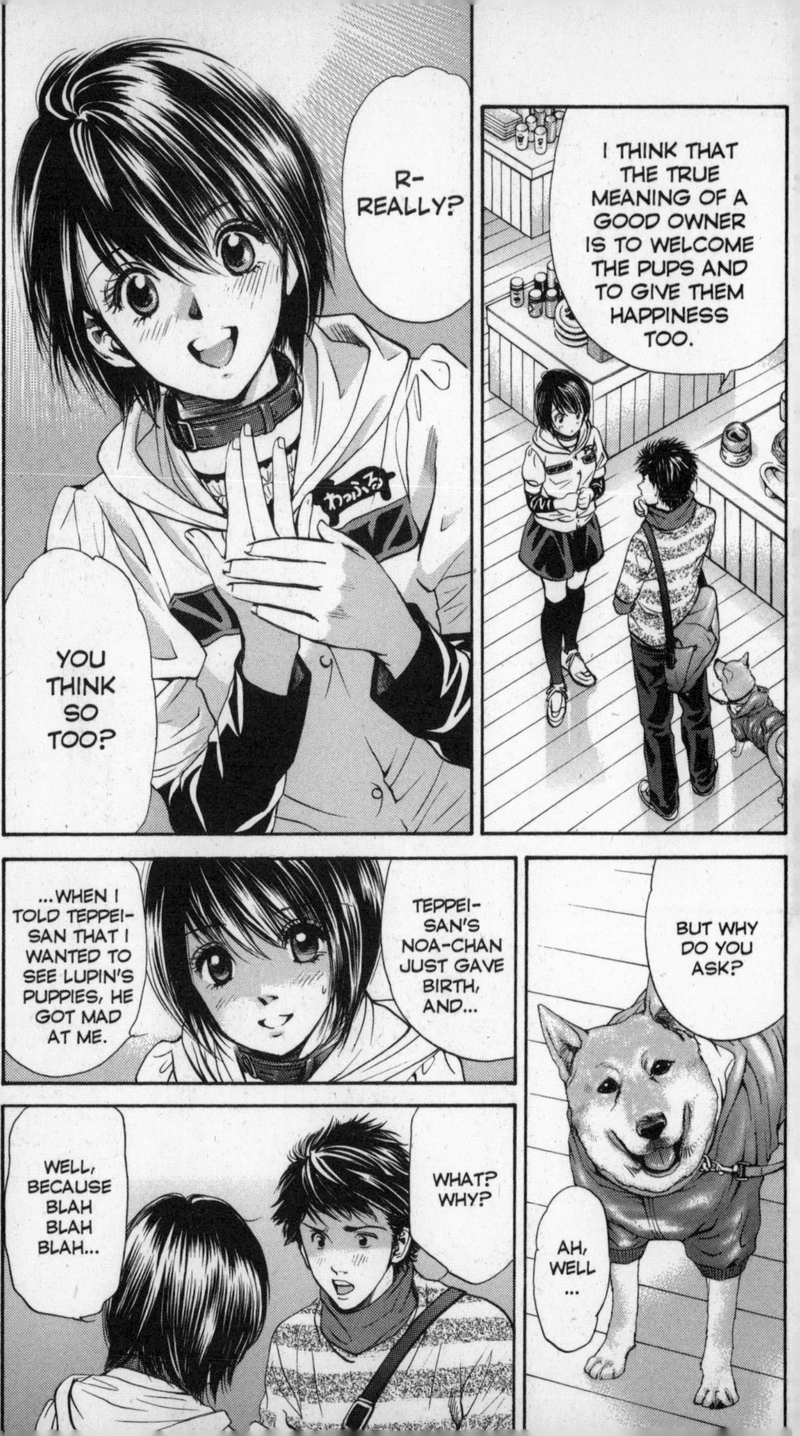
I THINK THAT THE TRUE MEANING OF A GOOD OWNER IS TO WELCOME THE PUPS AND TO GIVE THEM HAPPINESS TOO.
R- REALLY?
わっふる
YOU THINK SO TOO?
BUT WHY DO YOU ASK?
AH, WELL ...
TEPPEI-SAN'S NOA-CHAN JUST GAVE BIRTH, AND...
...WHEN I TOLD TEPPEI-SAN THAT I WANTED TO SEE LUPIN'S PUPPIES, HE GOT MAD AT ME.
WHAT? WHY?
WELL, BECAUSE BLAH BLAH BLAH...

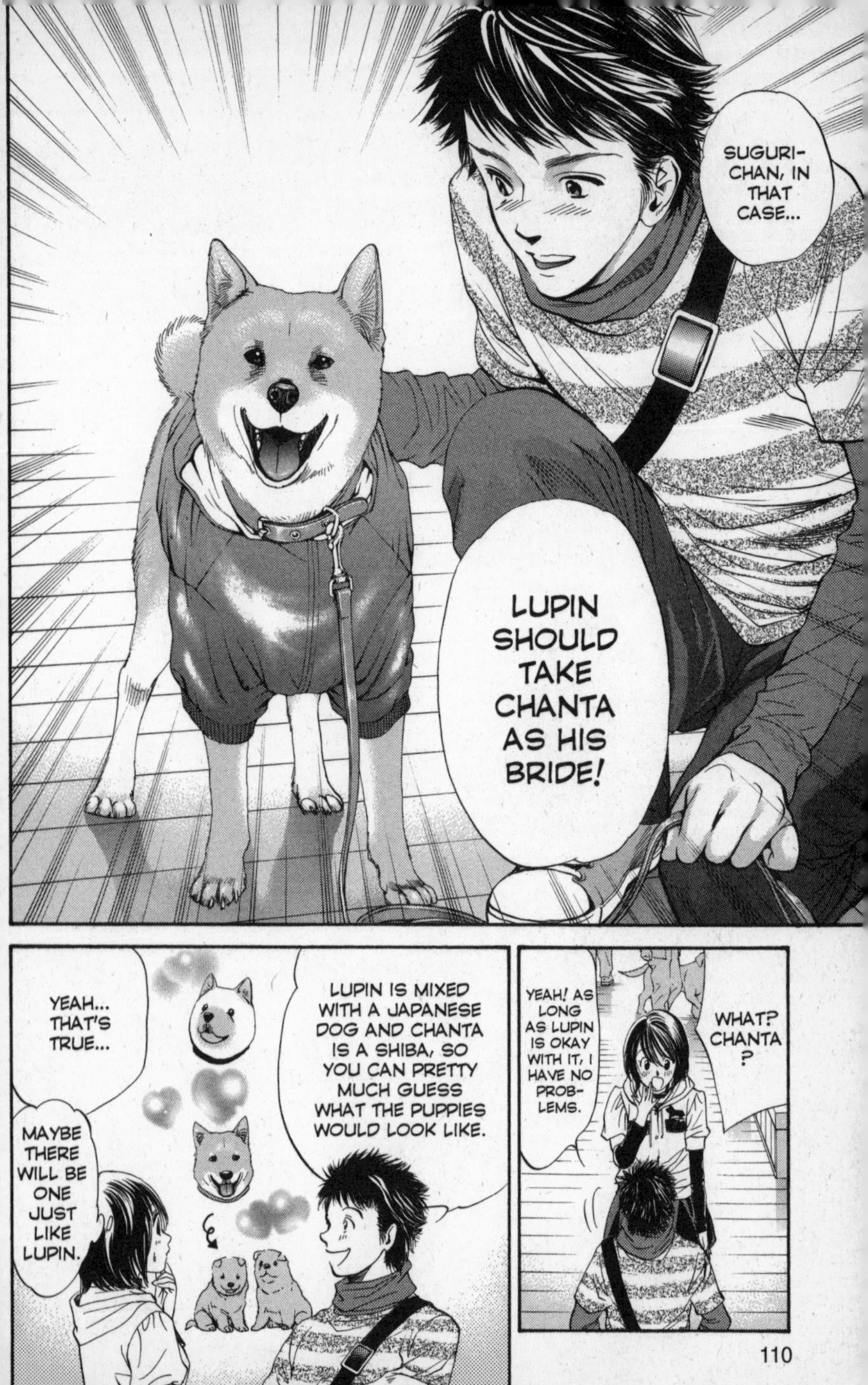
SUGURI-CHAN, IN THAT CASE...
LUPIN SHOULD TAKE CHANTA AS HIS BRIDE!
WHAT? CHANTA?
YEAH! AS LONG AS LUPIN IS OKAY WITH IT, I HAVE NO PROBLEMS.
LUPIN IS MIXED WITH A JAPANESE DOG AND CHANTA IS A SHIBA, SO YOU CAN PRETTY MUCH GUESS WHAT THE PUPPIES WOULD LOOK LIKE.
YEAH... THAT'S TRUE...
MAYBE THERE WILL BE ONE JUST LIKE LUPIN.

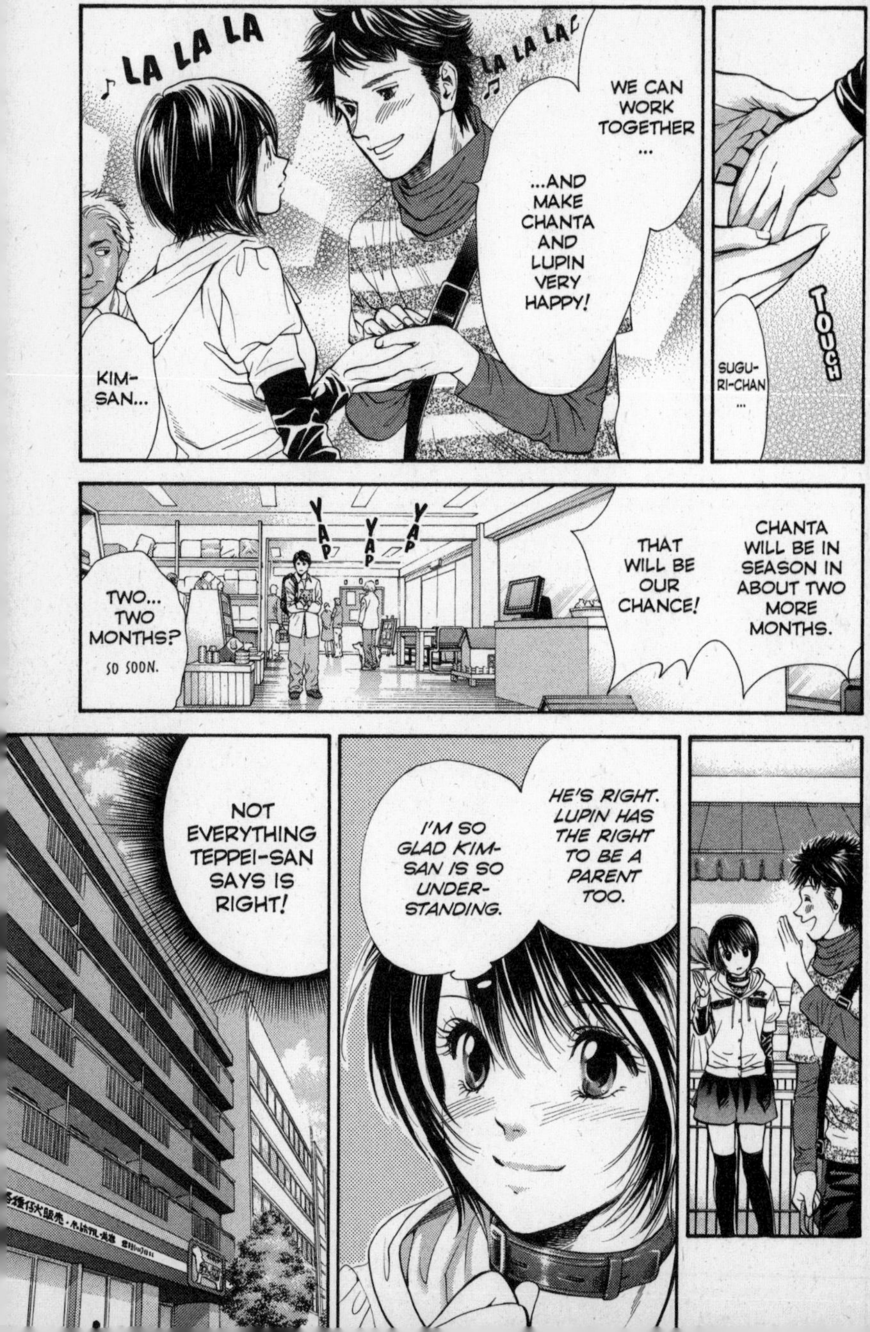
TOUCH
SUGU-RI-CHAN ...
LA LA LA
WE CAN WORK TOGETHER ...
...AND MAKE CHANTA AND LUPIN VERY HAPPY!
LA LA LA
KIM-SAN...
CHANTA WILL BE IN SEASON IN ABOUT TWO MORE MONTHS.
THAT WILL BE OUR CHANCE!
YAP YAP YAP
TWO... TWO MONTHS?
SO SOON.
HE'S RIGHT. LUPIN HAS THE RIGHT TO BE A PARENT TOO.
I'M SO GLAD KIM-SAN IS SO UNDER-STANDING.
NOT EVERYTHING TEPPEI-SAN SAYS IS RIGHT!

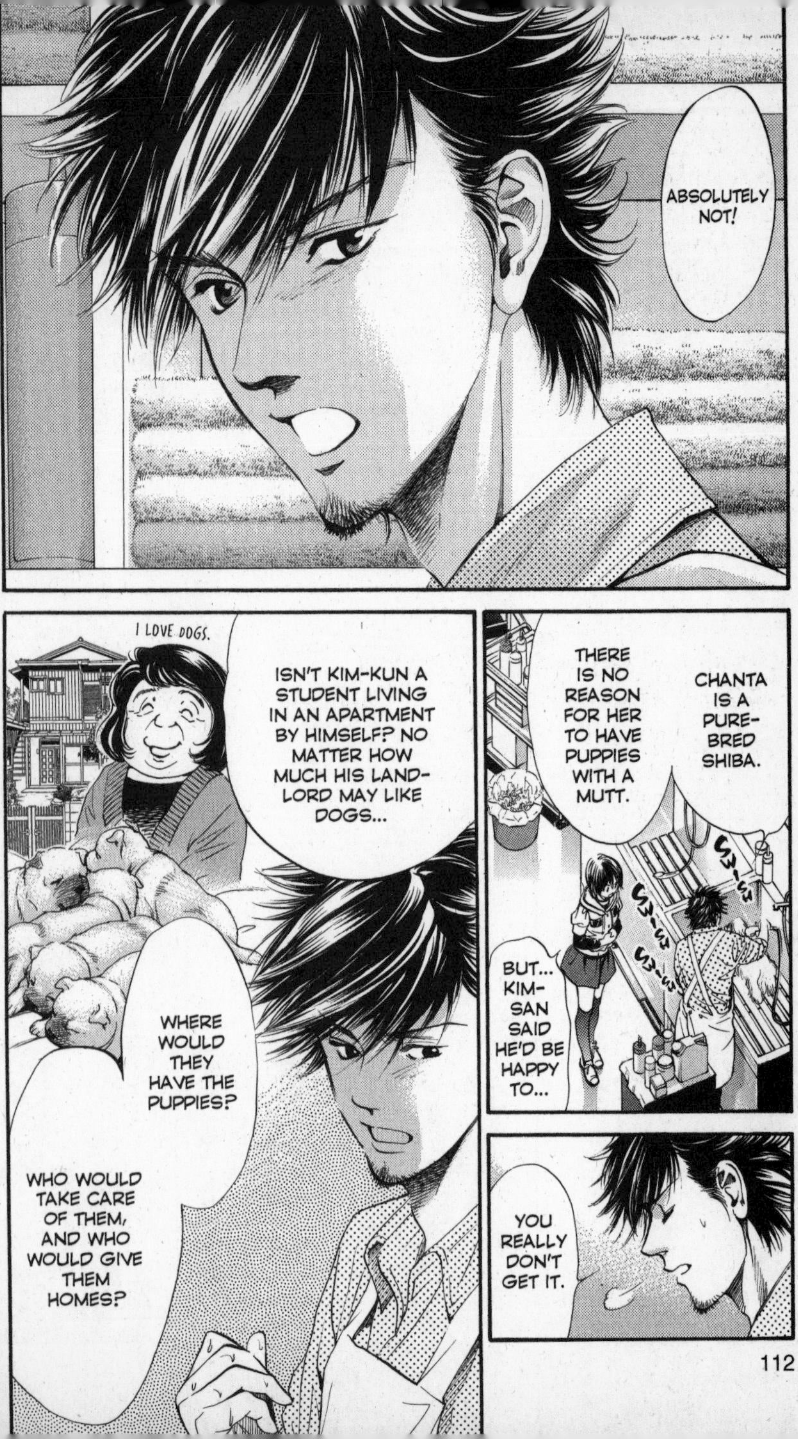
ABSOLUTELY NOT!
CHANTA IS A PUREBRED SHIBA.
THERE IS NO REASON FOR HER TO HAVE PUPPIES WITH A MUTT.
SWISH
SWISH
BUT... KIM-SAN SAID HE'D BE HAPPY TO...
YOU REALLY DON'T GET IT.
ISN'T KIM-KUN A STUDENT LIVING IN AN APARTMENT BY HIMSELF? NO MATTER HOW MUCH HIS LANDLORD MAY LIKE DOGS...
I LOVE DOGS.
WHERE WOULD THEY HAVE THE PUPPIES?
WHO WOULD TAKE CARE OF THEM, AND WHO WOULD GIVE THEM HOMES?

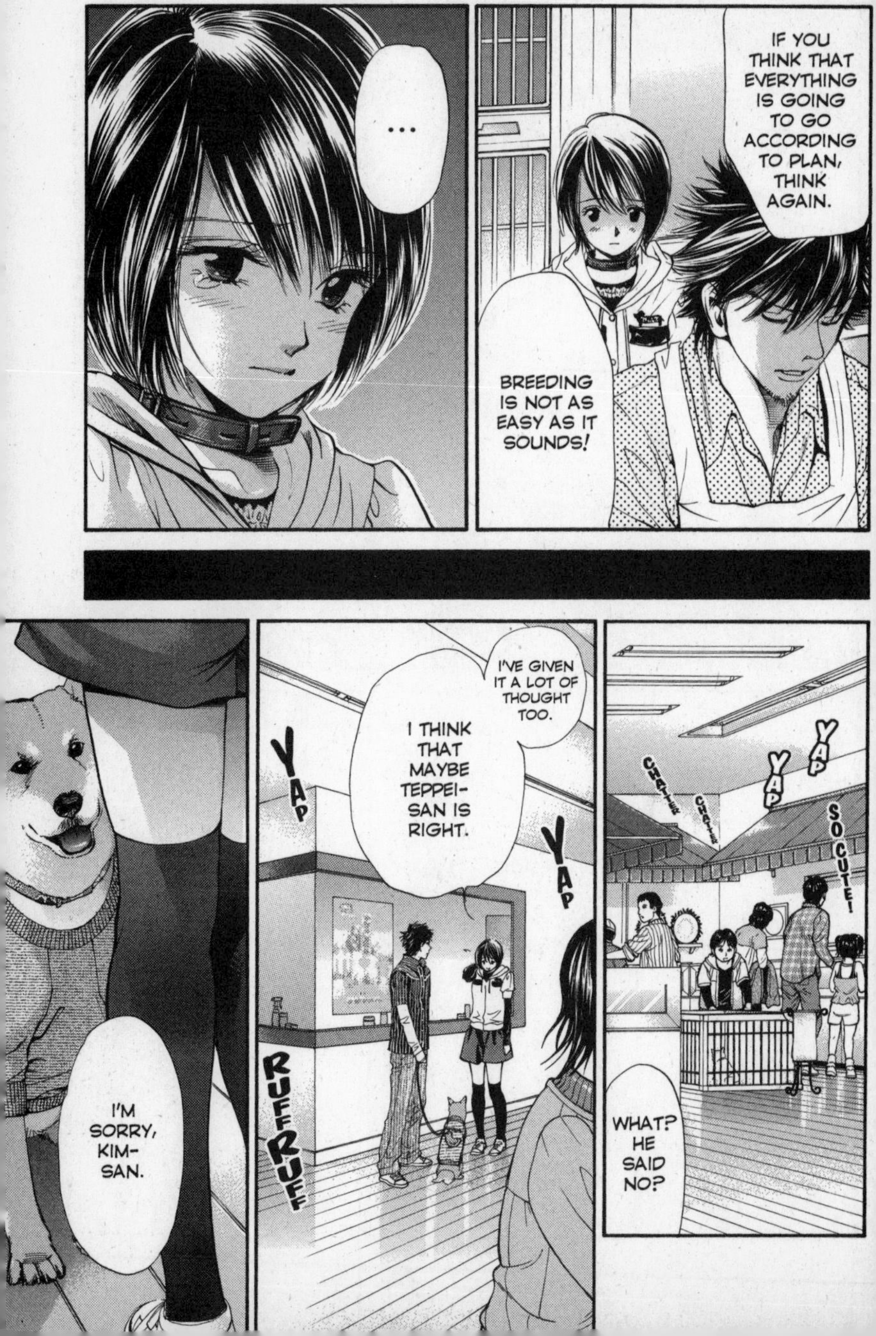
IF YOU THINK THAT EVERYTHING IS GOING TO GO ACCORDING TO PLAN, THINK AGAIN.
BREEDING IS NOT AS EASY AS IT SOUNDS!
...
YAP
YAP
CHATTER
CHATTER
SO CUTE!
WHAT? HE SAID NO?
I'VE GIVEN IT A LOT OF THOUGHT TOO.
I THINK THAT MAYBE TEPPEI-SAN IS RIGHT.
YAP
YAP
RUFF RUFF
I'M SORRY, KIM-SAN.

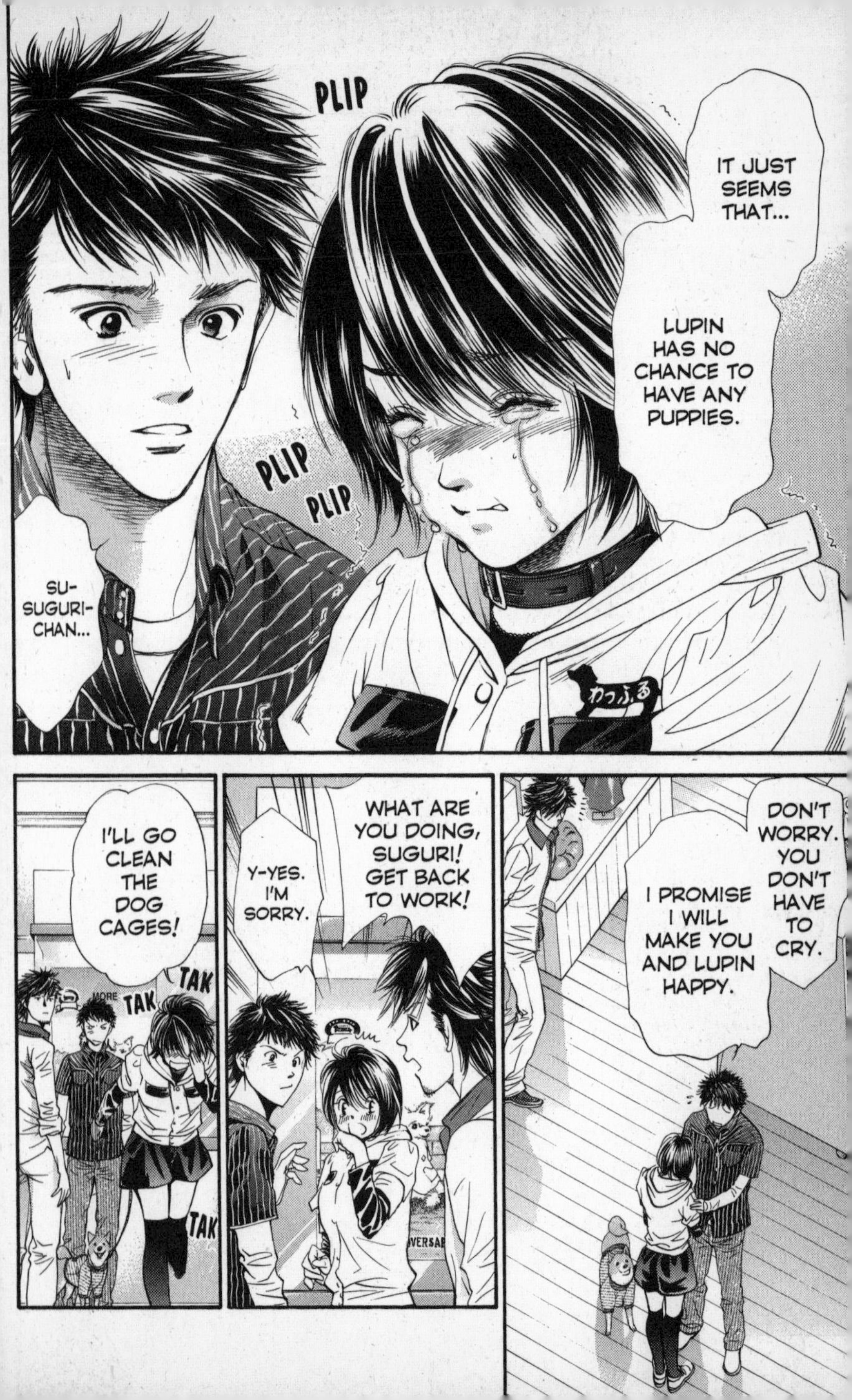
PLIP
IT JUST SEEMS THAT...
LUPIN HAS NO CHANCE TO HAVE ANY PUPPIES.
PLIP
PLIP
わっふる
SU-SUGURI-CHAN...
DON'T WORRY. YOU DON'T HAVE TO CRY.
I PROMISE I WILL MAKE YOU AND LUPIN HAPPY.
WHAT ARE YOU DOING, SUGURI! GET BACK TO WORK!
Y-YES. I'M SORRY.
I'LL GO CLEAN THE DOG CAGES!
TAK
MORE
TAK
TAK

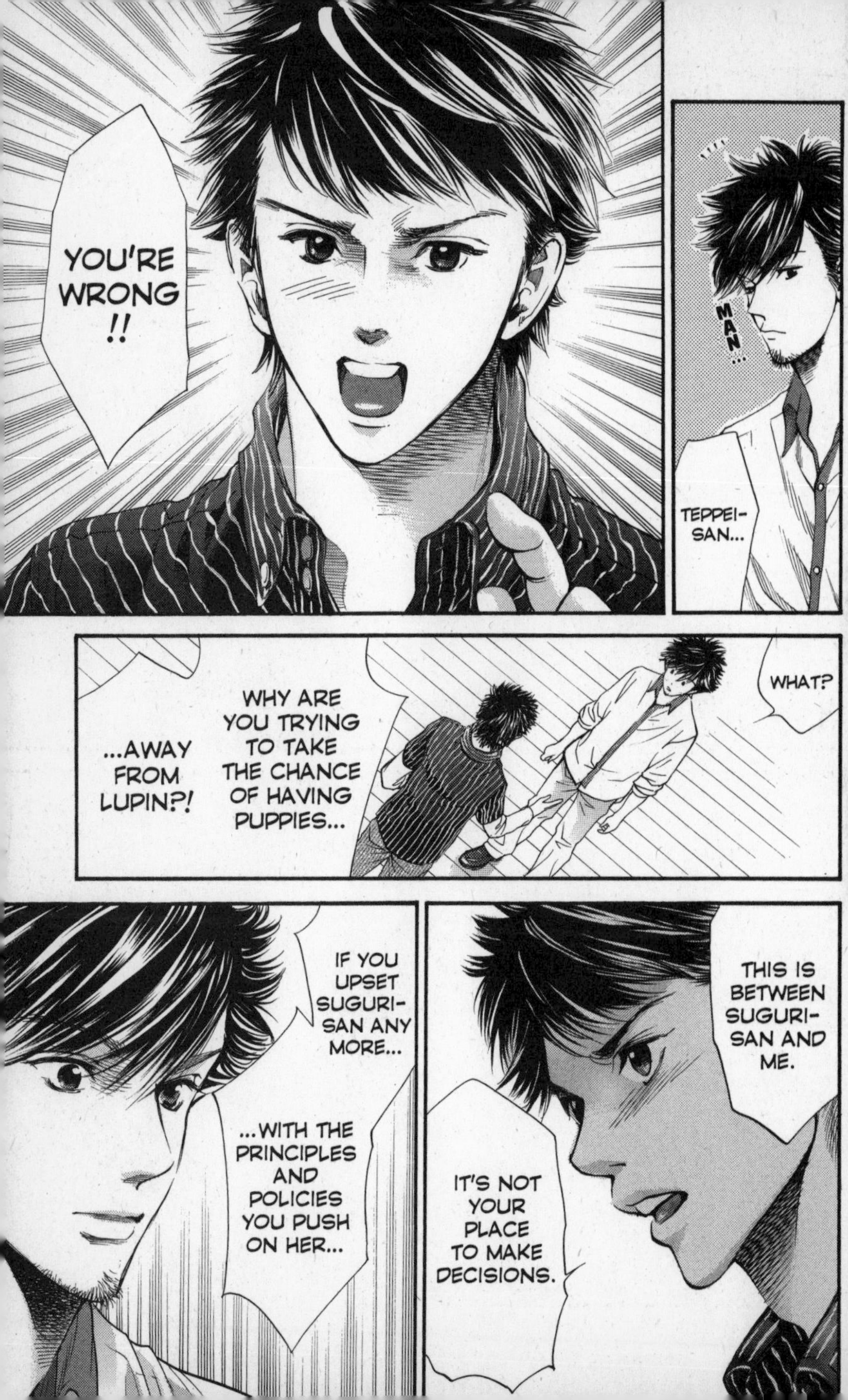
...
MAN...
TEPPEI-SAN...
YOU'RE WRONG!!
WHAT?
WHY ARE YOU TRYING TO TAKE THE CHANCE OF HAVING PUPPIES...
...AWAY FROM LUPIN?!
THIS IS BETWEEN SUGURI-SAN AND ME.
IT'S NOT YOUR PLACE TO MAKE DECISIONS.
IF YOU UPSET SUGURI-SAN ANY MORE...
...WITH THE PRINCIPLES AND POLICIES YOU PUSH ON HER...

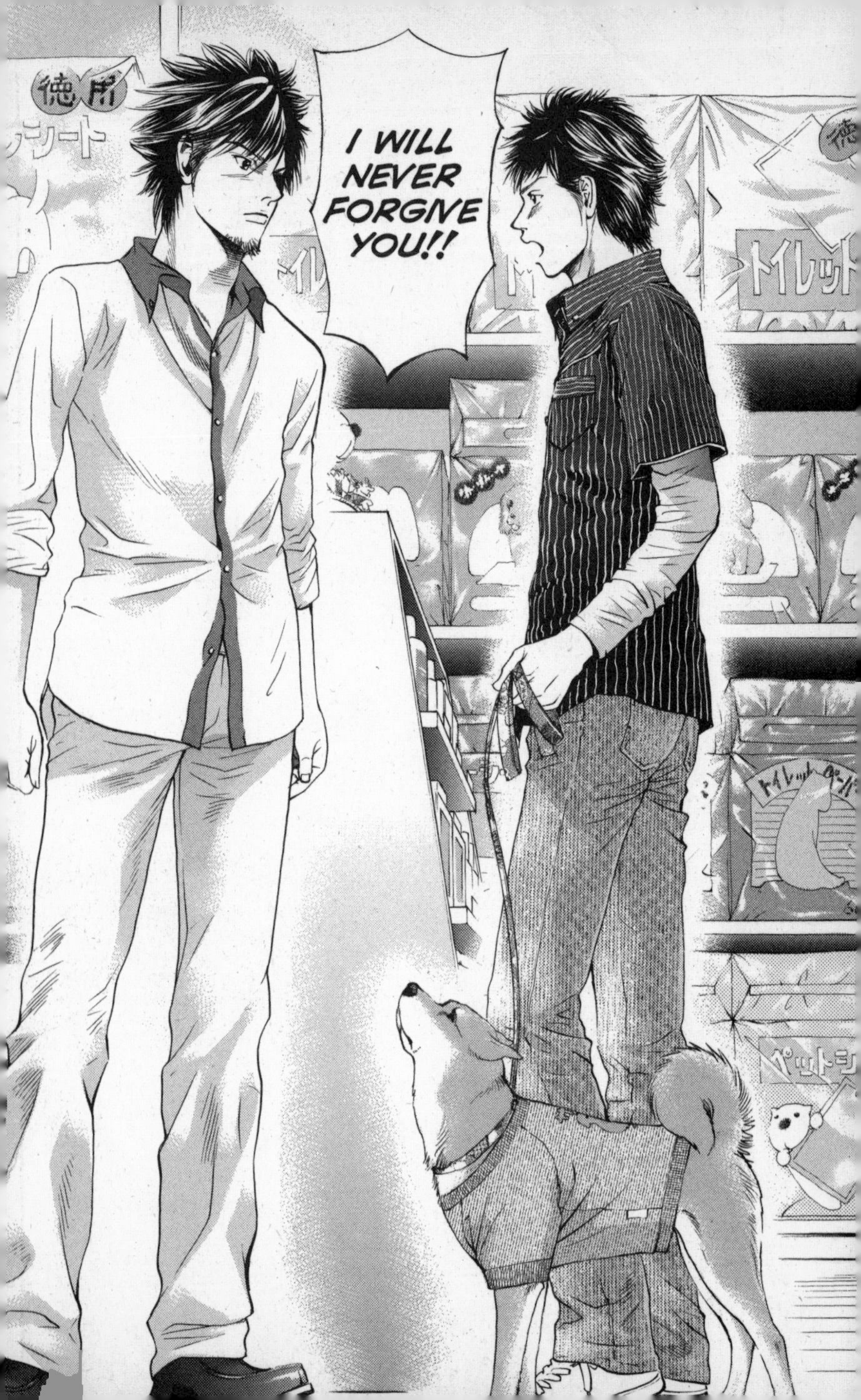
I WILL NEVER FORGIVE YOU!!

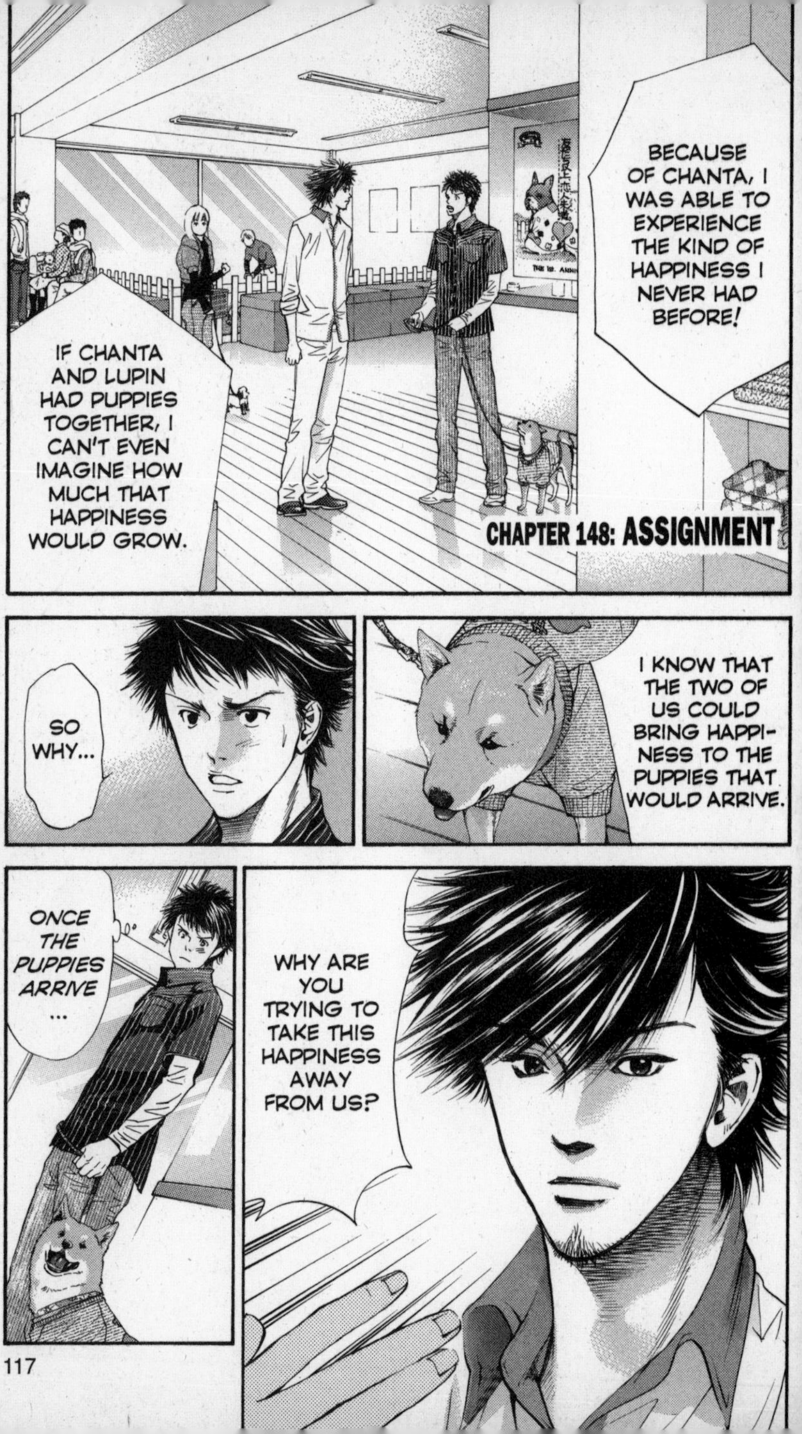
BECAUSE OF CHANTA, I WAS ABLE TO EXPERIENCE THE KIND OF HAPPINESS I NEVER HAD BEFORE!
IF CHANTA AND LUPIN HAD PUPPIES TOGETHER, I CAN'T EVEN IMAGINE HOW MUCH THAT HAPPINESS WOULD GROW.
CHAPTER 148: ASSIGNMENT
I KNOW THAT THE TWO OF US COULD BRING HAPPINESS TO THE PUPPIES THAT WOULD ARRIVE.
SO WHY...
WHY ARE YOU TRYING TO TAKE THIS HAPPINESS AWAY FROM US?
ONCE THE PUPPIES ARRIVE ...

CHAPTER 148: ASSIGNMENT

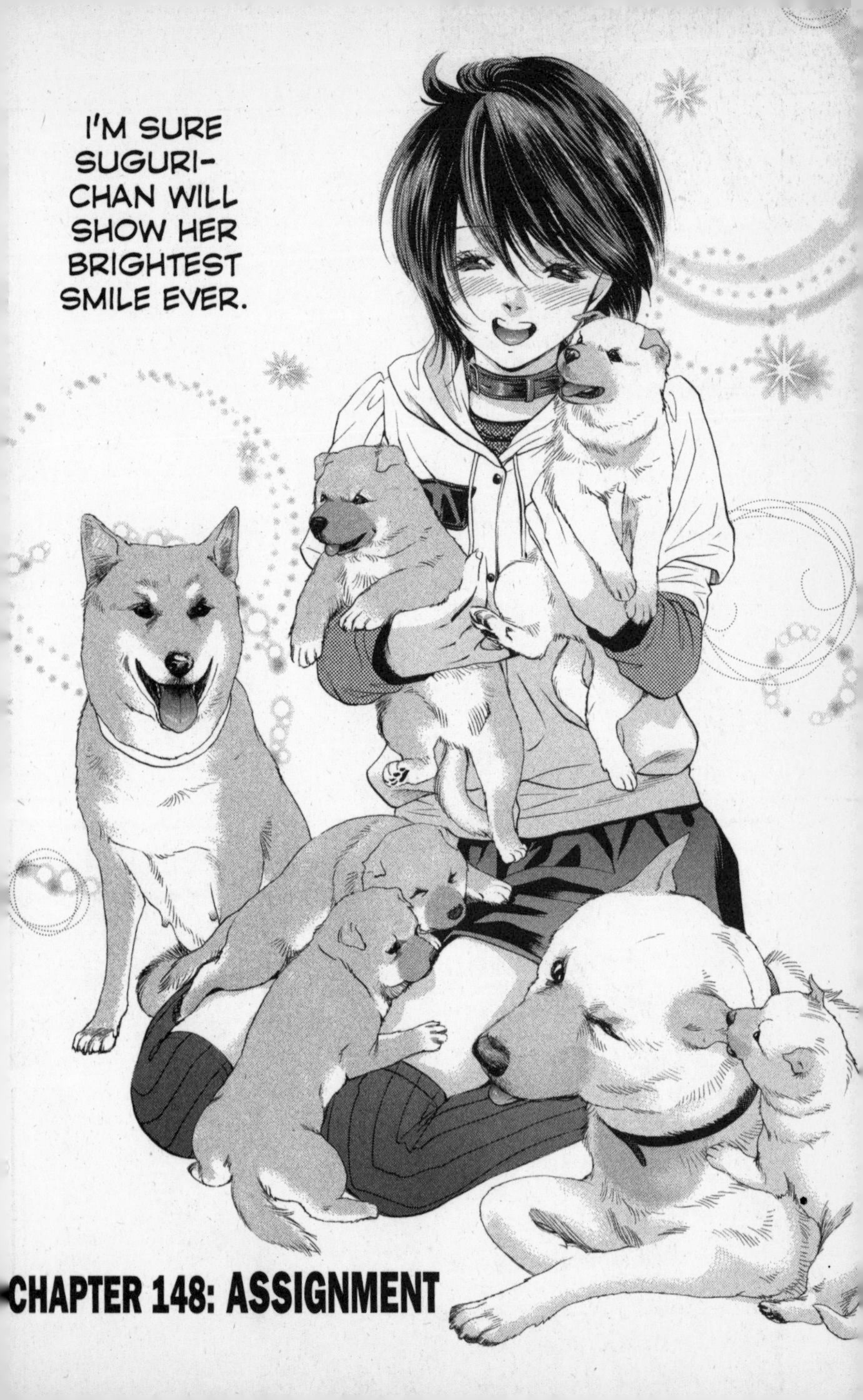
I'M SURE SUGURI-CHAN WILL SHOW HER BRIGHTEST SMILE EVER.

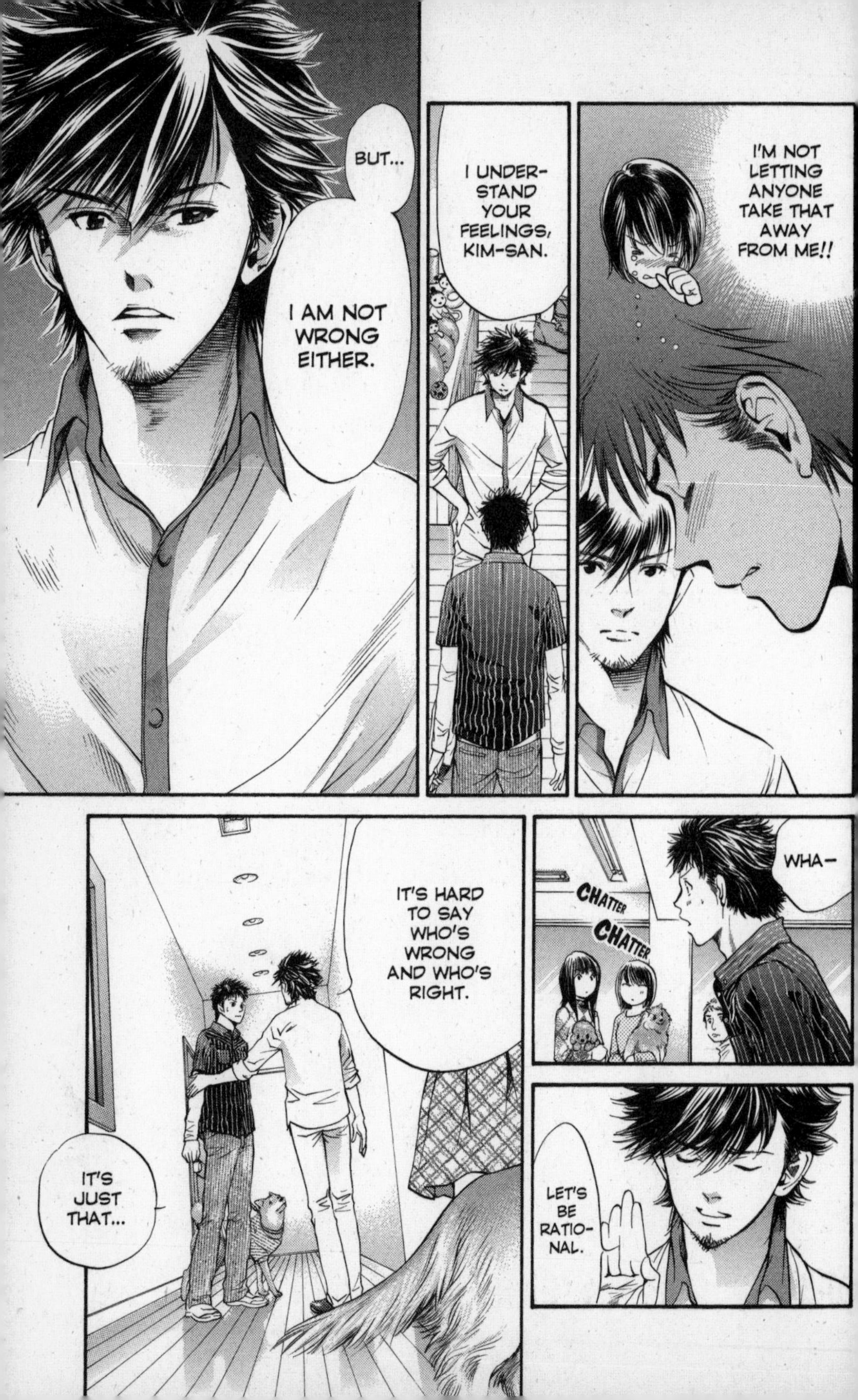

I'M NOT LETTING ANYONE TAKE THAT AWAY FROM ME!!
I UNDERSTAND YOUR FEELINGS, KIM-SAN.
BUT...
I AM NOT WRONG EITHER.
WHA-
CHATTER
CHATTER
LET'S BE RATIONAL.
IT'S HARD TO SAY WHO'S WRONG AND WHO'S RIGHT.
IT'S JUST THAT...

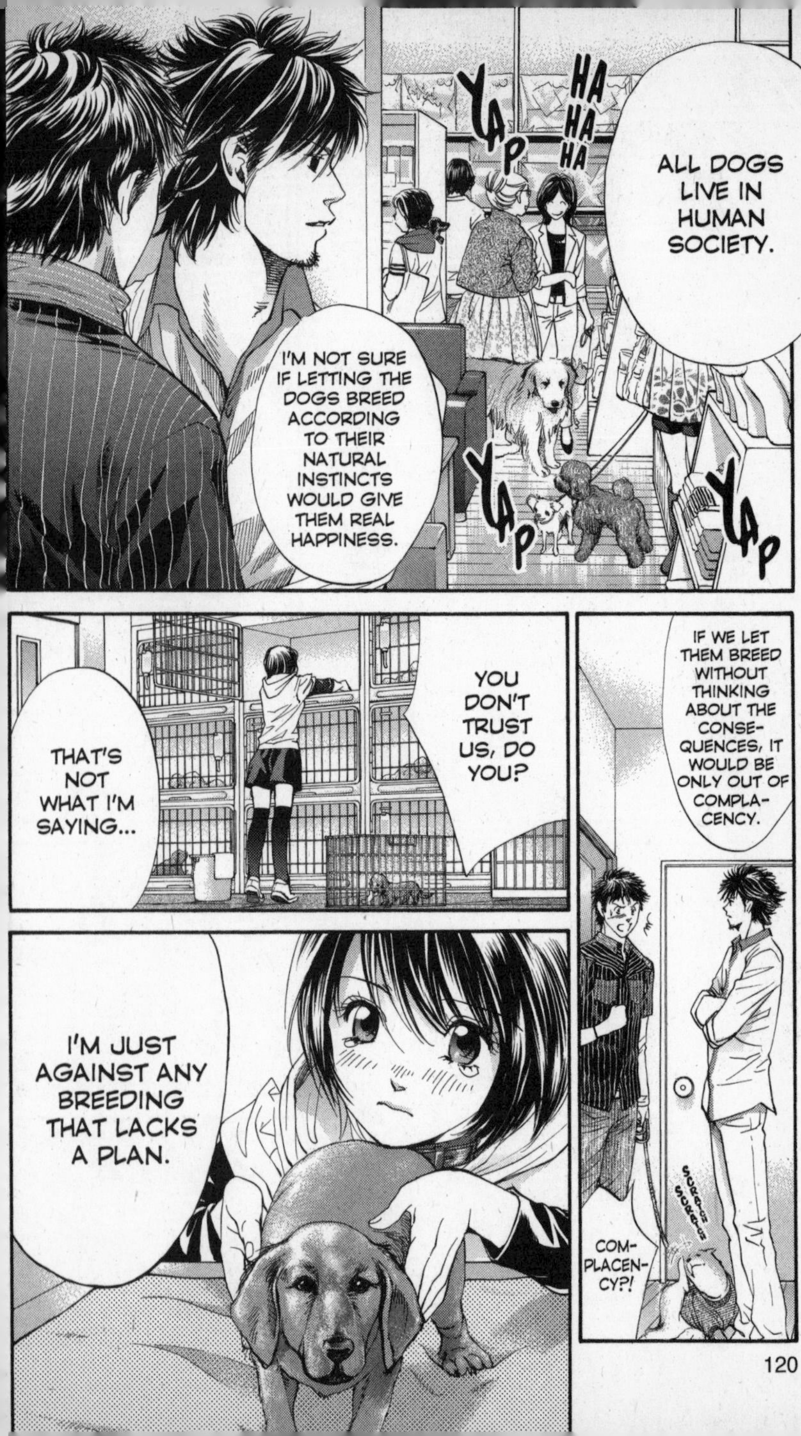
ALL DOGS LIVE IN HUMAN SOCIETY.
HA HA HA HA
YAP
I'M NOT SURE IF LETTING THE DOGS BREED ACCORDING TO THEIR NATURAL INSTINCTS WOULD GIVE THEM REAL HAPPINESS.
YAP
YAP
IF WE LET THEM BREED WITHOUT THINKING ABOUT THE CONSE-QUENCES, IT WOULD BE ONLY OUT OF COMPLA-CENCY.
SCRATCH SCRATCH
COM-PLACEN-CY?!
YOU DON'T TRUST US, DO YOU?
THAT'S NOT WHAT I'M SAYING...
I'M JUST AGAINST ANY BREEDING THAT LACKS A PLAN.

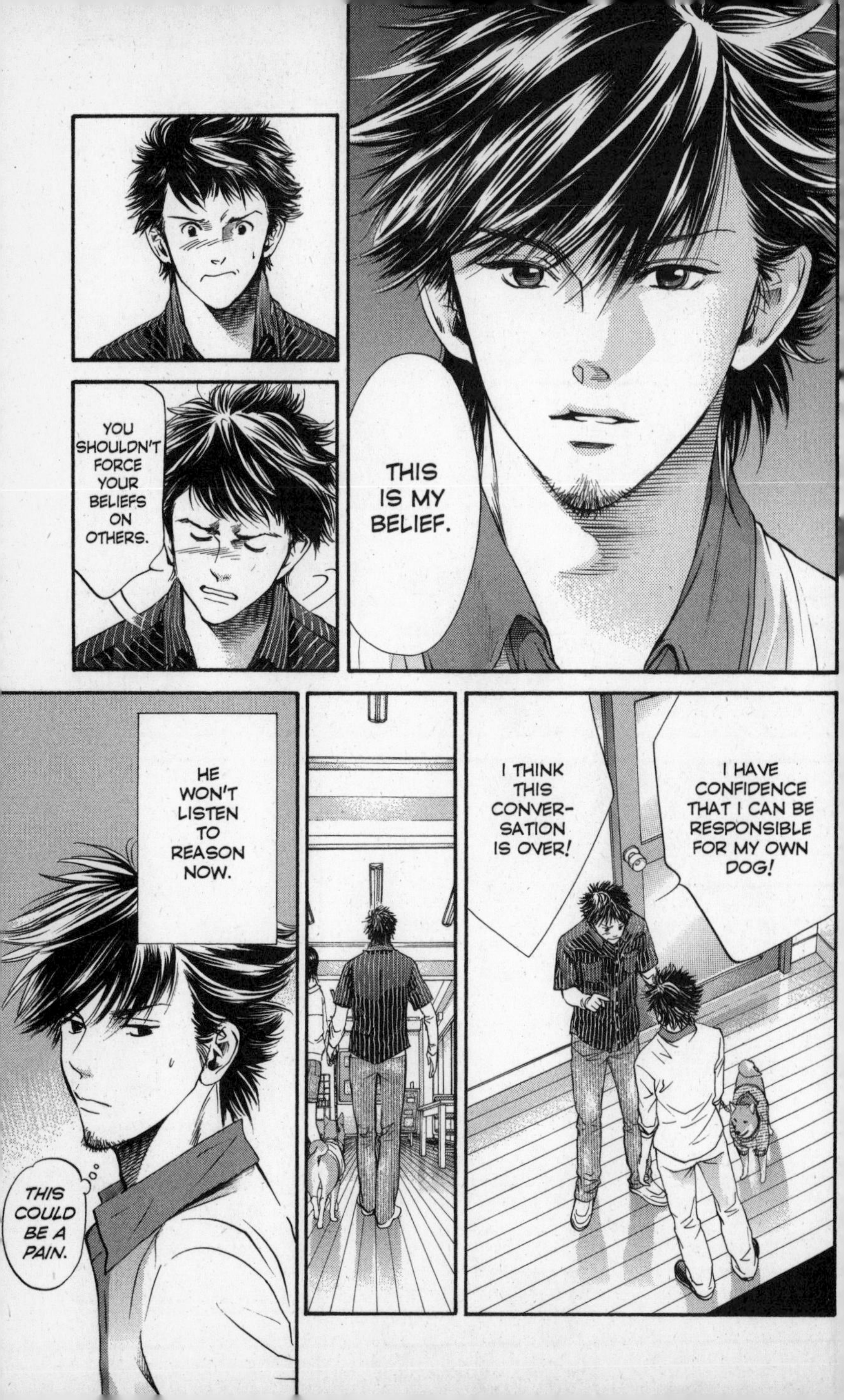
THIS IS MY BELIEF.
YOU SHOULDN'T FORCE YOUR BELIEFS ON OTHERS.
I HAVE CONFIDENCE THAT I CAN BE RESPONSIBLE FOR MY OWN DOG!
I THINK THIS CONVER-SATION IS OVER!
HE WON'T LISTEN TO REASON NOW.
THIS COULD BE A PAIN.

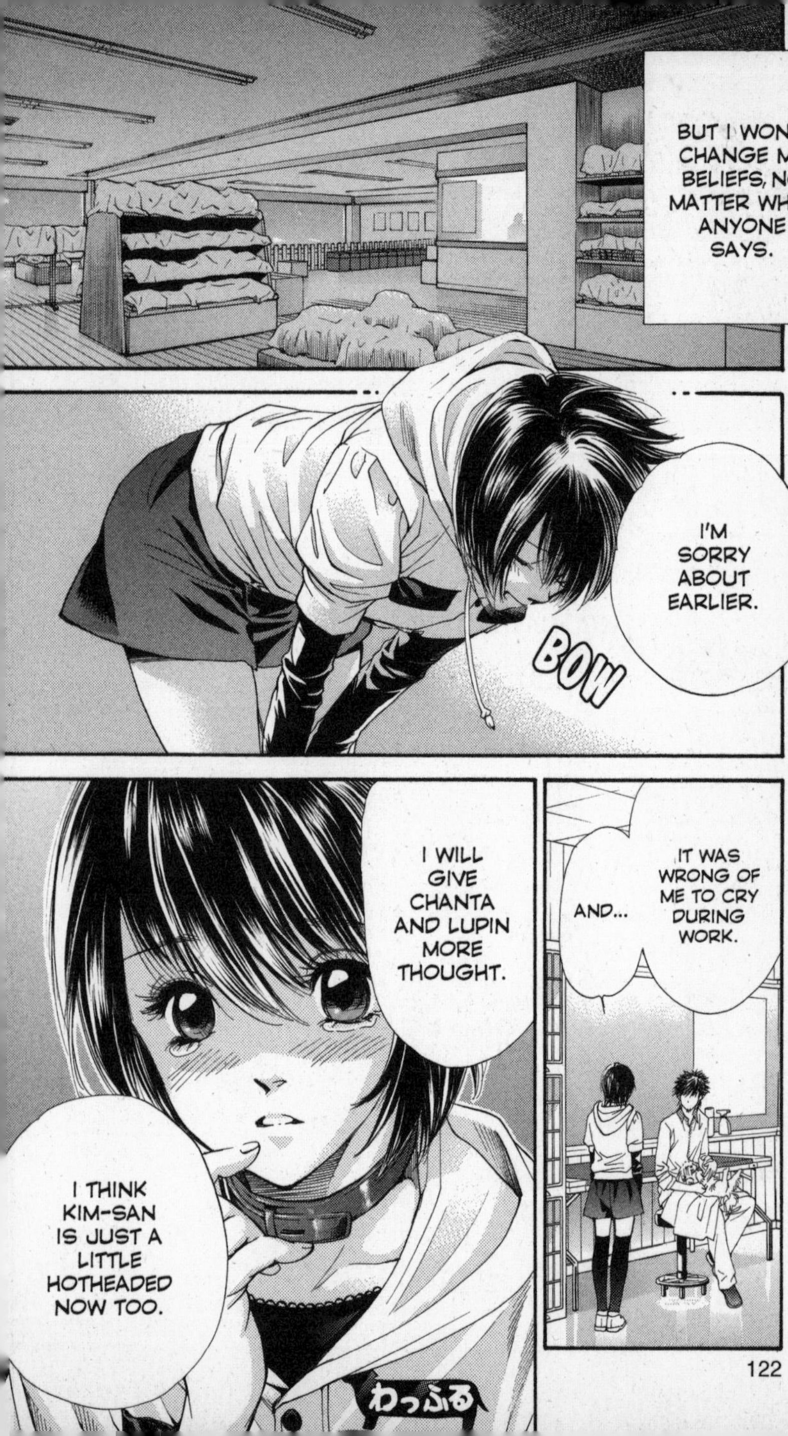
BUT I WON'T CHANGE MY BELIEFS, NO MATTER WHAT ANYONE SAYS.
I'M SORRY ABOUT EARLIER.
BOW
IT WAS WRONG OF ME TO CRY DURING WORK.
AND...
I WILL GIVE CHANTA AND LUPIN MORE THOUGHT.
I THINK KIM-SAN IS JUST A LITTLE HOTHEADED NOW TOO.
わっふる

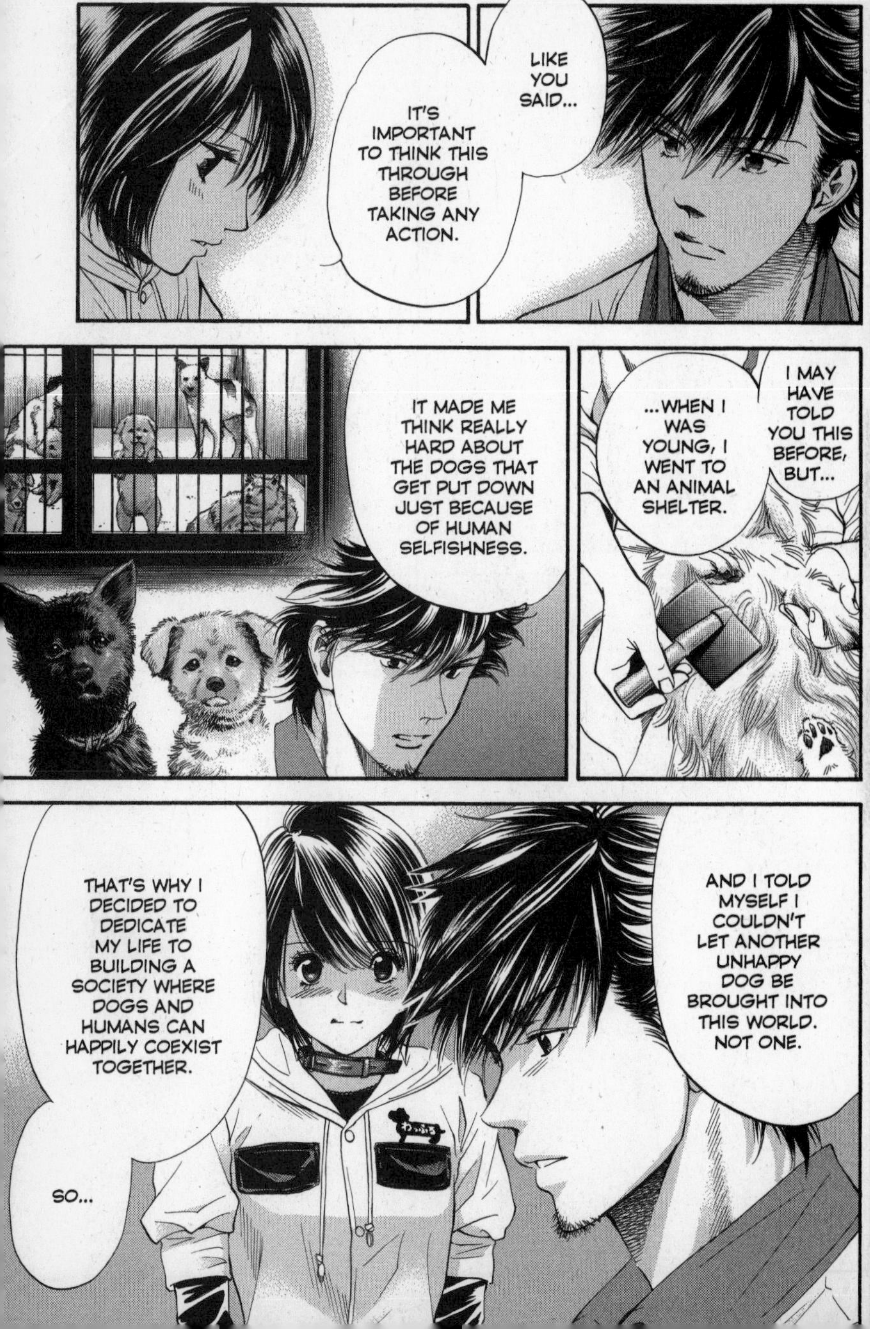
LIKE YOU SAID...
IT'S IMPORTANT TO THINK THIS THROUGH BEFORE TAKING ANY ACTION.
I MAY HAVE TOLD YOU THIS BEFORE, BUT...
...WHEN I WAS YOUNG, I WENT TO AN ANIMAL SHELTER.
IT MADE ME THINK REALLY HARD ABOUT THE DOGS THAT GET PUT DOWN JUST BECAUSE OF HUMAN SELFISHNESS.
AND I TOLD MYSELF I COULDN'T LET ANOTHER UNHAPPY DOG BE BROUGHT INTO THIS WORLD. NOT ONE.
THAT'S WHY I DECIDED TO DEDICATE MY LIFE TO BUILDING A SOCIETY WHERE DOGS AND HUMANS CAN HAPPILY COEXIST TOGETHER.
SO...

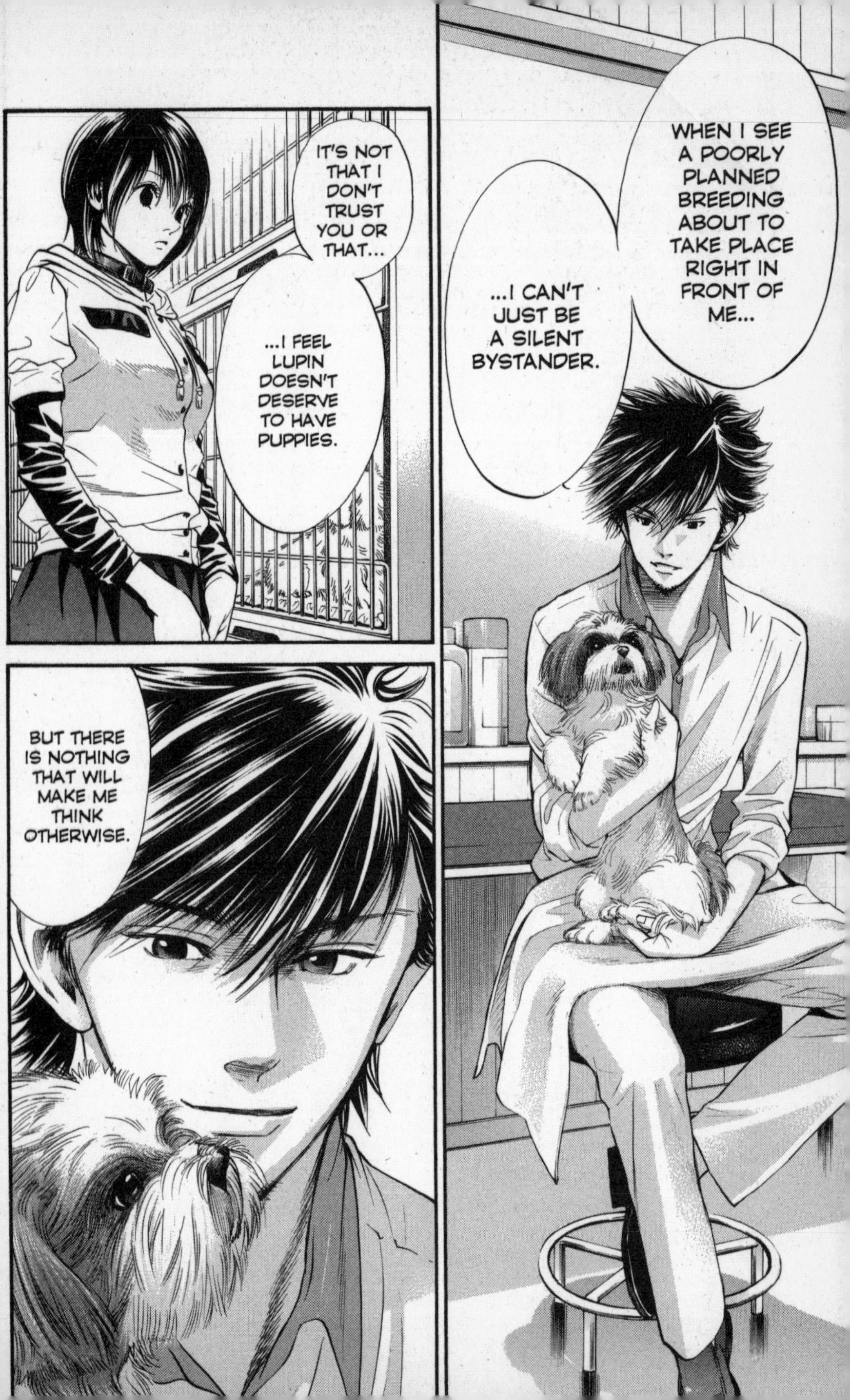
WHEN I SEE A POORLY PLANNED BREEDING ABOUT TO TAKE PLACE RIGHT IN FRONT OF ME...
...I CAN'T JUST BE A SILENT BYSTANDER.
IT'S NOT THAT I DON'T TRUST YOU OR THAT...
...I FEEL LUPIN DOESN'T DESERVE TO HAVE PUPPIES.
BUT THERE IS NOTHING THAT WILL MAKE ME THINK OTHERWISE.

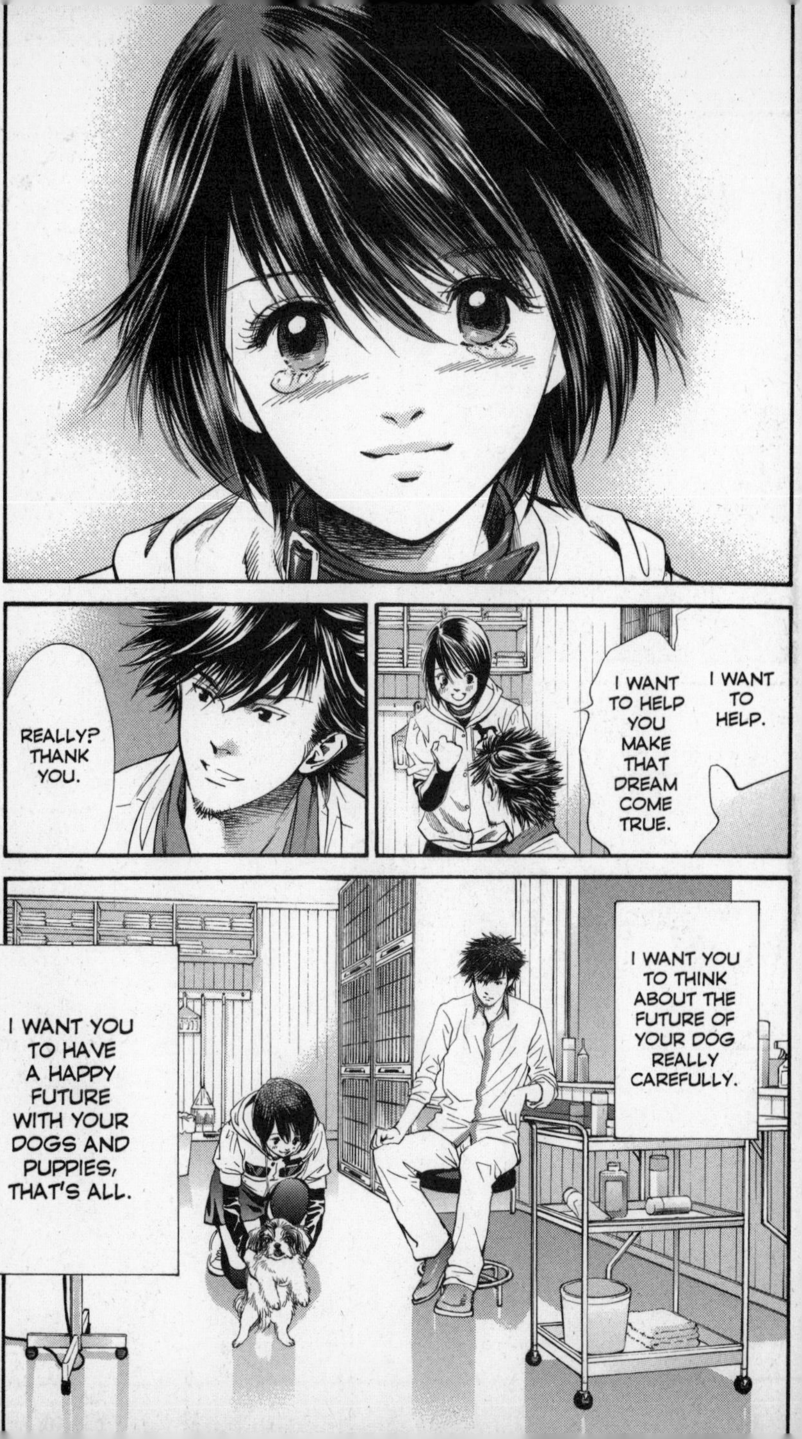
I WANT TO HELP.
I WANT TO HELP YOU MAKE THAT DREAM COME TRUE.
REALLY? THANK YOU.
I WANT YOU TO THINK ABOUT THE FUTURE OF YOUR DOG REALLY CAREFULLY.
I WANT YOU TO HAVE A HAPPY FUTURE WITH YOUR DOGS AND PUPPIES, THAT'S ALL.

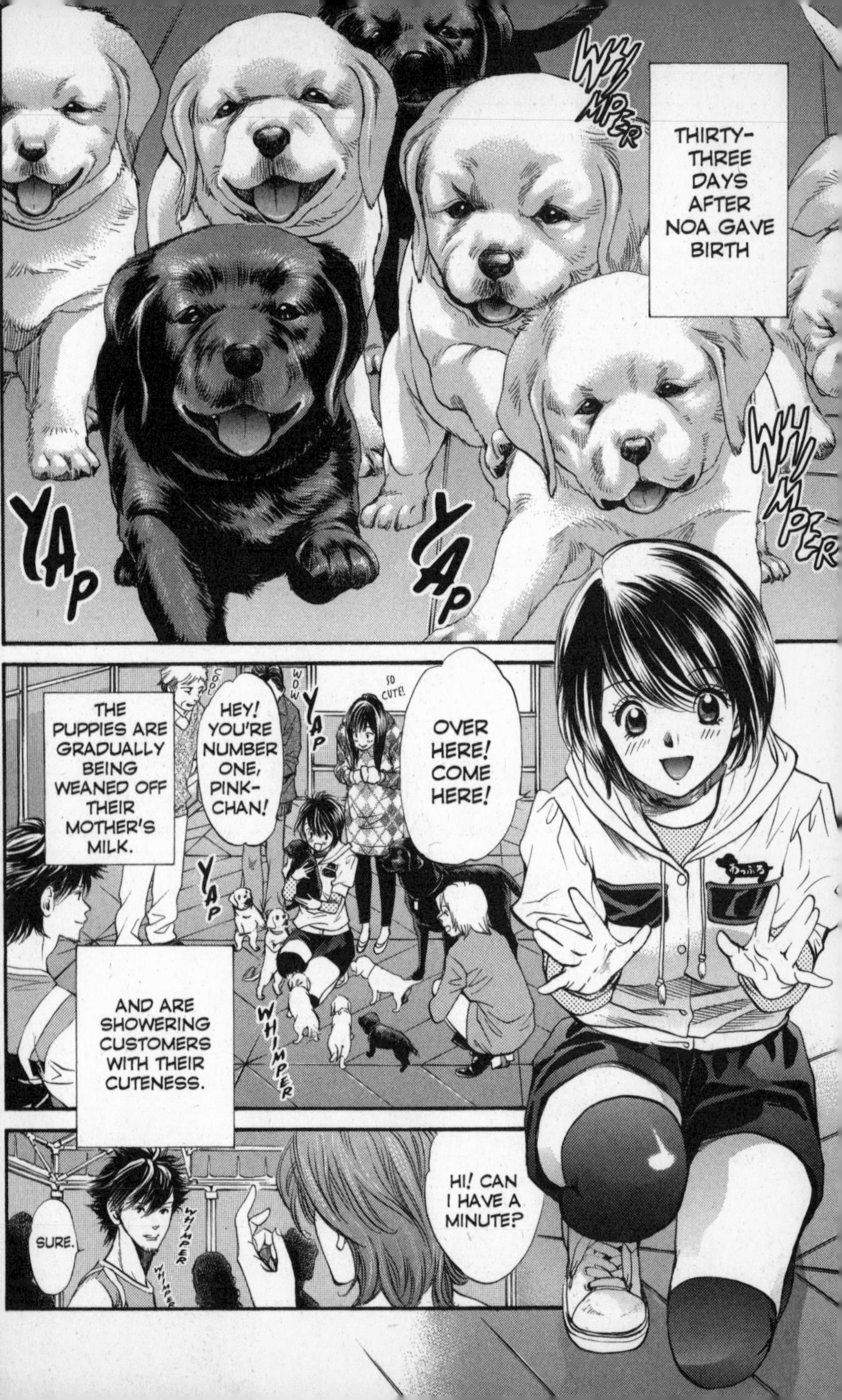
THIRTY-THREE DAYS AFTER NOA GAVE BIRTH
WHIMPER
WHIMPER
YAP
YAP
OVER HERE! COME HERE!
SO CUTE!
WOW
YAP
HEY! YOU'RE NUMBER ONE, PINK-CHAN!
COOL
THE PUPPIES ARE GRADUALLY BEING WEANED OFF THEIR MOTHER'S MILK.
YAP
WHIMPER
AND ARE SHOWERING CUSTOMERS WITH THEIR CUTENESS.
HI! CAN I HAVE A MINUTE?
WHIMPER
WHIMPER
SURE.

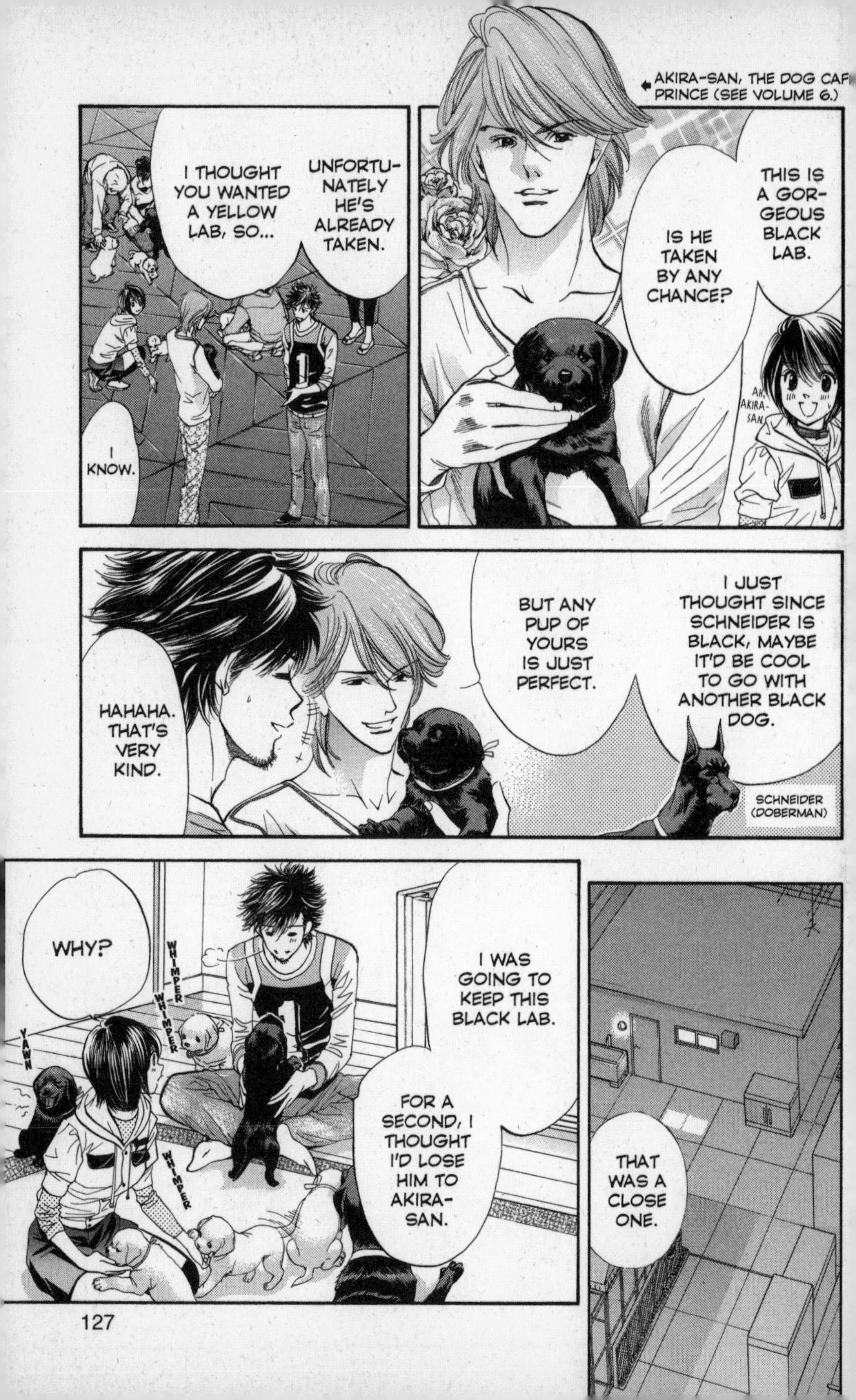
AKIRA-SAN, THE DOG CAF
PRINCE (SEE VOLUME 6.)
AH, AKIRA-SAN.
THIS IS A GORGEOUS BLACK LAB.
IS HE TAKEN BY ANY CHANCE?
UNFORTUNATELY HE'S ALREADY TAKEN.
I THOUGHT YOU WANTED A YELLOW LAB, SO...
I KNOW.
I JUST THOUGHT SINCE SCHNEIDER IS BLACK, MAYBE IT'D BE COOL TO GO WITH ANOTHER BLACK DOG.
BUT ANY PUP OF YOURS IS JUST PERFECT.
SCHNEIDER (DOBERMAN)
HAHAHA. THAT'S VERY KIND.
THAT WAS A CLOSE ONE.
I WAS GOING TO KEEP THIS BLACK LAB.
FOR A SECOND, I THOUGHT I'D LOSE HIM TO AKIRA-SAN.
WHIMPER
WHIMPER
WHY?
YAWN
WHIMPER

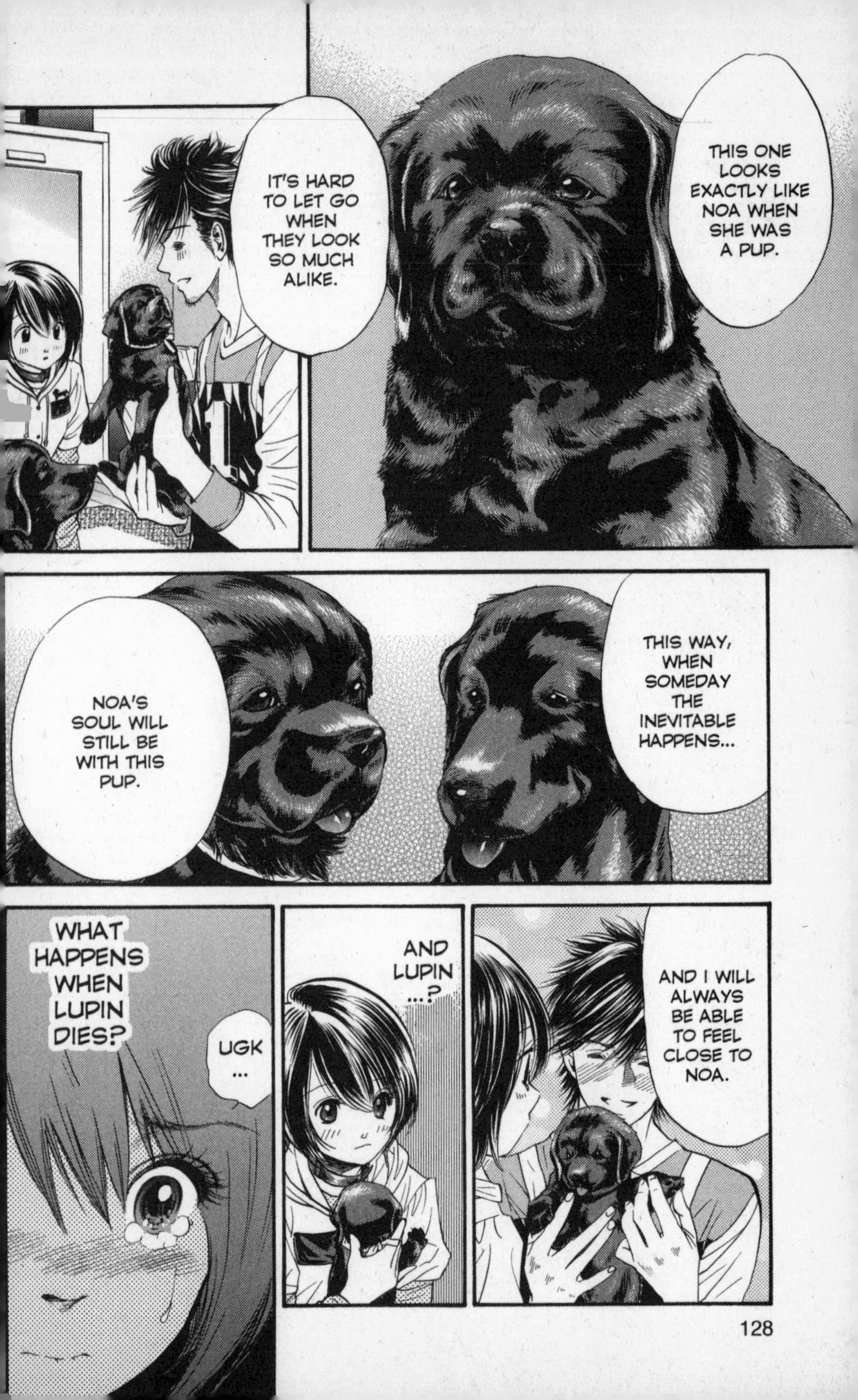
THIS ONE LOOKS EXACTLY LIKE NOA WHEN SHE WAS A PUP.
IT'S HARD TO LET GO WHEN THEY LOOK SO MUCH ALIKE.
THIS WAY, WHEN SOMEDAY THE INEVITABLE HAPPENS...
NOA'S SOUL WILL STILL BE WITH THIS PUP.
AND I WILL ALWAYS BE ABLE TO FEEL CLOSE TO NOA.
AND LUPIN ...?
WHAT HAPPENS WHEN LUPIN DIES?
UGK ...

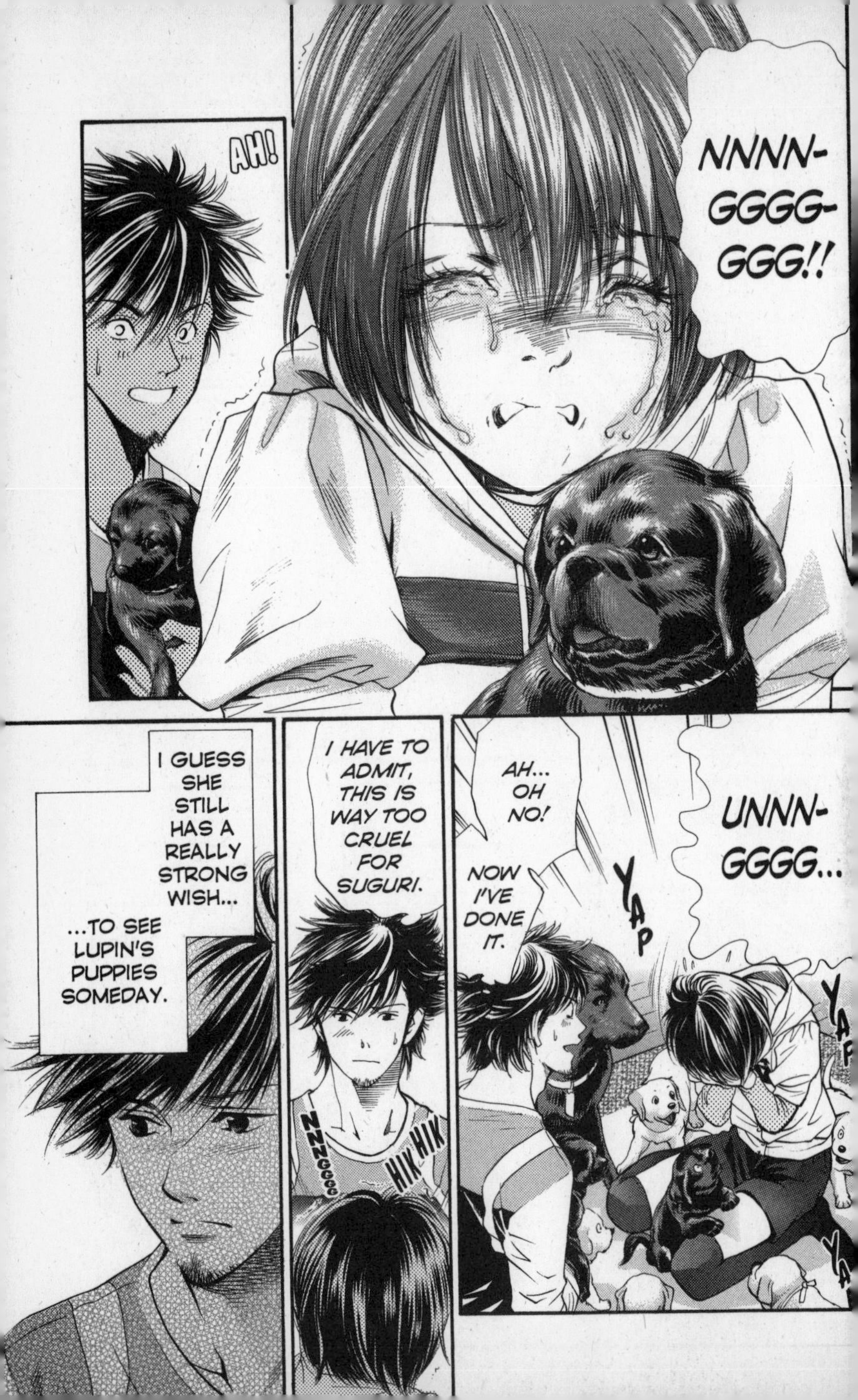
NNNN-GGGG-GGG!!
AH!
UNNN-GGGG...
AH... OH NO!
NOW I'VE DONE IT.
YAP
I HAVE TO ADMIT, THIS IS WAY TOO CRUEL FOR SUGURI.
NNNGGGG
HIK HIK
I GUESS SHE STILL HAS A REALLY STRONG WISH...
...TO SEE LUPIN'S PUPPIES SOMEDAY.

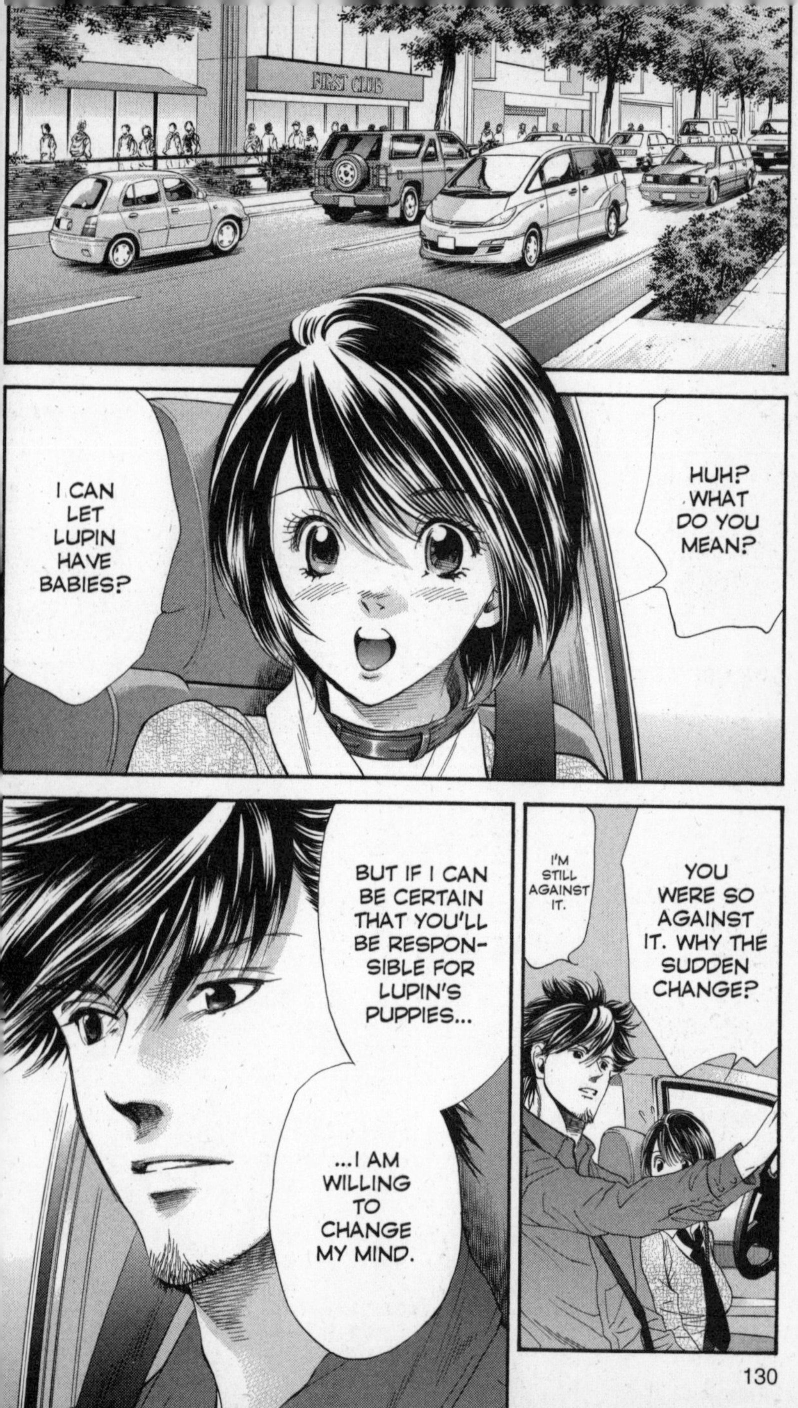

FIRST CLUB
HUH? WHAT DO YOU MEAN?
I CAN LET LUPIN HAVE BABIES?
YOU WERE SO AGAINST IT. WHY THE SUDDEN CHANGE?
I'M STILL AGAINST IT.
BUT IF I CAN BE CERTAIN THAT YOU'LL BE RESPONSIBLE FOR LUPIN'S PUPPIES...
...I AM WILLING TO CHANGE MY MIND.

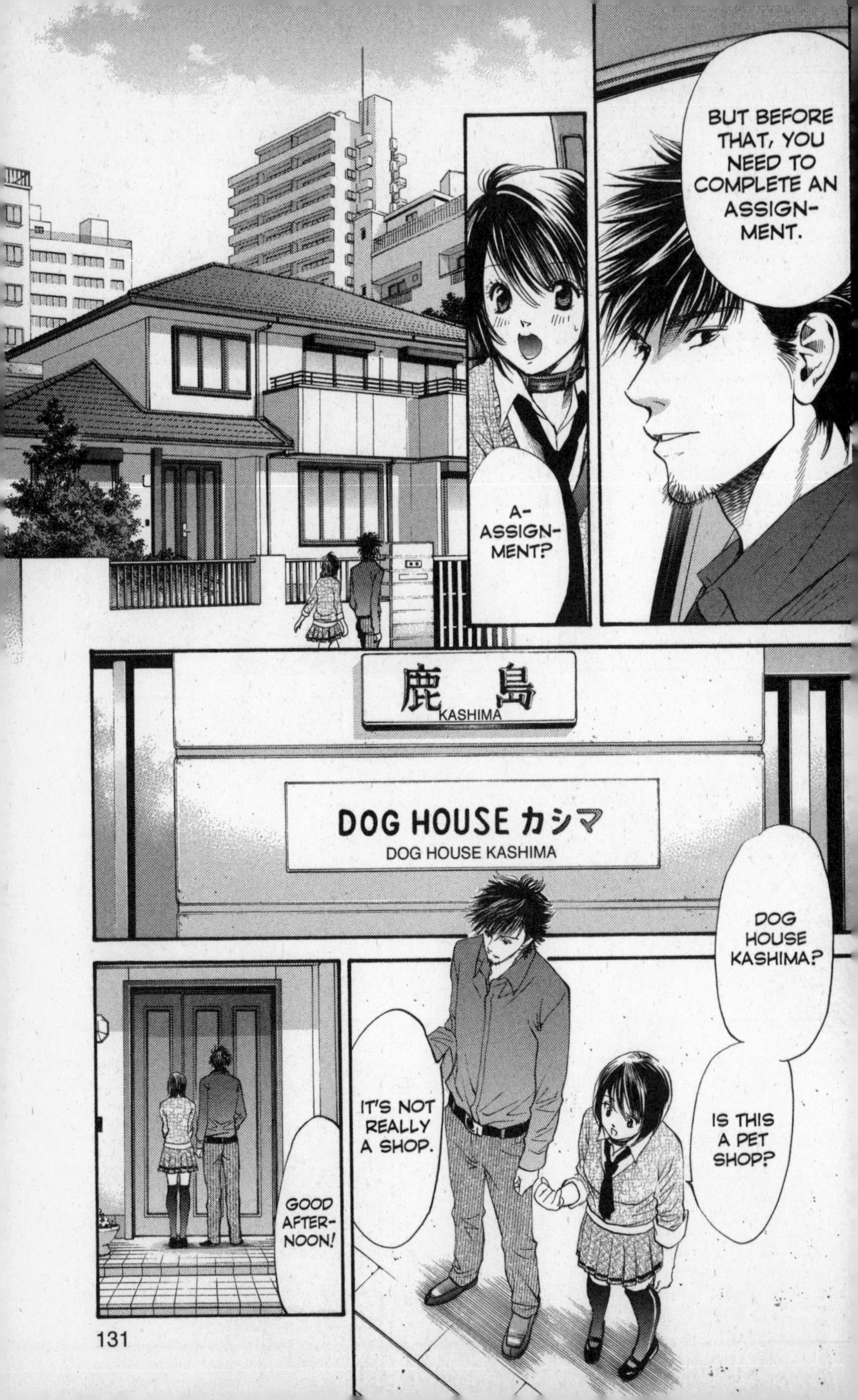
BUT BEFORE THAT, YOU NEED TO COMPLETE AN ASSIGN- MENT.
A- ASSIGN- MENT?
鹿島
KASHIMA
DOG HOUSE カシマ
DOG HOUSE KASHIMA
DOG HOUSE KASHIMA?
IS THIS A PET SHOP?
IT'S NOT REALLY A SHOP.
GOOD AFTER- NOON!

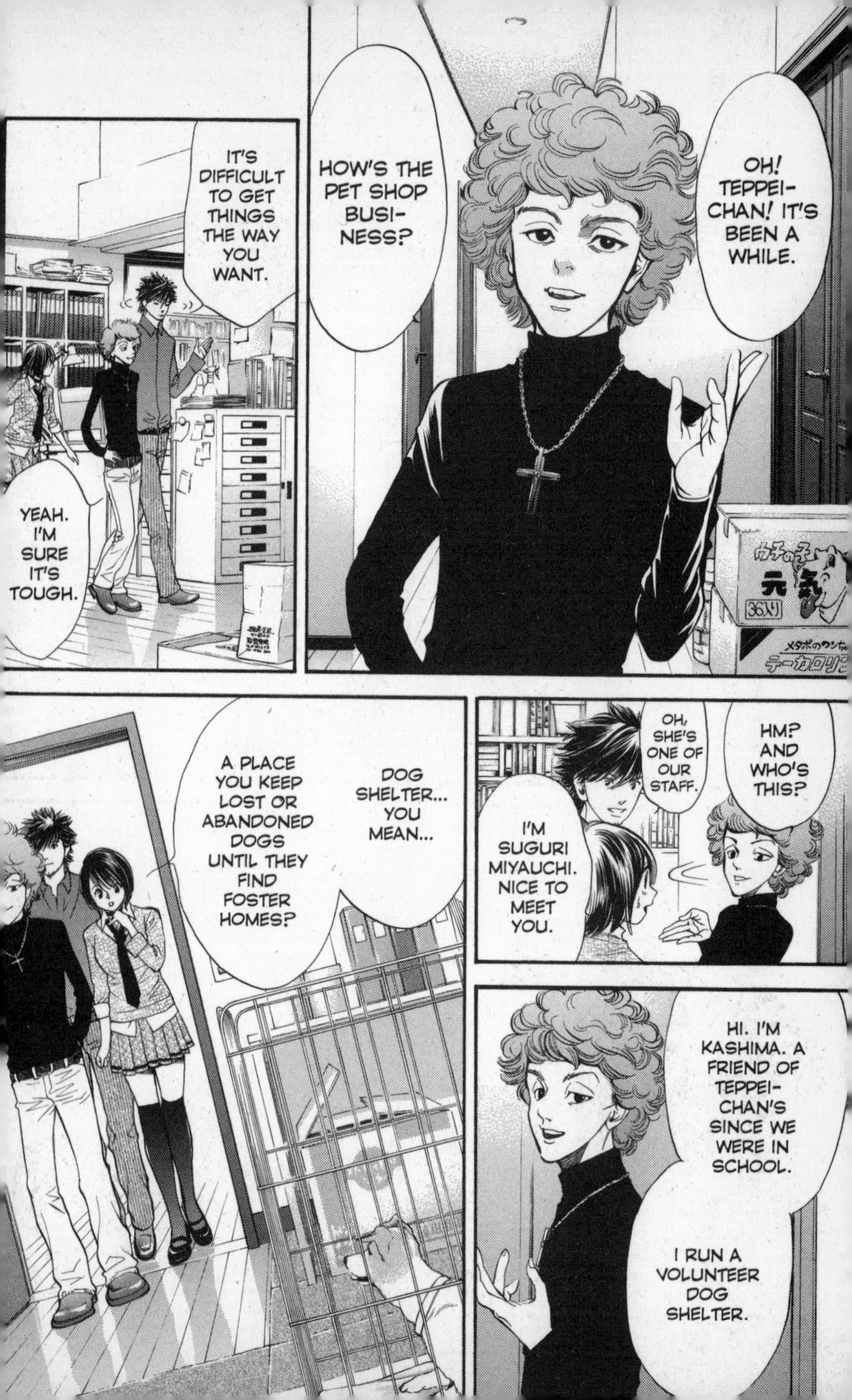
OH! TEPPEI-CHAN! IT'S BEEN A WHILE.
HOW'S THE PET SHOP BUSI-NESS?
IT'S DIFFICULT TO GET THINGS THE WAY YOU WANT.
YEAH. I'M SURE IT'S TOUGH.
HM? AND WHO'S THIS?
OH, SHE'S ONE OF OUR STAFF.
I'M SUGURI MIYAUCHI. NICE TO MEET YOU.
HI. I'M KASHIMA. A FRIEND OF TEPPEI-CHAN'S SINCE WE WERE IN SCHOOL.
I RUN A VOLUNTEER DOG SHELTER.
DOG SHELTER... YOU MEAN...
A PLACE YOU KEEP LOST OR ABANDONED DOGS UNTIL THEY FIND FOSTER HOMES?

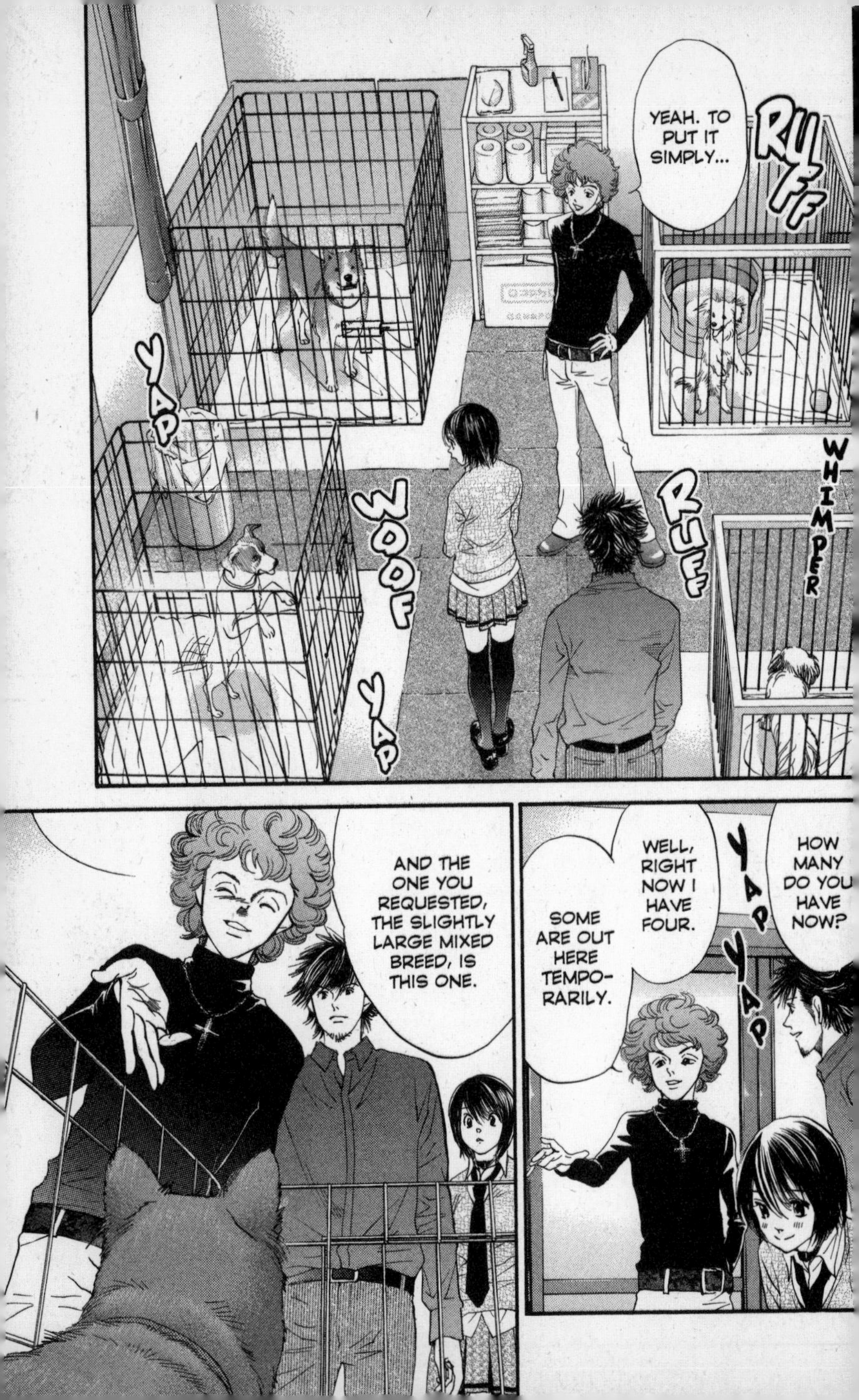
RUFF
YEAH. TO PUT IT SIMPLY...
WHIMPER
RUFF
YAP
WOOF
YAP
HOW MANY DO YOU HAVE NOW?
YAP YAP
YAP
WELL, RIGHT NOW I HAVE FOUR.
SOME ARE OUT HERE TEMPO-RARILY.
AND THE ONE YOU REQUESTED, THE SLIGHTLY LARGE MIXED BREED, IS THIS ONE.

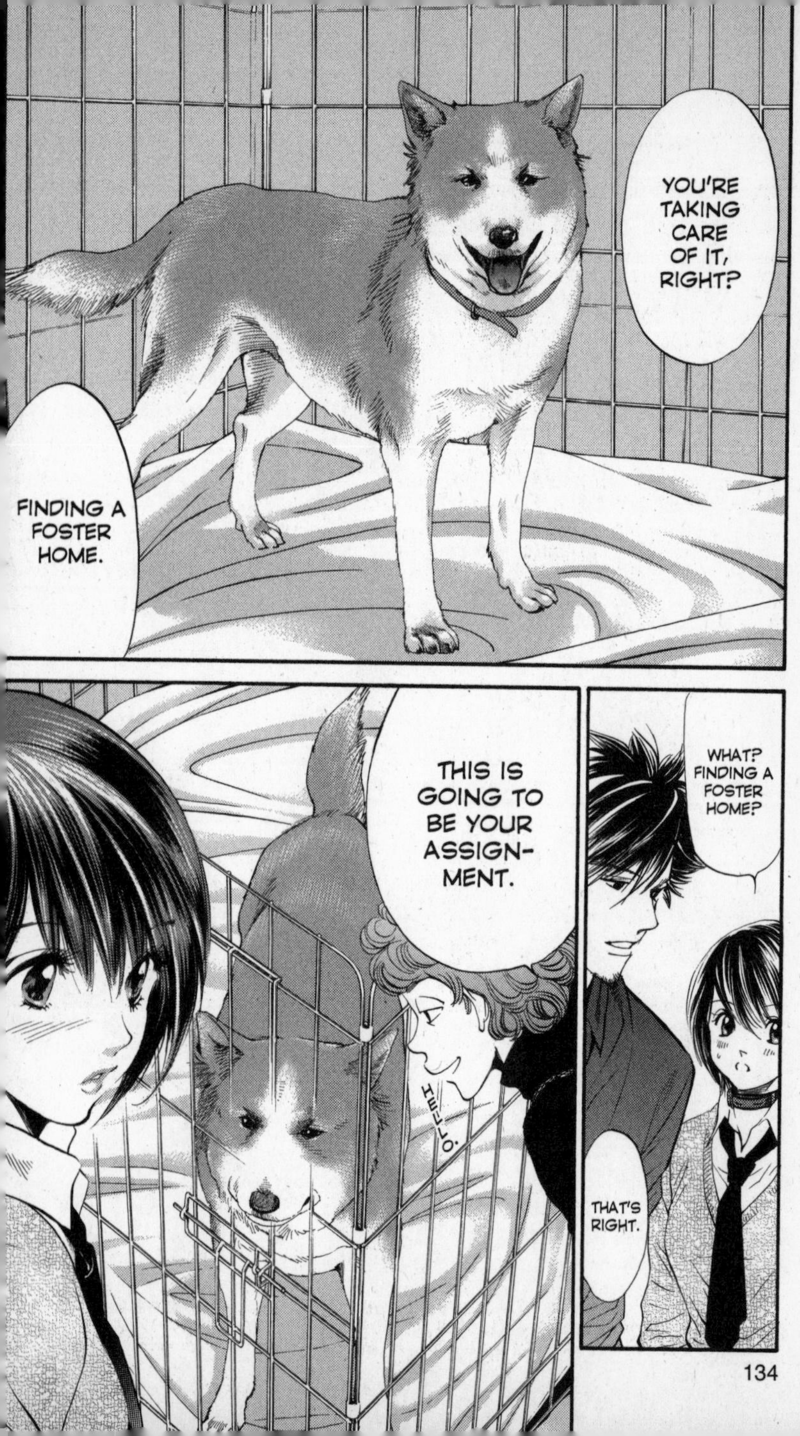
YOU'RE TAKING CARE OF IT, RIGHT?
FINDING A FOSTER HOME.
WHAT? FINDING A FOSTER HOME?
THAT'S RIGHT.
THIS IS GOING TO BE YOUR ASSIGN-MENT.
HELLO.

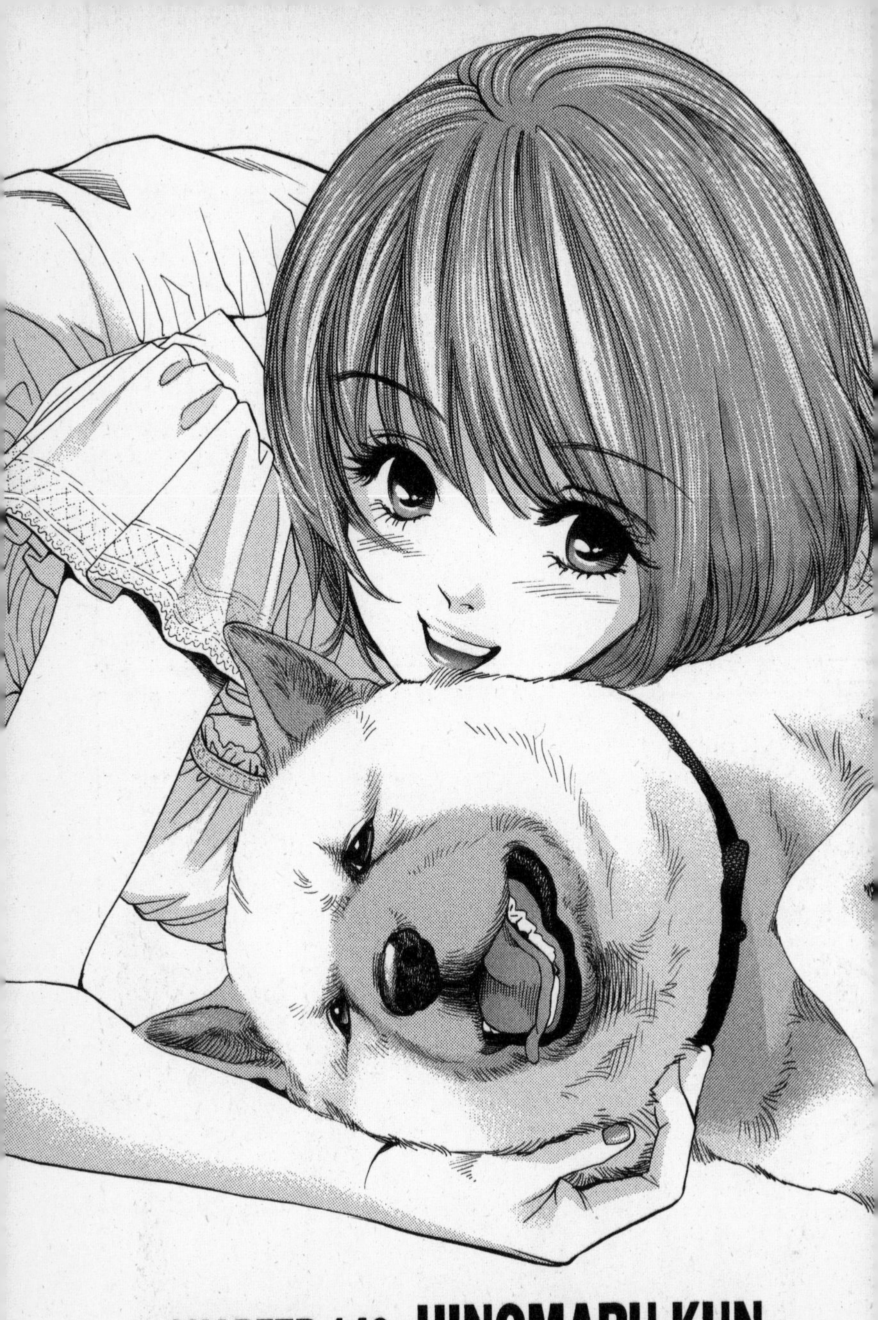

CHAPTER 149: HINOMARU-KUN

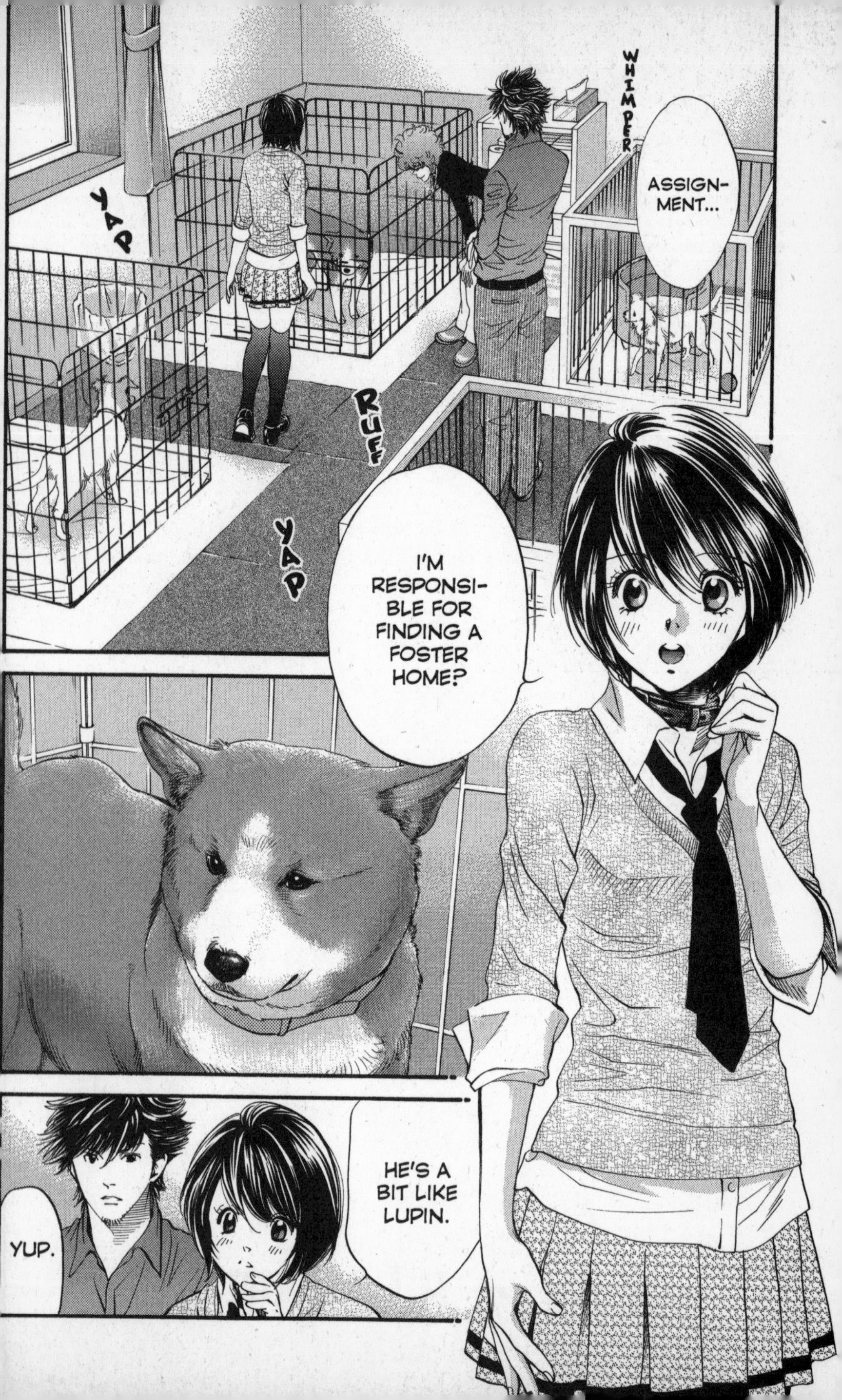
WHIMPER
ASSIGNMENT...
YAP
RUFF
YAP
I'M RESPONSIBLE FOR FINDING A FOSTER HOME?
HE'S A BIT LIKE LUPIN.
YUP.

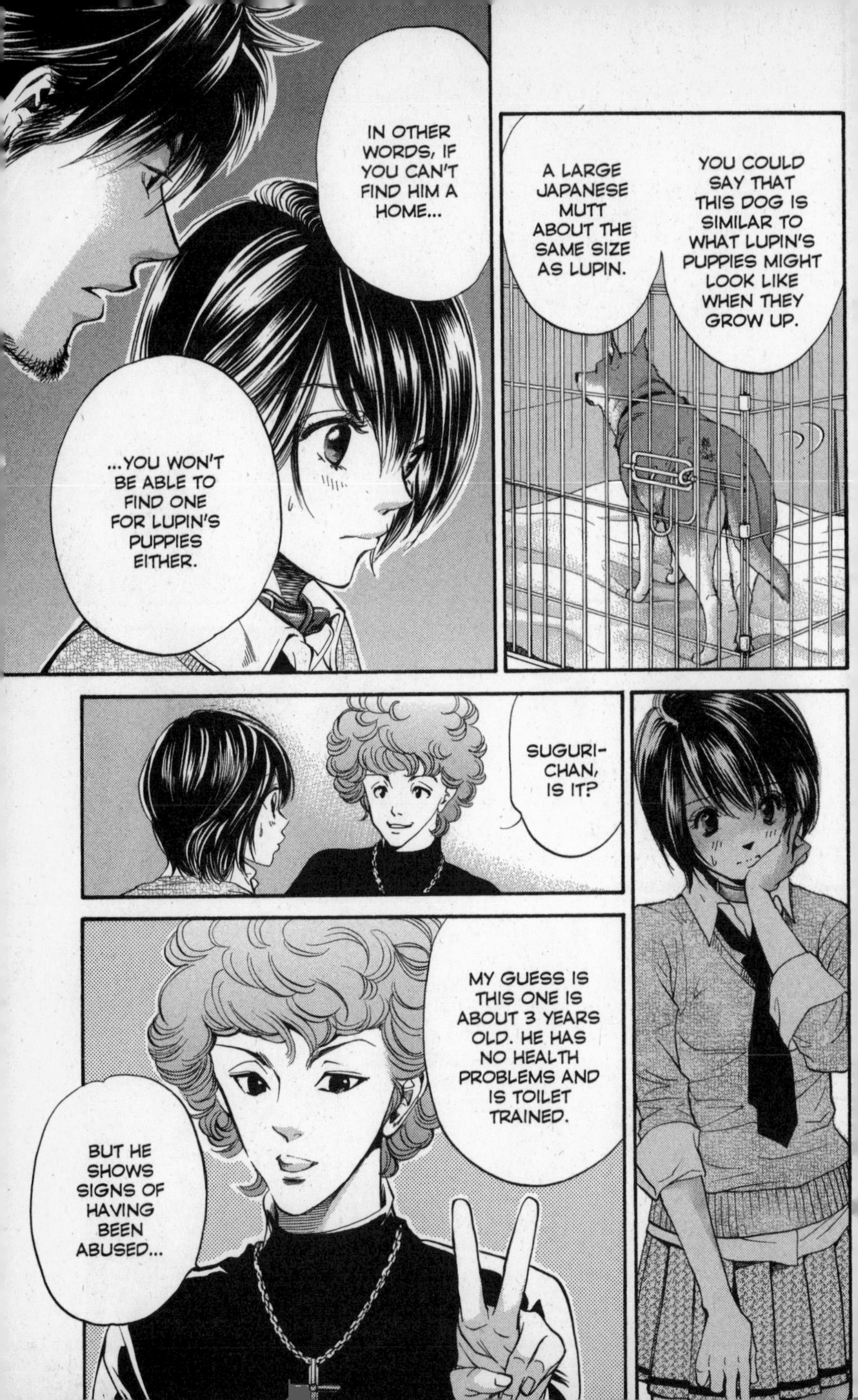
YOU COULD SAY THAT THIS DOG IS SIMILAR TO WHAT LUPIN'S PUPPIES MIGHT LOOK LIKE WHEN THEY GROW UP.
A LARGE JAPANESE MUTT ABOUT THE SAME SIZE AS LUPIN.
IN OTHER WORDS, IF YOU CAN'T FIND HIM A HOME...
...YOU WON'T BE ABLE TO FIND ONE FOR LUPIN'S PUPPIES EITHER.
SUGURI-CHAN, IS IT?
MY GUESS IS THIS ONE IS ABOUT 3 YEARS OLD. HE HAS NO HEALTH PROBLEMS AND IS TOILET TRAINED.
BUT HE SHOWS SIGNS OF HAVING BEEN ABUSED...

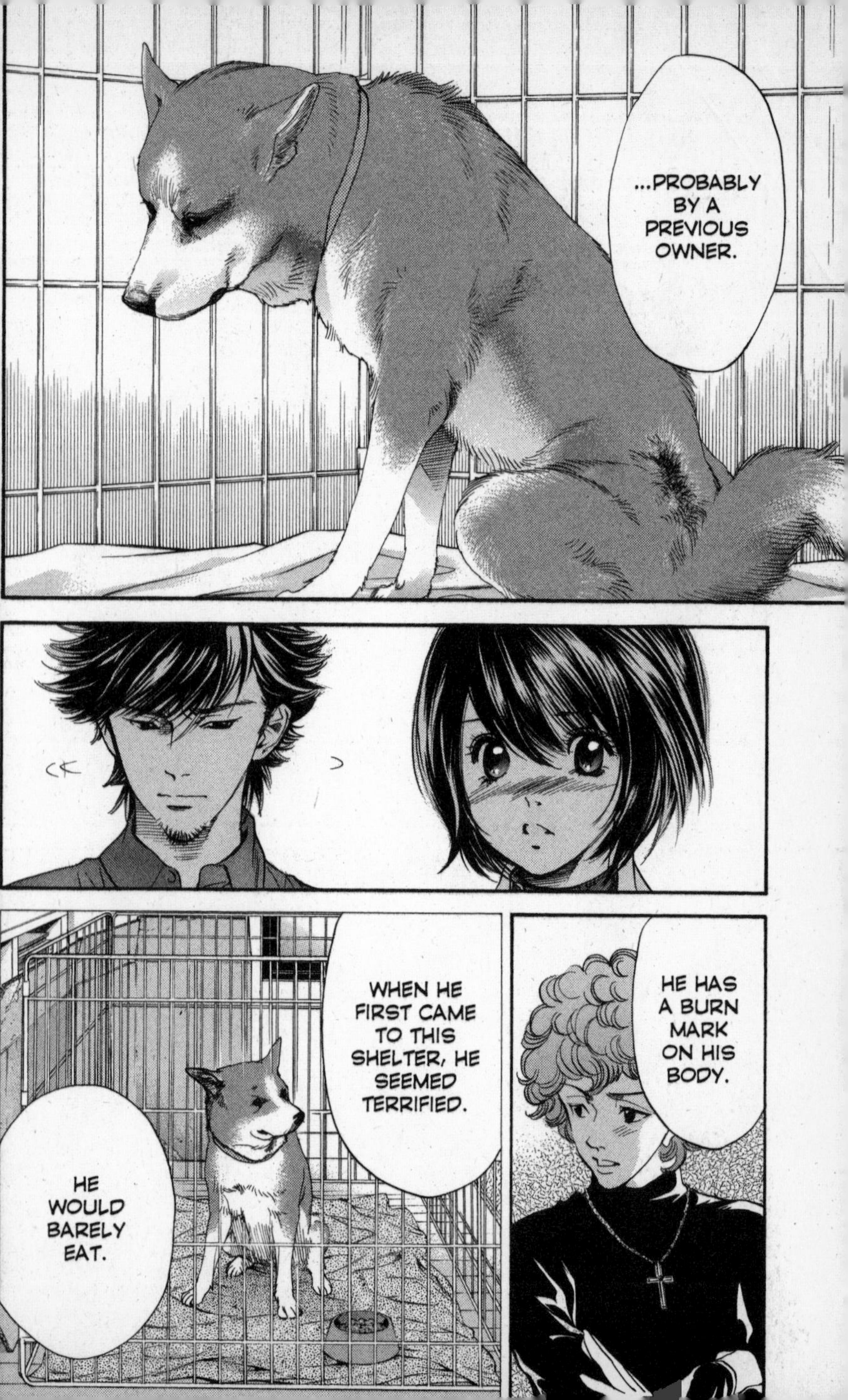
...PROBABLY BY A PREVIOUS OWNER.
HE HAS A BURN MARK ON HIS BODY.
WHEN HE FIRST CAME TO THIS SHELTER, HE SEEMED TERRIFIED.
HE WOULD BARELY EAT.

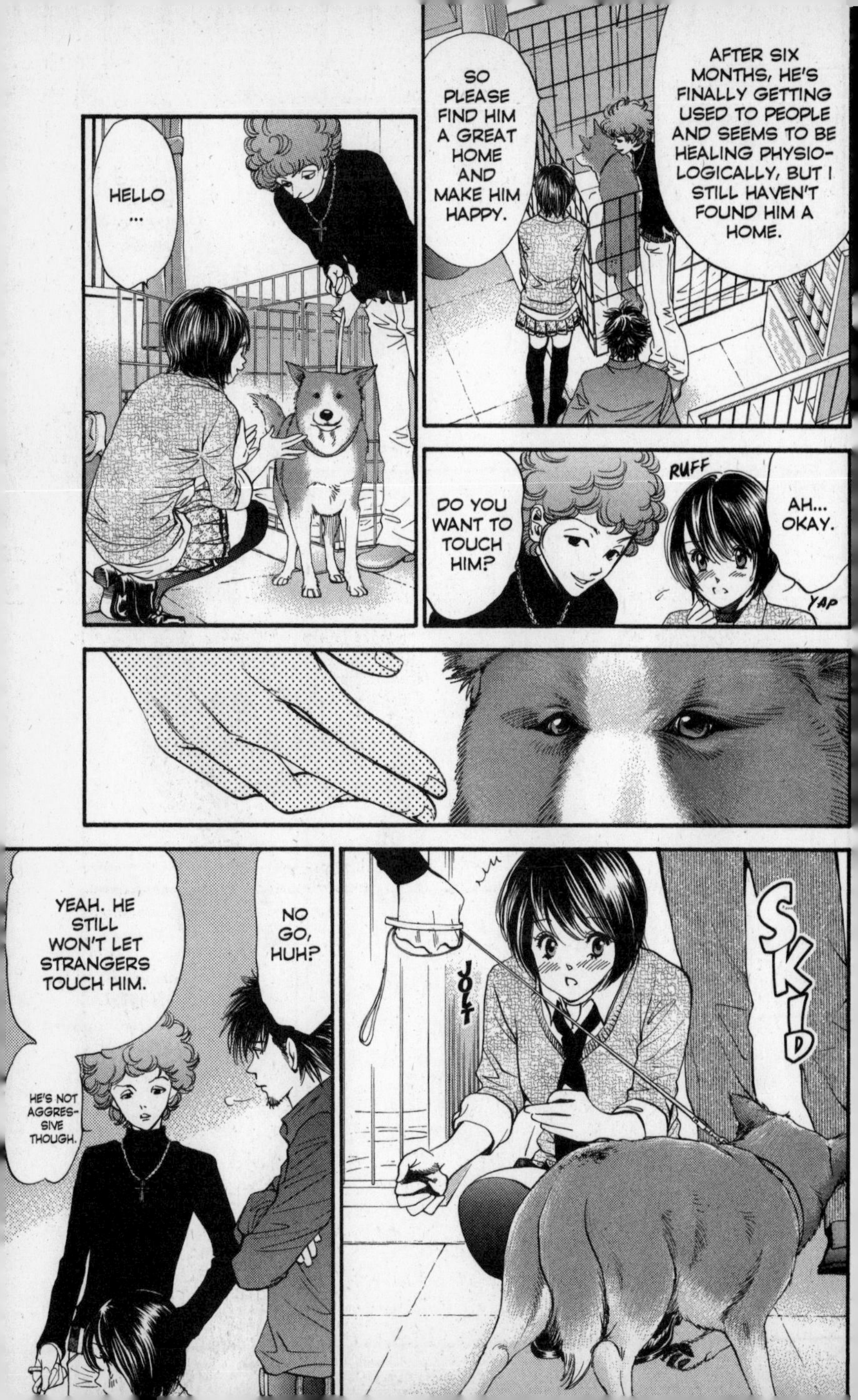
AFTER SIX MONTHS, HE'S FINALLY GETTING USED TO PEOPLE AND SEEMS TO BE HEALING PHYSIO-LOGICALLY, BUT I STILL HAVEN'T FOUND HIM A HOME.
SO PLEASE FIND HIM A GREAT HOME AND MAKE HIM HAPPY.
AH... OKAY.
RUFF
DO YOU WANT TO TOUCH HIM?
YAP
HELLO ...
SKID
JOLT
NO GO, HUH?
YEAH. HE STILL WON'T LET STRANGERS TOUCH HIM.
HE'S NOT AGGRES-SIVE THOUGH.

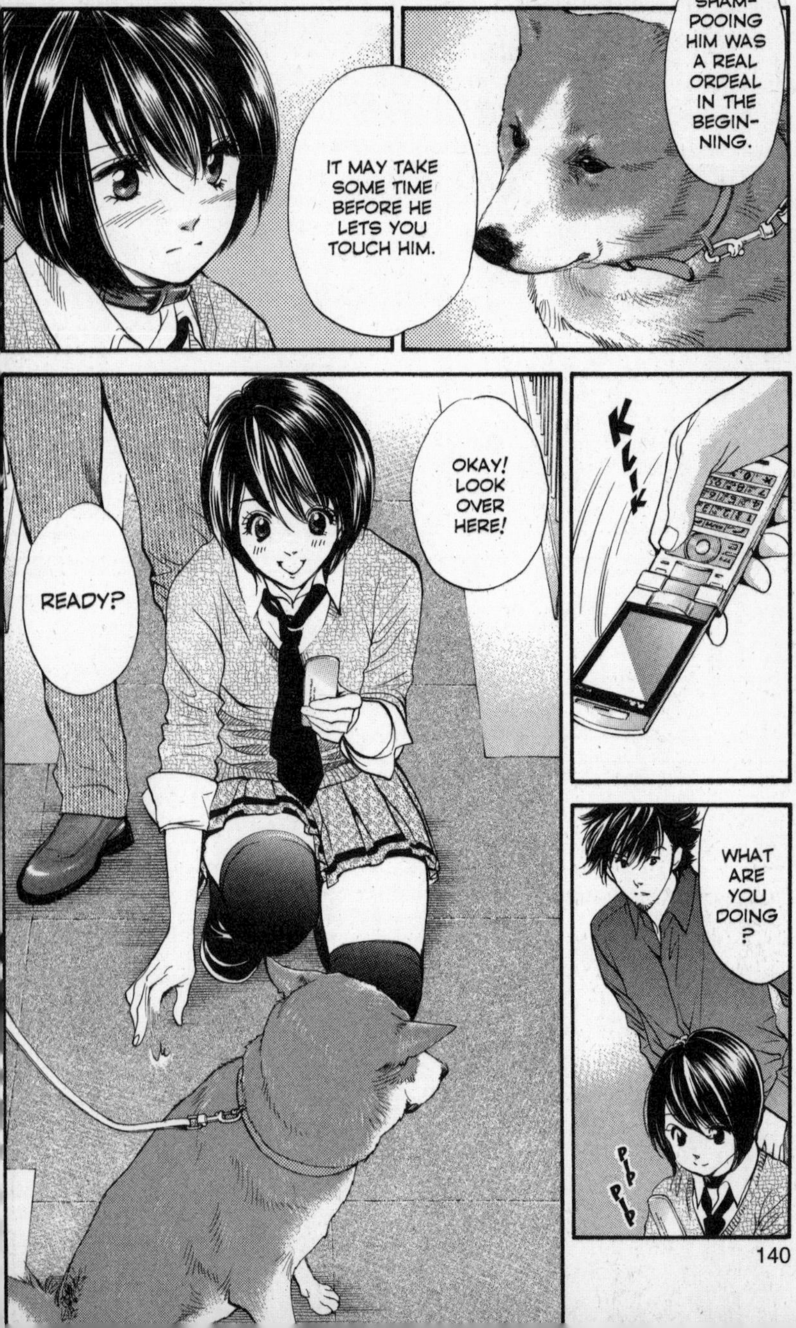
SHAMPOOING HIM WAS A REAL ORDEAL IN THE BEGINNING.
IT MAY TAKE SOME TIME BEFORE HE LETS YOU TOUCH HIM.
KLIK
WHAT ARE YOU DOING?
PIP PIP
OKAY! LOOK OVER HERE!
READY?

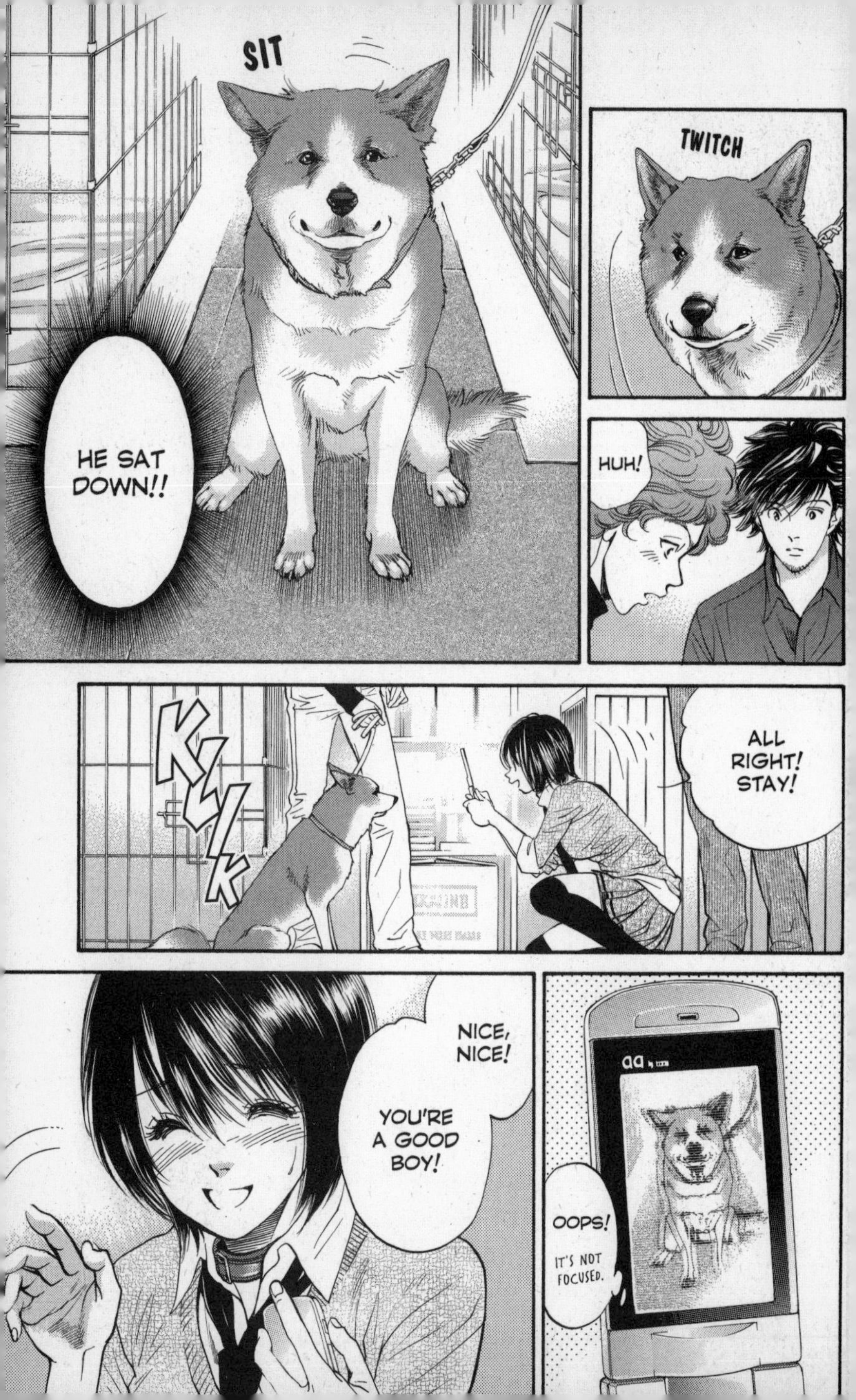
TWITCH
HUH!
SIT
HE SAT DOWN!!
ALL RIGHT! STAY!
KLIK
OOPS!
IT'S NOT FOCUSED.
NICE, NICE!
YOU'RE A GOOD BOY!

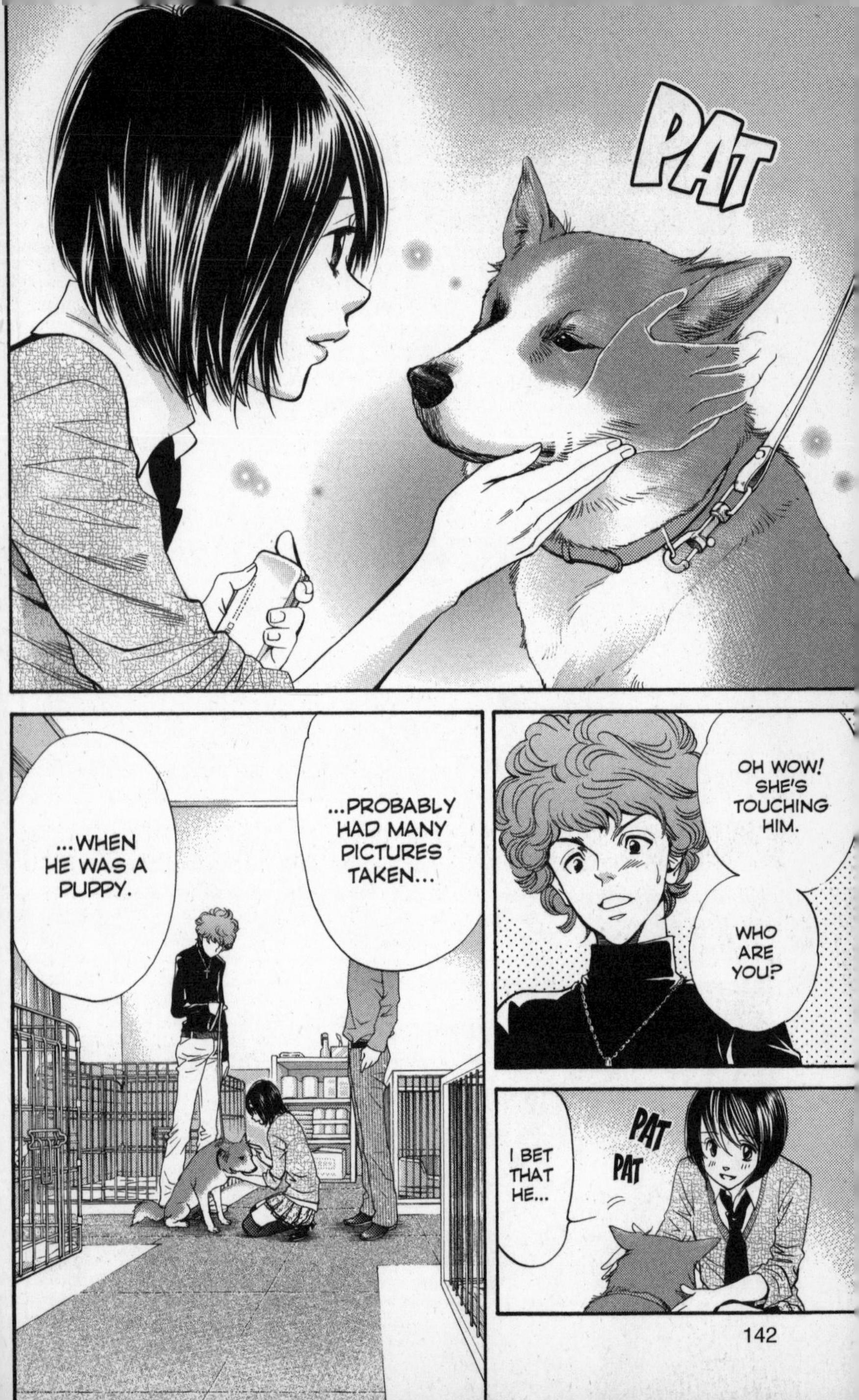
PAT
OH WOW! SHE'S TOUCHING HIM.
WHO ARE YOU?
PAT
PAT
I BET THAT HE...
...PROBABLY HAD MANY PICTURES TAKEN...
...WHEN HE WAS A PUPPY.

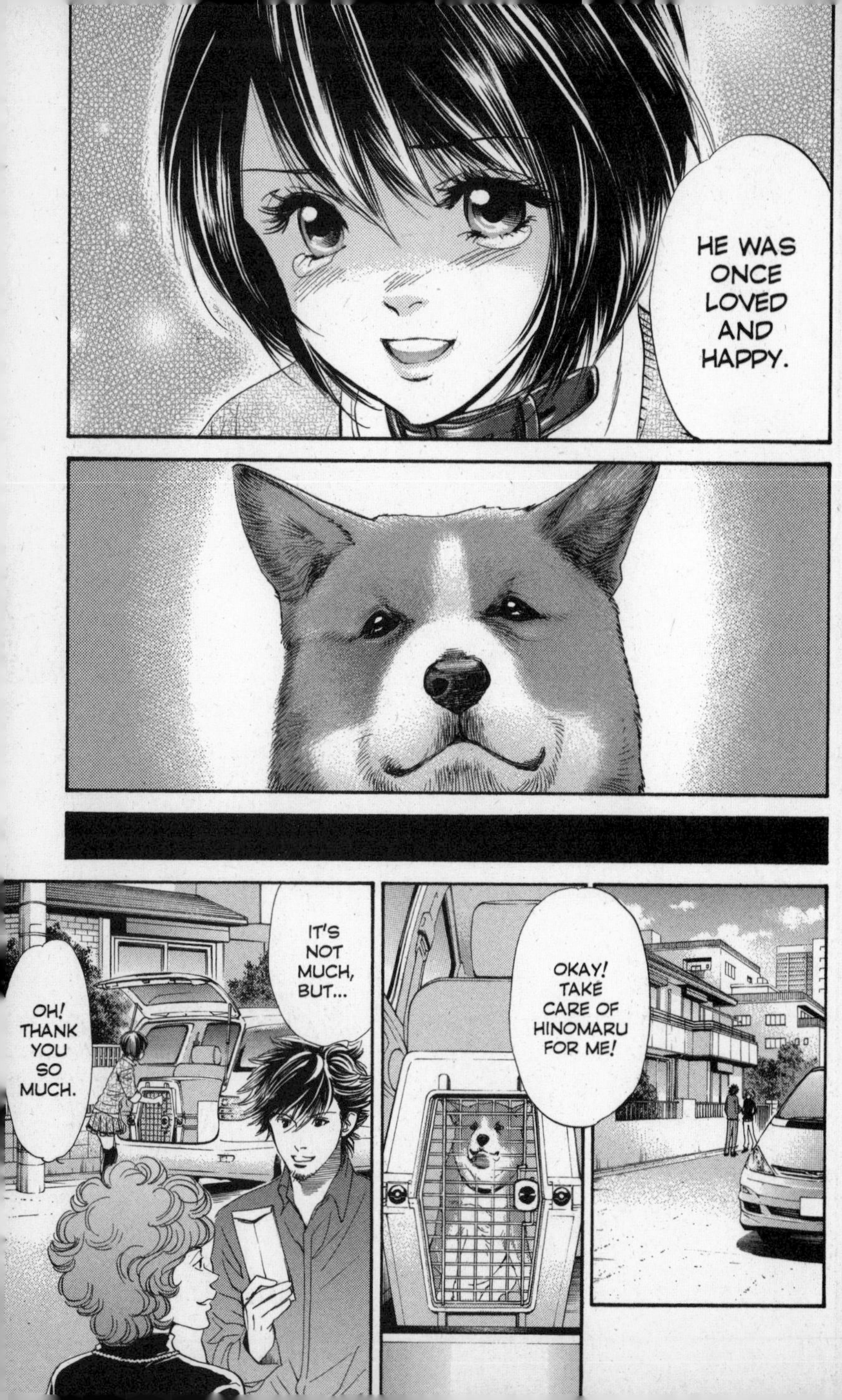
HE WAS ONCE LOVED AND HAPPY.
OKAY! TAKE CARE OF HINOMARU FOR ME!
IT'S NOT MUCH, BUT...
OH! THANK YOU SO MUCH.

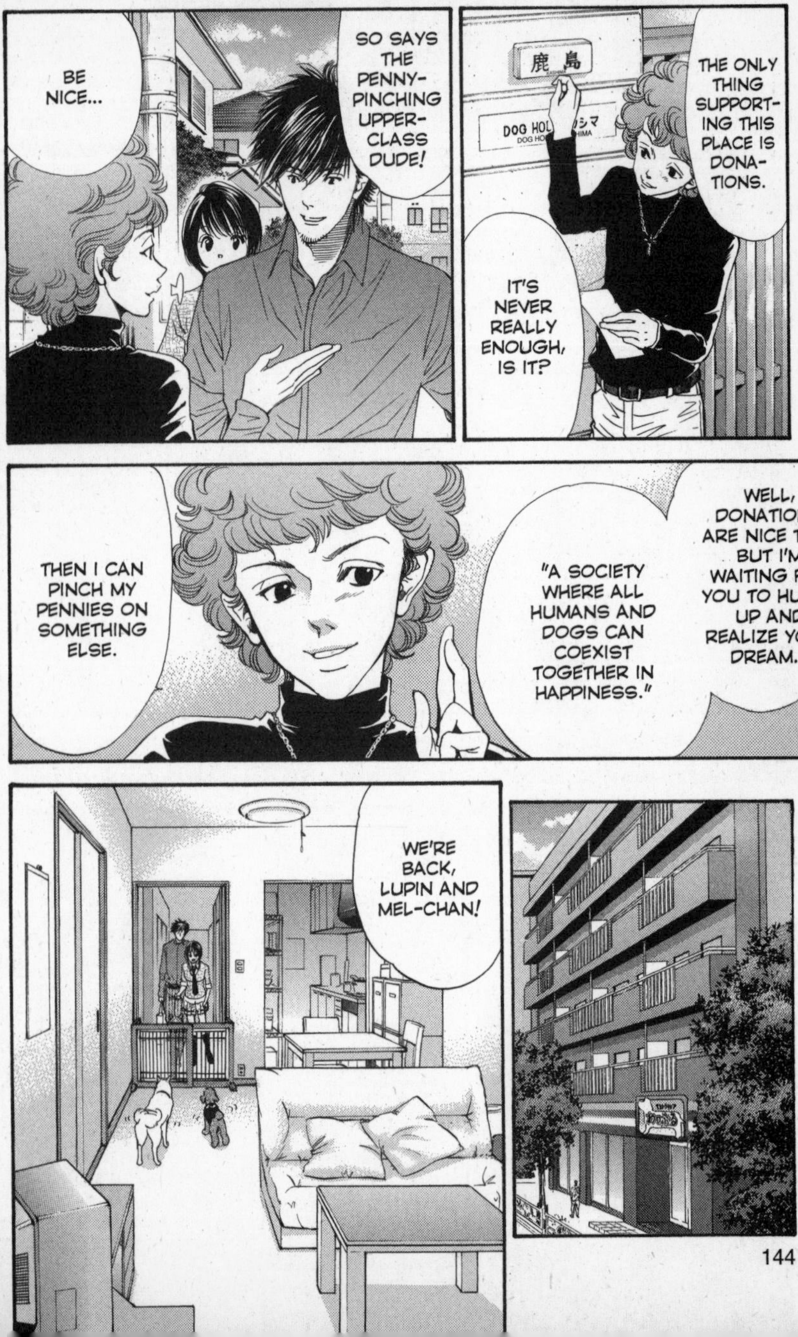
鹿島
THE ONLY THING SUPPORT-ING THIS PLACE IS DONA-TIONS.
IT'S NEVER REALLY ENOUGH, IS IT?
SO SAYS THE PENNY-PINCHING UPPER-CLASS DUDE!
BE NICE...
WELL, DONATIONS ARE NICE TOO, BUT I'M WAITING FOR YOU TO HURRY UP AND REALIZE YOUR DREAM...
"A SOCIETY WHERE ALL HUMANS AND DOGS CAN COEXIST TOGETHER IN HAPPINESS."
THEN I CAN PINCH MY PENNIES ON SOMETHING ELSE.
WE'RE BACK, LUPIN AND MEL-CHAN!

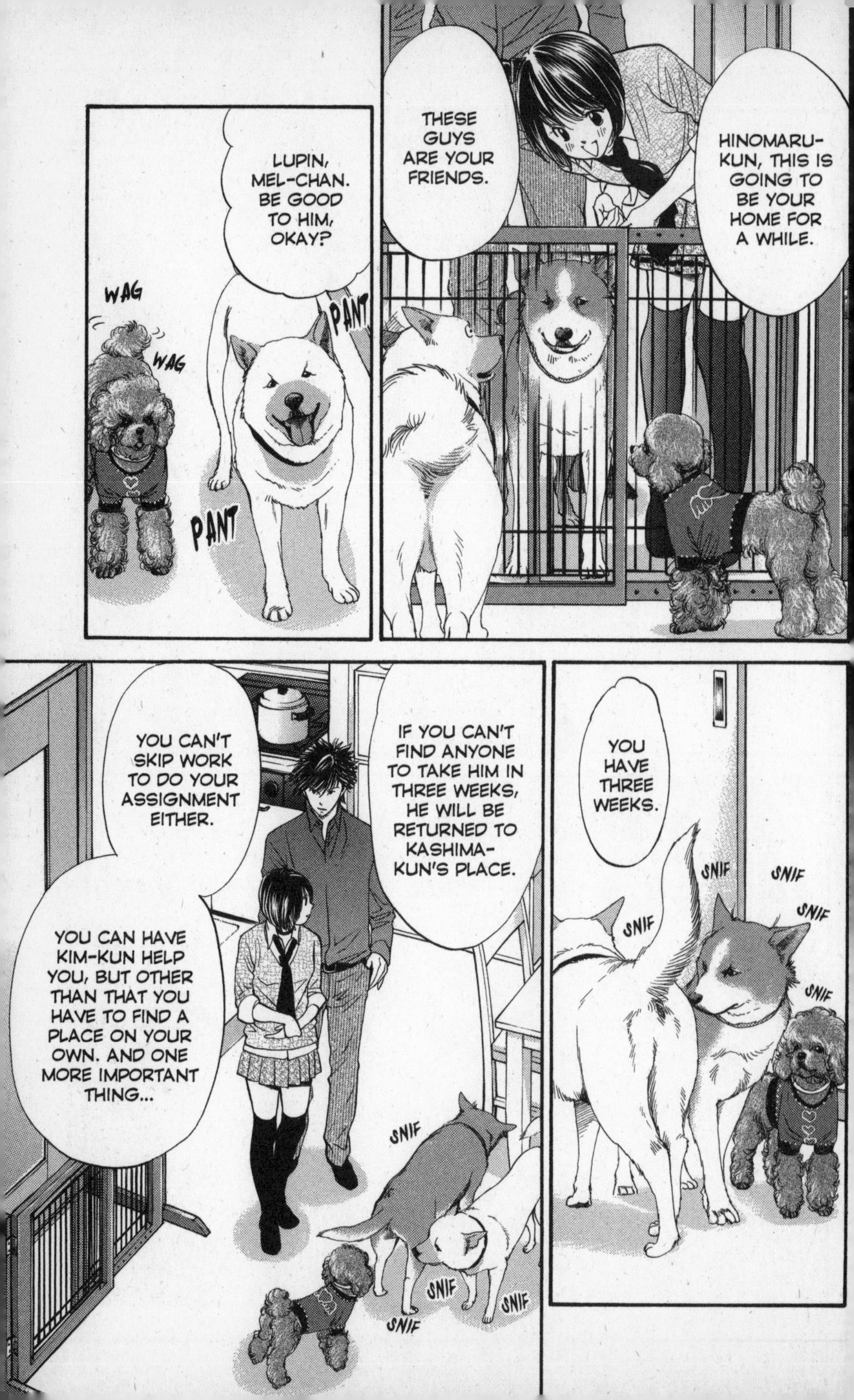

HINOMARU-KUN, THIS IS GOING TO BE YOUR HOME FOR A WHILE.
THESE GUYS ARE YOUR FRIENDS.
LUPIN, MEL-CHAN. BE GOOD TO HIM, OKAY?
PANT
WAG
WAG
PANT
YOU HAVE THREE WEEKS.
SNIF
SNIF
SNIF
SNIF
SNIF
IF YOU CAN'T FIND ANYONE TO TAKE HIM IN THREE WEEKS, HE WILL BE RETURNED TO KASHIMA-KUN'S PLACE.
YOU CAN'T SKIP WORK TO DO YOUR ASSIGNMENT EITHER.
YOU CAN HAVE KIM-KUN HELP YOU, BUT OTHER THAN THAT YOU HAVE TO FIND A PLACE ON YOUR OWN. AND ONE MORE IMPORTANT THING...
SNIF
SNIF
SNIF
SNIF

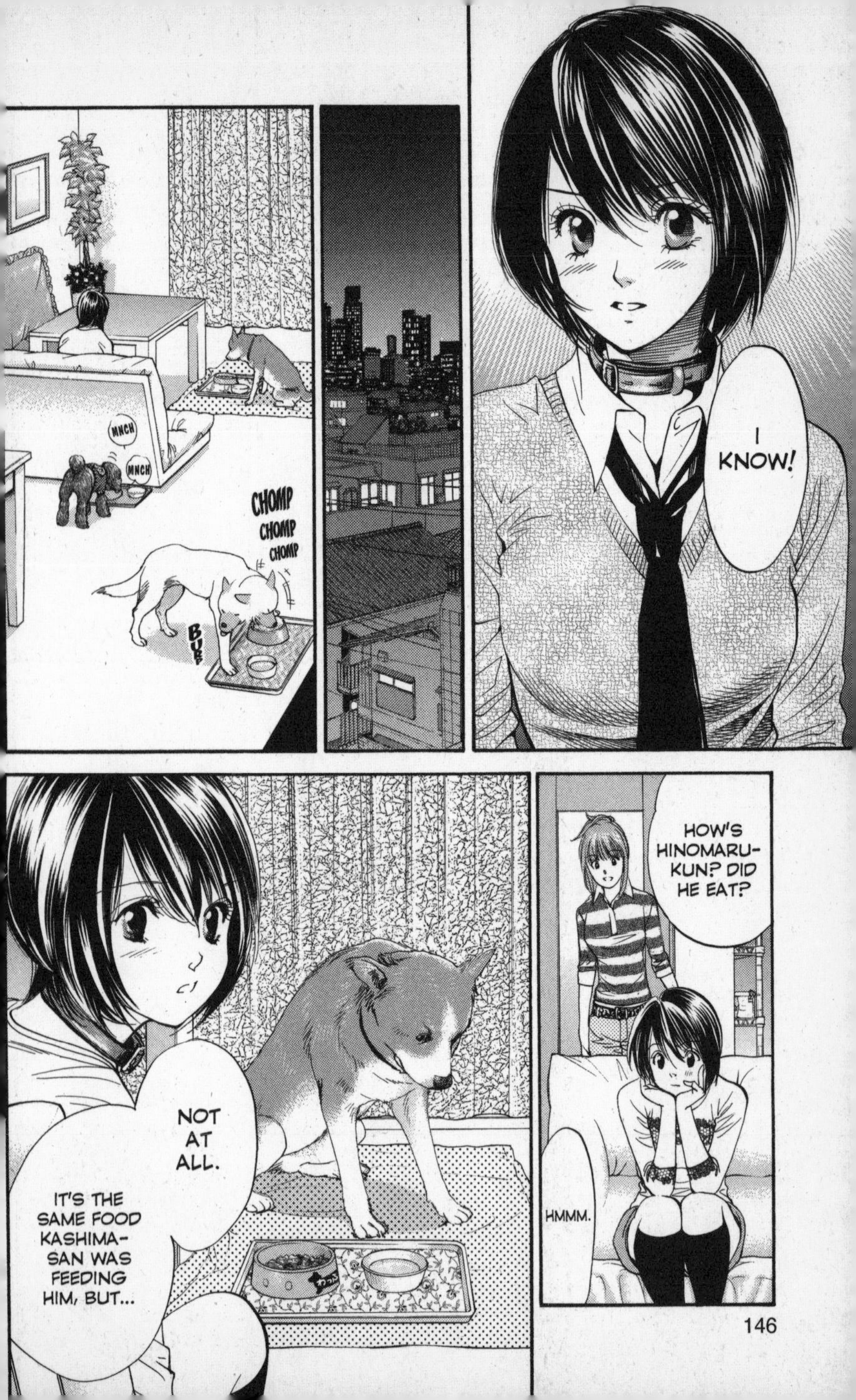
I KNOW!
MNCH
MNCH
CHOMP
CHOMP
CHOMP
HOW'S HINOMARU-KUN? DID HE EAT?
HMMM.
NOT AT ALL.
IT'S THE SAME FOOD KASHIMA-SAN WAS FEEDING HIM, BUT...

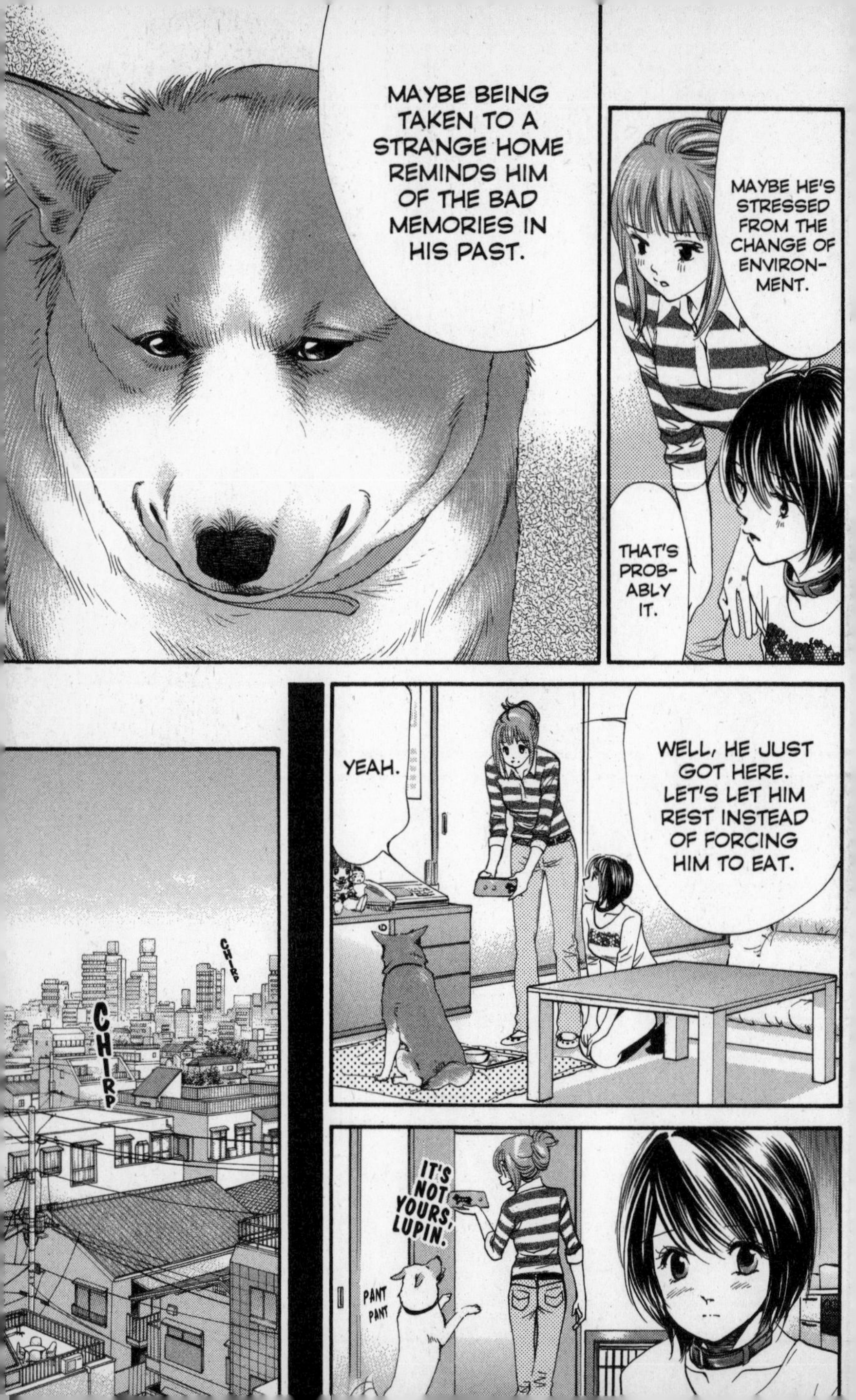
MAYBE HE'S STRESSED FROM THE CHANGE OF ENVIRON-MENT.
THAT'S PROB-ABLY IT.
MAYBE BEING TAKEN TO A STRANGE HOME REMINDS HIM OF THE BAD MEMORIES IN HIS PAST.
WELL, HE JUST GOT HERE. LET'S LET HIM REST INSTEAD OF FORCING HIM TO EAT.
YEAH.
IT'S NOT YOURS, LUPIN.
PANT PANT
CHIRP
CHIRP

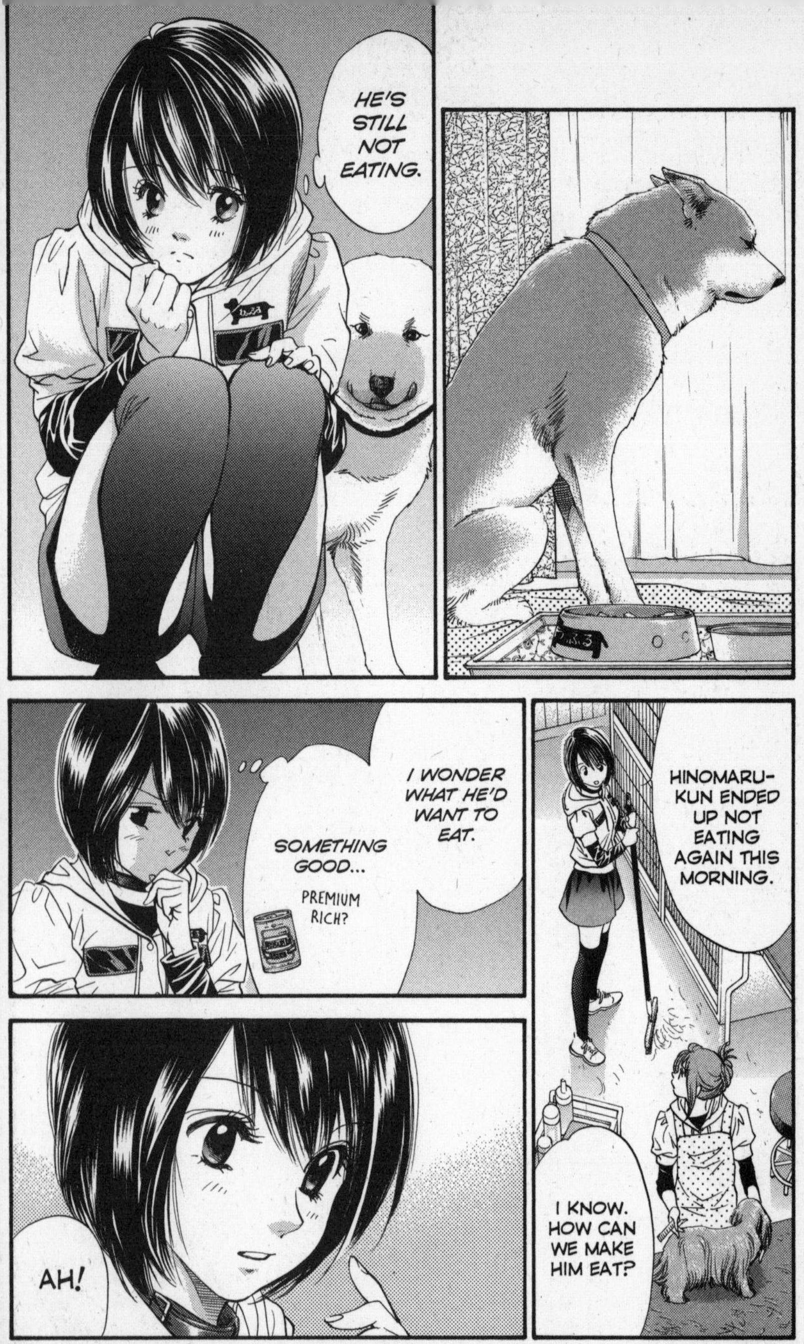
HE'S STILL NOT EATING.
HINOMARU-KUN ENDED UP NOT EATING AGAIN THIS MORNING.
I KNOW. HOW CAN WE MAKE HIM EAT?
I WONDER WHAT HE'D WANT TO EAT.
SOMETHING GOOD...
PREMIUM RICH?
AH!

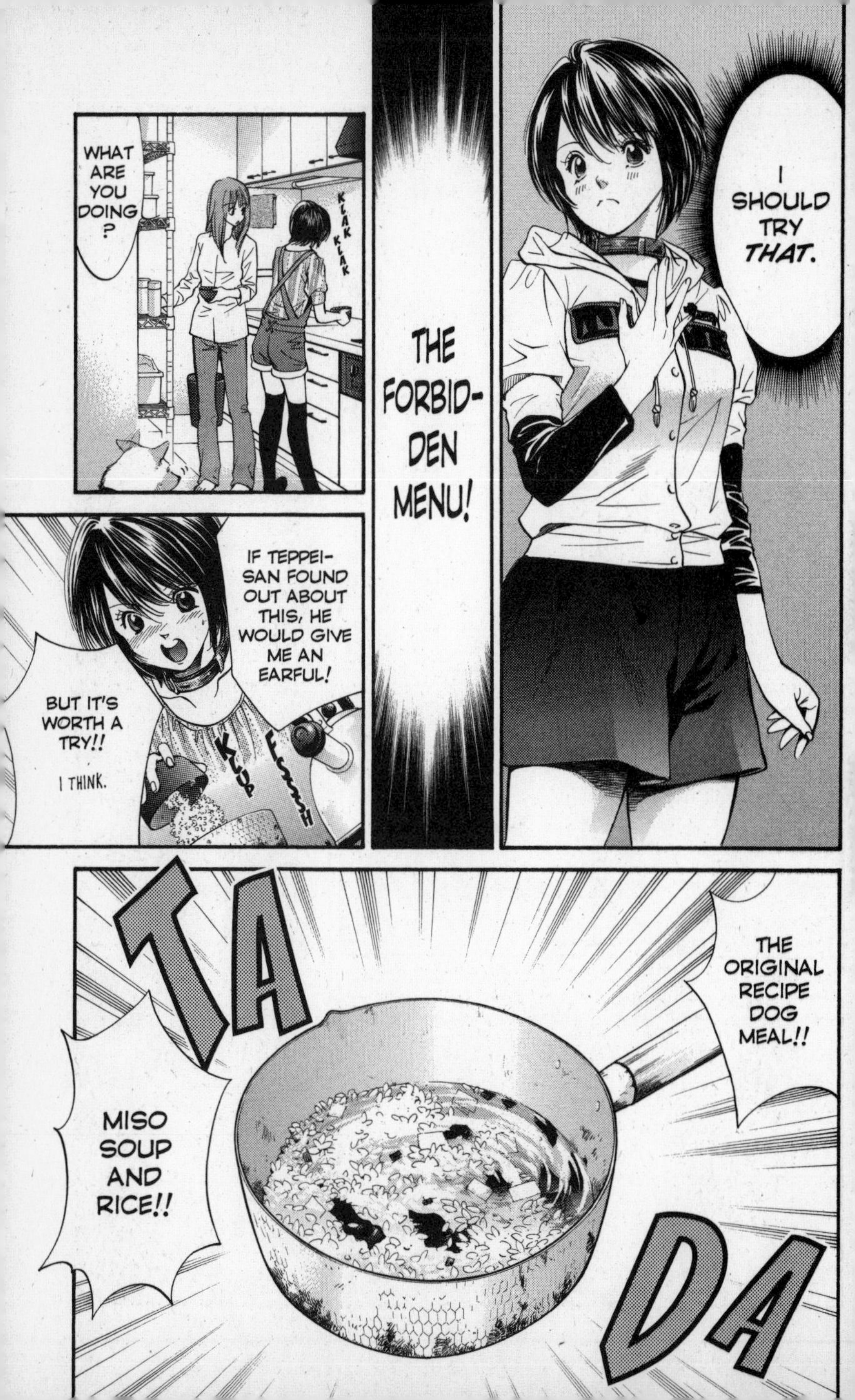
I SHOULD TRY *THAT*.
THE FORBID-DEN MENU!
WHAT ARE YOU DOING?
KLAK KLAK
IF TEPPEI-SAN FOUND OUT ABOUT THIS, HE WOULD GIVE ME AN EARFUL!
BUT IT'S WORTH A TRY!!
I THINK.
FSSSSH
KLUP
TA
THE ORIGINAL RECIPE DOG MEAL!!
MISO SOUP AND RICE!!
DA

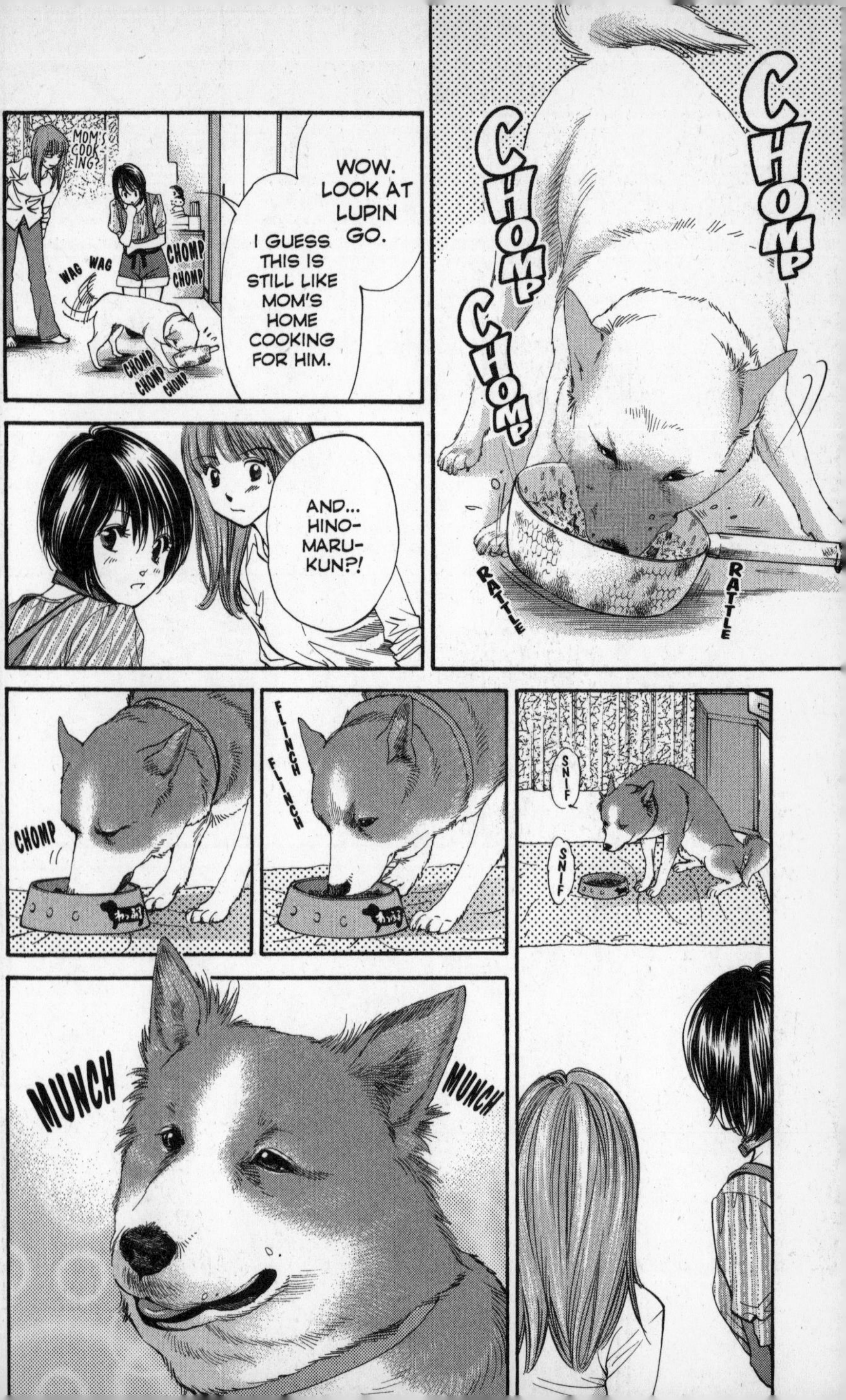
CHOMP
CHOMP
CHOMP
RATTLE
RATTLE
WOW. LOOK AT LUPIN GO.
I GUESS THIS IS STILL LIKE MOM'S HOME COOKING FOR HIM.
MOM'S COOKING?
CHOMP CHOMP
WAG WAG
CHOMP CHOMP CHOMP
AND... HINOMARU-KUN?!
SNIF
SNIF
FLINCH FLINCH
CHOMP
MUNCH
MUNCH

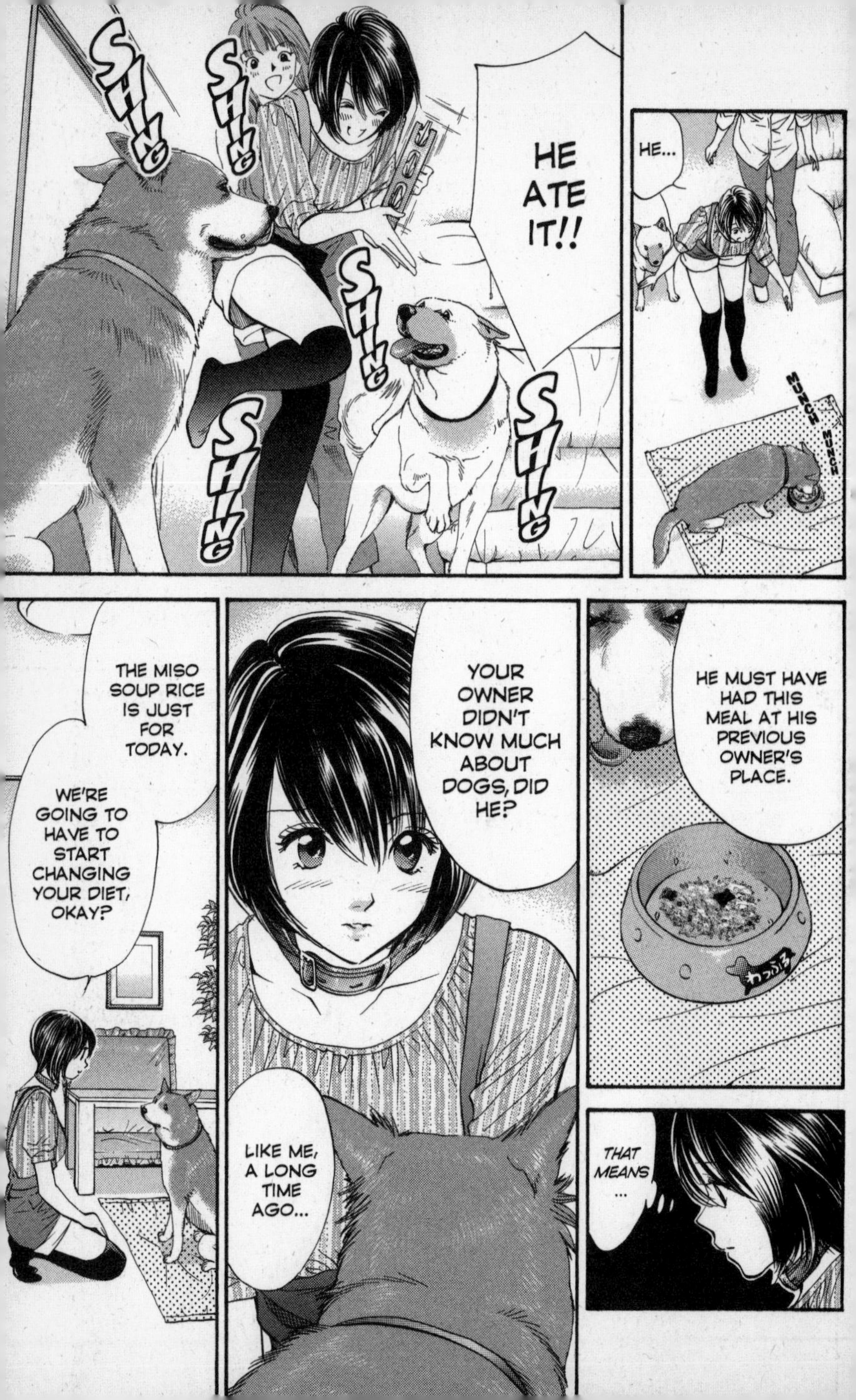
HE...
MUNCH MUNCH
HE ATE IT!!
SHING SHING SHING SHING SHING
HE MUST HAVE HAD THIS MEAL AT HIS PREVIOUS OWNER'S PLACE.
わっふる
THAT MEANS...
YOUR OWNER DIDN'T KNOW MUCH ABOUT DOGS, DID HE?
LIKE ME, A LONG TIME AGO...
THE MISO SOUP RICE IS JUST FOR TODAY.
WE'RE GOING TO HAVE TO START CHANGING YOUR DIET, OKAY?

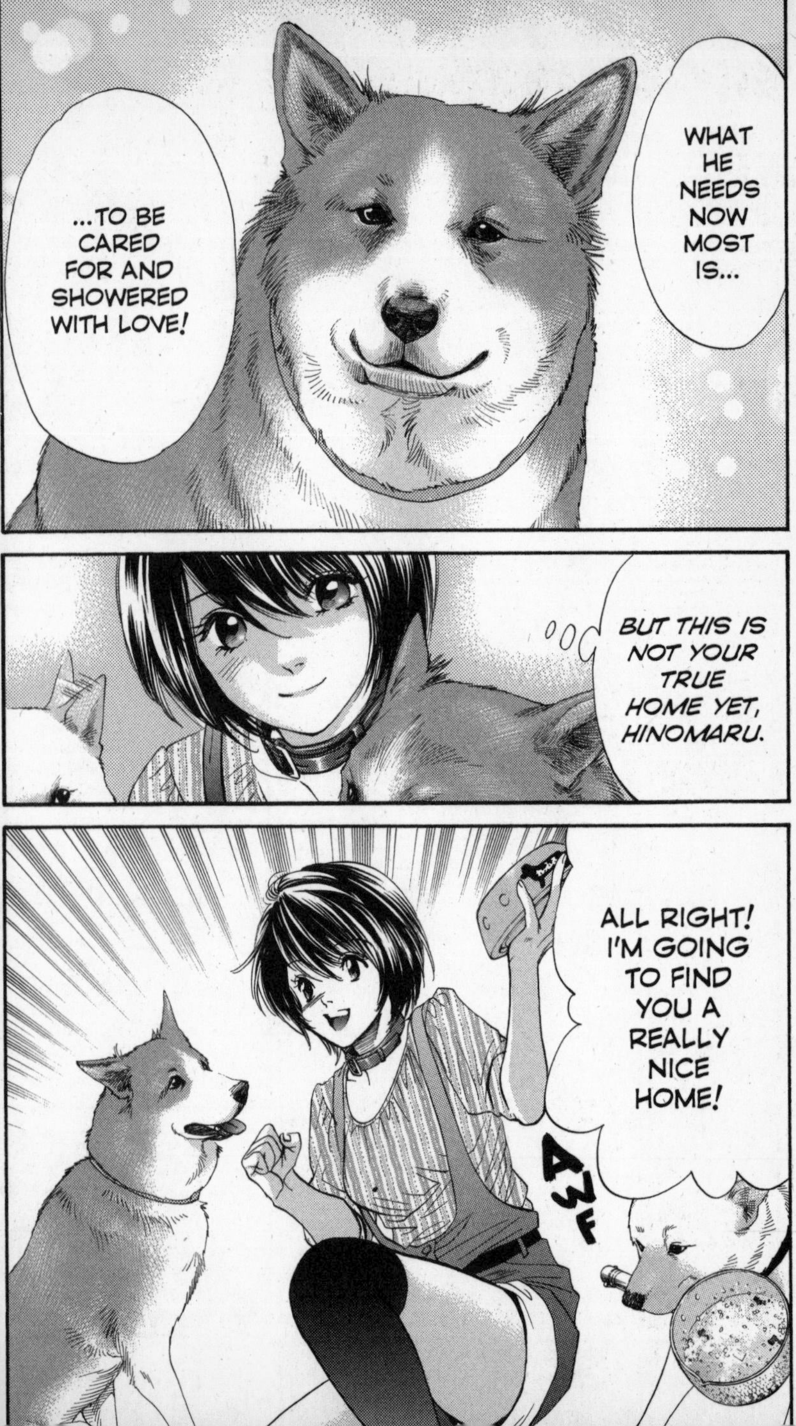
WHAT HE NEEDS NOW MOST IS...
...TO BE CARED FOR AND SHOWERED WITH LOVE!
BUT THIS IS NOT YOUR TRUE HOME YET, HINOMARU.
ALL RIGHT! I'M GOING TO FIND YOU A REALLY NICE HOME!
AWF

FUN DRAFTS AND STORYBOARDS PART 2

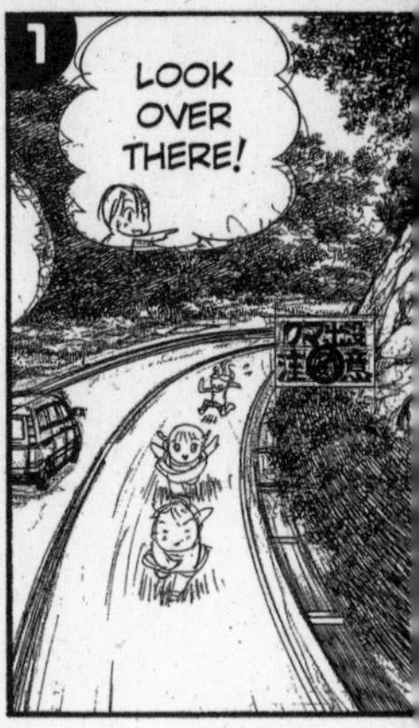
1
LOOK OVER THERE!

RUN!

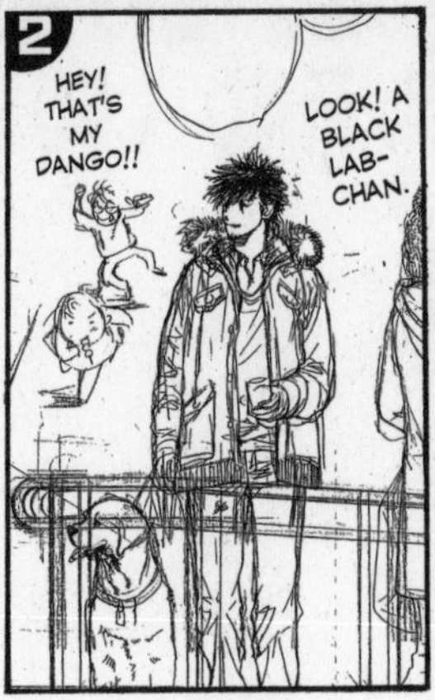
2
LOOK! A BLACK LAB-CHAN.
HEY! THAT'S MY DANGO!!

RUN!!

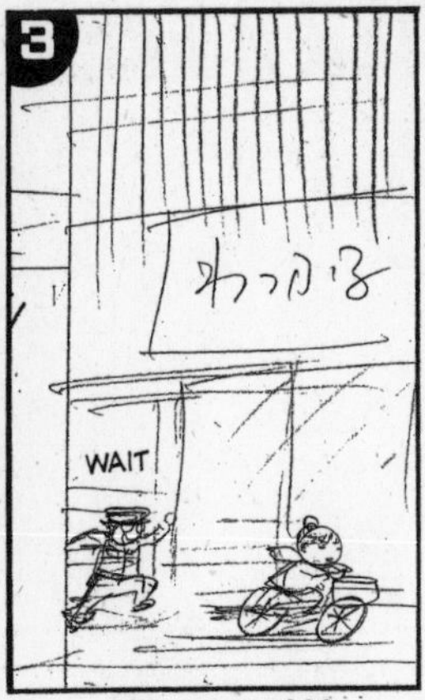
3
WAIT

RUUUN!!!

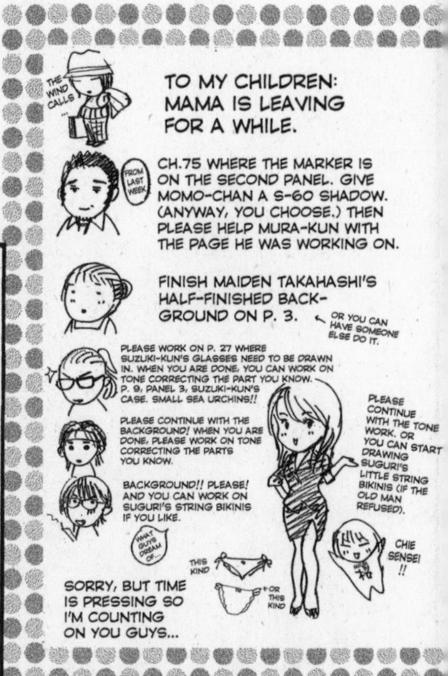
THE WIND CALLS...
TO MY CHILDREN: MAMA IS LEAVING FOR A WHILE.
FROM LAST WEEK
CH.75 WHERE THE MARKER IS ON THE SECOND PANEL. GIVE MOMO-CHAN A S-60 SHADOW. (ANYWAY, YOU CHOOSE.) THEN PLEASE HELP MURA-KUN WITH THE PAGE HE WAS WORKING ON.
FINISH MAIDEN TAKAHASHI'S HALF-FINISHED BACK-GROUND ON P. 3.
OR YOU CAN HAVE SOMEONE ELSE DO IT.
PLEASE WORK ON P. 27 WHERE SUZUKI-KUN'S GLASSES NEED TO BE DRAWN IN. WHEN YOU ARE DONE, YOU CAN WORK ON TONE CORRECTING THE PART YOU KNOW. P. 9, PANEL 3, SUZUKI-KUN'S CASE. SMALL SEA URCHINS!!
PLEASE CONTINUE WITH THE BACKGROUND! WHEN YOU ARE DONE, PLEASE WORK ON TONE CORRECTING THE PARTS YOU KNOW.
BACKGROUND!! PLEASE! AND YOU CAN WORK ON SUGURI'S STRING BIKINIS IF YOU LIKE.
WHAT GUYS DREAM OF...
PLEASE CONTINUE WITH THE TONE WORK. OR YOU CAN START DRAWING SUGURI'S LITTLE STRING BIKINIS (IF THE OLD MAN REFUSED).
THIS KIND
OR THIS KIND
CHIE SENSEI !!
SORRY, BUT TIME IS PRESSING SO I'M COUNTING ON YOU GUYS...

THE MEMO YUKIYAN SENSEI WROTE TO HER STAFF WHEN SHE LEFT WHILE WORKING ON THE STORY OF LITTLE LUPIN. THE WORDS "TIME IS PRESSING" SOUND QUITE REAL. (LAUGH)

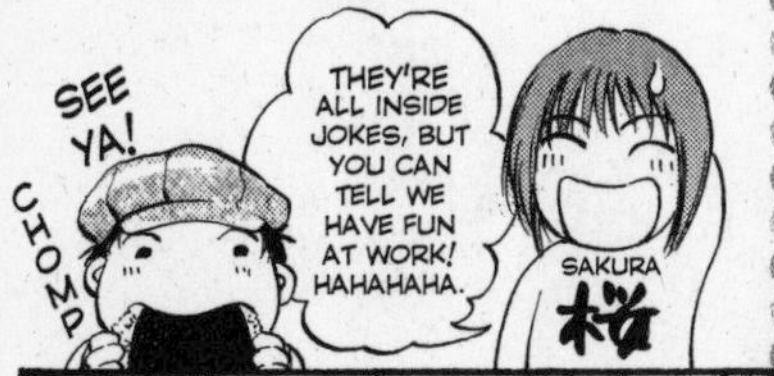
THEY'RE ALL INSIDE JOKES, BUT YOU CAN TELL WE HAVE FUN AT WORK! HAHAHAHA.
SAKURA
桜
SEE YA!
CHOMP

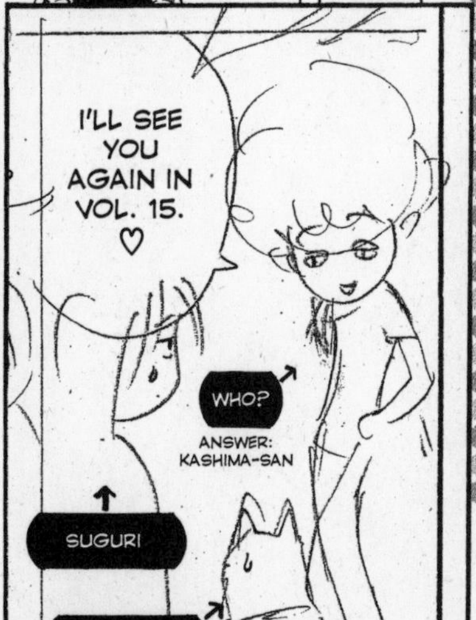
I'LL SEE YOU AGAIN IN VOL. 15. ♡
WHO?
ANSWER: KASHIMA-SAN
SUGURI
HINOMARU

STORYBOARD OF A SCENE IN VOL. 15. WHO IS ON THE RIGHT? (LAUGH)

(1) VOL. 14, CH. 143, P. 35, PANEL 5. (2) VOL. 14, CH. 145, P. 70, PANEL 5. (3) VOL. 14, CH. 145, P. 75, PANEL 5.

ANSWERS TO THE SCENES ON PAGE 80
(A) VOL. 6, CH. 57, P. 90, PANEL 5. (B) VOL. 13, CH. 133, P. 52, PANEL 4. (C) VOL. 8, CH. 78, P. 24, PANEL 3. (D) VOL. 6, CH. 58, P. 113, PANEL 5. (E) VOL. 11, CH. 111, P. 47, PANEL 5.

CHAPTER 150:
OPERATION: FIND A FOSTER HOME!

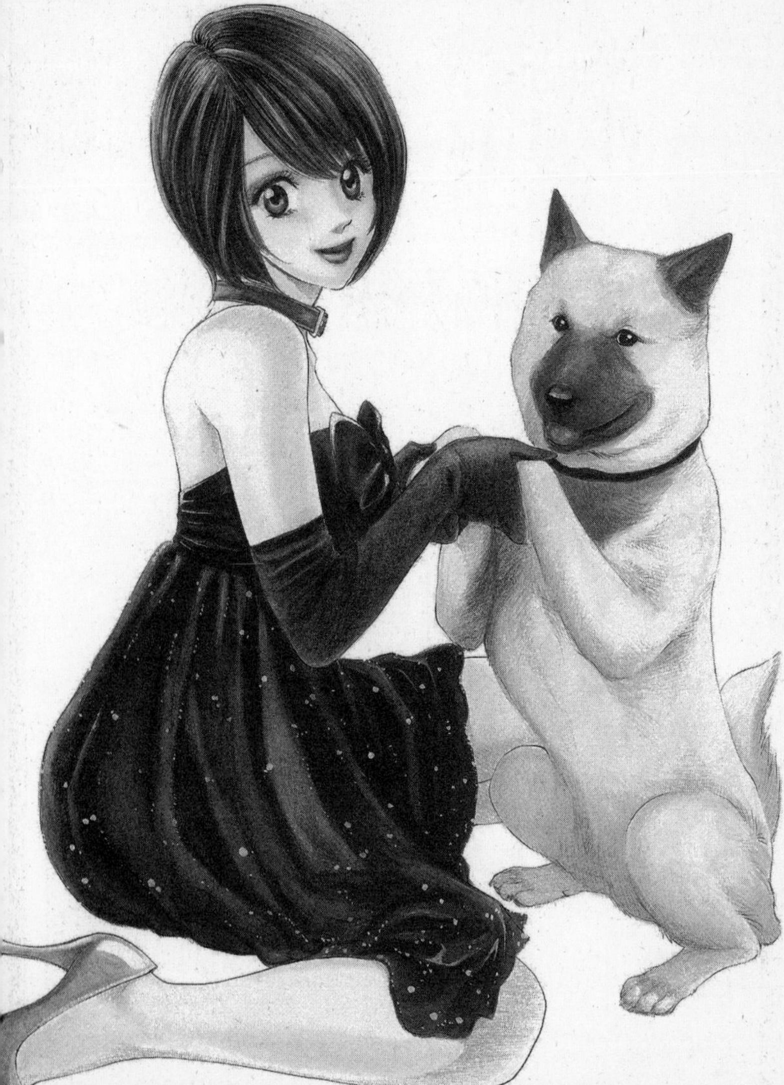

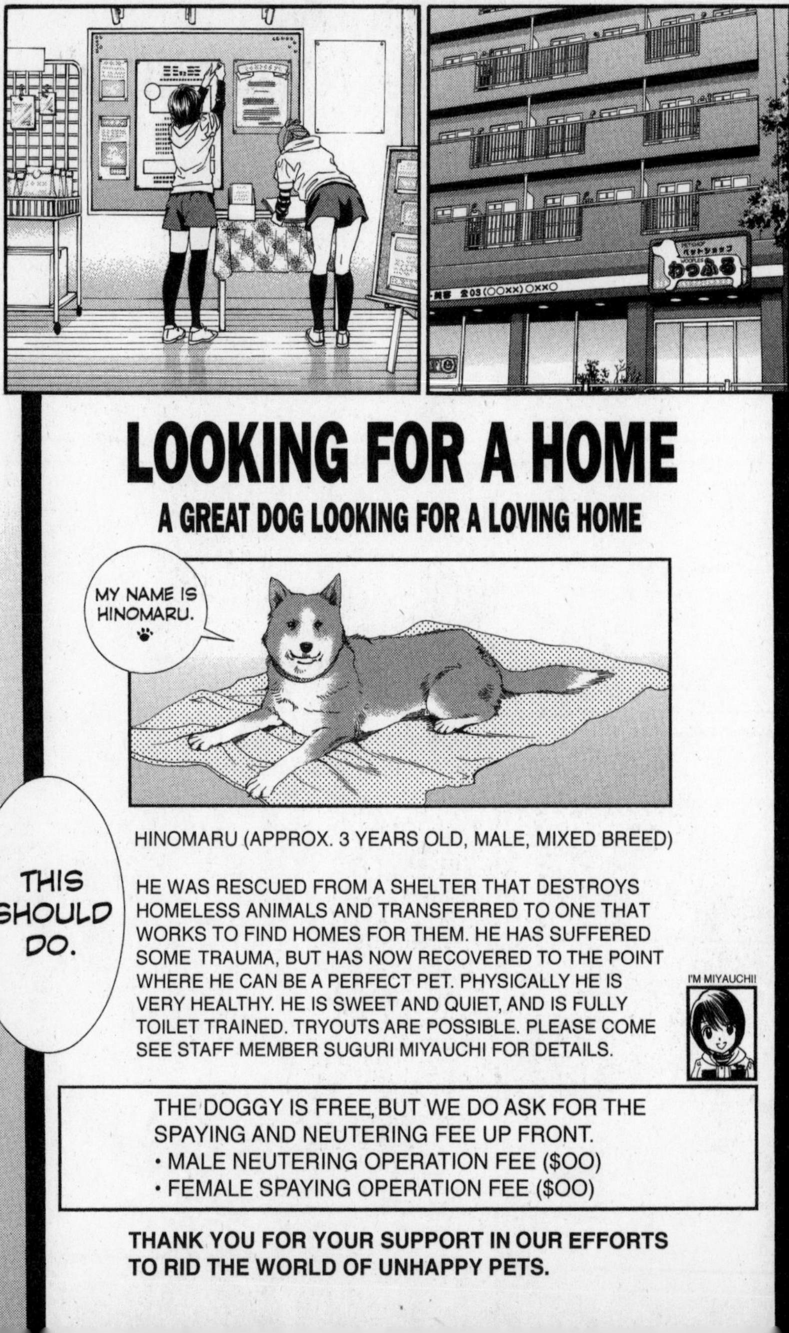
LOOKING FOR A HOME
A GREAT DOG LOOKING FOR A LOVING HOME
MY NAME IS HINOMARU.
HINOMARU (APPROX. 3 YEARS OLD, MALE, MIXED BREED)
HE WAS RESCUED FROM A SHELTER THAT DESTROYS HOMELESS ANIMALS AND TRANSFERRED TO ONE THAT WORKS TO FIND HOMES FOR THEM. HE HAS SUFFERED SOME TRAUMA, BUT HAS NOW RECOVERED TO THE POINT WHERE HE CAN BE A PERFECT PET. PHYSICALLY HE IS VERY HEALTHY. HE IS SWEET AND QUIET, AND IS FULLY TOILET TRAINED. TRYOUTS ARE POSSIBLE. PLEASE COME SEE STAFF MEMBER SUGURI MIYAUCHI FOR DETAILS.
I'M MIYAUCHI!
THE DOGGY IS FREE, BUT WE DO ASK FOR THE SPAYING AND NEUTERING FEE UP FRONT.
• MALE NEUTERING OPERATION FEE ($OO)
• FEMALE SPAYING OPERATION FEE ($OO)
THANK YOU FOR YOUR SUPPORT IN OUR EFFORTS TO RID THE WORLD OF UNHAPPY PETS.
THIS SHOULD DO.

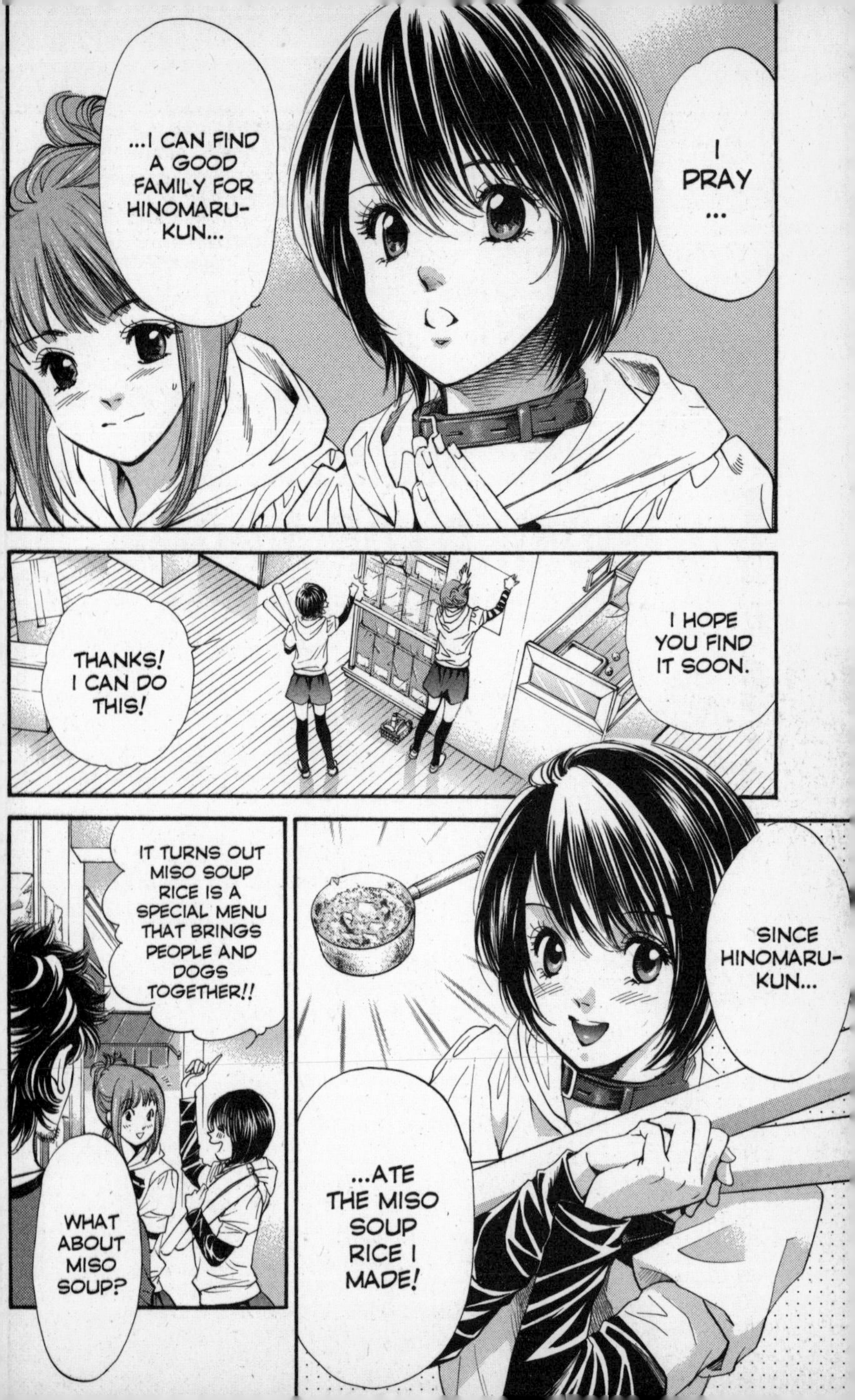
I PRAY...
...I CAN FIND A GOOD FAMILY FOR HINOMARU-KUN...
I HOPE YOU FIND IT SOON.
THANKS! I CAN DO THIS!
SINCE HINOMARU-KUN...
...ATE THE MISO SOUP RICE I MADE!
IT TURNS OUT MISO SOUP RICE IS A SPECIAL MENU THAT BRINGS PEOPLE AND DOGS TOGETHER!!
WHAT ABOUT MISO SOUP?

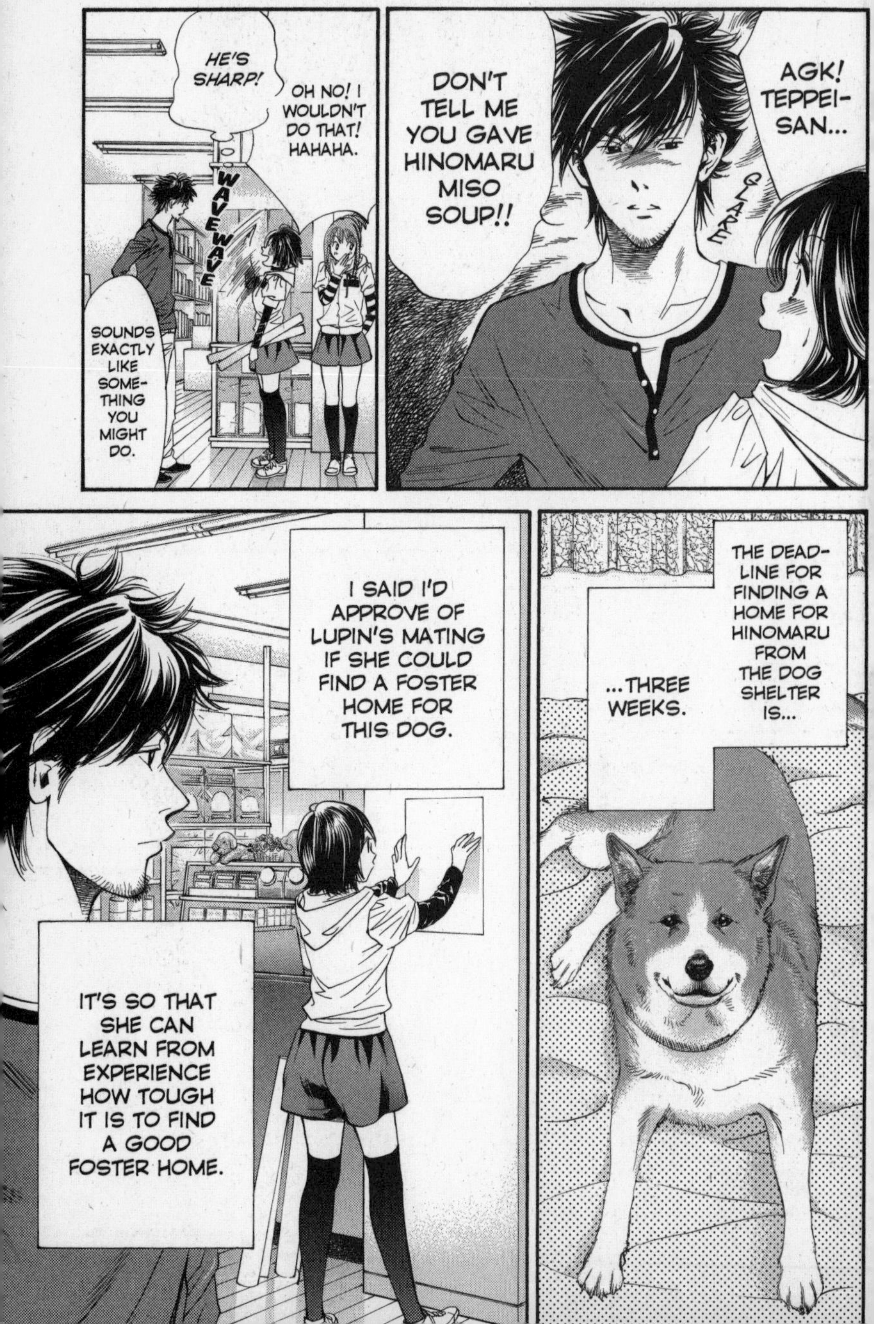
AGK! TEPPEI-SAN...
GLARE
DON'T TELL ME YOU GAVE HINOMARU MISO SOUP!!
OH NO! I WOULDN'T DO THAT! HAHAHA.
HE'S SHARP!
WAVE WAVE
SOUNDS EXACTLY LIKE SOME-THING YOU MIGHT DO.
THE DEAD-LINE FOR FINDING A HOME FOR HINOMARU FROM THE DOG SHELTER IS...
...THREE WEEKS.
I SAID I'D APPROVE OF LUPIN'S MATING IF SHE COULD FIND A FOSTER HOME FOR THIS DOG.
IT'S SO THAT SHE CAN LEARN FROM EXPERIENCE HOW TOUGH IT IS TO FIND A GOOD FOSTER HOME.

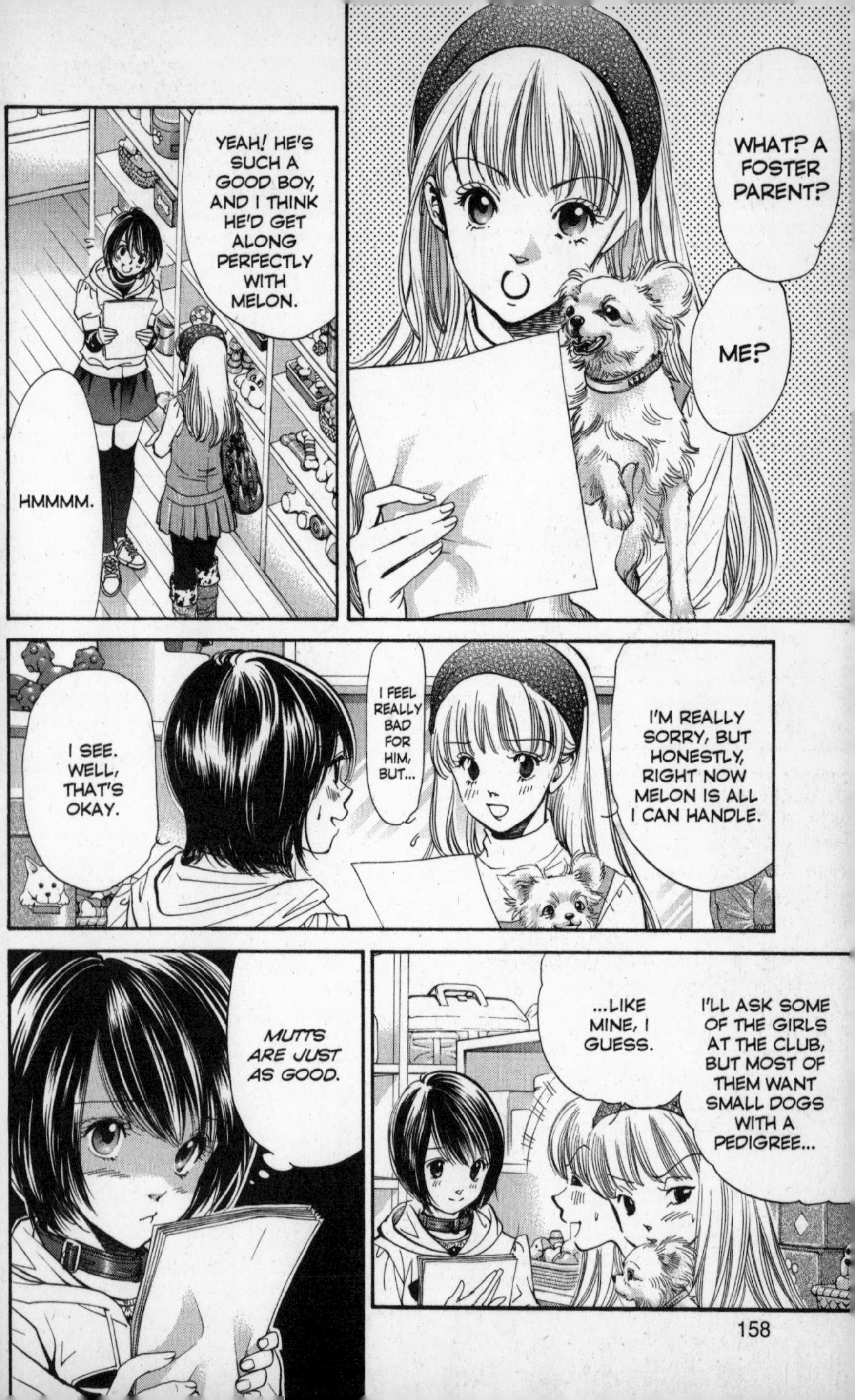
WHAT? A FOSTER PARENT?
ME?
YEAH! HE'S SUCH A GOOD BOY, AND I THINK HE'D GET ALONG PERFECTLY WITH MELON.
HMMMM.
I'M REALLY SORRY, BUT HONESTLY, RIGHT NOW MELON IS ALL I CAN HANDLE.
I FEEL REALLY BAD FOR HIM, BUT...
I SEE. WELL, THAT'S OKAY.
I'LL ASK SOME OF THE GIRLS AT THE CLUB, BUT MOST OF THEM WANT SMALL DOGS WITH A PEDIGREE...
...LIKE MINE, I GUESS.
MUTTS ARE JUST AS GOOD.

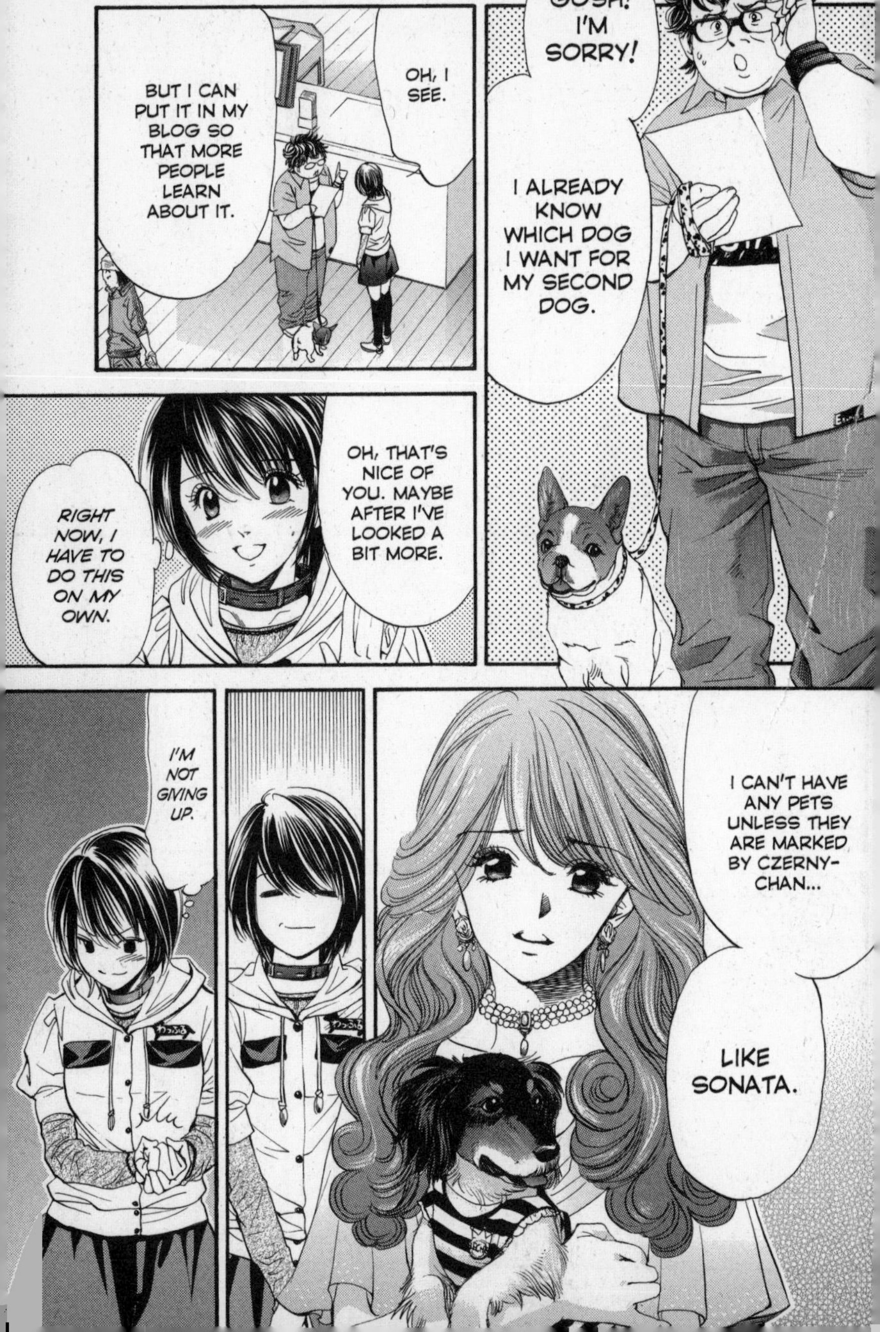
GOSH! I'M SORRY!
I ALREADY KNOW WHICH DOG I WANT FOR MY SECOND DOG.
OH, I SEE.
BUT I CAN PUT IT IN MY BLOG SO THAT MORE PEOPLE LEARN ABOUT IT.
OH, THAT'S NICE OF YOU. MAYBE AFTER I'VE LOOKED A BIT MORE.
RIGHT NOW, I HAVE TO DO THIS ON MY OWN.
I CAN'T HAVE ANY PETS UNLESS THEY ARE MARKED BY CZERNY-CHAN...
LIKE SONATA.
I'M NOT GIVING UP.

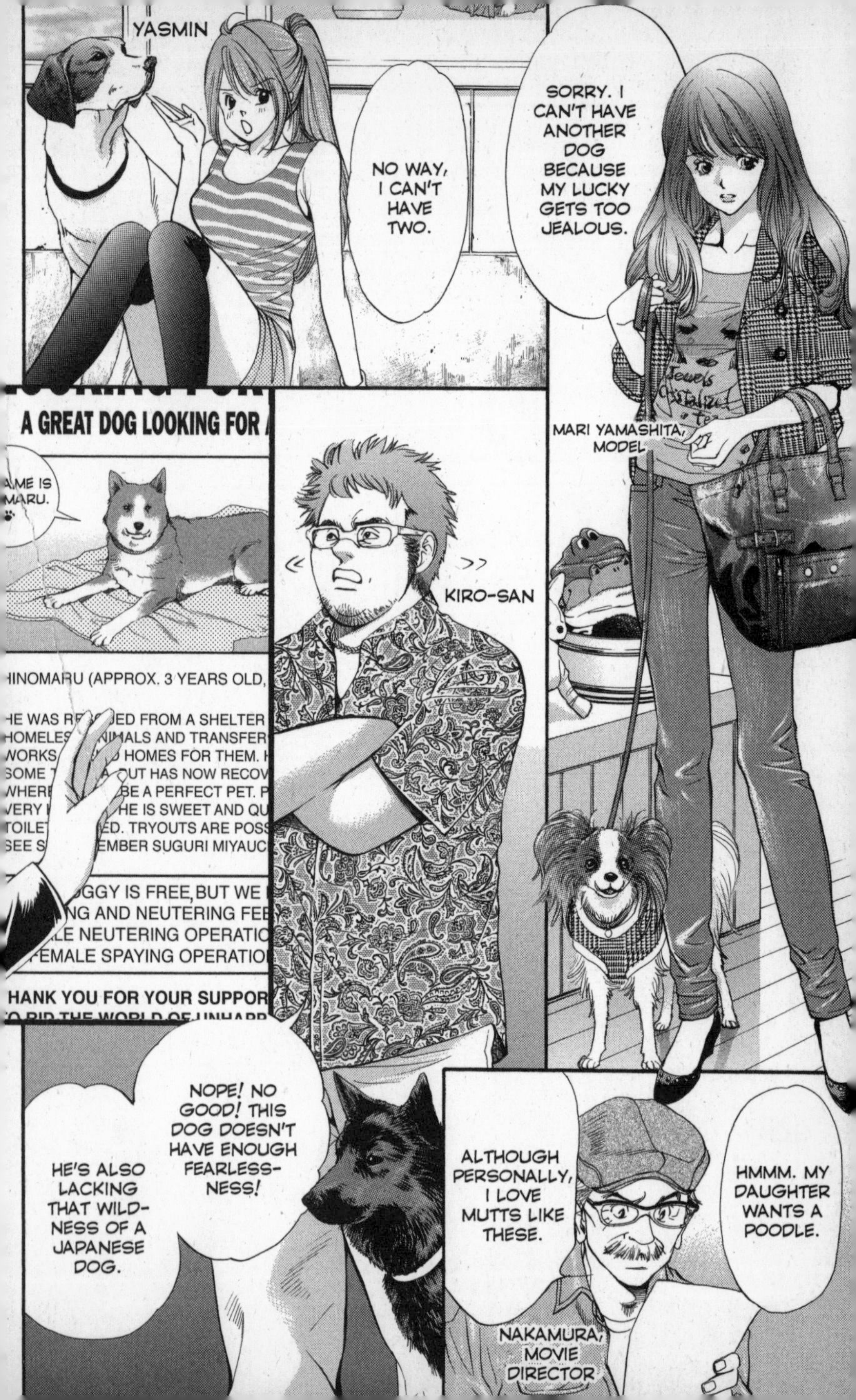
SORRY. I CAN'T HAVE ANOTHER DOG BECAUSE MY LUCKY GETS TOO JEALOUS.
MARI YAMASHITA, MODEL
YASMIN
NO WAY, I CAN'T HAVE TWO.
KIRO-SAN
A GREAT DOG LOOKING FOR
AME IS
MARU.
HINOMARU (APPROX. 3 YEARS OLD,
HE WAS RE ED FROM A SHELTER
HOMELES NIMALS AND TRANSFER
WORKS HOMES FOR THEM. H
SOME T UT HAS NOW RECOV
WHERE BE A PERFECT PET. P
VERY HE IS SWEET AND QU
TOILET ED. TRYOUTS ARE POSS
SEE S EMBER SUGURI MIYAUC
OGGY IS FREE, BUT WE
NG AND NEUTERING FEE
LE NEUTERING OPERATIO
FEMALE SPAYING OPERATIO
HANK YOU FOR YOUR SUPPOR
HMMM. MY DAUGHTER WANTS A POODLE.
ALTHOUGH PERSONALLY, I LOVE MUTTS LIKE THESE.
NAKAMURA, MOVIE DIRECTOR
NOPE! NO GOOD! THIS DOG DOESN'T HAVE ENOUGH FEARLESS-NESS!
HE'S ALSO LACKING THAT WILD-NESS OF A JAPANESE DOG.

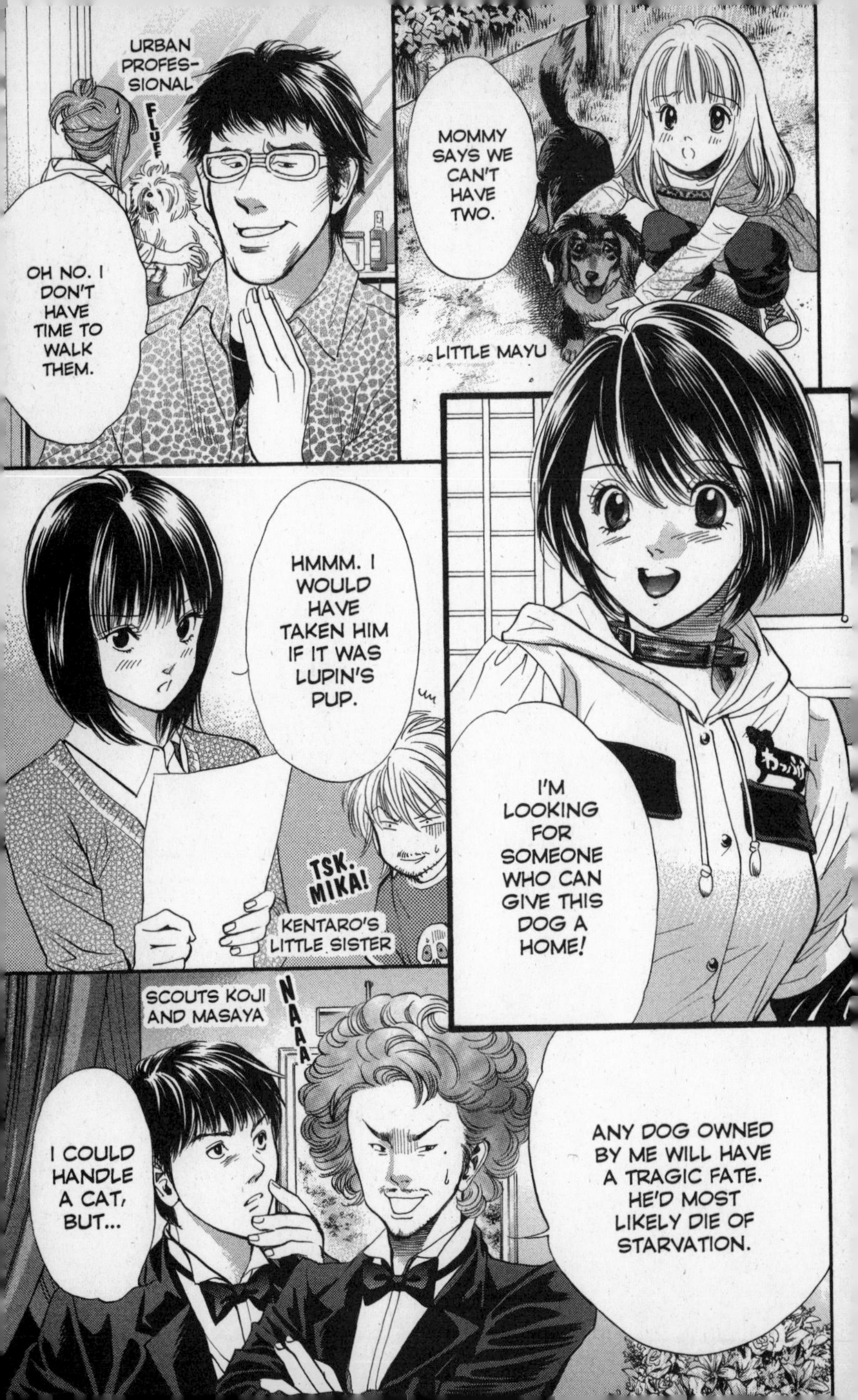
MOMMY SAYS WE CAN'T HAVE TWO.
LITTLE MAYU
URBAN PROFESSIONAL
FLUFF
OH NO. I DON'T HAVE TIME TO WALK THEM.
I'M LOOKING FOR SOMEONE WHO CAN GIVE THIS DOG A HOME!
HMMM. I WOULD HAVE TAKEN HIM IF IT WAS LUPIN'S PUP.
TSK. MIKA!
KENTARO'S LITTLE SISTER
ANY DOG OWNED BY ME WILL HAVE A TRAGIC FATE. HE'D MOST LIKELY DIE OF STARVATION.
SCOUTS KOJI AND MASAYA
NAAA
I COULD HANDLE A CAT, BUT...

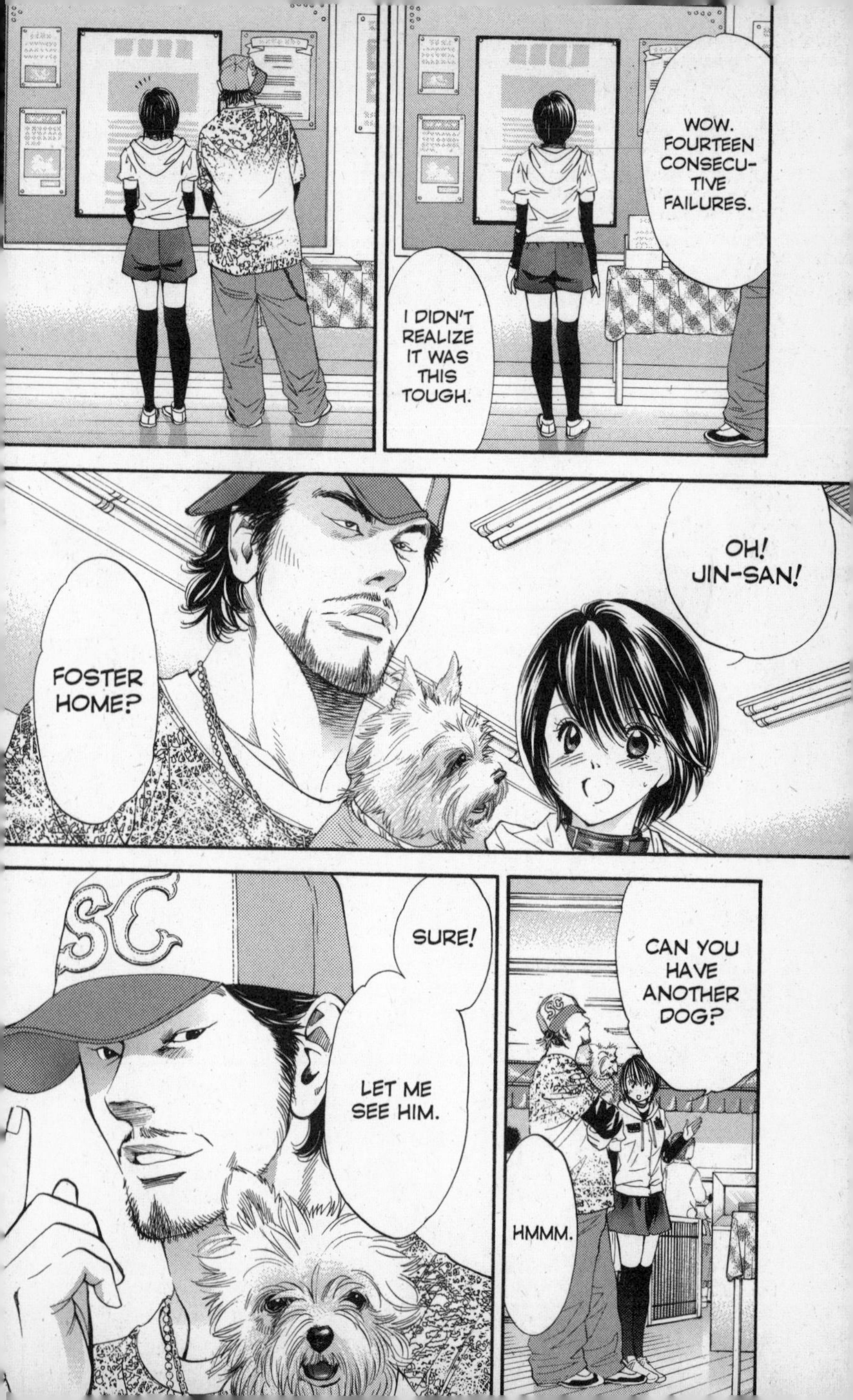
WOW. FOURTEEN CONSECU-TIVE FAILURES.
I DIDN'T REALIZE IT WAS THIS TOUGH.
OH! JIN-SAN!
FOSTER HOME?
CAN YOU HAVE ANOTHER DOG?
HMMM.
SURE!
LET ME SEE HIM.

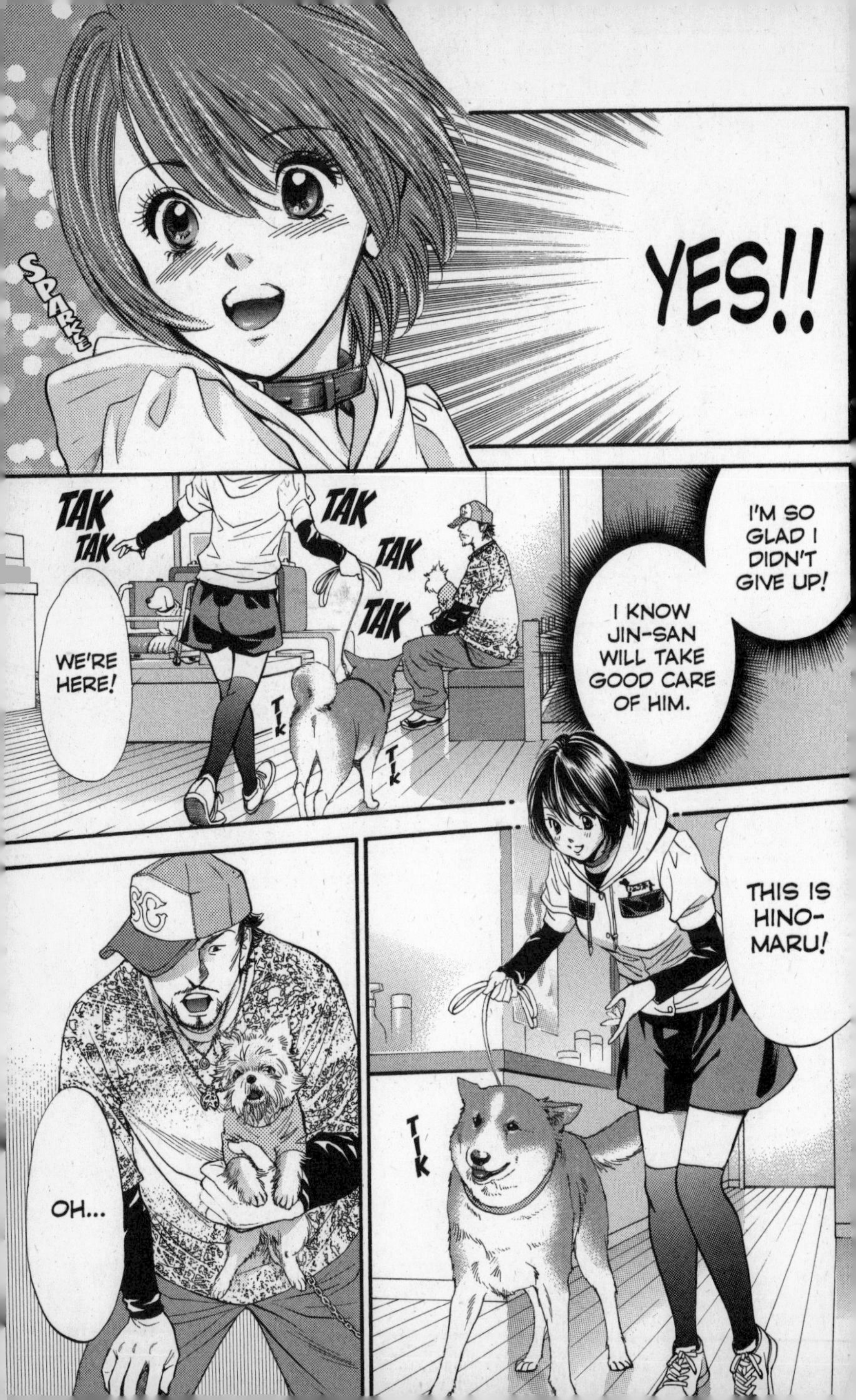
YES!!
SPARKLE
I'M SO GLAD I DIDN'T GIVE UP!
I KNOW JIN-SAN WILL TAKE GOOD CARE OF HIM.
TAK
TAK
TAK
TAK
TAK
WE'RE HERE!
TIK
TIK
THIS IS HINO-MARU!
TIK
OH...

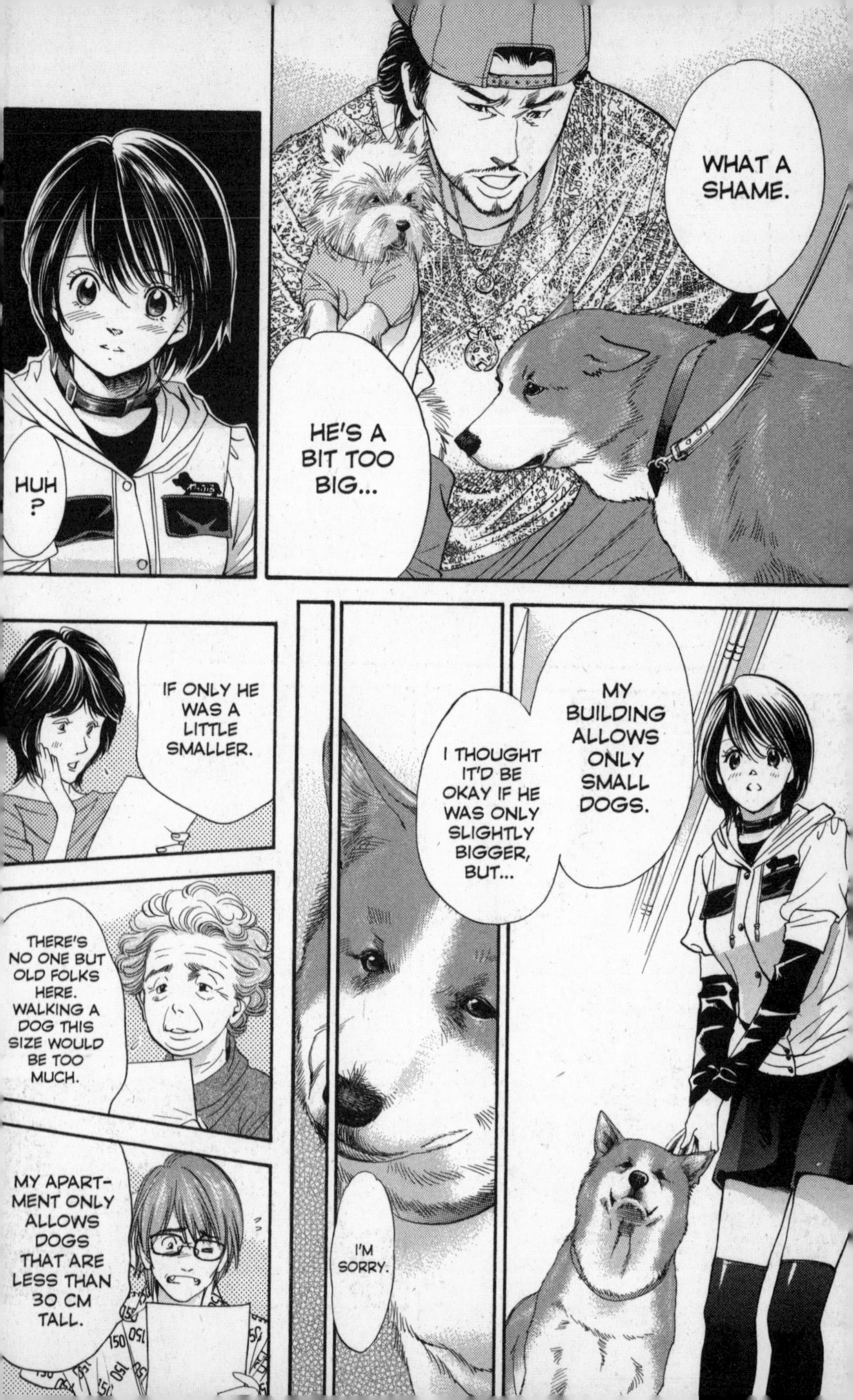
WHAT A SHAME.
HE'S A BIT TOO BIG...
HUH?
MY BUILDING ALLOWS ONLY SMALL DOGS.
I THOUGHT IT'D BE OKAY IF HE WAS ONLY SLIGHTLY BIGGER, BUT...
I'M SORRY.
IF ONLY HE WAS A LITTLE SMALLER.
THERE'S NO ONE BUT OLD FOLKS HERE. WALKING A DOG THIS SIZE WOULD BE TOO MUCH.
MY APART-MENT ONLY ALLOWS DOGS THAT ARE LESS THAN 30 CM TALL.

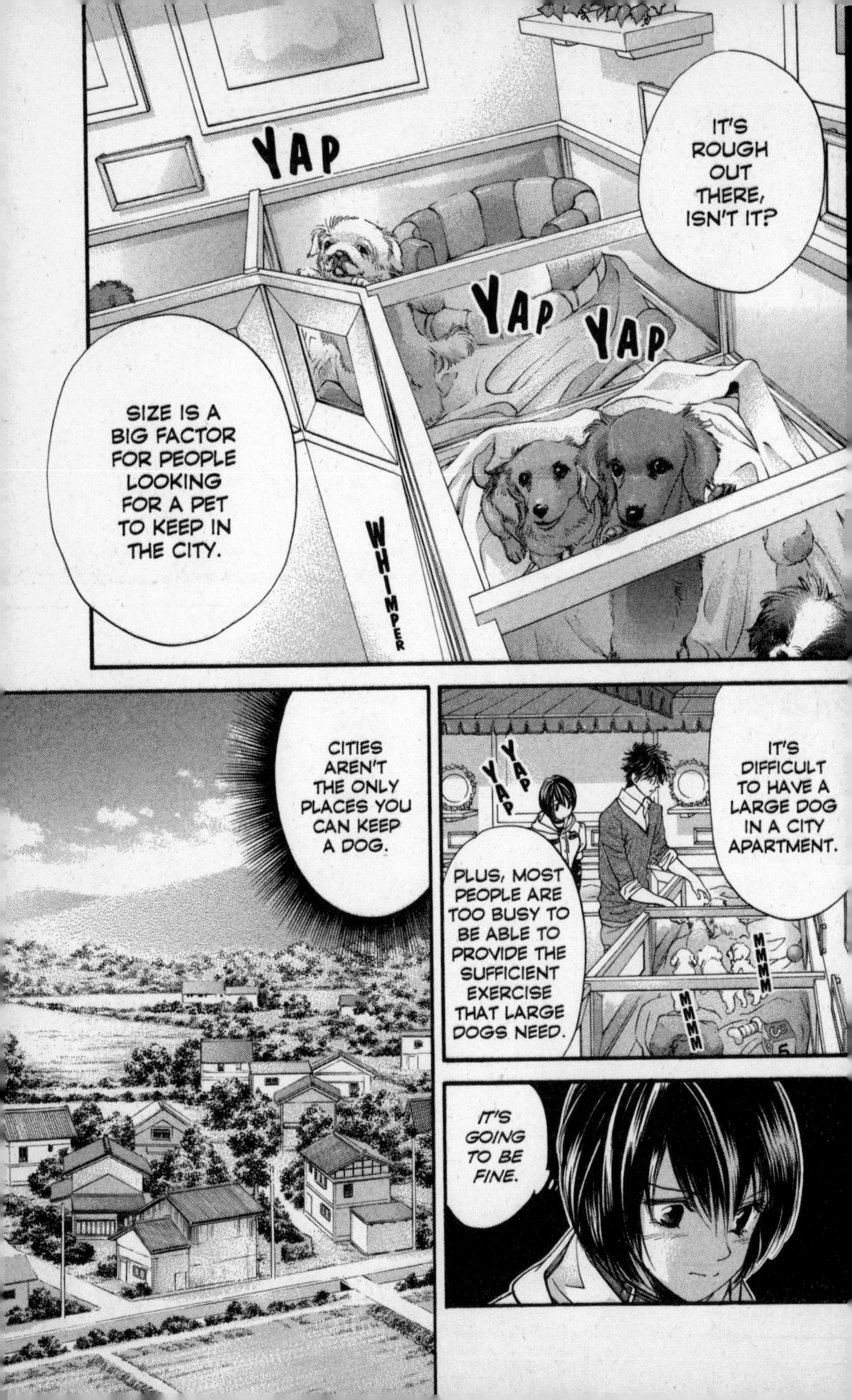
IT'S ROUGH OUT THERE, ISN'T IT?
YAP
YAP
YAP
SIZE IS A BIG FACTOR FOR PEOPLE LOOKING FOR A PET TO KEEP IN THE CITY.
WHIMPER
IT'S DIFFICULT TO HAVE A LARGE DOG IN A CITY APARTMENT.
YAP
YAP
PLUS, MOST PEOPLE ARE TOO BUSY TO BE ABLE TO PROVIDE THE SUFFICIENT EXERCISE THAT LARGE DOGS NEED.
MMMM
MMMM
IT'S GOING TO BE FINE.
CITIES AREN'T THE ONLY PLACES YOU CAN KEEP A DOG.

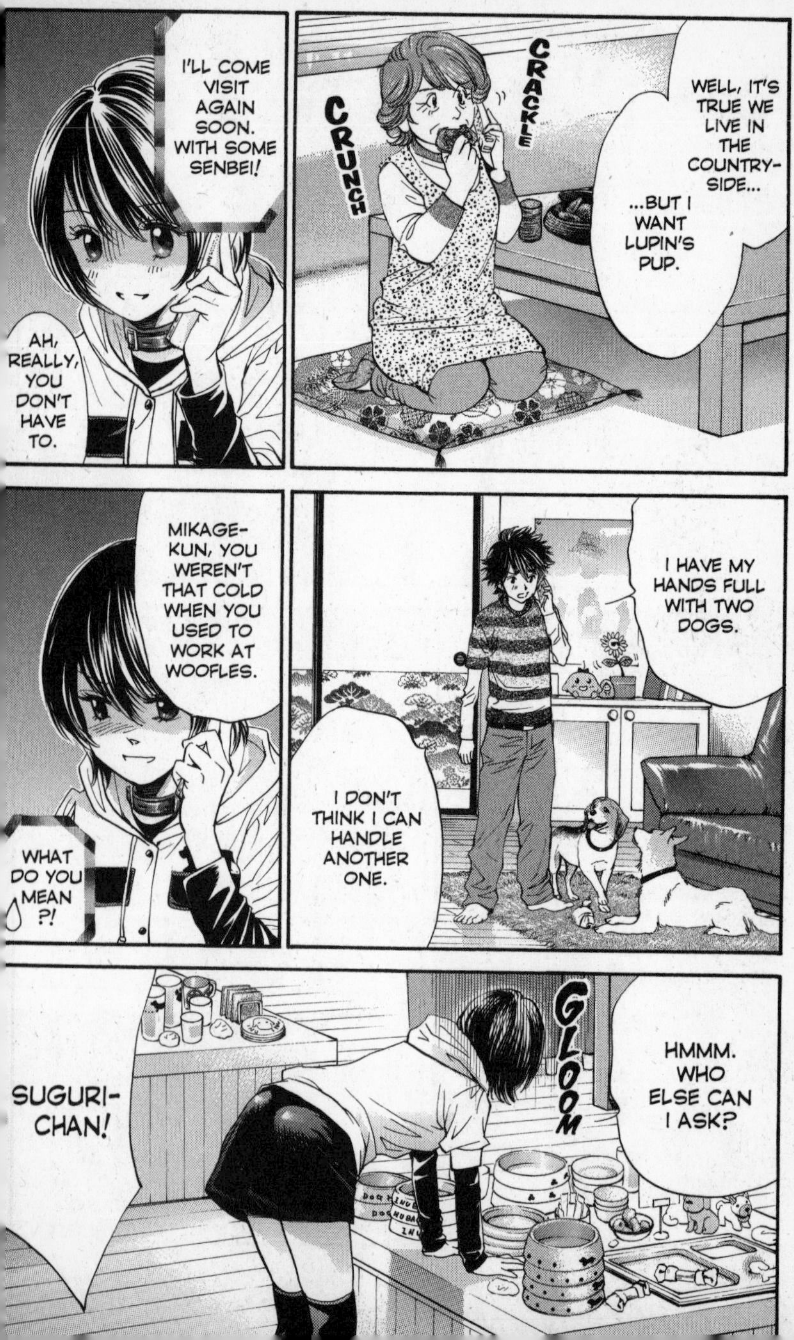

CRACKLE
CRUNCH
WELL, IT'S TRUE WE LIVE IN THE COUNTRY-SIDE...
...BUT I WANT LUPIN'S PUP.
I'LL COME VISIT AGAIN SOON. WITH SOME SENBEI!
AH, REALLY, YOU DON'T HAVE TO.
I HAVE MY HANDS FULL WITH TWO DOGS.
I DON'T THINK I CAN HANDLE ANOTHER ONE.
MIKAGE-KUN, YOU WEREN'T THAT COLD WHEN YOU USED TO WORK AT WOOFLES.
WHAT DO YOU MEAN?!
HMMM. WHO ELSE CAN I ASK?
GLOOM
SUGURI-CHAN!

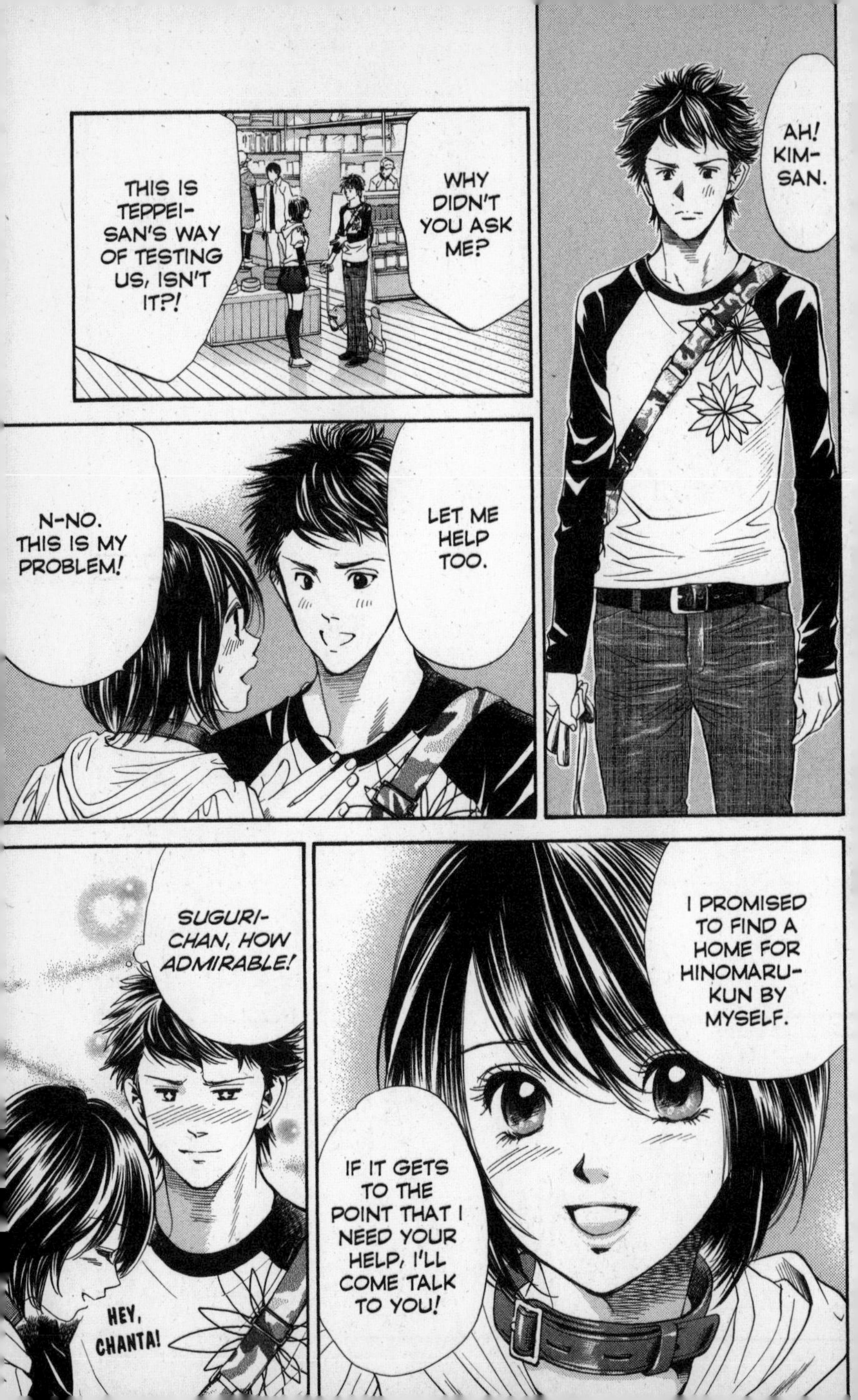
AH! KIM-SAN.
WHY DIDN'T YOU ASK ME?
THIS IS TEPPEI-SAN'S WAY OF TESTING US, ISN'T IT?!
LET ME HELP TOO.
N-NO. THIS IS MY PROBLEM!
I PROMISED TO FIND A HOME FOR HINOMARU-KUN BY MYSELF.
IF IT GETS TO THE POINT THAT I NEED YOUR HELP, I'LL COME TALK TO YOU!
SUGURI-CHAN, HOW ADMIRABLE!
HEY, CHANTA!

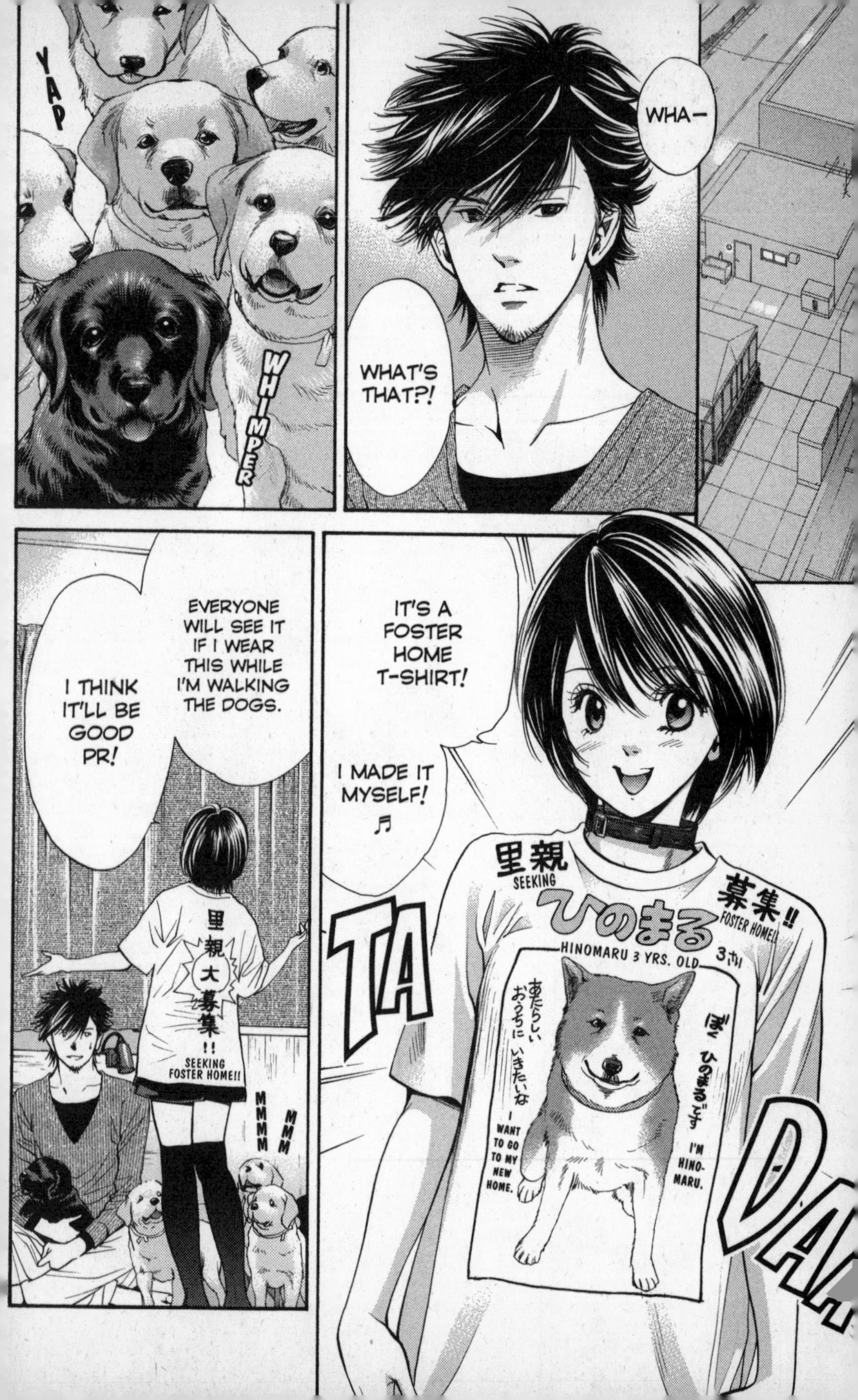
WHA—
WHAT'S THAT?!
YAP
WHIMPER
IT'S A FOSTER HOME T-SHIRT!
I MADE IT MYSELF! ♫
TA
DA
里親 SEEKING
ひのまる
募集!! FOSTER HOME!!
HINOMARU 3 YRS. OLD
3さい
ぼく ひのまるです
I'M HINOMARU.
あたらしい おうちに いきたいな
I WANT TO GO TO MY NEW HOME.
EVERYONE WILL SEE IT IF I WEAR THIS WHILE I'M WALKING THE DOGS.
I THINK IT'LL BE GOOD PR!
里親大募集!!
SEEKING FOSTER HOME!!
MMMM
MMM

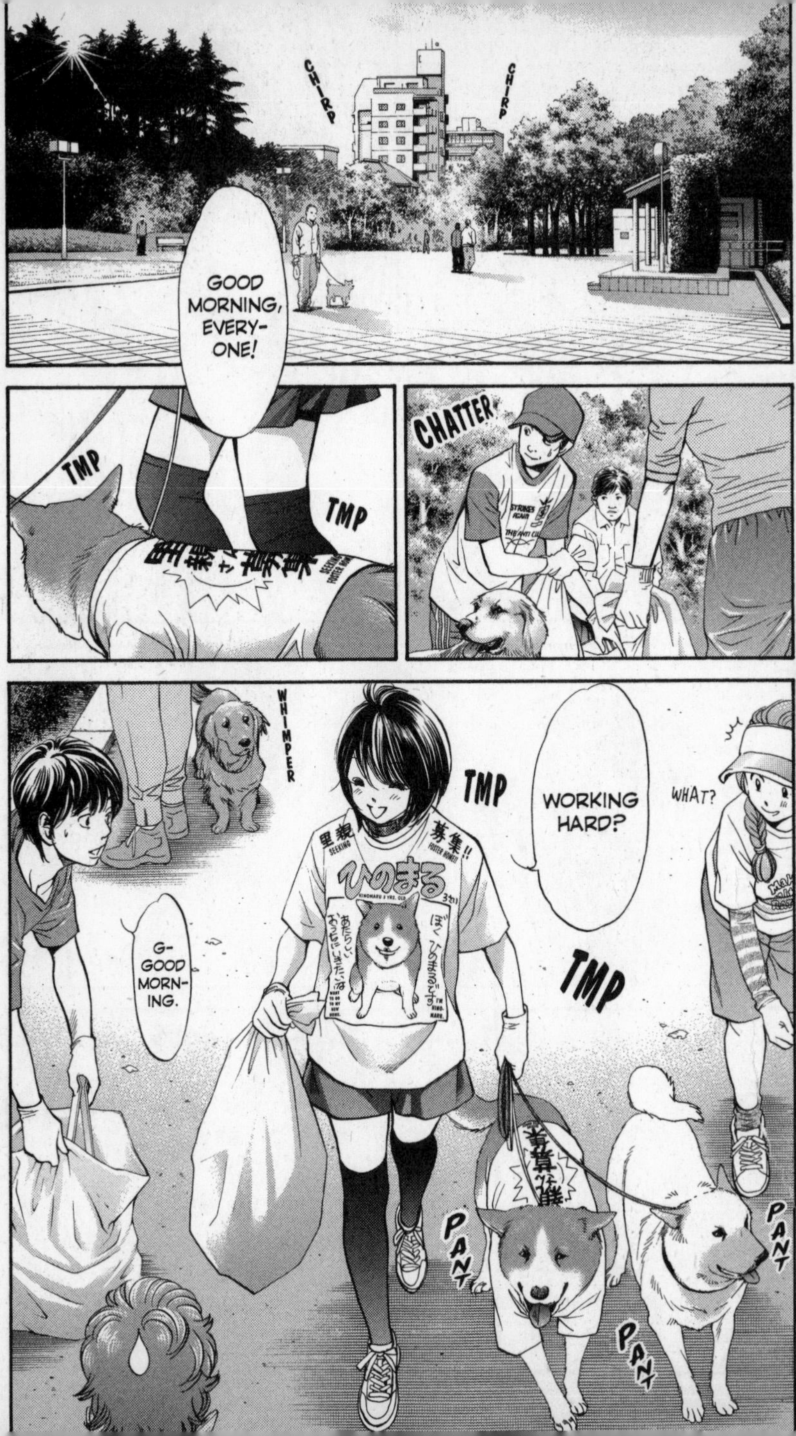
CHIRP
CHIRP
GOOD MORNING, EVERY-ONE!
CHATTER
TMP
TMP
WHAT?
WORKING HARD?
TMP
TMP
WHIMPER
G-GOOD MORN-ING.
PANT
PANT
PANT

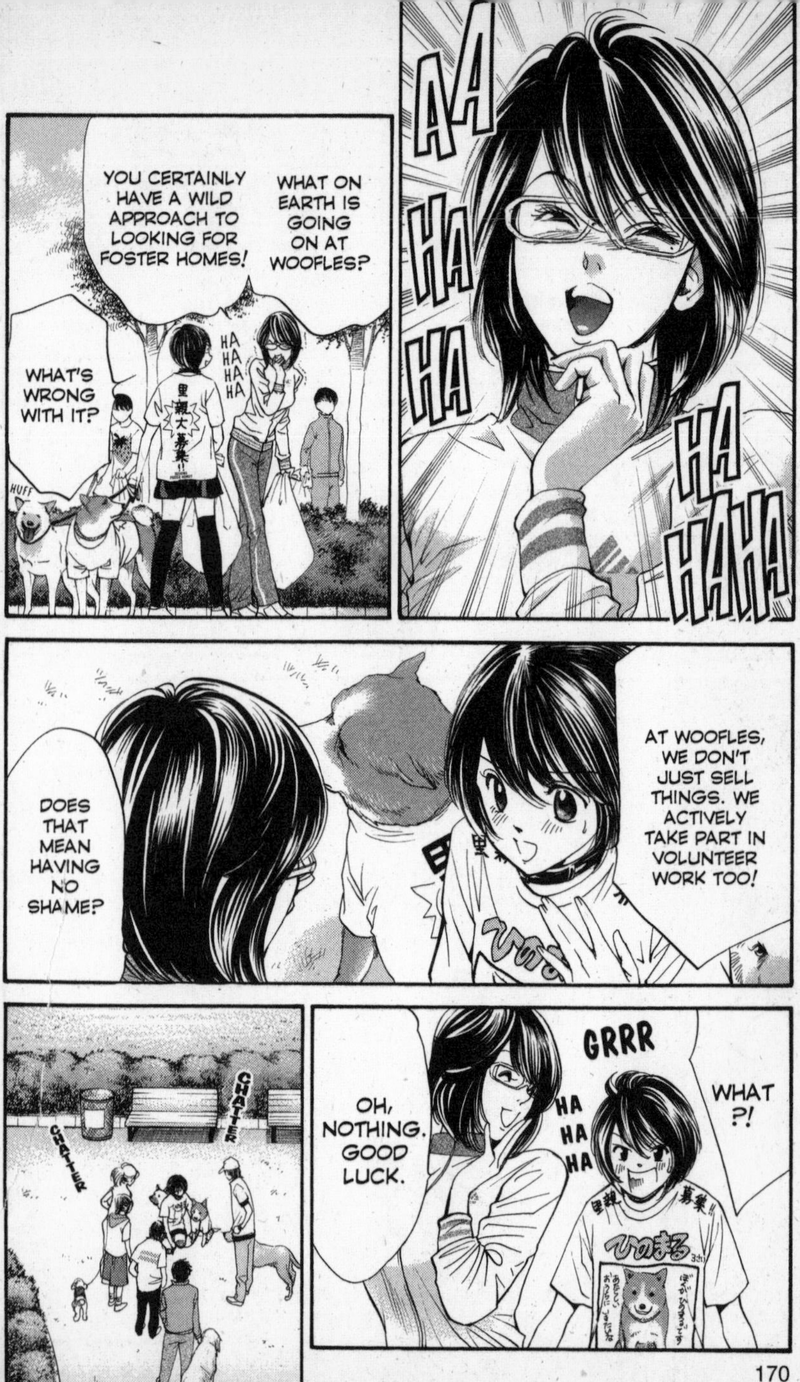
AA
HA
HA
HA
HAHA
WHAT ON EARTH IS GOING ON AT WOOFLES?
YOU CERTAINLY HAVE A WILD APPROACH TO LOOKING FOR FOSTER HOMES!
HA HA HA HA
WHAT'S WRONG WITH IT?
HUFF
AT WOOFLES, WE DON'T JUST SELL THINGS. WE ACTIVELY TAKE PART IN VOLUNTEER WORK TOO!
DOES THAT MEAN HAVING NO SHAME?
WHAT?!
GRRR
HA HA HA
OH, NOTHING. GOOD LUCK.
CHATTER
CHATTER

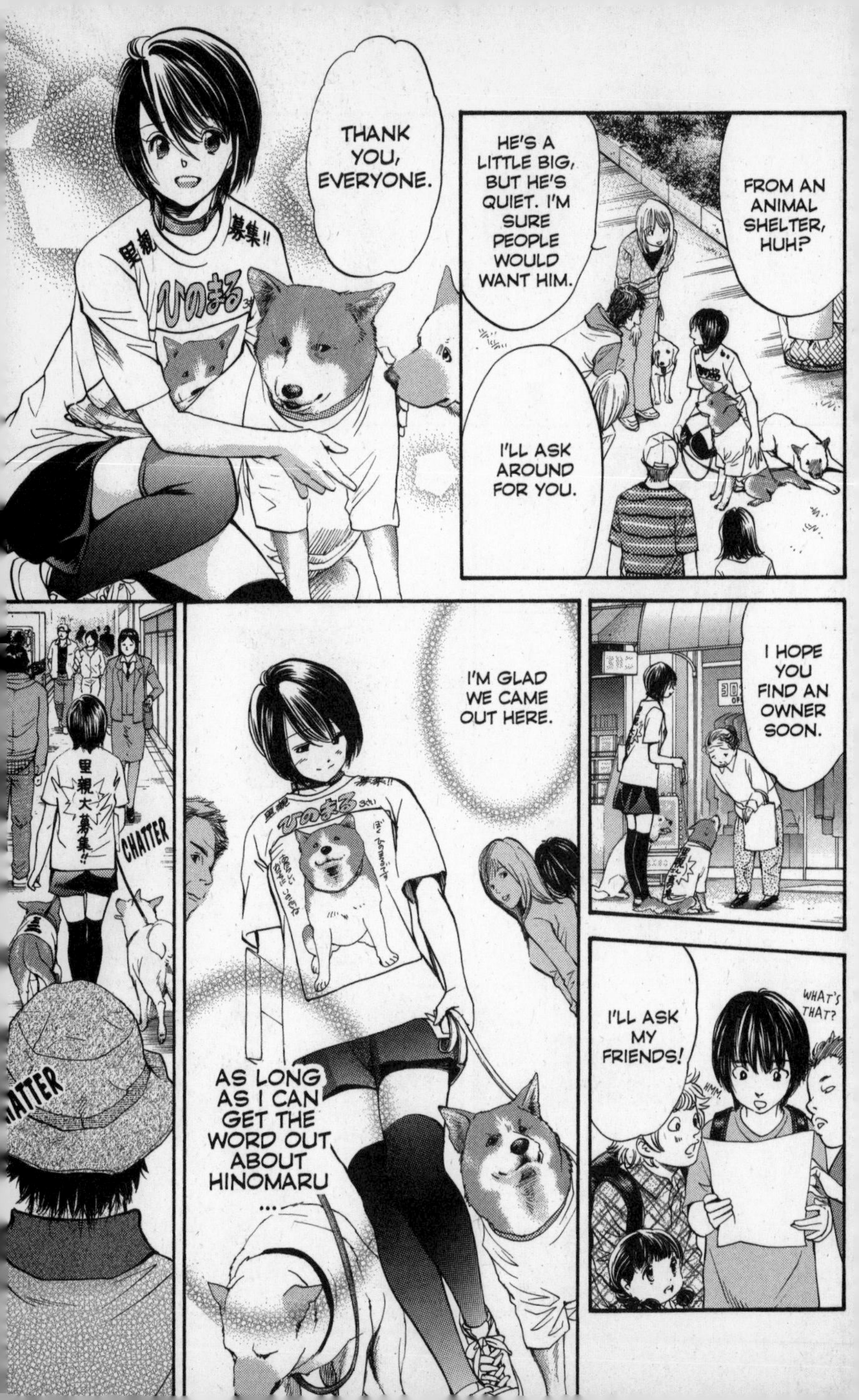
FROM AN ANIMAL SHELTER, HUH?
HE'S A LITTLE BIG, BUT HE'S QUIET. I'M SURE PEOPLE WOULD WANT HIM.
I'LL ASK AROUND FOR YOU.
THANK YOU, EVERYONE.
里親 募集!!
ひのまる
I HOPE YOU FIND AN OWNER SOON.
I'LL ASK MY FRIENDS!
HMM.
WHAT'S THAT?
I'M GLAD WE CAME OUT HERE.
AS LONG AS I CAN GET THE WORD OUT ABOUT HINOMARU...
里親大募集!!
CHATTER

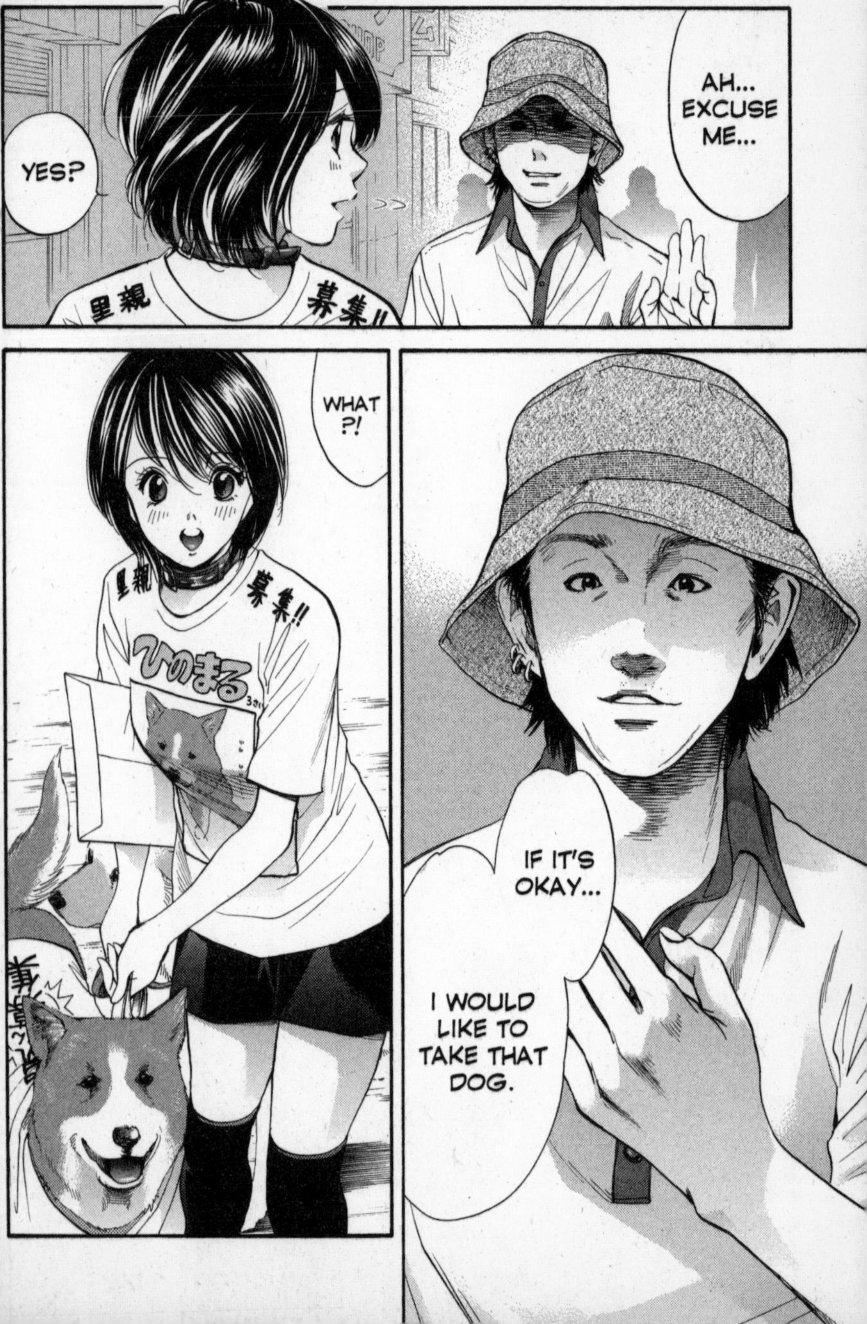
AH... EXCUSE ME...
YES?
里親 募集!!
IF IT'S OKAY...
I WOULD LIKE TO TAKE THAT DOG.
WHAT ?!
里親 募集!!
ひのまる

CHAPTER 151: FOSTER HOME CANDIDATE

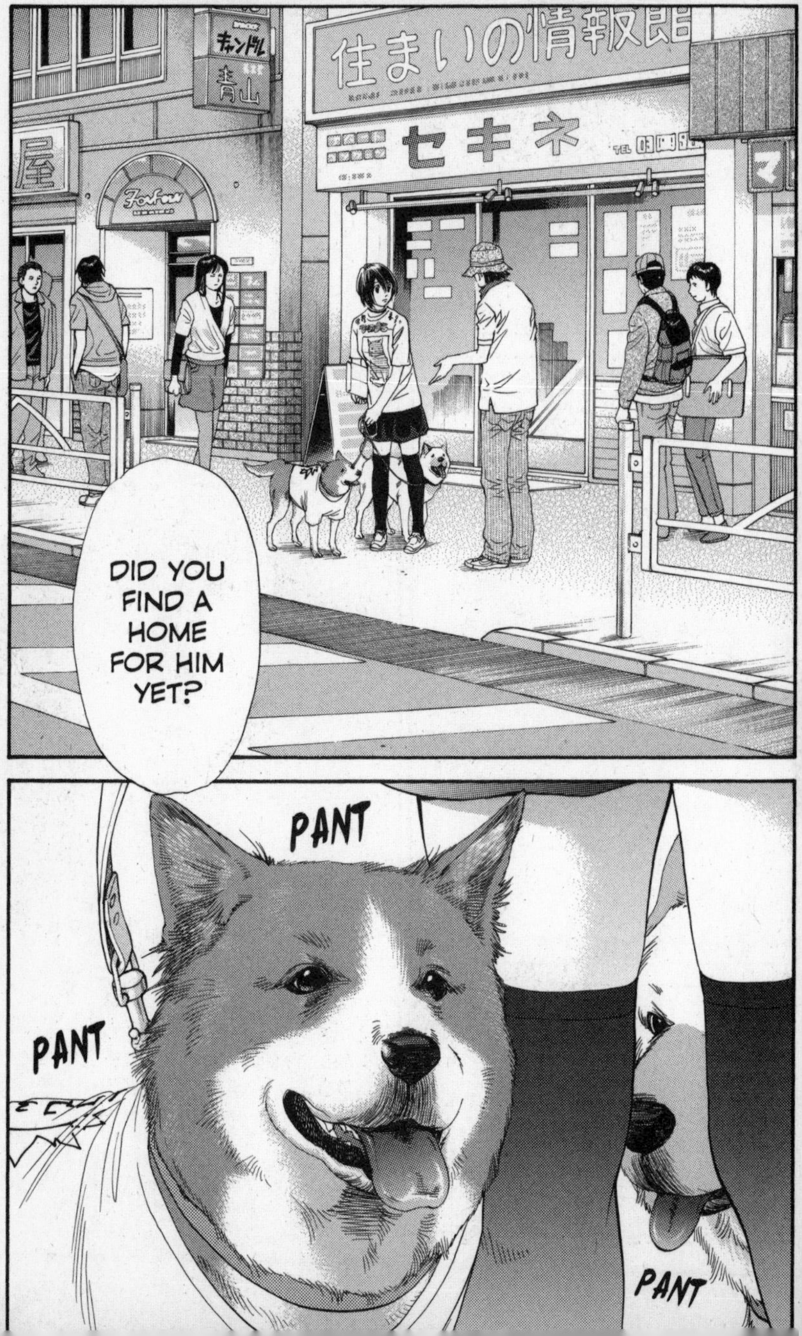
青山
セキネ
DID YOU FIND A HOME FOR HIM YET?
PANT
PANT
PANT

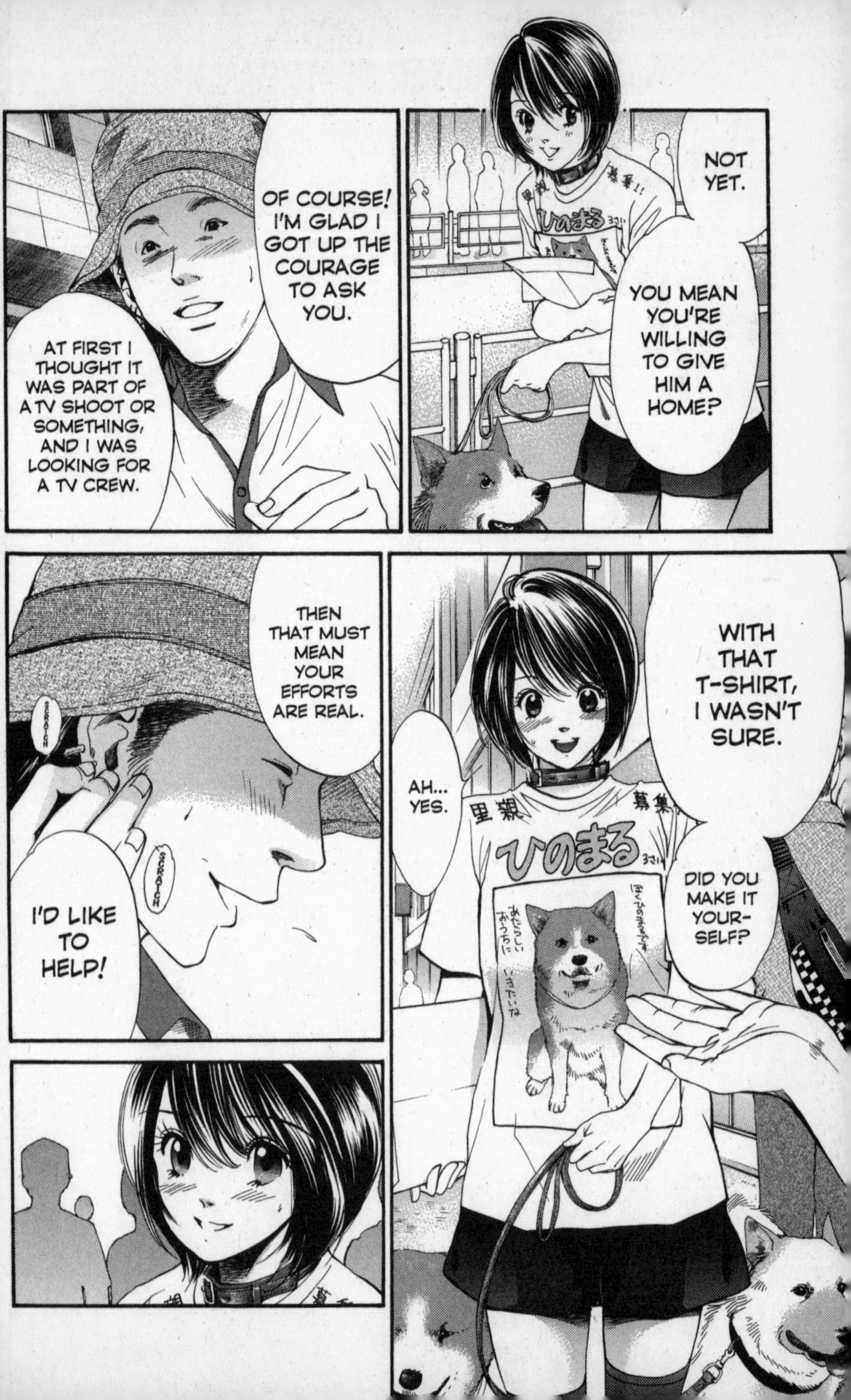
NOT YET.
YOU MEAN YOU'RE WILLING TO GIVE HIM A HOME?
OF COURSE! I'M GLAD I GOT UP THE COURAGE TO ASK YOU.
AT FIRST I THOUGHT IT WAS PART OF A TV SHOOT OR SOMETHING, AND I WAS LOOKING FOR A TV CREW.
WITH THAT T-SHIRT, I WASN'T SURE.
DID YOU MAKE IT YOURSELF?
AH... YES.
里親 募集
ひのまる 3さい
THEN THAT MUST MEAN YOUR EFFORTS ARE REAL.
SCRATCH
SCRATCH
I'D LIKE TO HELP!

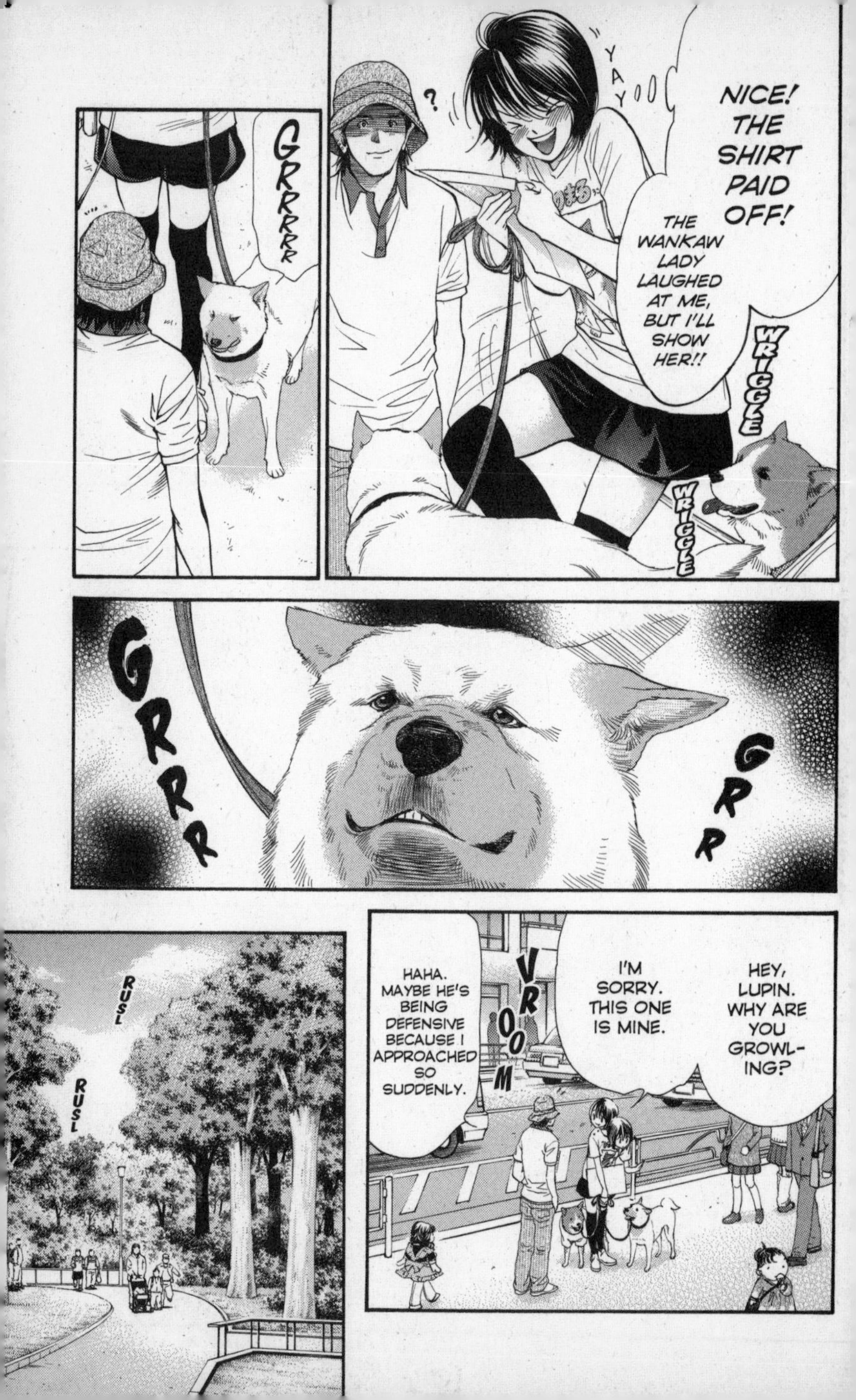

YAY
?
NICE! THE SHIRT PAID OFF!
THE WANKAW LADY LAUGHED AT ME, BUT I'LL SHOW HER!!
WRIGGLE
WRIGGLE
GRRRRRR
GRRR
GRR
HEY, LUPIN. WHY ARE YOU GROWL-ING?
I'M SORRY. THIS ONE IS MINE.
VROOM
HAHA. MAYBE HE'S BEING DEFENSIVE BECAUSE I APPROACHED SO SUDDENLY.
RUSL
RUSL

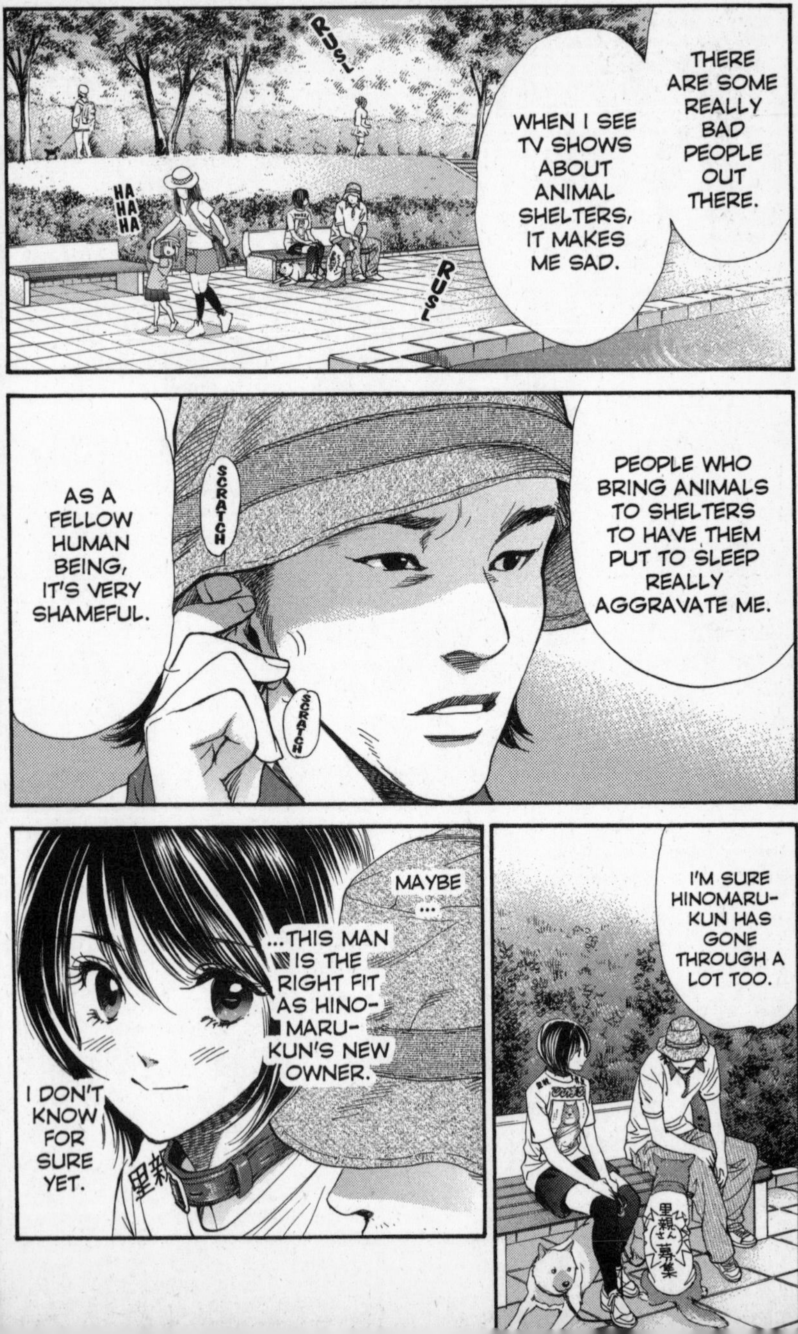
RUSL
THERE ARE SOME REALLY BAD PEOPLE OUT THERE.
WHEN I SEE TV SHOWS ABOUT ANIMAL SHELTERS, IT MAKES ME SAD.
HA HA HA
RUSL
PEOPLE WHO BRING ANIMALS TO SHELTERS TO HAVE THEM PUT TO SLEEP REALLY AGGRAVATE ME.
SCRATCH
AS A FELLOW HUMAN BEING, IT'S VERY SHAMEFUL.
SCRATCH
I'M SURE HINOMARU-KUN HAS GONE THROUGH A LOT TOO.
里親さん募集
MAYBE...
...THIS MAN IS THE RIGHT FIT AS HINO-MARU-KUN'S NEW OWNER.
I DON'T KNOW FOR SURE YET.

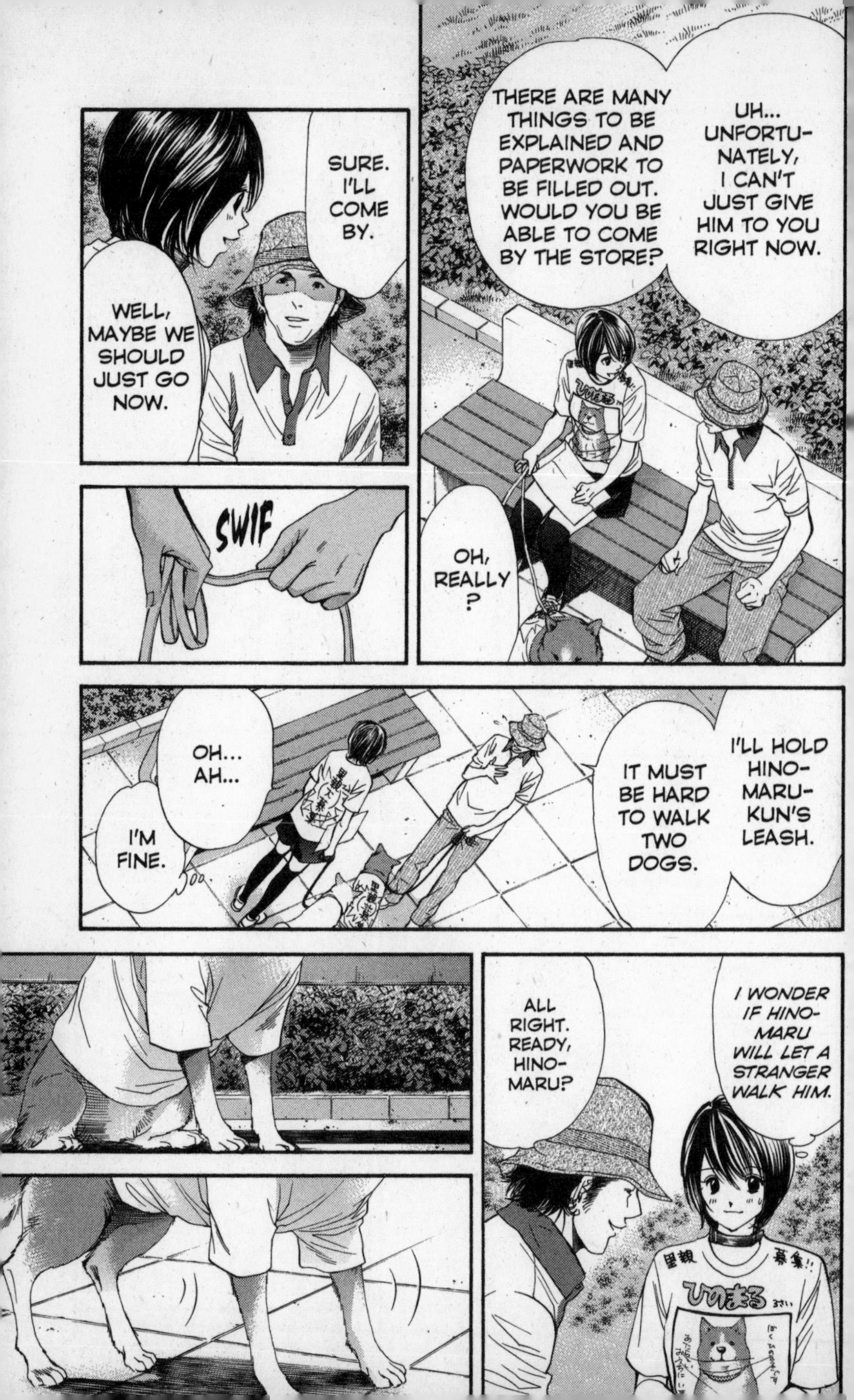
UH... UNFORTU-NATELY, I CAN'T JUST GIVE HIM TO YOU RIGHT NOW.
THERE ARE MANY THINGS TO BE EXPLAINED AND PAPERWORK TO BE FILLED OUT. WOULD YOU BE ABLE TO COME BY THE STORE?
OH, REALLY?
SURE. I'LL COME BY.
WELL, MAYBE WE SHOULD JUST GO NOW.
SWIF
I'LL HOLD HINO-MARU-KUN'S LEASH.
IT MUST BE HARD TO WALK TWO DOGS.
OH... AH...
I'M FINE.
I WONDER IF HINO-MARU WILL LET A STRANGER WALK HIM.
ALL RIGHT. READY, HINO-MARU?

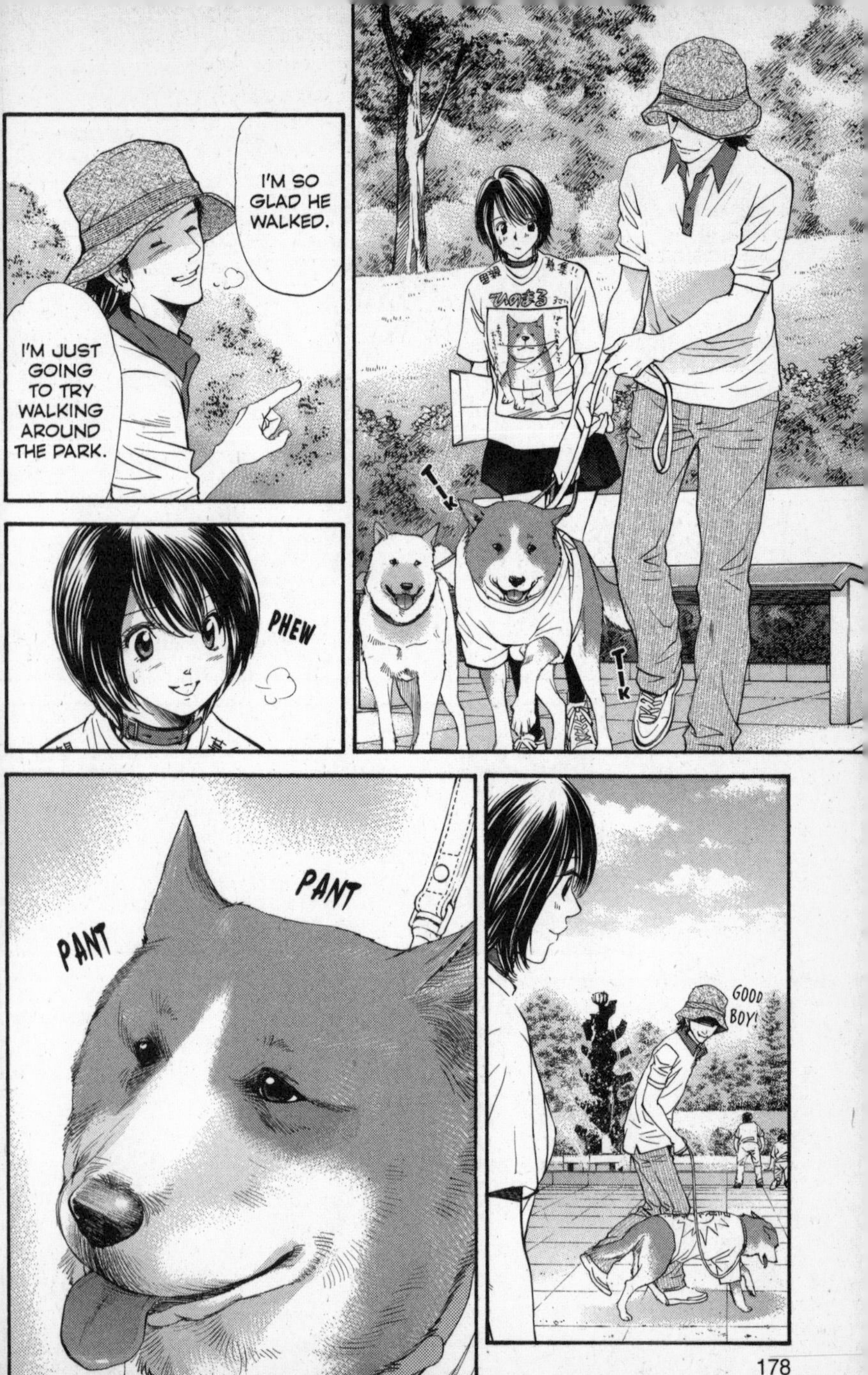
TIK
TIK
I'M SO GLAD HE WALKED.
I'M JUST GOING TO TRY WALKING AROUND THE PARK.
PHEW
GOOD BOY!
PANT
PANT

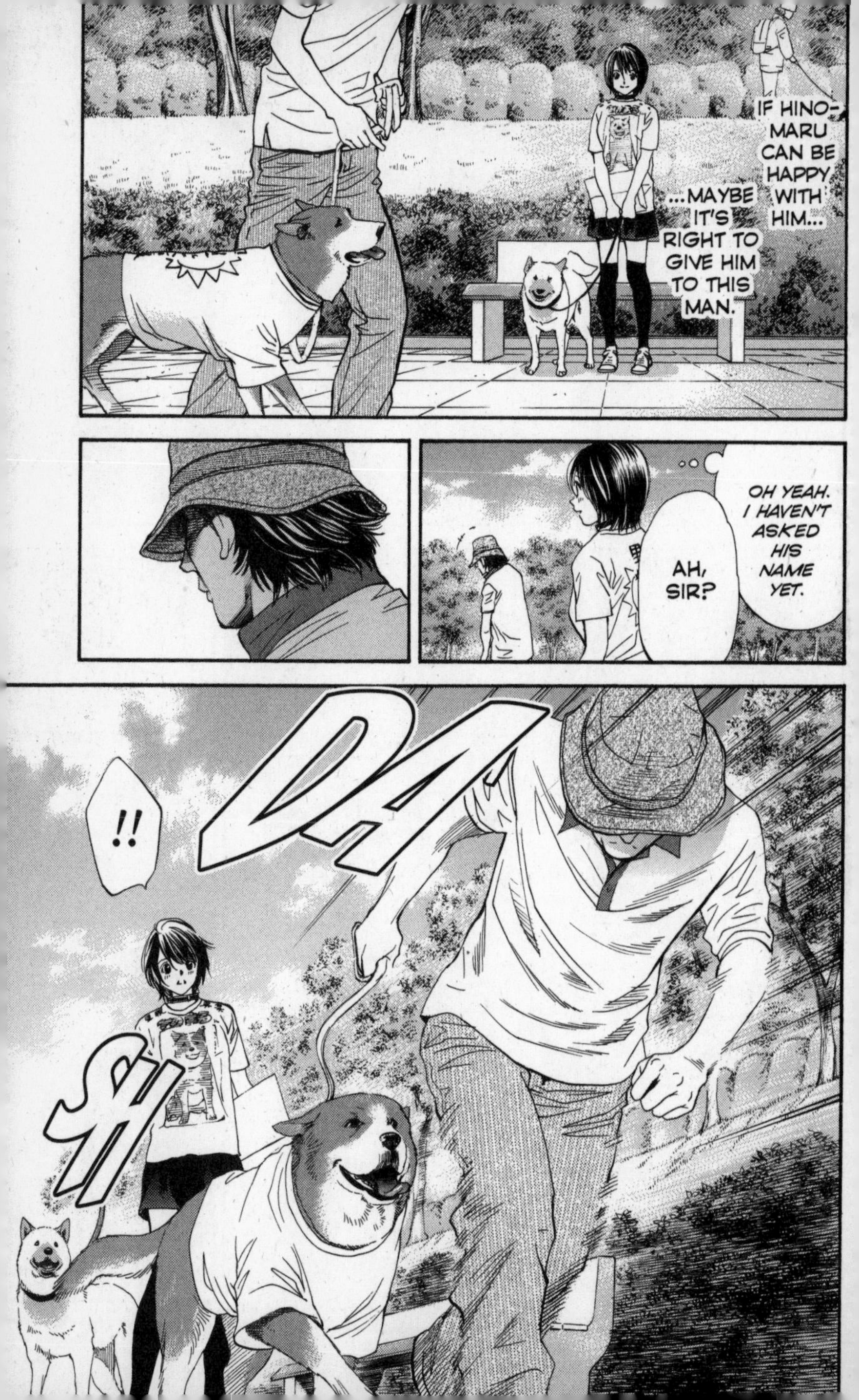
IF HINO-MARU CAN BE HAPPY WITH HIM...
...MAYBE IT'S RIGHT TO GIVE HIM TO THIS MAN.
OH YEAH. I HAVEN'T ASKED HIS NAME YET.
AH, SIR?
!!
DA
SH

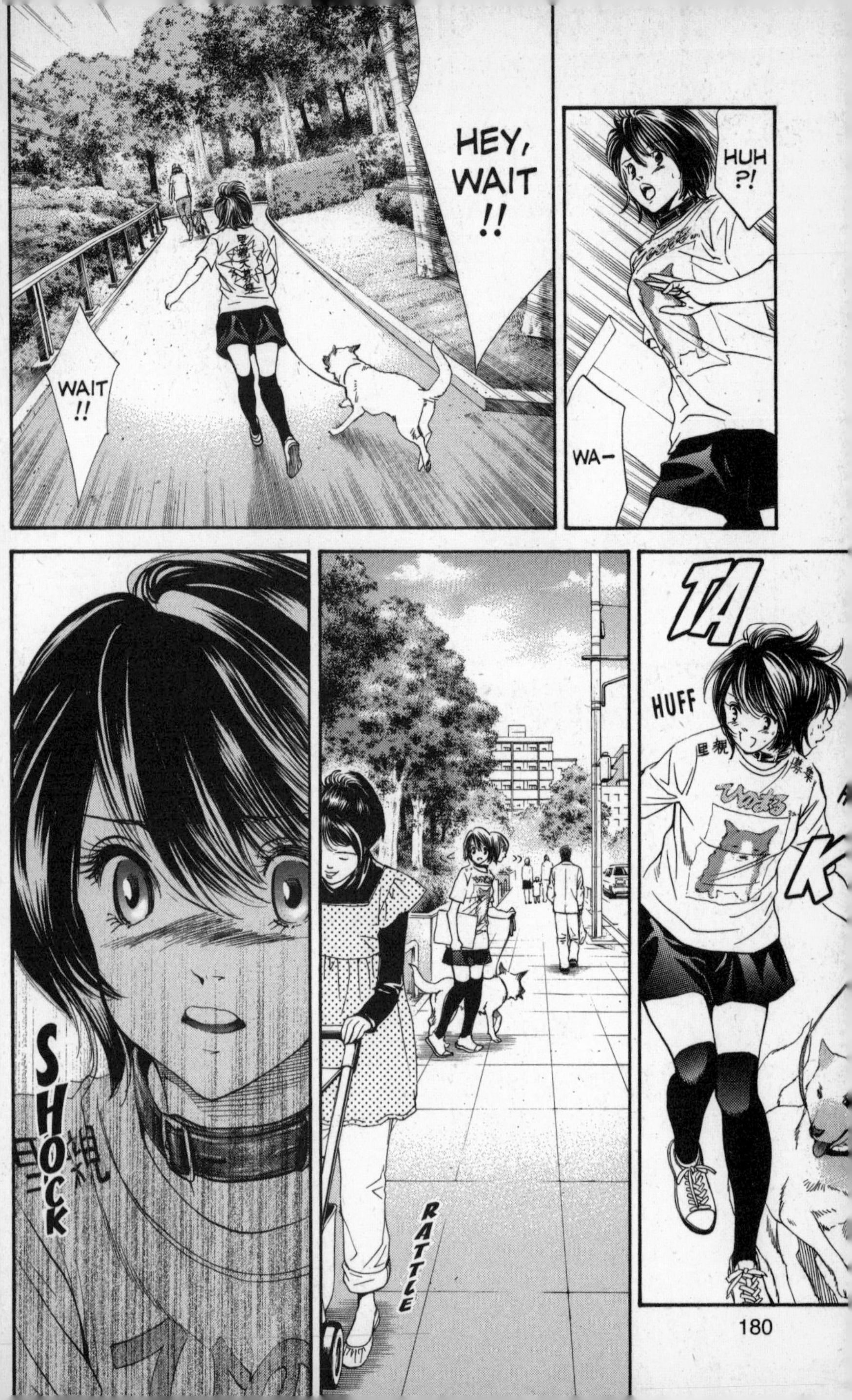
HUH ?!
WA-
HEY, WAIT !!
WAIT !!
TA
HUFF
K
RATTLE
SHOCK

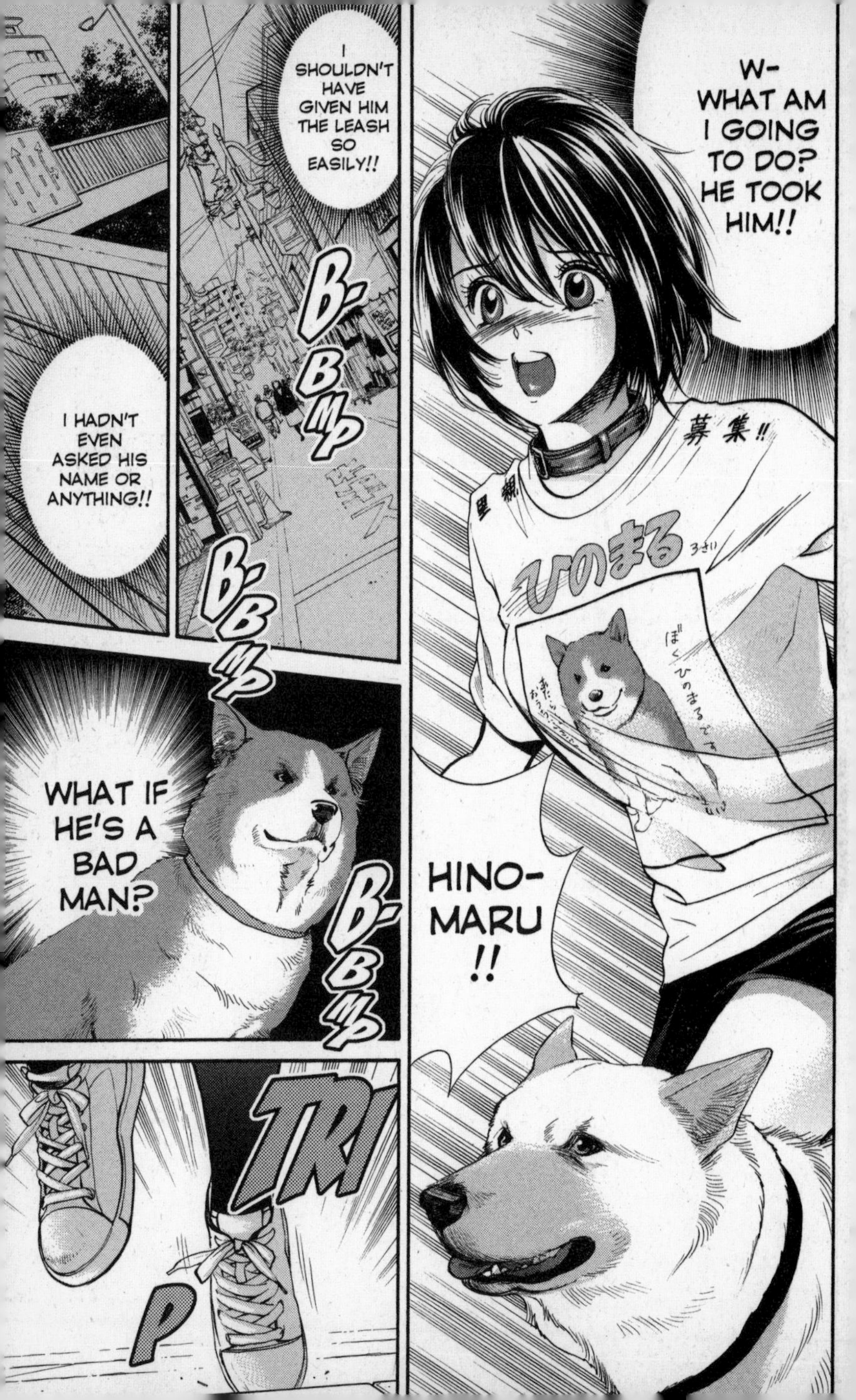
W- WHAT AM I GOING TO DO? HE TOOK HIM!!
里親
募集!!
ひのまる
ぼくひのまるです
HINO- MARU !!
I SHOULDN'T HAVE GIVEN HIM THE LEASH SO EASILY!!
B-BMP
I HADN'T EVEN ASKED HIS NAME OR ANYTHING!!
B-BMP
WHAT IF HE'S A BAD MAN?
B-BMP
TRAP

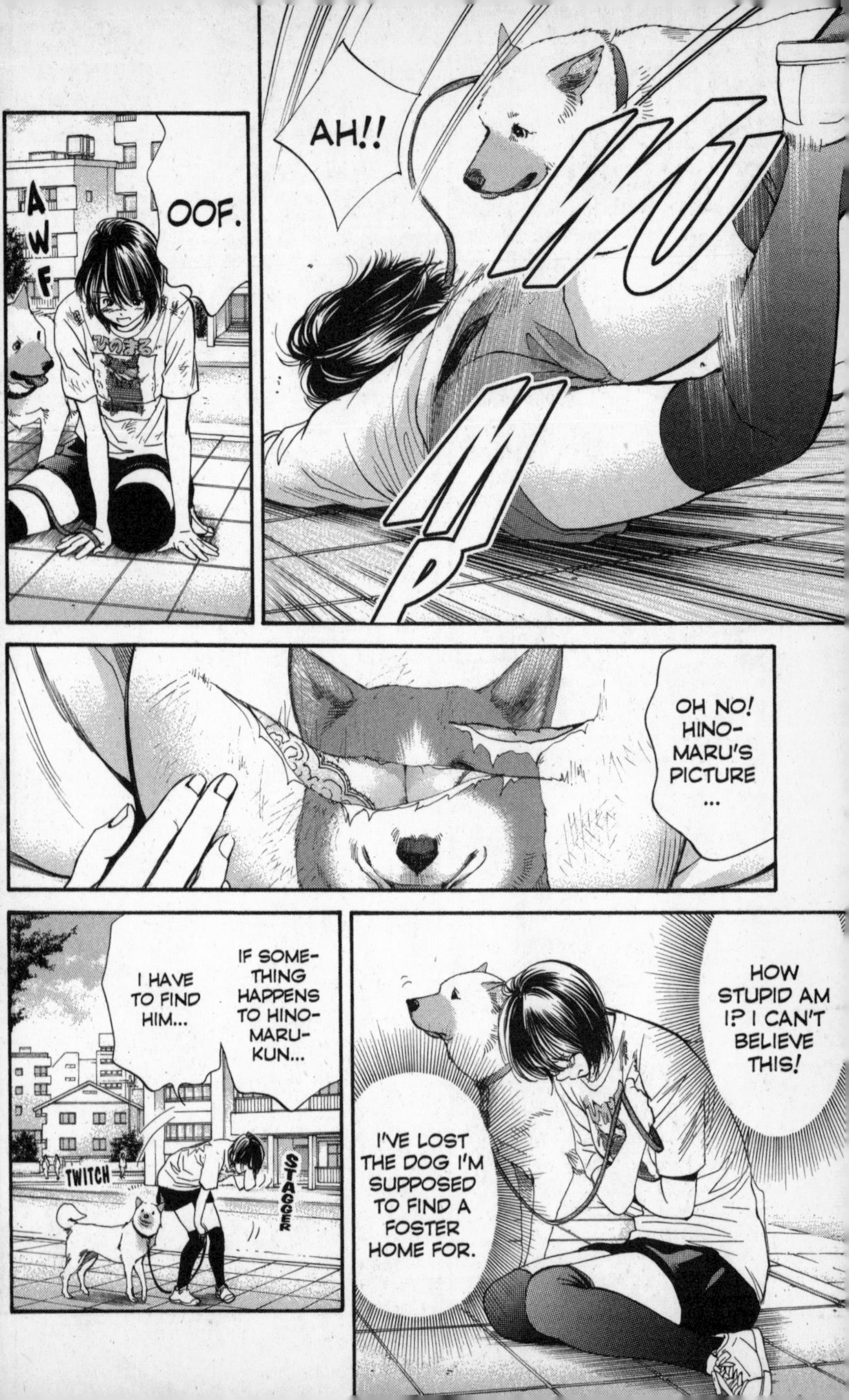
AH!!
WUMP
OOF.
AWF
OH NO! HINO-MARU'S PICTURE...
HOW STUPID AM I!? I CAN'T BELIEVE THIS!
I'VE LOST THE DOG I'M SUPPOSED TO FIND A FOSTER HOME FOR.
IF SOME-THING HAPPENS TO HINO-MARU-KUN...
I HAVE TO FIND HIM...
STAGGER
TWITCH

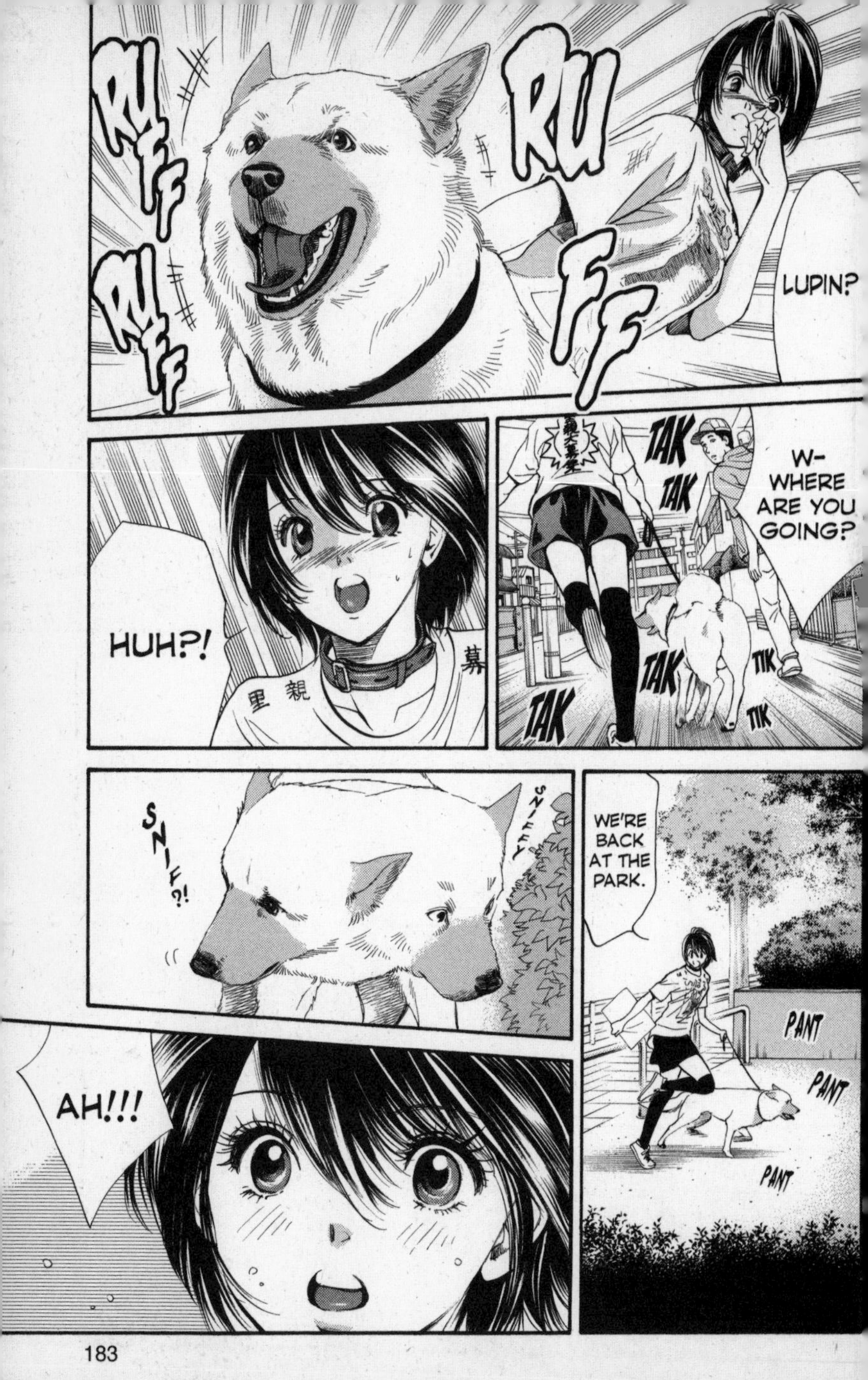
RUFF
LUPIN?
RUFF
RUFF
TAK
TAK
W-WHERE ARE YOU GOING?
TAK
TAK
TIK
TIK
HUH?!
募
里親
WE'RE BACK AT THE PARK.
PANT
PANT
PANT
SNIFFY
SNIFF?!
AH!!!

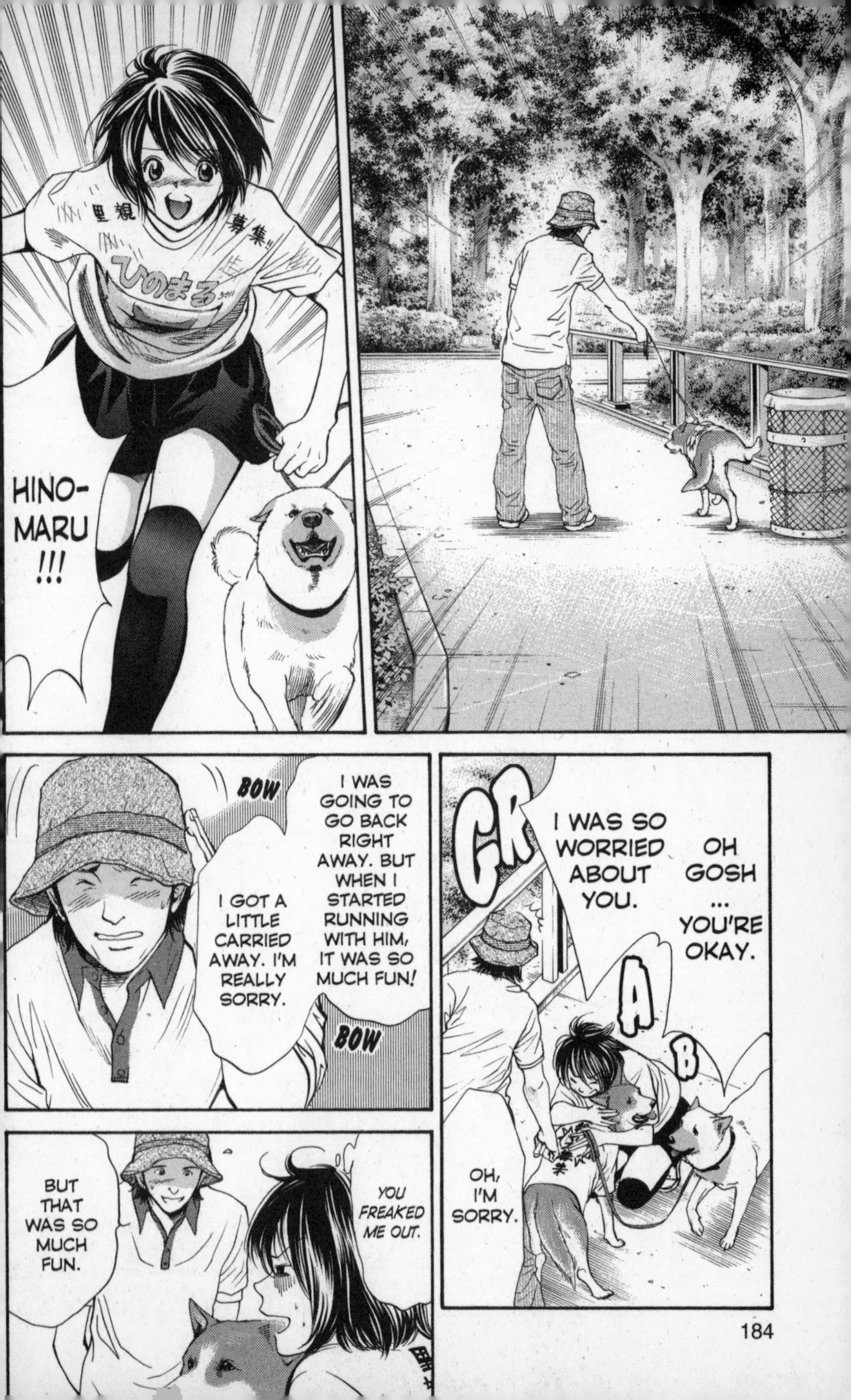

里親 募集
ひのまる
HINO-MARU!!!
CR
OH GOSH ... YOU'RE OKAY.
I WAS SO WORRIED ABOUT YOU.
A
B
OH, I'M SORRY.
BOW
I WAS GOING TO GO BACK RIGHT AWAY. BUT WHEN I STARTED RUNNING WITH HIM, IT WAS SO MUCH FUN!
I GOT A LITTLE CARRIED AWAY. I'M REALLY SORRY.
BOW
YOU FREAKED ME OUT.
BUT THAT WAS SO MUCH FUN.

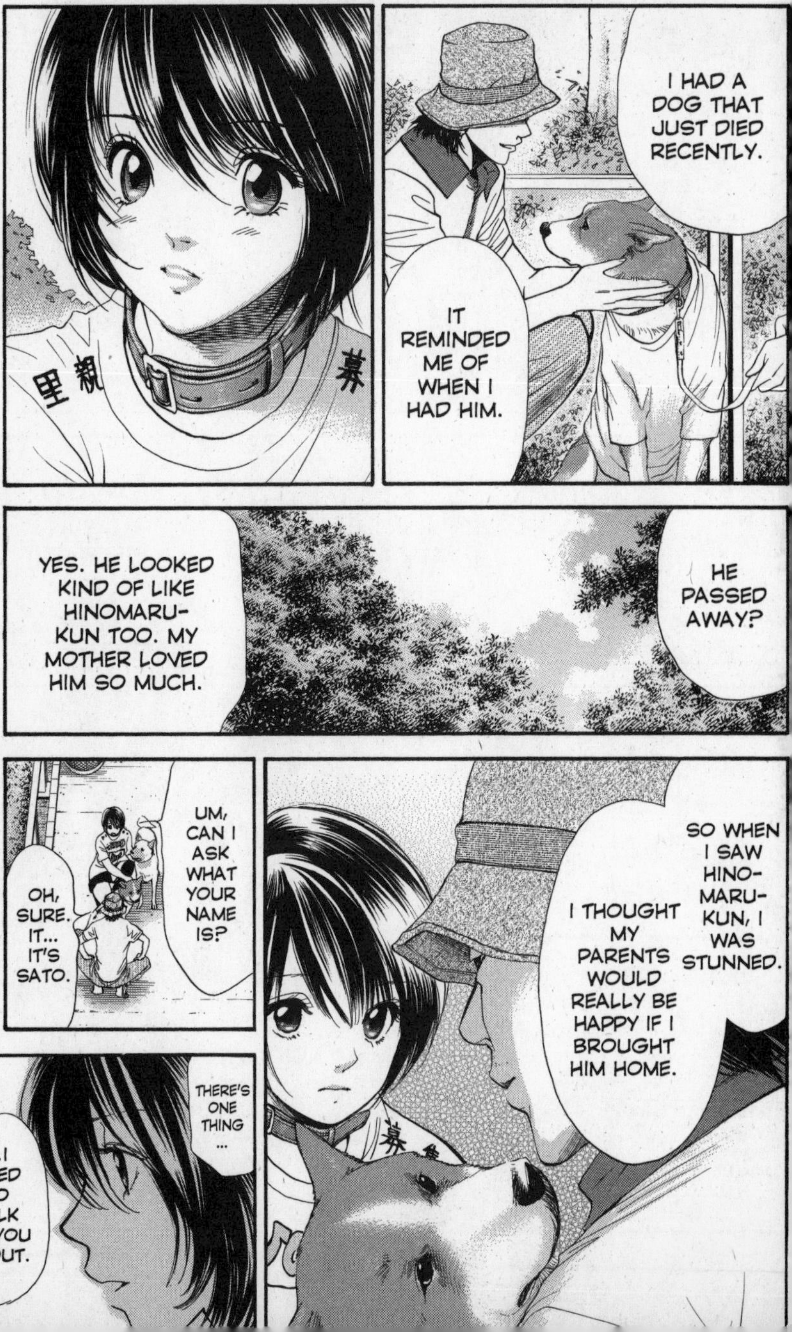
I HAD A DOG THAT JUST DIED RECENTLY.
IT REMINDED ME OF WHEN I HAD HIM.
HE PASSED AWAY?
YES. HE LOOKED KIND OF LIKE HINOMARU-KUN TOO. MY MOTHER LOVED HIM SO MUCH.
SO WHEN I SAW HINO-MARU-KUN, I WAS STUNNED.
I THOUGHT MY PARENTS WOULD REALLY BE HAPPY IF I BROUGHT HIM HOME.
UM, CAN I ASK WHAT YOUR NAME IS?
OH, SURE. IT... IT'S SATO.
THERE'S ONE THING...
...I NEED TO TALK TO YOU ABOUT.

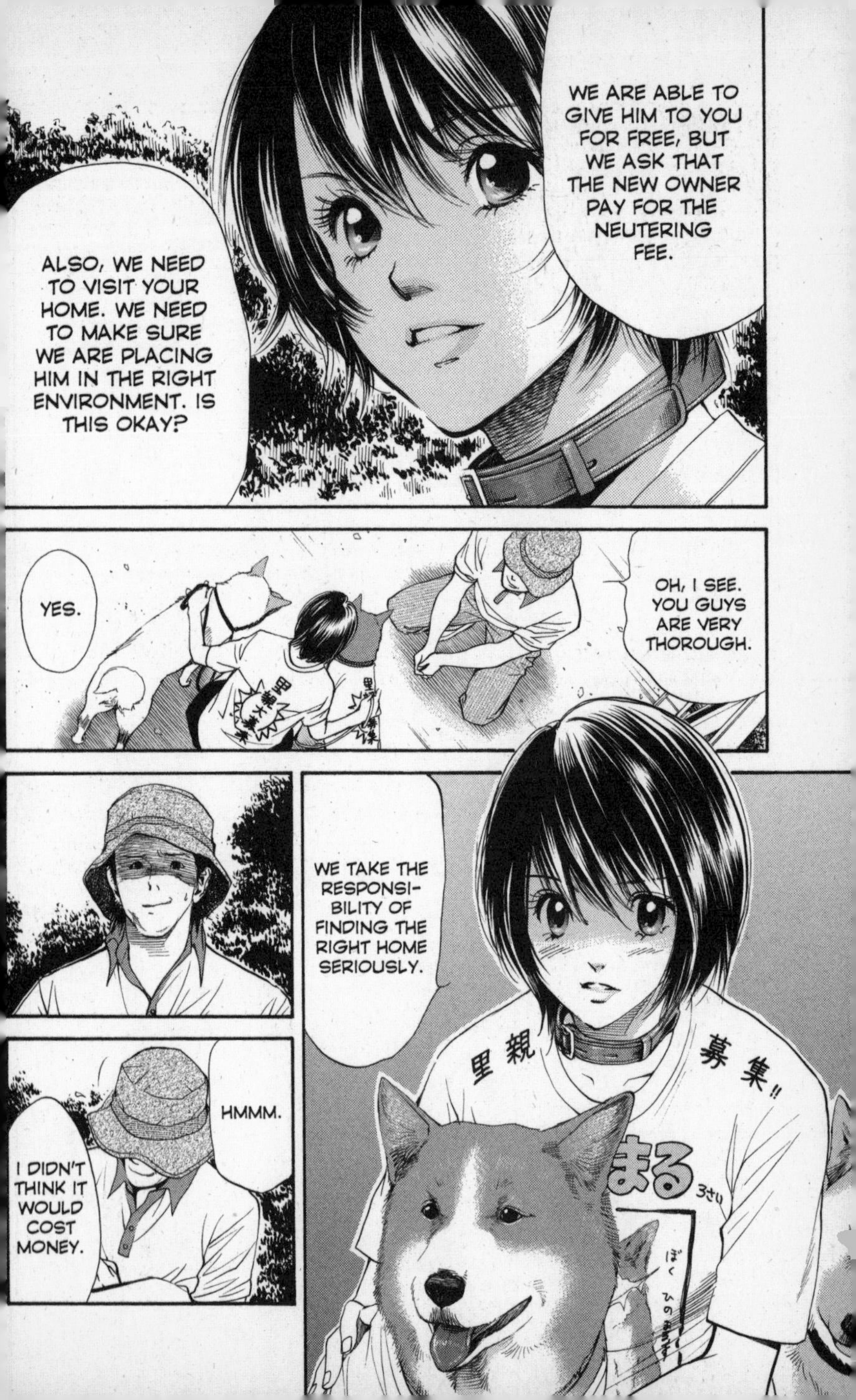
WE ARE ABLE TO GIVE HIM TO YOU FOR FREE, BUT WE ASK THAT THE NEW OWNER PAY FOR THE NEUTERING FEE.
ALSO, WE NEED TO VISIT YOUR HOME. WE NEED TO MAKE SURE WE ARE PLACING HIM IN THE RIGHT ENVIRONMENT. IS THIS OKAY?
OH, I SEE. YOU GUYS ARE VERY THOROUGH.
YES.
WE TAKE THE RESPONSI-BILITY OF FINDING THE RIGHT HOME SERIOUSLY.
里親 募集!!
まる 3さい
ぼく
HMMM.
I DIDN'T THINK IT WOULD COST MONEY.

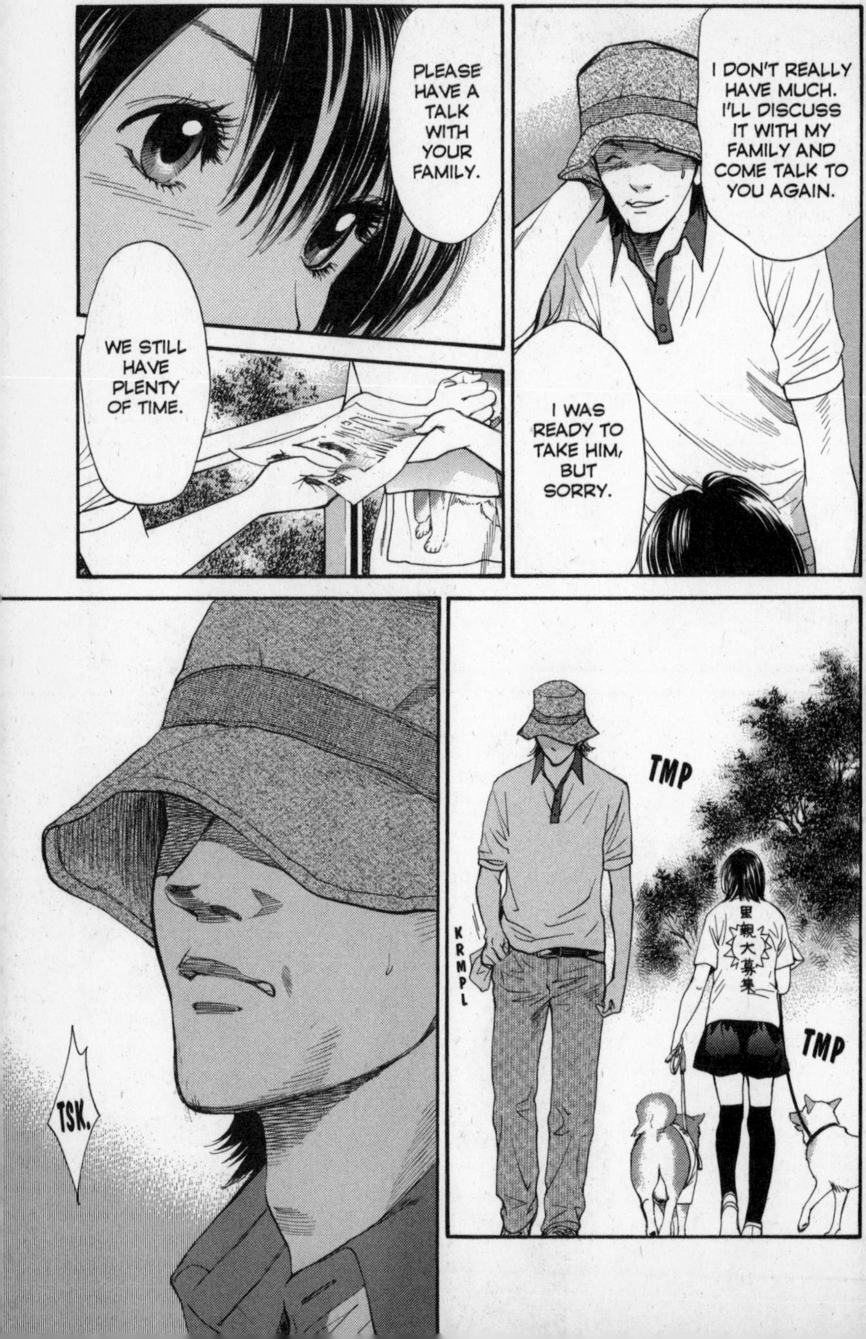
I DON'T REALLY HAVE MUCH. I'LL DISCUSS IT WITH MY FAMILY AND COME TALK TO YOU AGAIN.
I WAS READY TO TAKE HIM, BUT SORRY.
PLEASE HAVE A TALK WITH YOUR FAMILY.
WE STILL HAVE PLENTY OF TIME.
TMP
里親大募集
TMP
KRMPL
TSK.

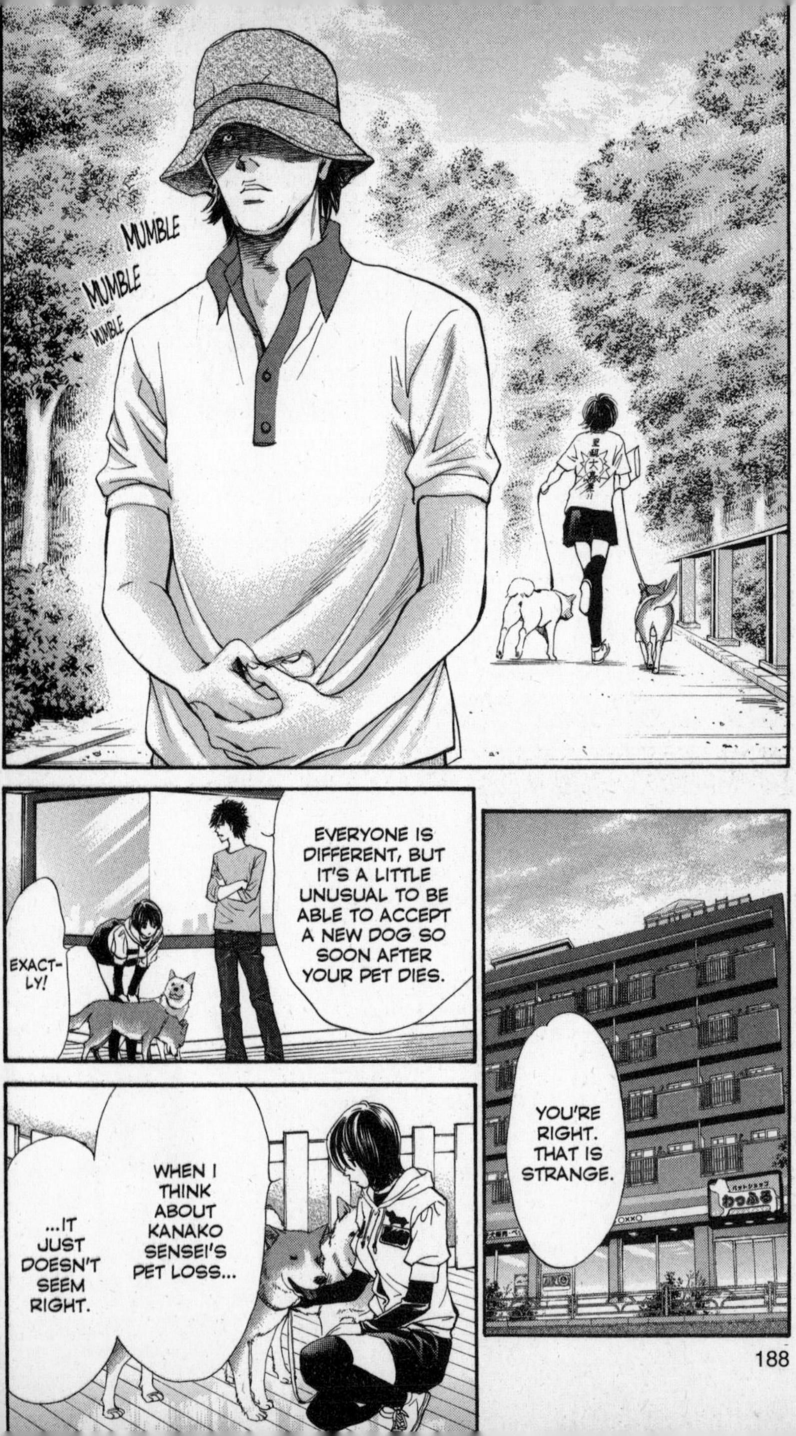
MUMBLE
MUMBLE
MUMBLE
YOU'RE RIGHT. THAT IS STRANGE.
EVERYONE IS DIFFERENT, BUT IT'S A LITTLE UNUSUAL TO BE ABLE TO ACCEPT A NEW DOG SO SOON AFTER YOUR PET DIES.
EXACT-LY!
WHEN I THINK ABOUT KANAKO SENSEI'S PET LOSS...
...IT JUST DOESN'T SEEM RIGHT.

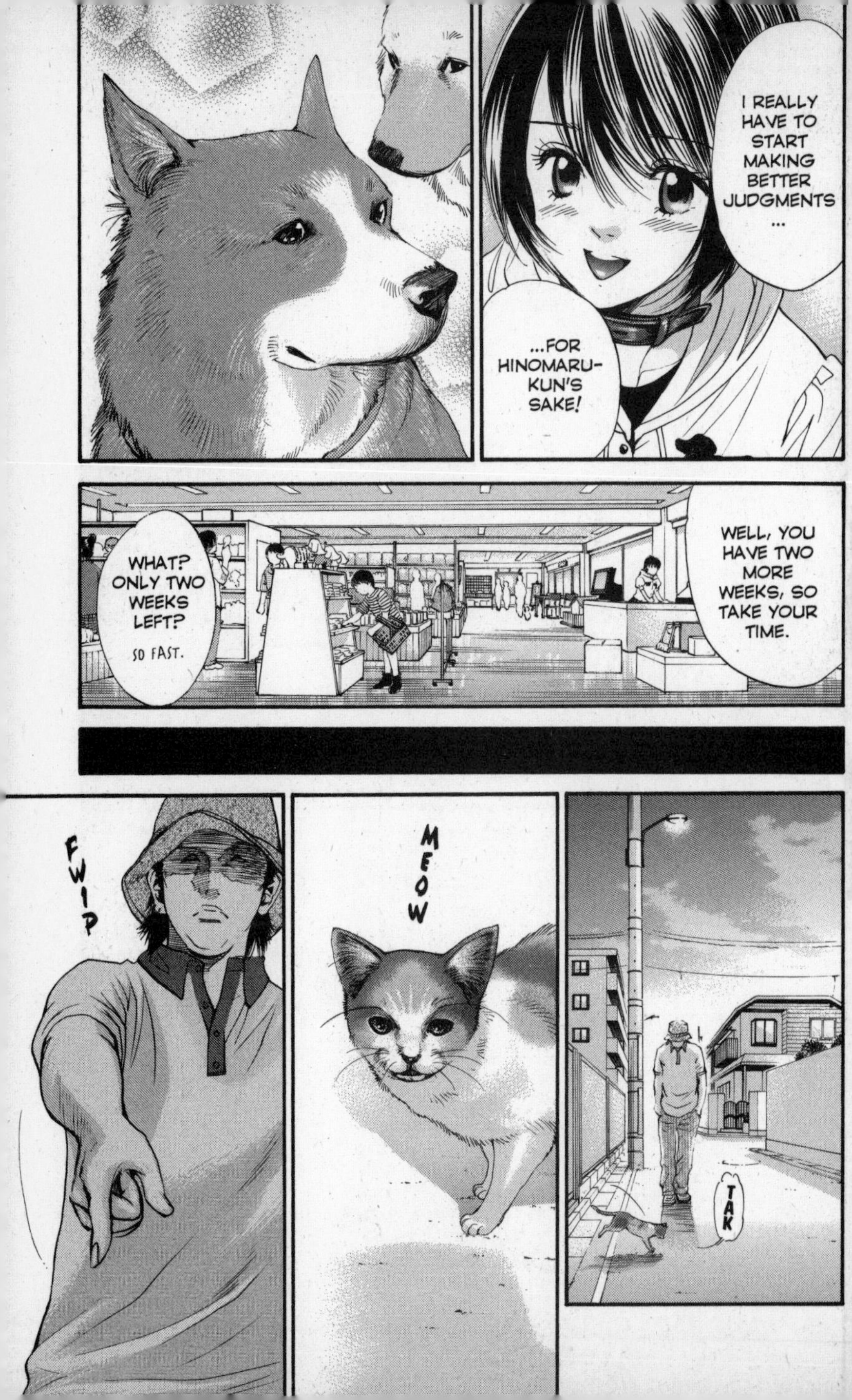
I REALLY HAVE TO START MAKING BETTER JUDGMENTS ...
...FOR HINOMARU-KUN'S SAKE!
WELL, YOU HAVE TWO MORE WEEKS, SO TAKE YOUR TIME.
WHAT? ONLY TWO WEEKS LEFT?
SO FAST.
TAK
MEOW
FWIP

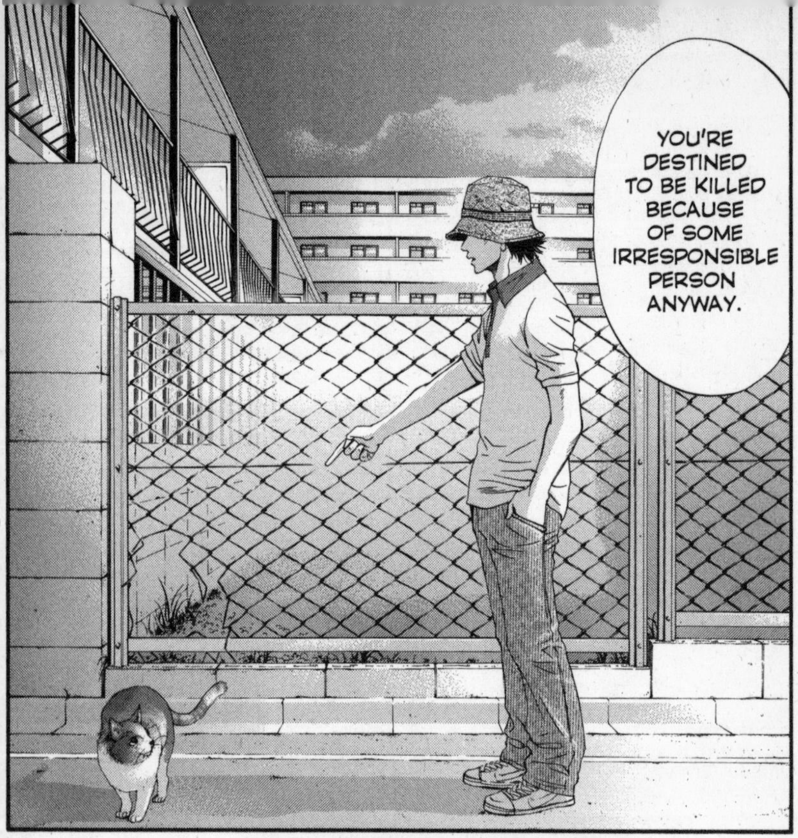
YOU'RE DESTINED TO BE KILLED BECAUSE OF SOME IRRESPONSIBLE PERSON ANYWAY.

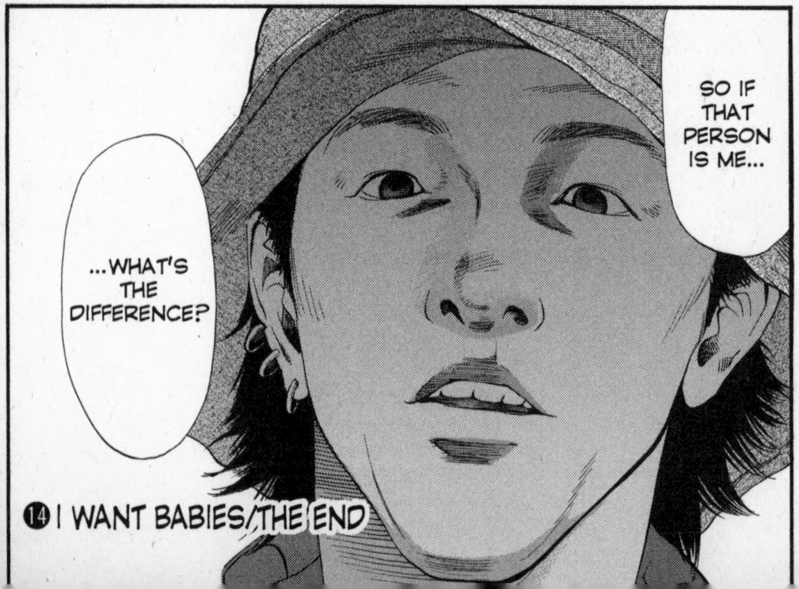
SO IF THAT PERSON IS ME...
...WHAT'S THE DIFFERENCE?
14 I WANT BABIES/THE END

INUBA☆KA

SPECIAL CHAPTER

STORY OF LITTLE LUPIN

THIEF DOG GOES WILD!

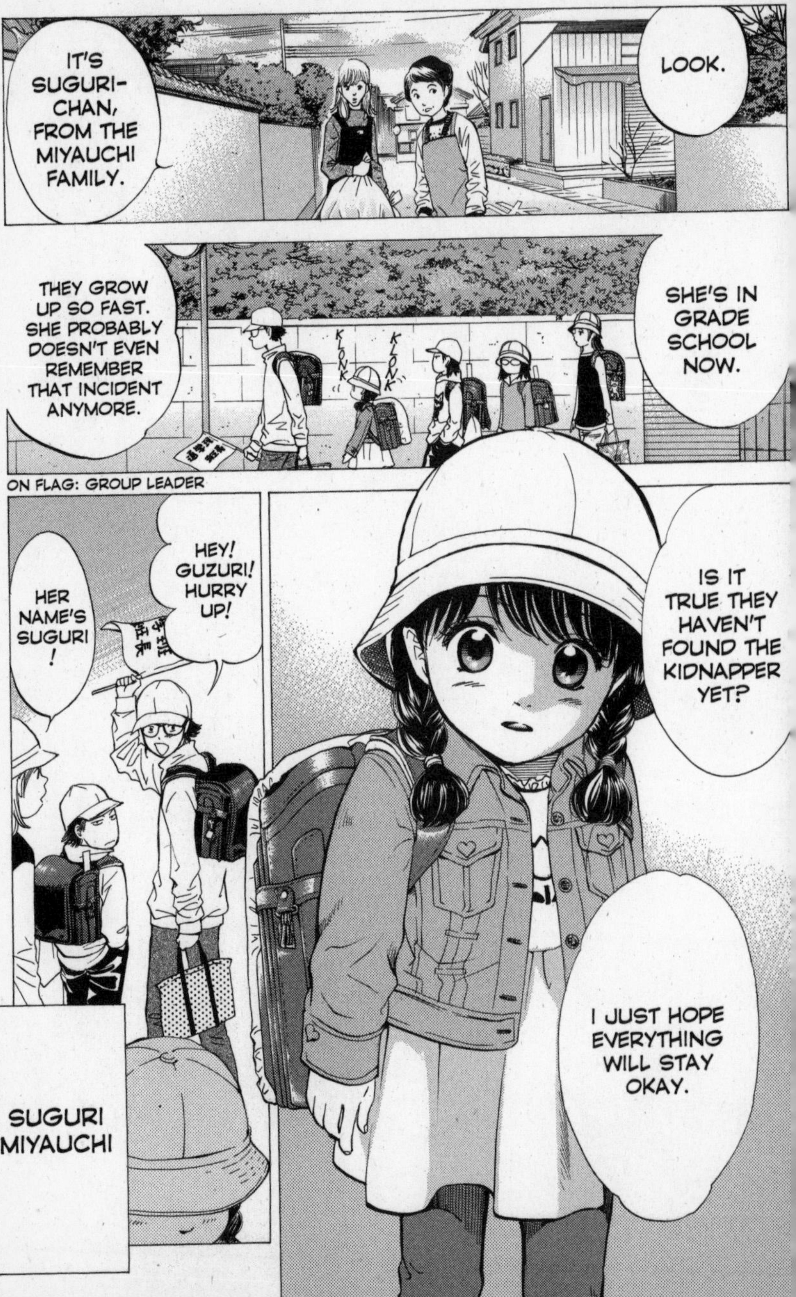
LOOK.
IT'S SUGURI-CHAN, FROM THE MIYAUCHI FAMILY.
SHE'S IN GRADE SCHOOL NOW.
THEY GROW UP SO FAST. SHE PROBABLY DOESN'T EVEN REMEMBER THAT INCIDENT ANYMORE.
KLONK
KLONK
ON FLAG: GROUP LEADER
IS IT TRUE THEY HAVEN'T FOUND THE KIDNAPPER YET?
I JUST HOPE EVERYTHING WILL STAY OKAY.
HEY! GUZURI! HURRY UP!
HER NAME'S SUGURI!
SUGURI MIYAUCHI

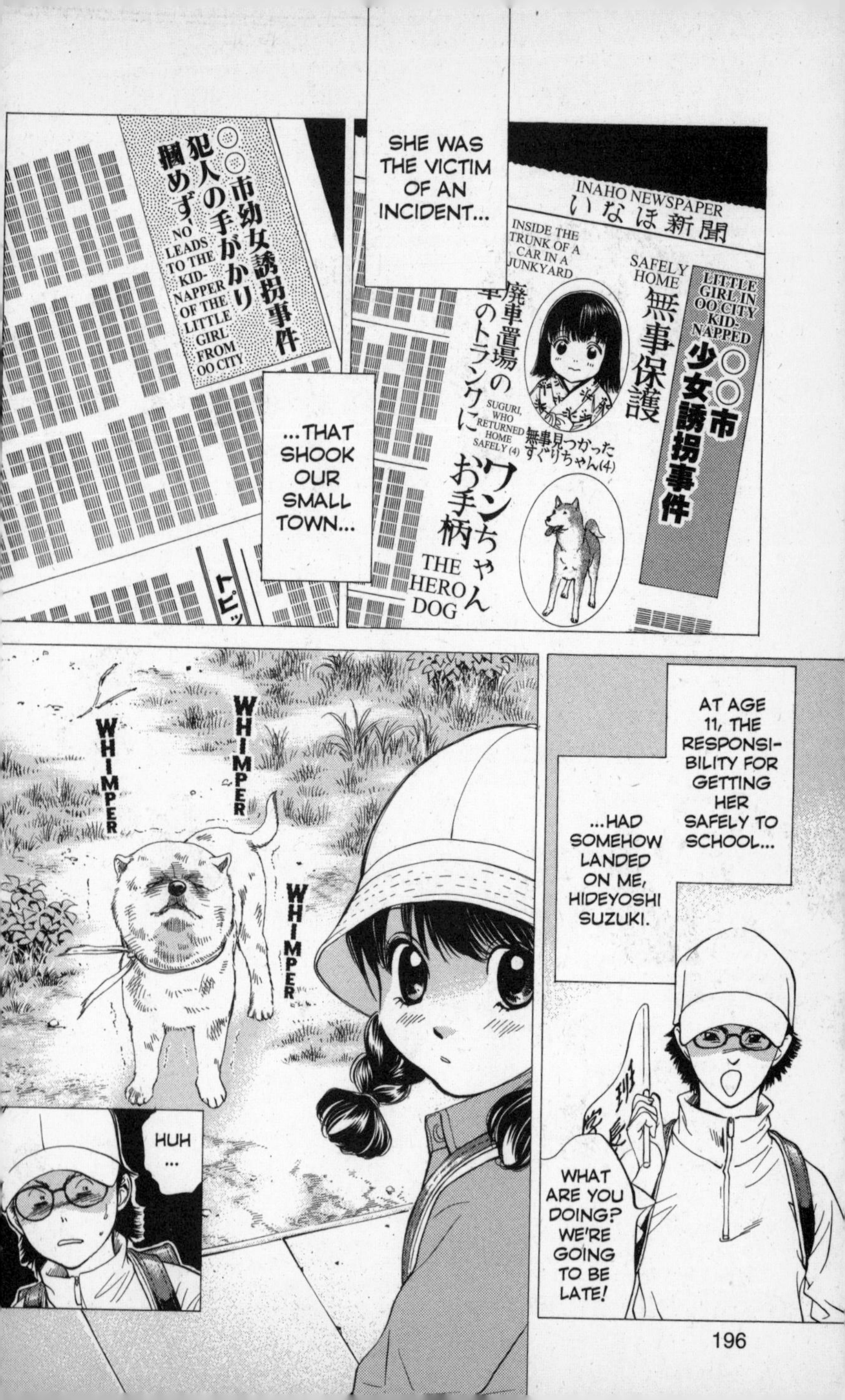
SHE WAS THE VICTIM OF AN INCIDENT...
INAHO NEWSPAPER
いなほ新聞
LITTLE GIRL IN OO CITY KID-NAPPED
○○市少女誘拐事件
SAFELY HOME
無事保護
INSIDE THE TRUNK OF A CAR IN A JUNKYARD
廃車置場のトランクに
SUGURI, WHO RETURNED HOME SAFELY (4)
無事見つかったすぐりちゃん(4)
THE HERO DOG
ワンちゃんお手柄
...THAT SHOOK OUR SMALL TOWN...
○○市幼女誘拐事件
犯人の手がかり掴めず
NO LEADS TO THE KID-NAPPER OF THE LITTLE GIRL FROM OO CITY
トピッ
AT AGE 11, THE RESPONSI-BILITY FOR GETTING HER SAFELY TO SCHOOL...
...HAD SOMEHOW LANDED ON ME, HIDEYOSHI SUZUKI.
WHAT ARE YOU DOING? WE'RE GOING TO BE LATE!
WHIMPER
WHIMPER
WHIMPER
HUH...

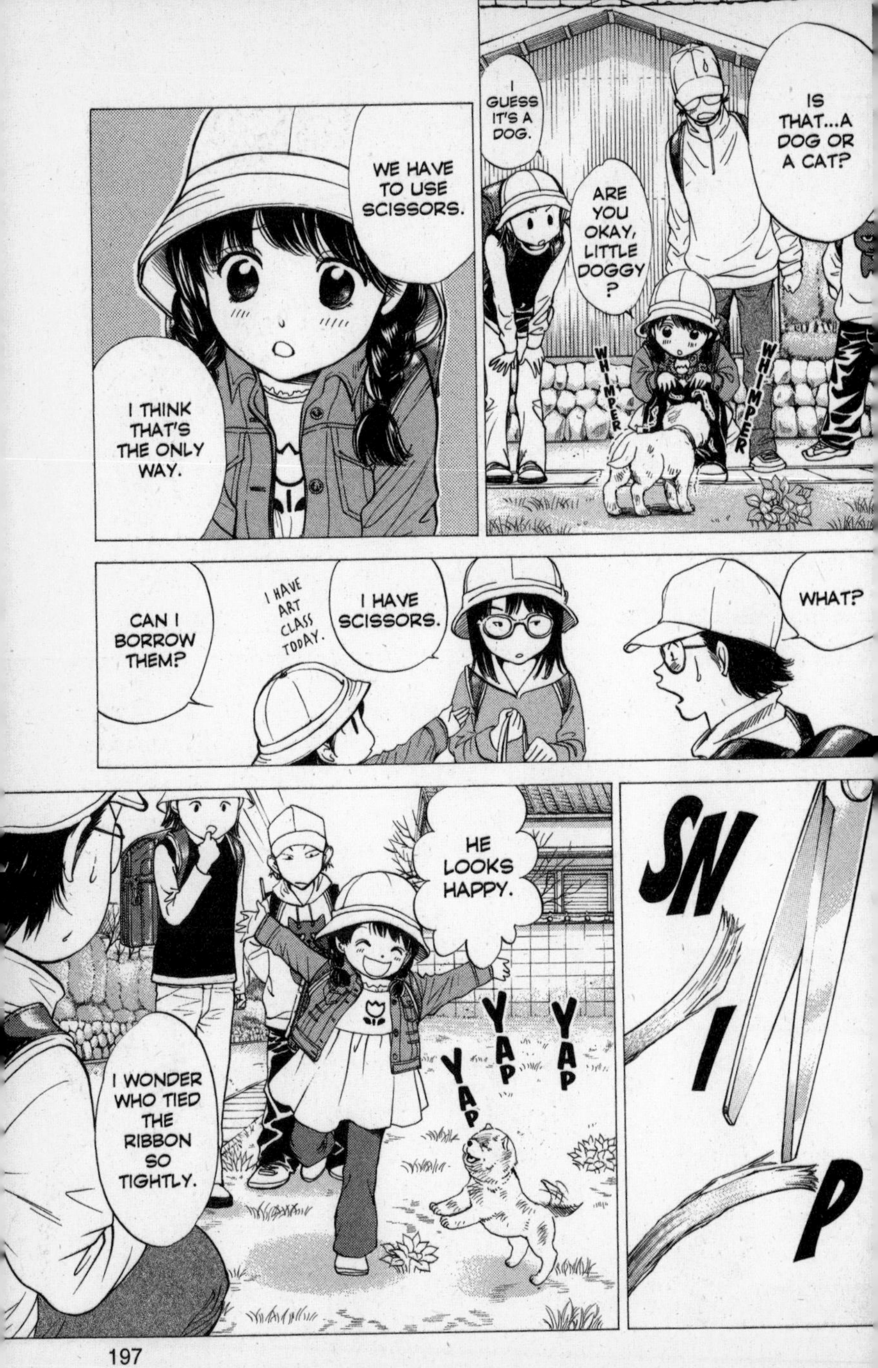
IS THAT...A DOG OR A CAT?
I GUESS IT'S A DOG.
ARE YOU OKAY, LITTLE DOGGY?
WHIMPER
WHIMPER
WE HAVE TO USE SCISSORS.
I THINK THAT'S THE ONLY WAY.
WHAT?
I HAVE SCISSORS.
I HAVE ART CLASS TODAY.
CAN I BORROW THEM?
SNIP
HE LOOKS HAPPY.
YAP
YAP
YAP
I WONDER WHO TIED THE RIBBON SO TIGHTLY.

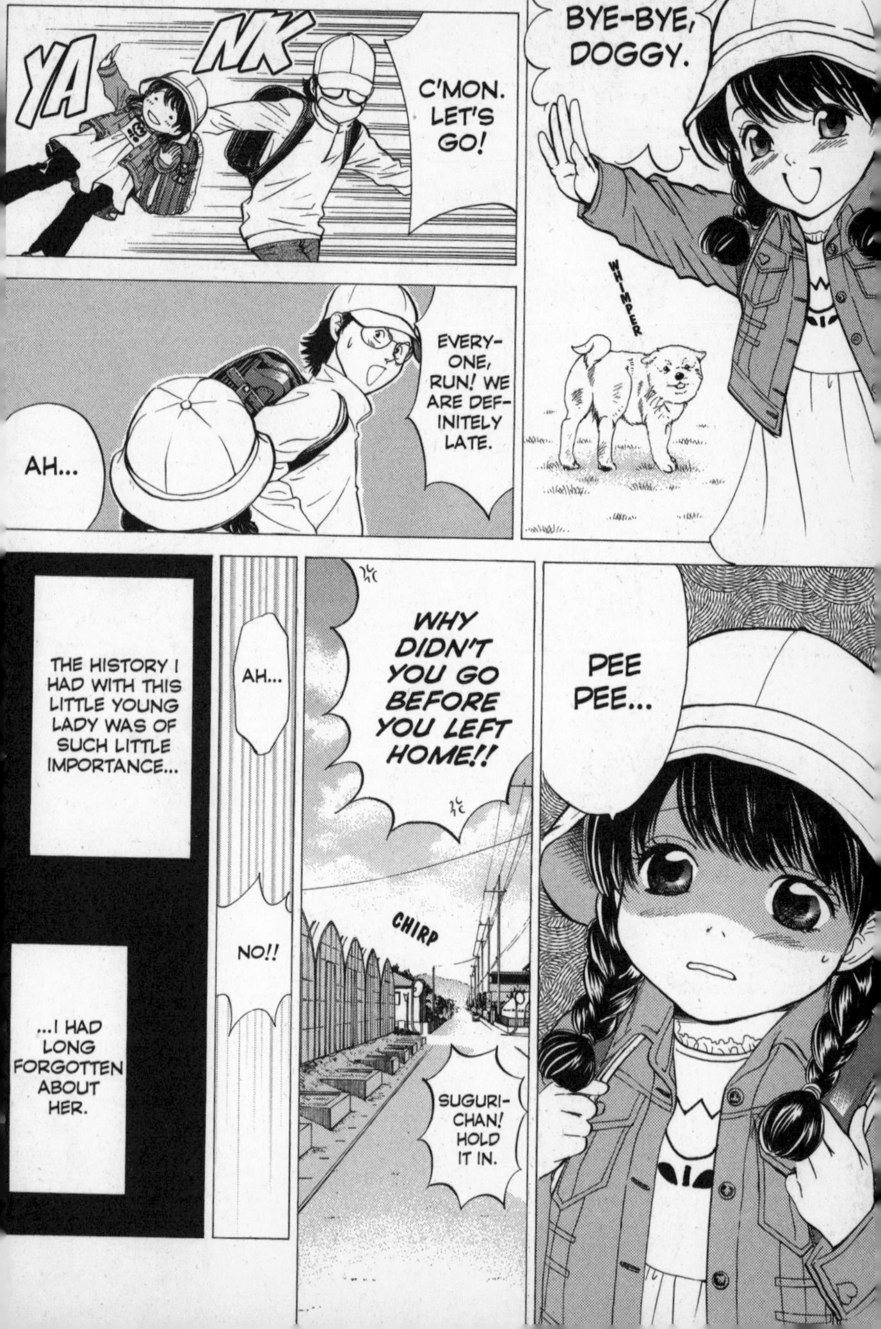
BYE-BYE, DOGGY.
WHIMPER
C'MON. LET'S GO!
YANK
EVERY-ONE, RUN! WE ARE DEF-INITELY LATE.
AH...
PEE PEE...
WHY DIDN'T YOU GO BEFORE YOU LEFT HOME!!
CHIRP
SUGURI-CHAN! HOLD IT IN.
AH...
NO!!
THE HISTORY I HAD WITH THIS LITTLE YOUNG LADY WAS OF SUCH LITTLE IMPORTANCE...
...I HAD LONG FORGOTTEN ABOUT HER.

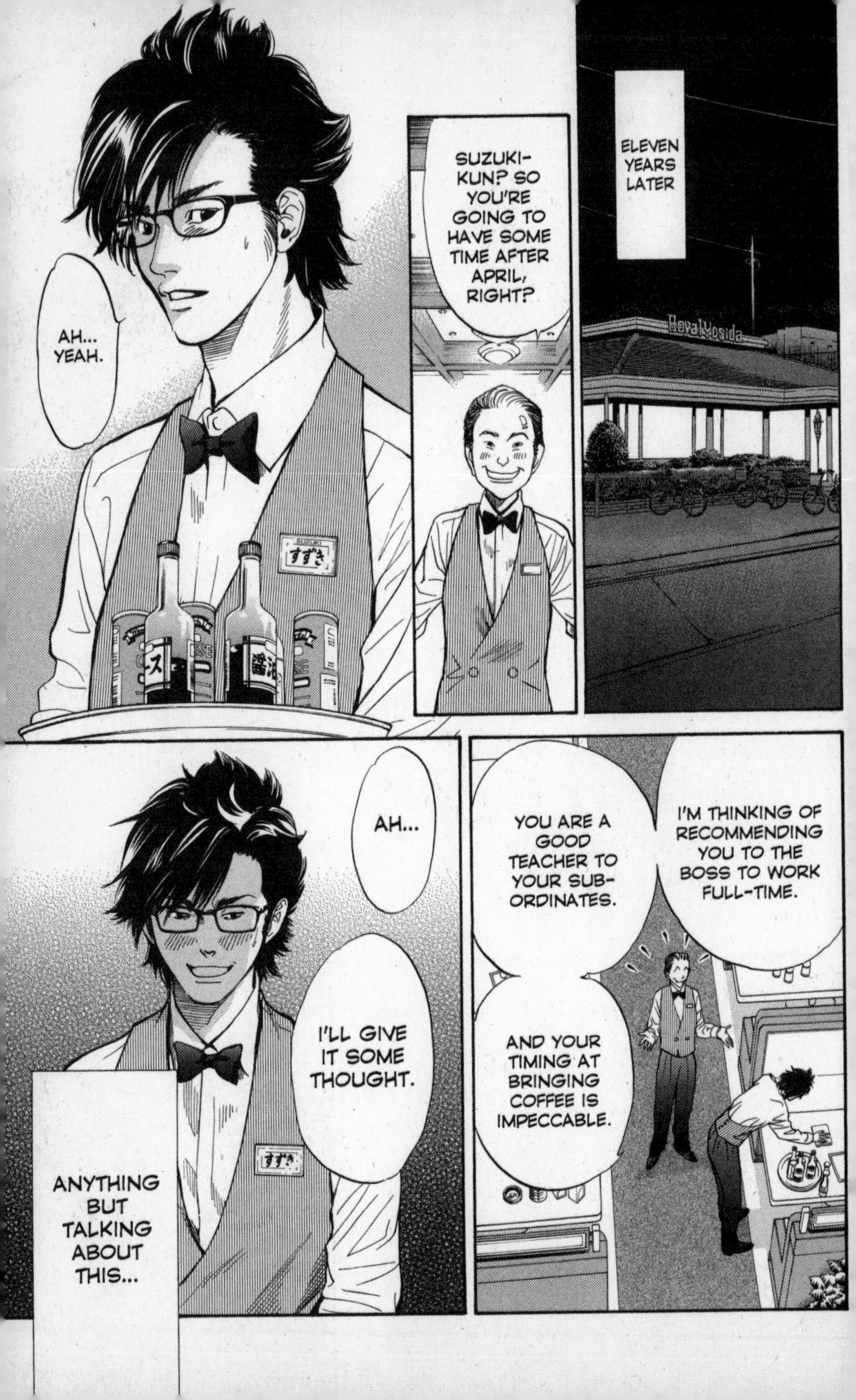
ELEVEN YEARS LATER
SUZUKI-KUN? SO YOU'RE GOING TO HAVE SOME TIME AFTER APRIL, RIGHT?
AH... YEAH.
I'M THINKING OF RECOMMENDING YOU TO THE BOSS TO WORK FULL-TIME.
YOU ARE A GOOD TEACHER TO YOUR SUB-ORDINATES.
AND YOUR TIMING AT BRINGING COFFEE IS IMPECCABLE.
AH...
I'LL GIVE IT SOME THOUGHT.
ANYTHING BUT TALKING ABOUT THIS...

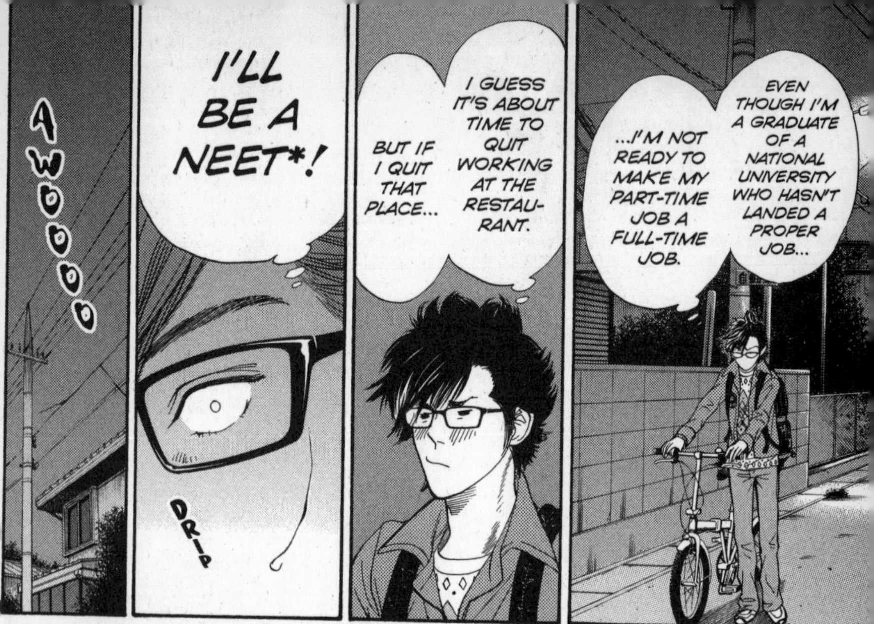
EVEN THOUGH I'M A GRADUATE OF A NATIONAL UNIVERSITY WHO HASN'T LANDED A PROPER JOB...
...I'M NOT READY TO MAKE MY PART-TIME JOB A FULL-TIME JOB.
I GUESS IT'S ABOUT TIME TO QUIT WORKING AT THE RESTAU-RANT.
BUT IF I QUIT THAT PLACE...
I'LL BE A NEET*!
DRIP
AWOOOO

* "NOT IN EMPLOYMENT, EDUCATION OR TRAINING"

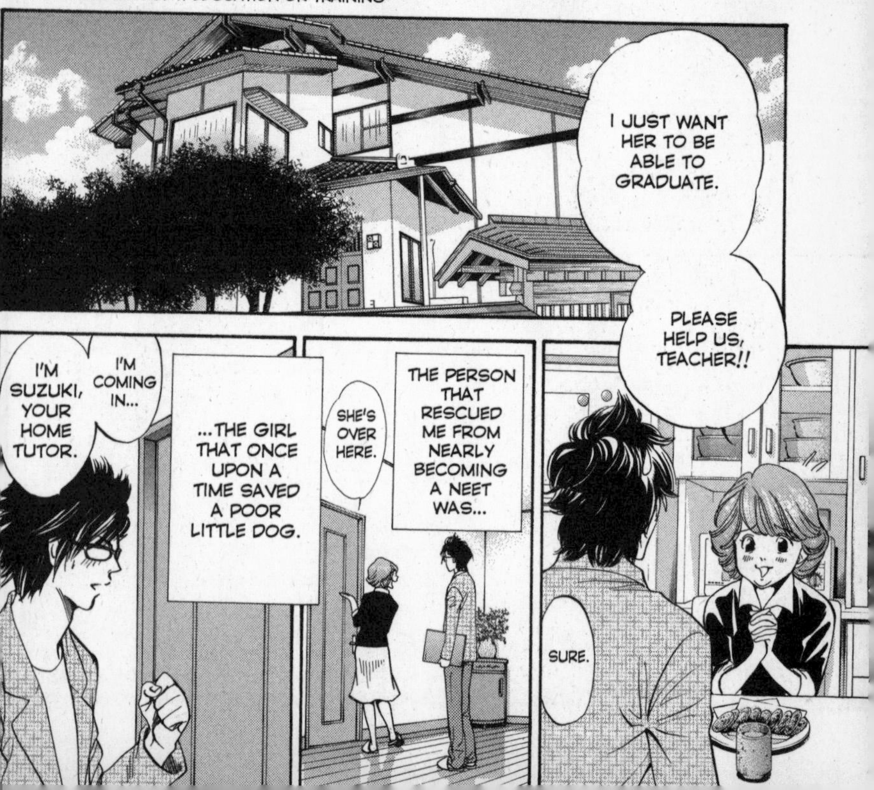
I JUST WANT HER TO BE ABLE TO GRADUATE.
PLEASE HELP US, TEACHER!!
SURE.
THE PERSON THAT RESCUED ME FROM NEARLY BECOMING A NEET WAS...
SHE'S OVER HERE.
...THE GIRL THAT ONCE UPON A TIME SAVED A POOR LITTLE DOG.
I'M COMING IN...
I'M SUZUKI, YOUR HOME TUTOR.

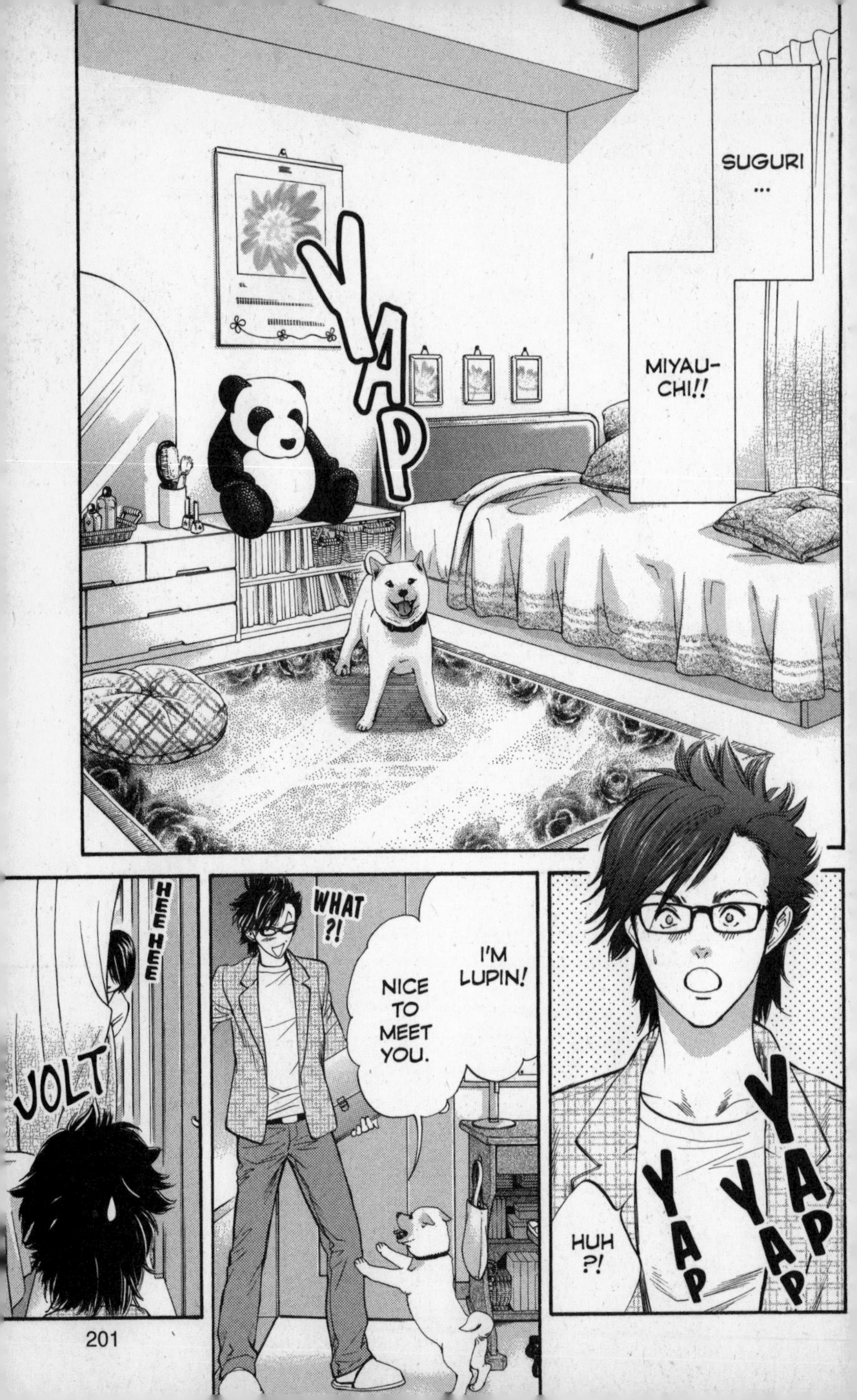
SUGURI
...
MIYAU-CHI!!
YAP
YAP
YAP
YAP
HUH?!
WHAT?!
I'M LUPIN!
NICE TO MEET YOU.
HEE HEE
JOLT

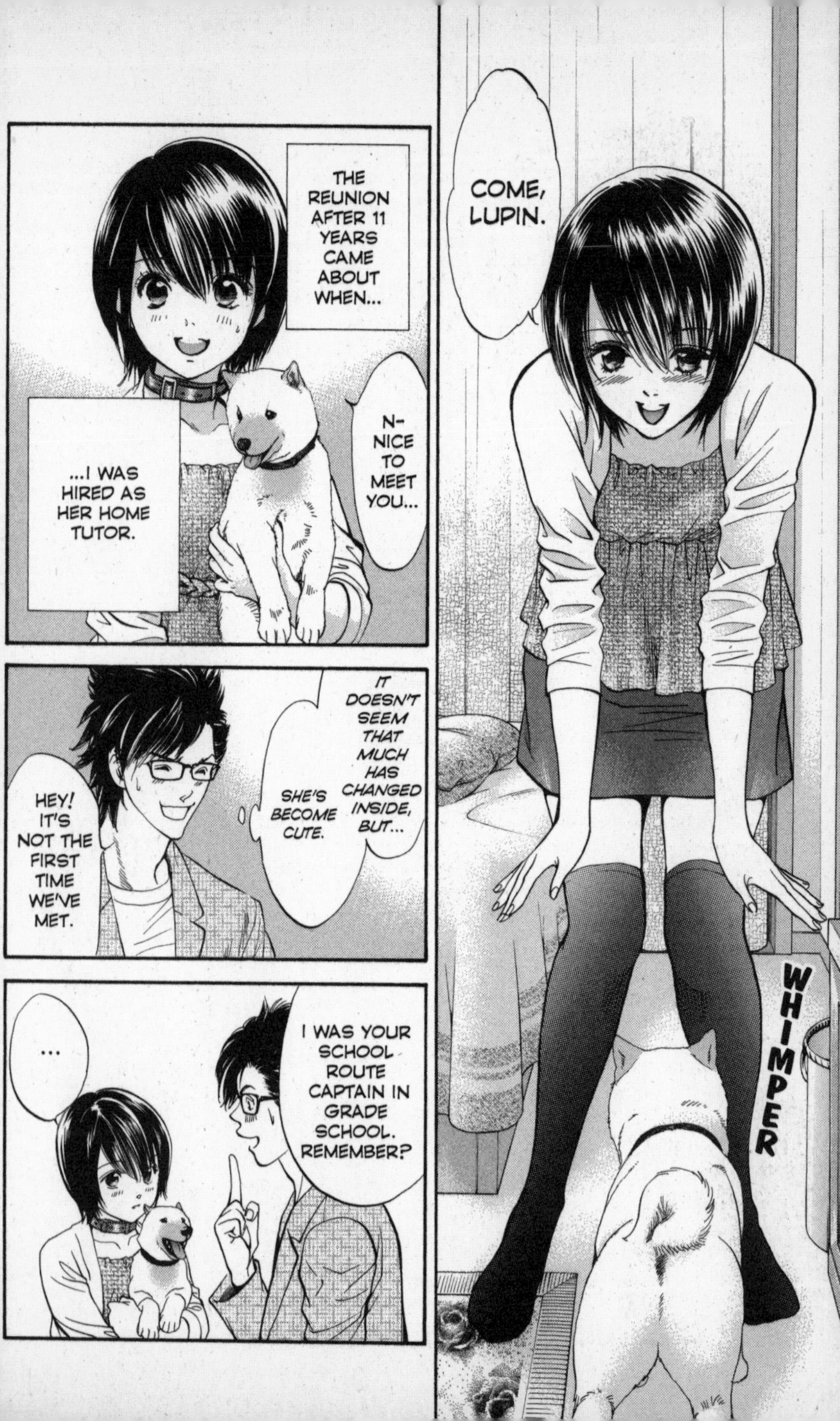
COME, LUPIN.
WHIMPER
THE REUNION AFTER 11 YEARS CAME ABOUT WHEN...
N-NICE TO MEET YOU...
...I WAS HIRED AS HER HOME TUTOR.
IT DOESN'T SEEM THAT MUCH HAS CHANGED INSIDE, BUT...
SHE'S BECOME CUTE.
HEY! IT'S NOT THE FIRST TIME WE'VE MET.
I WAS YOUR SCHOOL ROUTE CAPTAIN IN GRADE SCHOOL. REMEMBER?
...

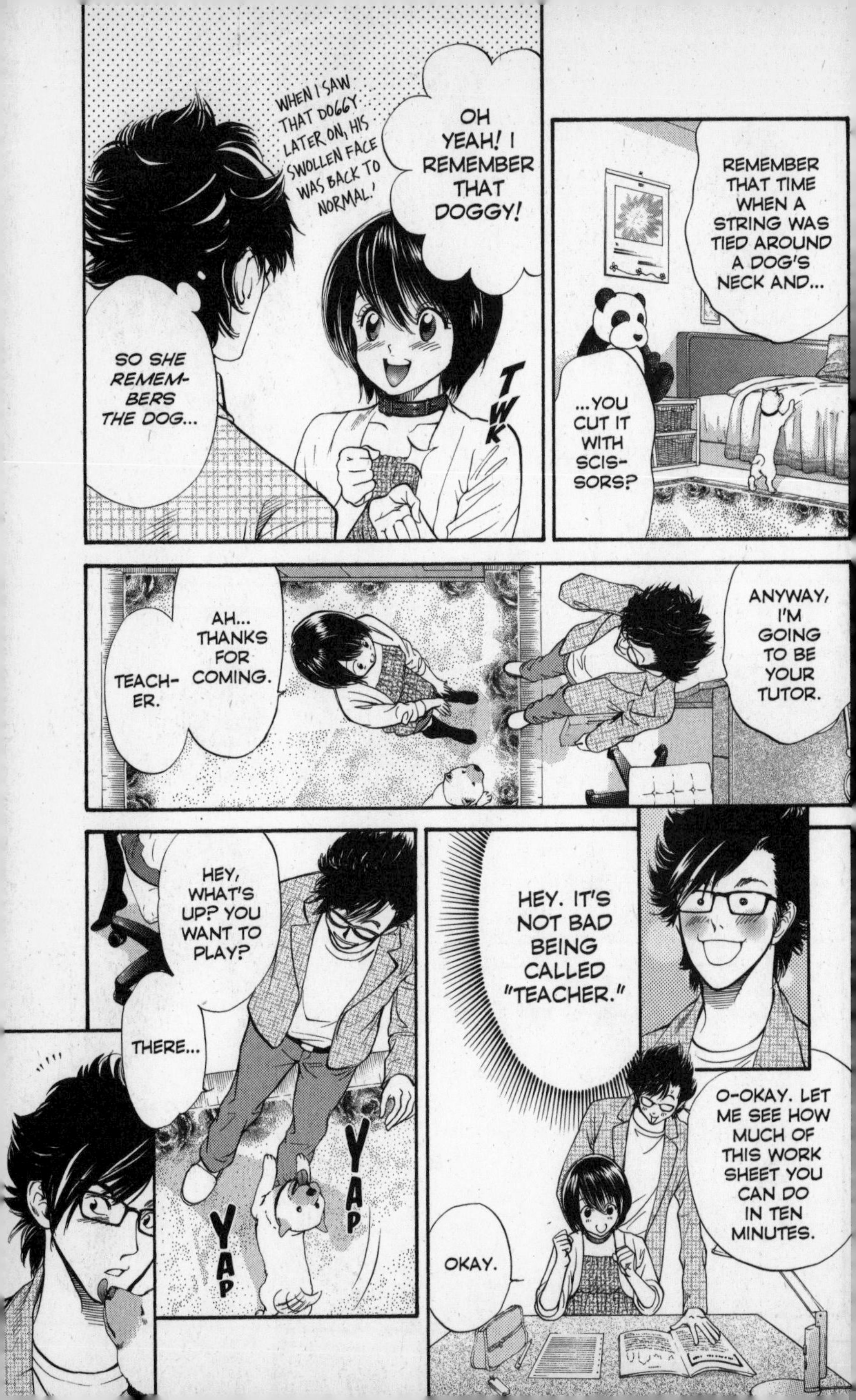
REMEMBER THAT TIME WHEN A STRING WAS TIED AROUND A DOG'S NECK AND...
...YOU CUT IT WITH SCIS-SORS?
OH YEAH! I REMEMBER THAT DOGGY!
WHEN I SAW THAT DOGGY LATER ON, HIS SWOLLEN FACE WAS BACK TO NORMAL!
TWK
SO SHE REMEM-BERS THE DOG...
ANYWAY, I'M GOING TO BE YOUR TUTOR.
AH... THANKS FOR COMING.
TEACH-ER.
HEY. IT'S NOT BAD BEING CALLED "TEACHER."
O-OKAY. LET ME SEE HOW MUCH OF THIS WORK SHEET YOU CAN DO IN TEN MINUTES.
OKAY.
HEY, WHAT'S UP? YOU WANT TO PLAY?
YAP
YAP
THERE...

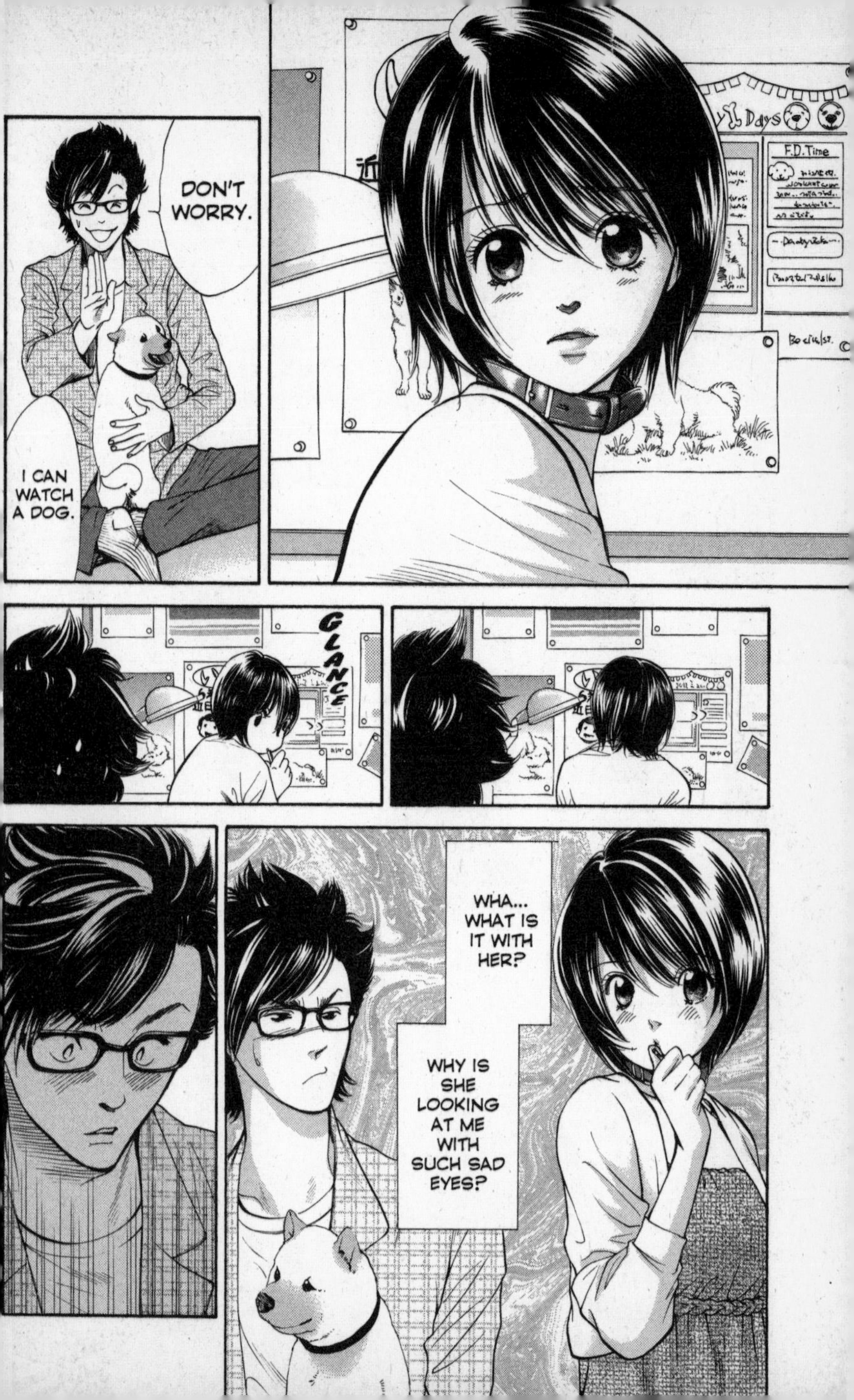
F.D.Time
DON'T WORRY.
I CAN WATCH A DOG.
GLANCE
WHA... WHAT IS IT WITH HER?
WHY IS SHE LOOKING AT ME WITH SUCH SAD EYES?

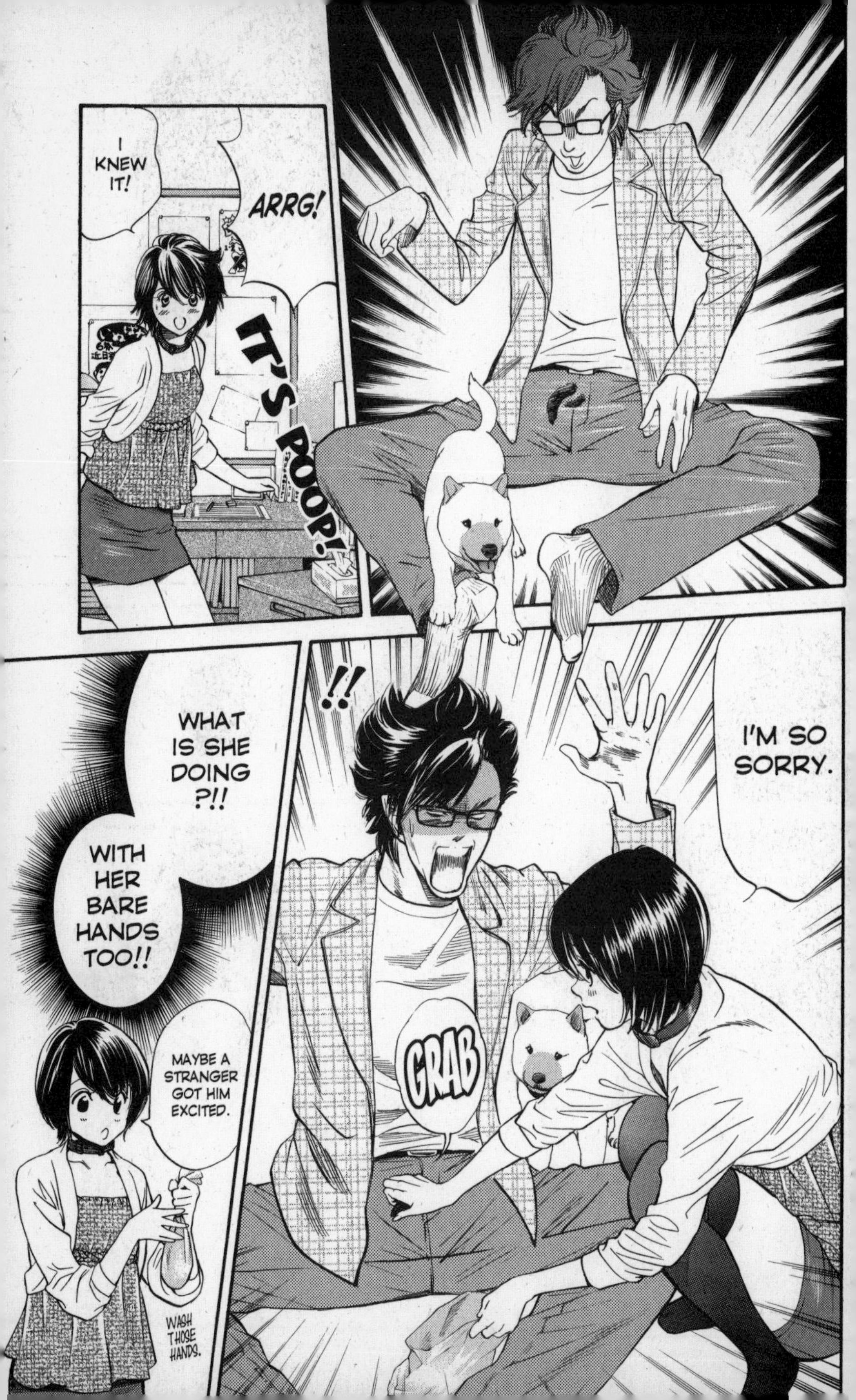
I KNEW IT!
ARRG!
IT'S POOP!
I'M SO SORRY.
!!
GRAB
WHAT IS SHE DOING?!!
WITH HER BARE HANDS TOO!!
MAYBE A STRANGER GOT HIM EXCITED.
WASH THOSE HANDS.

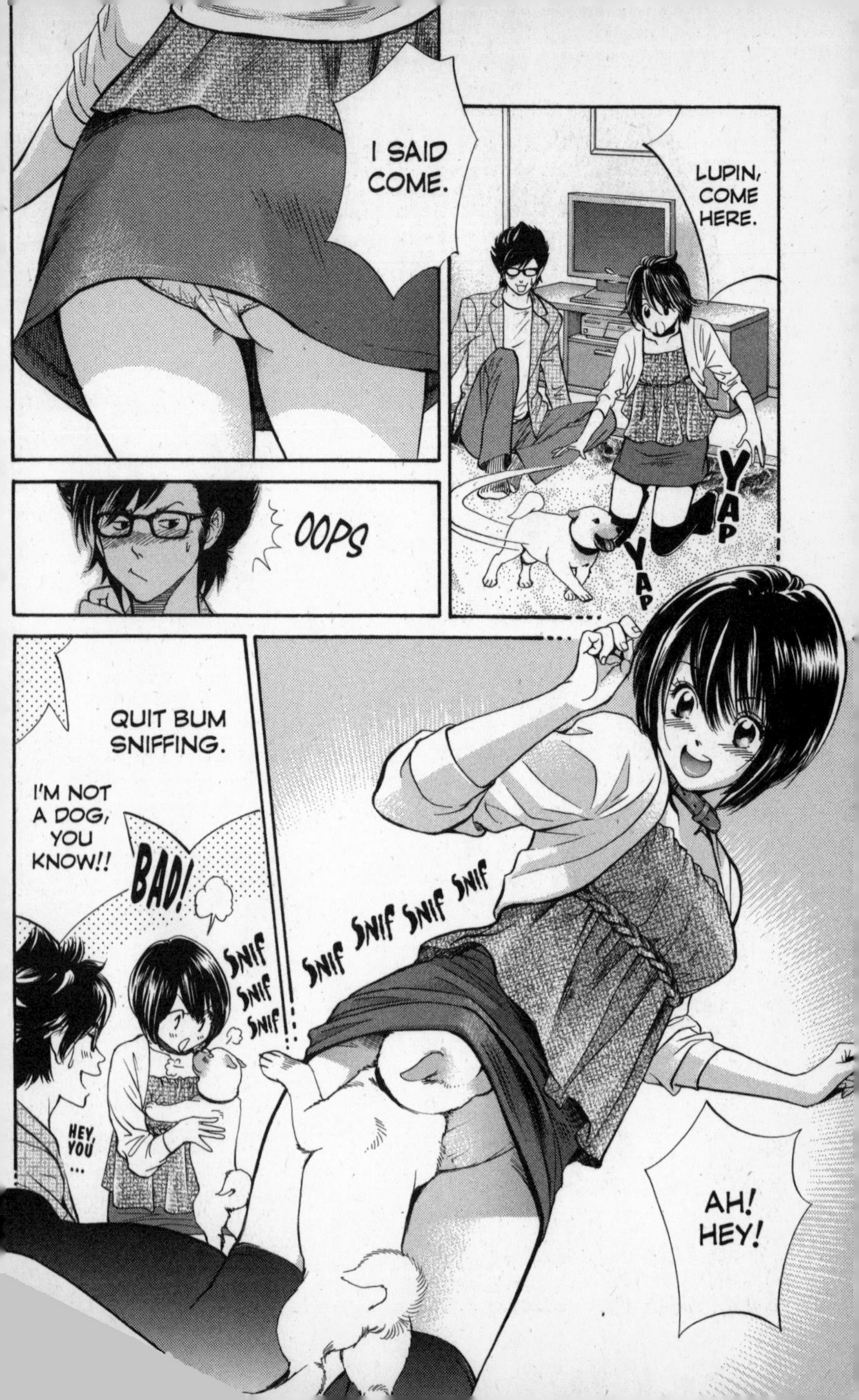
LUPIN, COME HERE.
YAP YAP
YAP YAP
I SAID COME.
OOPS
SNIF SNIF SNIF SNIF SNIF
AH! HEY!
QUIT BUM SNIFFING.
I'M NOT A DOG, YOU KNOW!!
BAD!
SNIF SNIF SNIF
HEY, YOU...

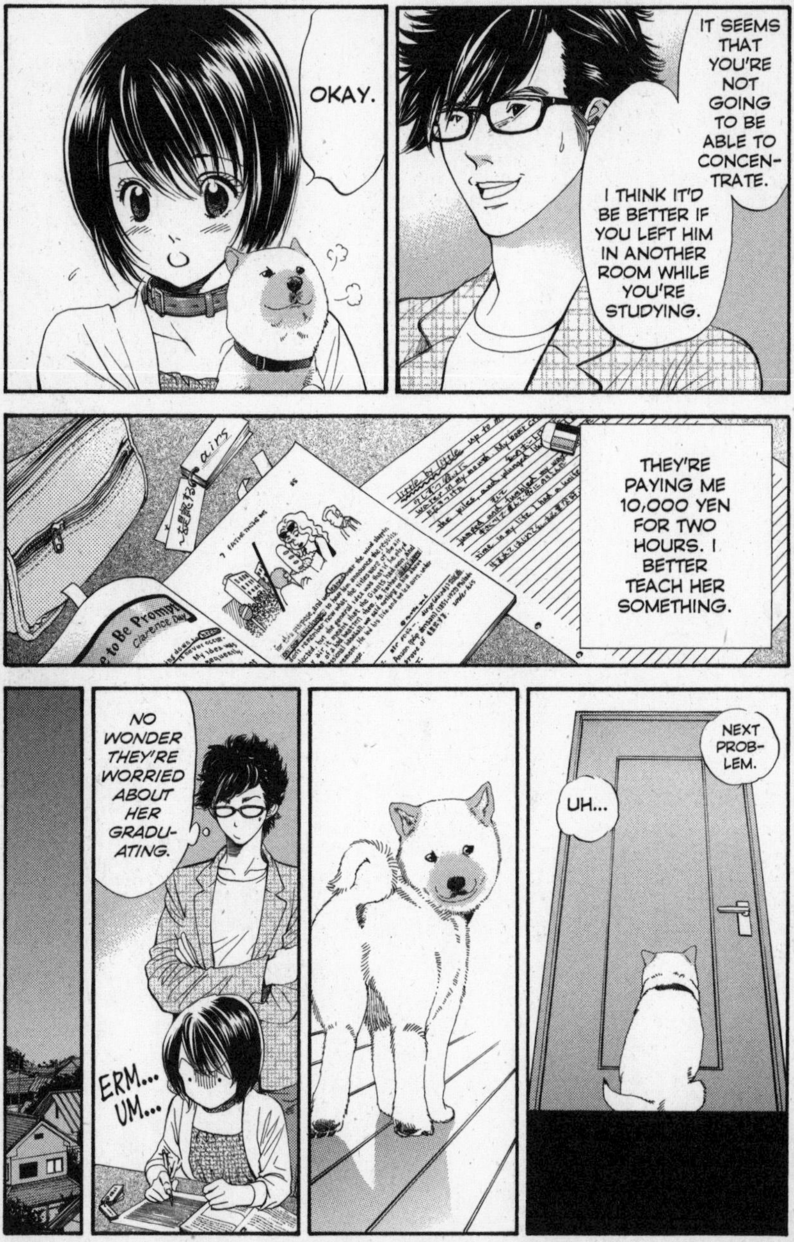
IT SEEMS THAT YOU'RE NOT GOING TO BE ABLE TO CONCENTRATE.
I THINK IT'D BE BETTER IF YOU LEFT HIM IN ANOTHER ROOM WHILE YOU'RE STUDYING.
OKAY.
THEY'RE PAYING ME 10,000 YEN FOR TWO HOURS. I BETTER TEACH HER SOMETHING.
NEXT PROB-LEM.
UH...
NO WONDER THEY'RE WORRIED ABOUT HER GRADU-ATING.
ERM... UM...

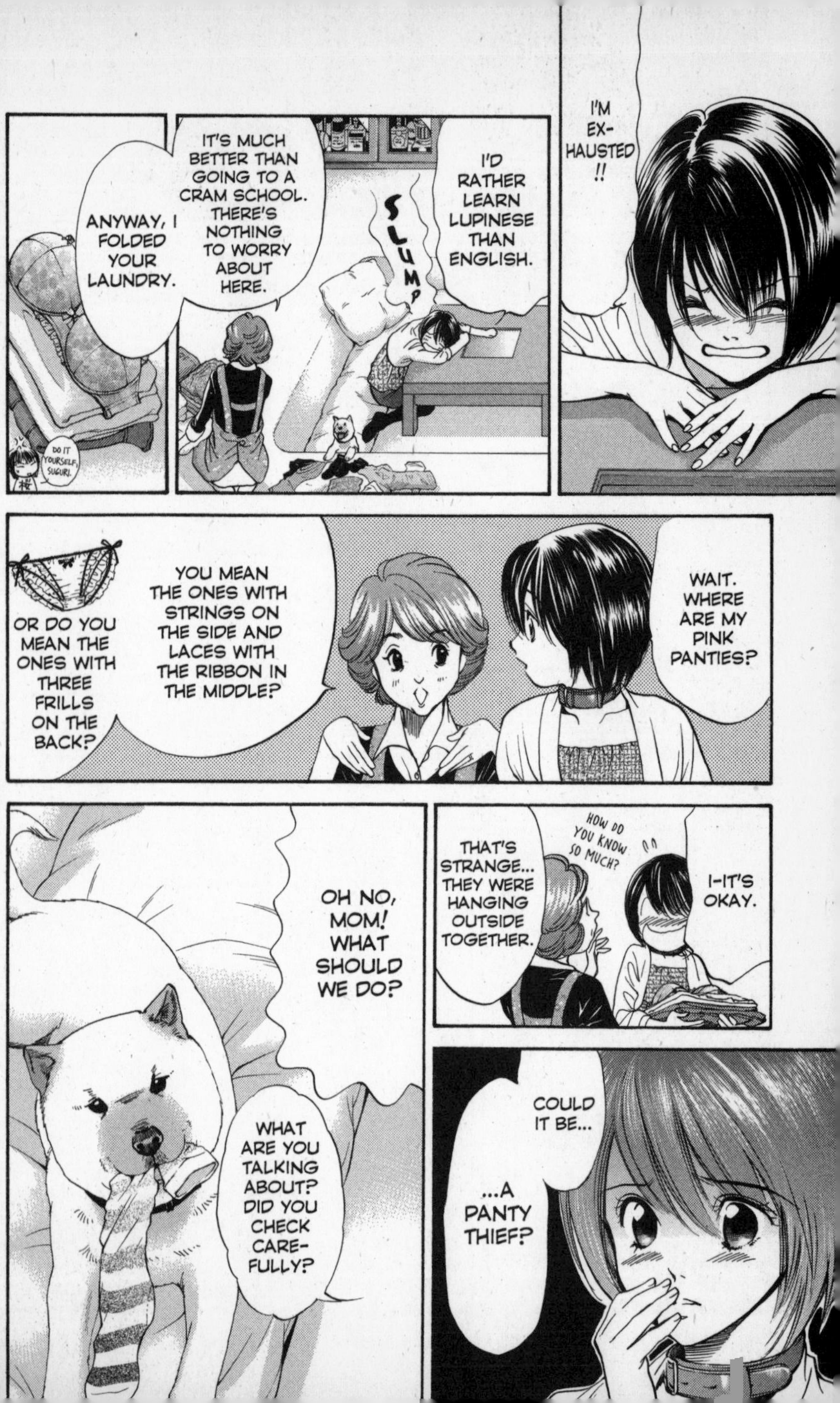
I'M EX-HAUSTED!!
I'D RATHER LEARN LUPINESE THAN ENGLISH.
SLUMP
IT'S MUCH BETTER THAN GOING TO A CRAM SCHOOL. THERE'S NOTHING TO WORRY ABOUT HERE.
ANYWAY, I FOLDED YOUR LAUNDRY.
DO IT YOURSELF, SUGURI.
WAIT. WHERE ARE MY PINK PANTIES?
YOU MEAN THE ONES WITH STRINGS ON THE SIDE AND LACES WITH THE RIBBON IN THE MIDDLE?
OR DO YOU MEAN THE ONES WITH THREE FRILLS ON THE BACK?
I-IT'S OKAY.
HOW DO YOU KNOW SO MUCH?
THAT'S STRANGE... THEY WERE HANGING OUTSIDE TOGETHER.
COULD IT BE...
...A PANTY THIEF?
OH NO, MOM! WHAT SHOULD WE DO?
WHAT ARE YOU TALKING ABOUT? DID YOU CHECK CAREFULLY?

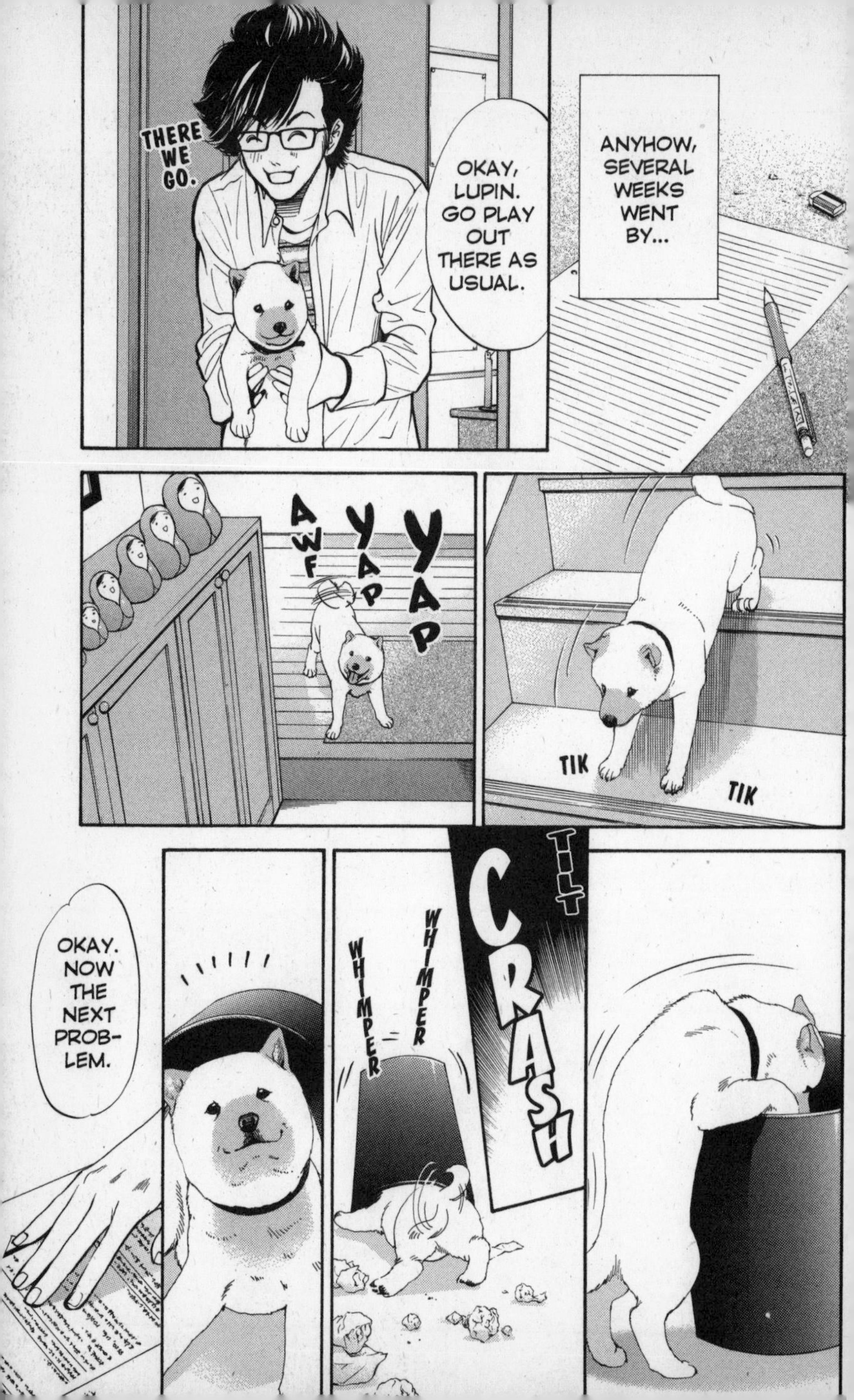
ANYHOW, SEVERAL WEEKS WENT BY...
OKAY, LUPIN. GO PLAY OUT THERE AS USUAL.
THERE WE GO.
TIK
TIK
YAP
YAP
AWF
TILT
CRASH
WHIMPER
WHIMPER
OKAY. NOW THE NEXT PROB-LEM.

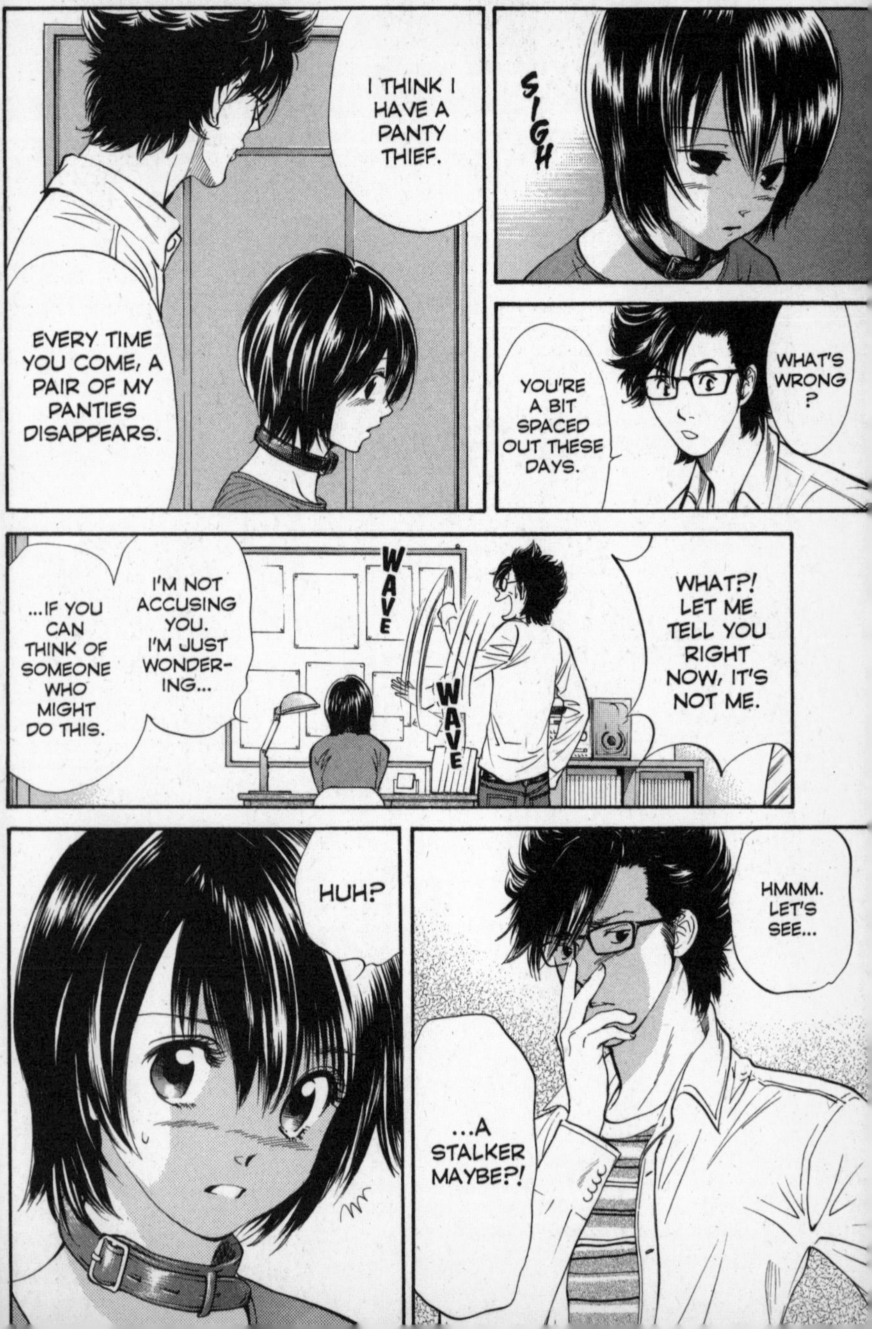
SIGH
WHAT'S WRONG?
YOU'RE A BIT SPACED OUT THESE DAYS.
I THINK I HAVE A PANTY THIEF.
EVERY TIME YOU COME, A PAIR OF MY PANTIES DISAPPEARS.
WHAT?! LET ME TELL YOU RIGHT NOW, IT'S NOT ME.
WAVE
WAVE
I'M NOT ACCUSING YOU. I'M JUST WONDERING...
...IF YOU CAN THINK OF SOMEONE WHO MIGHT DO THIS.
HMMM. LET'S SEE...
...A STALKER MAYBE?!
HUH?

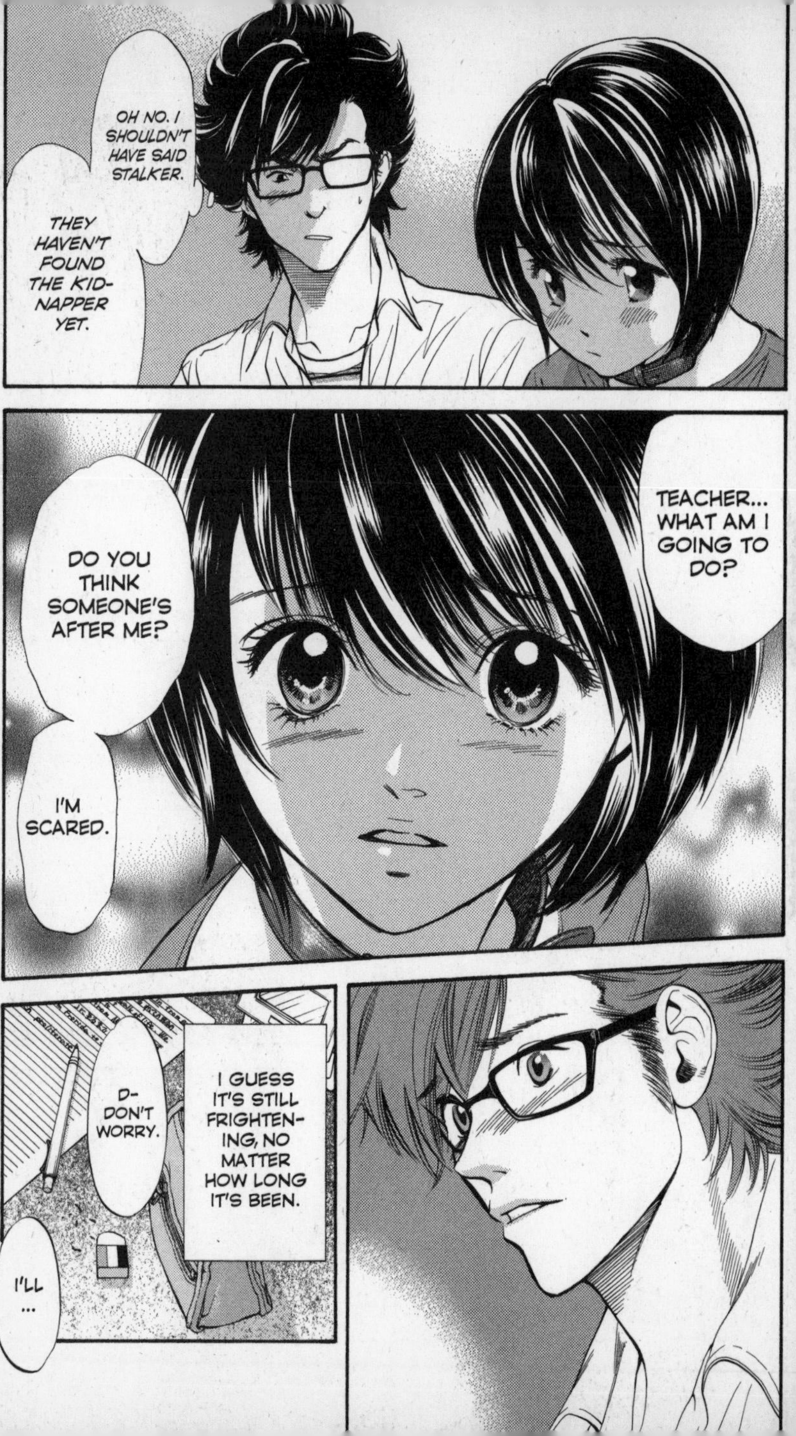
OH NO. I SHOULDN'T HAVE SAID STALKER.
THEY HAVEN'T FOUND THE KID-NAPPER YET.
TEACHER... WHAT AM I GOING TO DO?
DO YOU THINK SOMEONE'S AFTER ME?
I'M SCARED.
I GUESS IT'S STILL FRIGHTEN-ING, NO MATTER HOW LONG IT'S BEEN.
D-DON'T WORRY.
I'LL ...

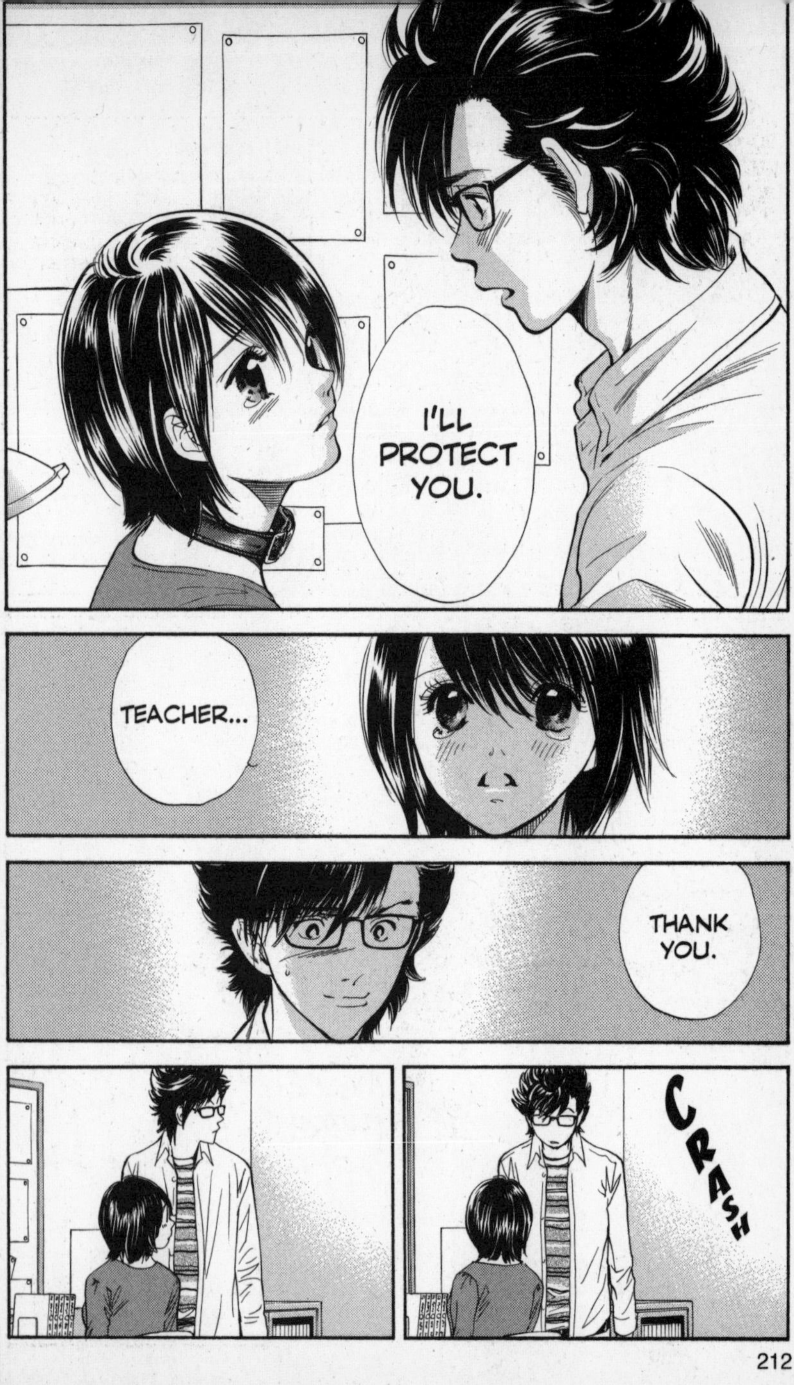
I'LL PROTECT YOU.
TEACHER...
THANK YOU.
CRASH

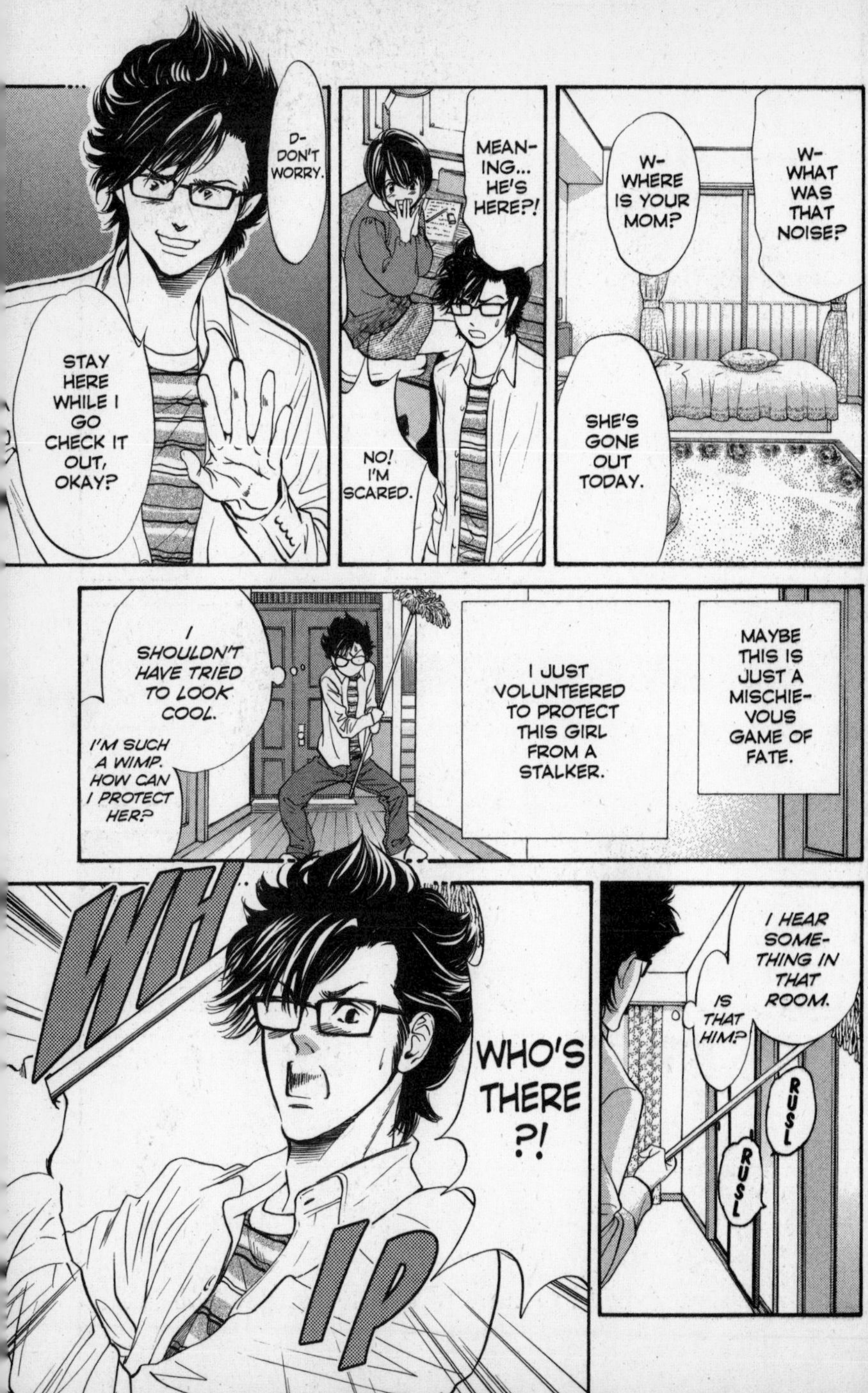
W-WHAT WAS THAT NOISE?
W-WHERE IS YOUR MOM?
SHE'S GONE OUT TODAY.
MEANING... HE'S HERE?!
NO! I'M SCARED.
D-DON'T WORRY.
STAY HERE WHILE I GO CHECK IT OUT, OKAY?
MAYBE THIS IS JUST A MISCHIEVOUS GAME OF FATE.
I JUST VOLUNTEERED TO PROTECT THIS GIRL FROM A STALKER.
I SHOULDN'T HAVE TRIED TO LOOK COOL.
I'M SUCH A WIMP. HOW CAN I PROTECT HER?
I HEAR SOMETHING IN THAT ROOM.
IS THAT HIM?
RUSL
RUSL
WHO'S THERE?!
WH
IP

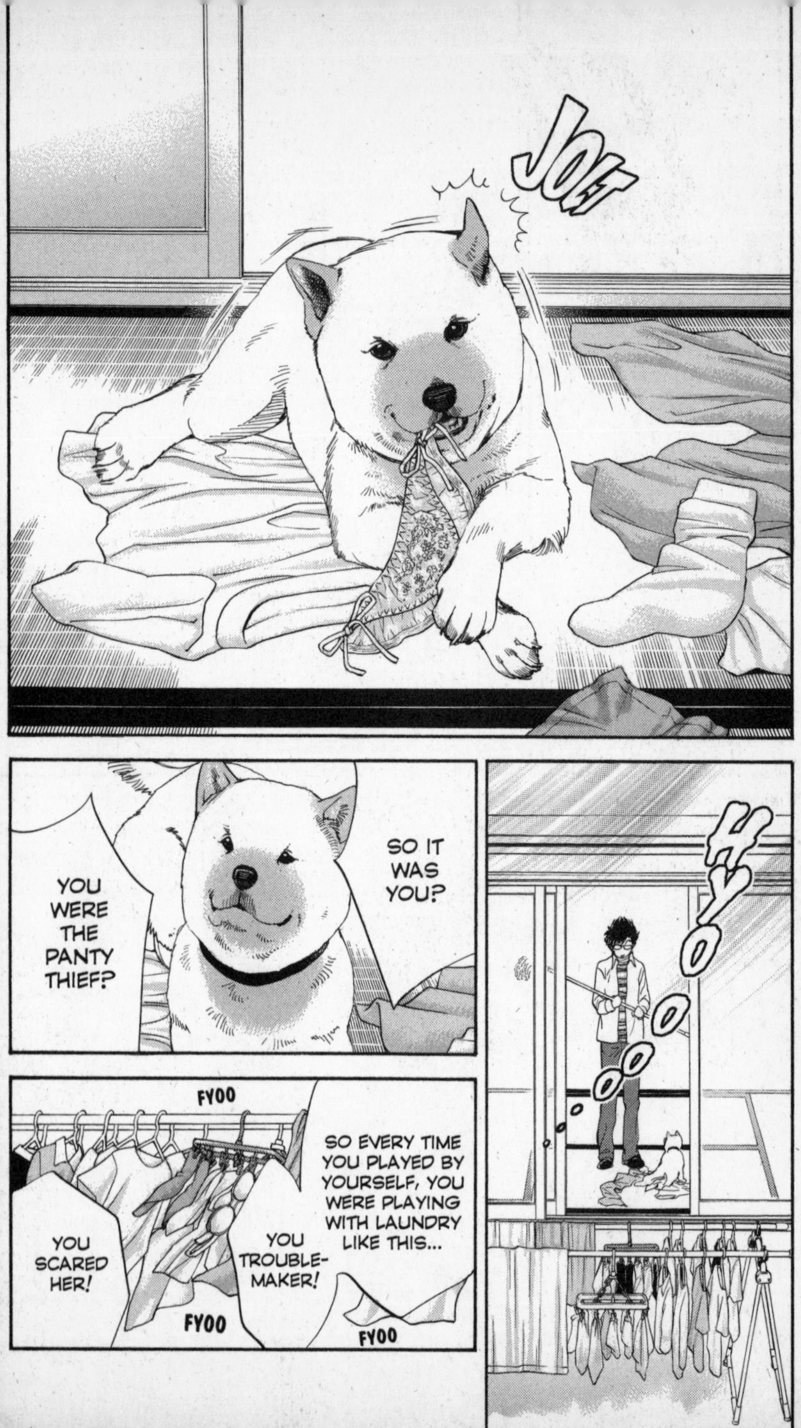
JOLT
HYOOOOOO
SO IT WAS YOU?
YOU WERE THE PANTY THIEF?
FYOO
SO EVERY TIME YOU PLAYED BY YOURSELF, YOU WERE PLAYING WITH LAUNDRY LIKE THIS...
YOU TROUBLE-MAKER!
YOU SCARED HER!
FYOO
FYOO

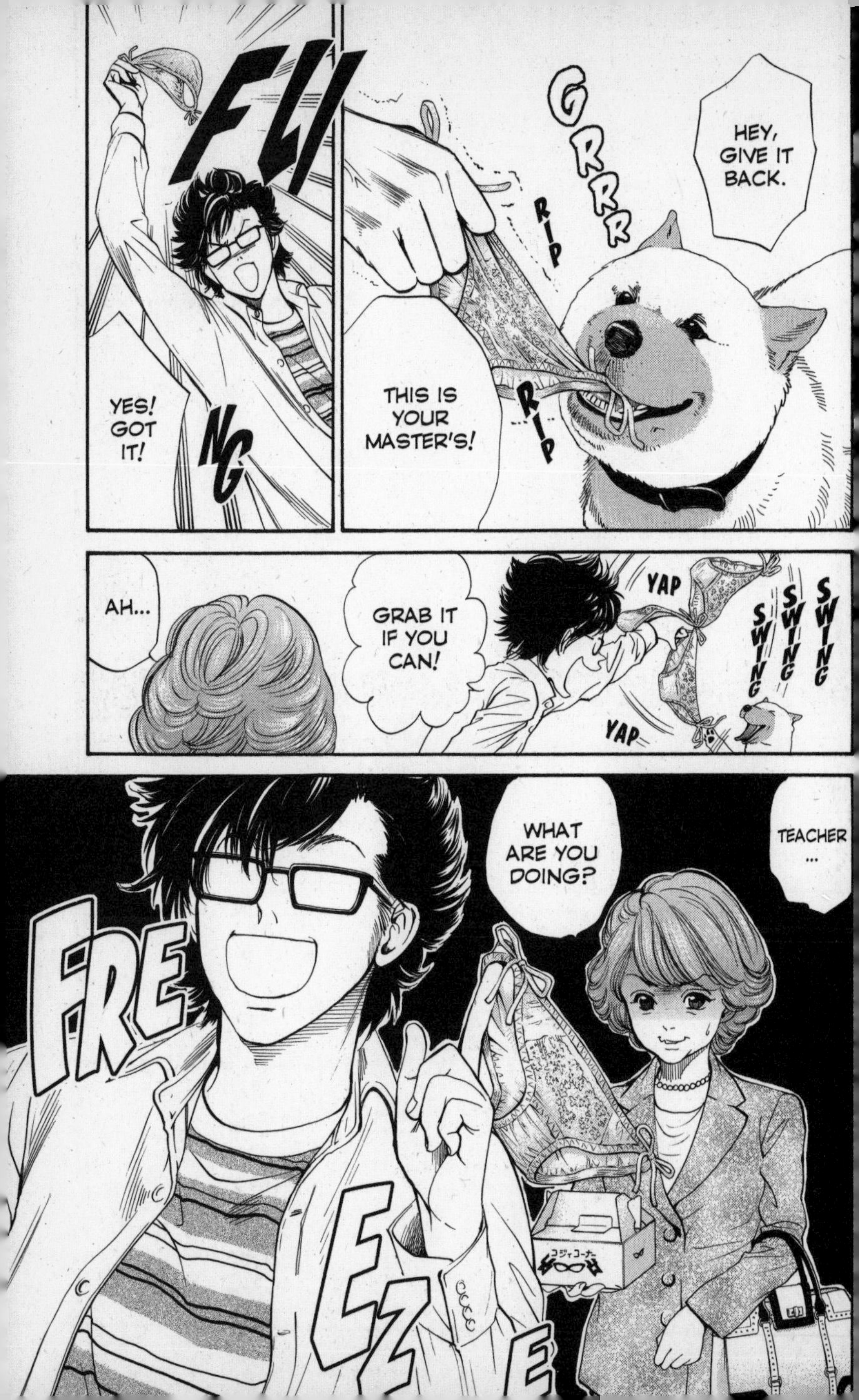
HEY, GIVE IT BACK.
GRRR
RIP
THIS IS YOUR MASTER'S!
RIP
FLI
NG
YES! GOT IT!
SWING
SWING
SWING
YAP
YAP
GRAB IT IF YOU CAN!
AH...
TEACHER ...
WHAT ARE YOU DOING?
FRE
EZE

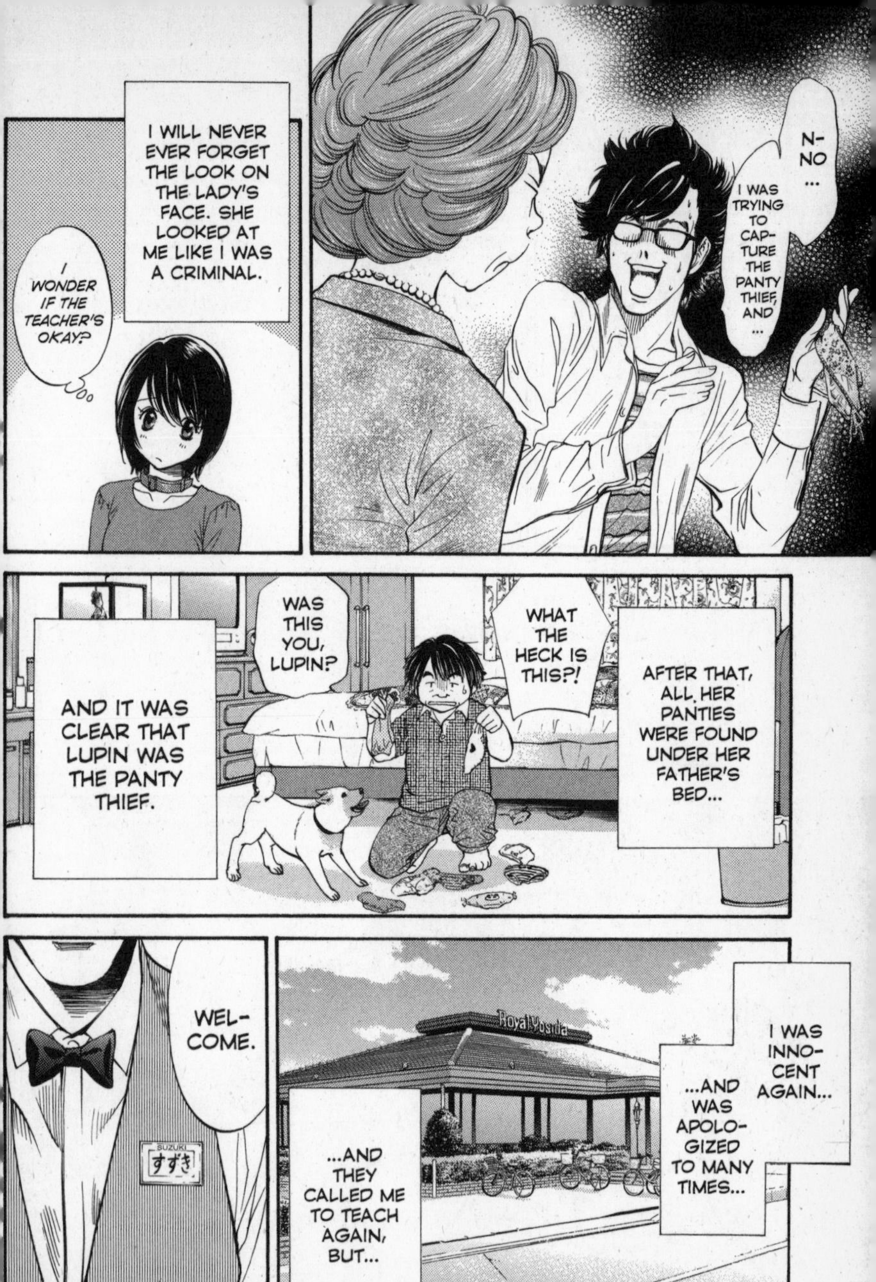
N-NO ...
I WAS TRYING TO CAPTURE THE PANTY THIEF, AND ...
I WILL NEVER EVER FORGET THE LOOK ON THE LADY'S FACE. SHE LOOKED AT ME LIKE I WAS A CRIMINAL.
I WONDER IF THE TEACHER'S OKAY?
AFTER THAT, ALL HER PANTIES WERE FOUND UNDER HER FATHER'S BED...
WHAT THE HECK IS THIS?!
WAS THIS YOU, LUPIN?
AND IT WAS CLEAR THAT LUPIN WAS THE PANTY THIEF.
I WAS INNOCENT AGAIN...
...AND WAS APOLOGIZED TO MANY TIMES...
...AND THEY CALLED ME TO TEACH AGAIN, BUT...
WELCOME.
SUZUKI
すずき

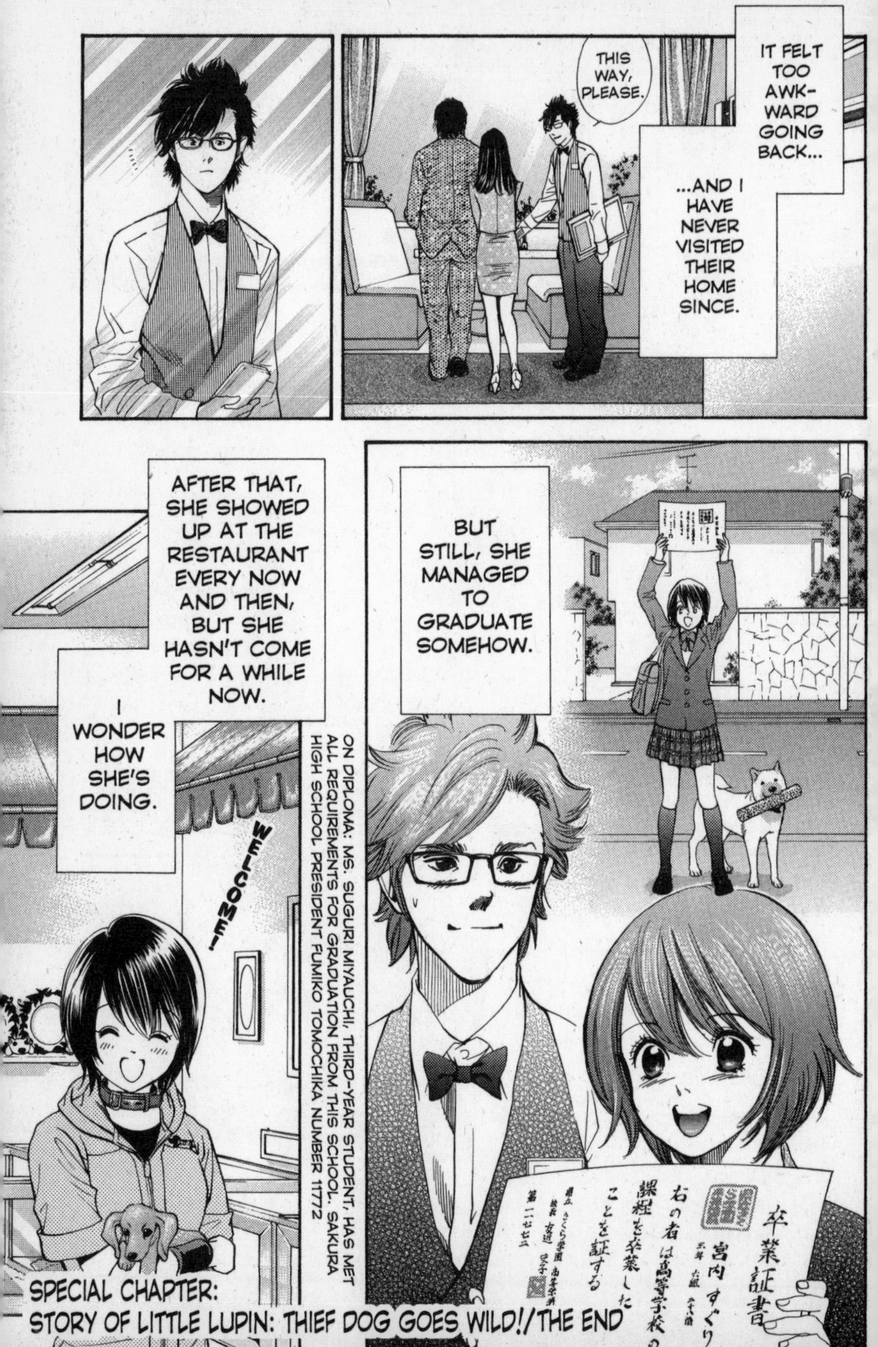
IT FELT TOO AWK-WARD GOING BACK...
THIS WAY, PLEASE.
...AND I HAVE NEVER VISITED THEIR HOME SINCE.
BUT STILL, SHE MANAGED TO GRADUATE SOMEHOW.
ON DIPLOMA: MS. SUGURI MIYAUCHI, THIRD-YEAR STUDENT, HAS MET ALL REQUIREMENTS FOR GRADUATION FROM THIS SCHOOL. SAKURA HIGH SCHOOL PRESIDENT FUMIKO TOMOCHIKA NUMBER 1772
AFTER THAT, SHE SHOWED UP AT THE RESTAURANT EVERY NOW AND THEN, BUT SHE HASN'T COME FOR A WHILE NOW.
I WONDER HOW SHE'S DOING.
WELCOME!
SPECIAL CHAPTER:
STORY OF LITTLE LUPIN: THIEF DOG GOES WILD!/THE END

INUBAKA

Everybody's Crazy for Dogs!

From Ae-san in Hyogo Prefecture

🐾 Miu-chan (Shiba)

Huh!! Σ(˚ ∇ ˚ ✳) Look at the two look-alikes! It's adorable. Although born on the "Day for Cats," February 22, I guess he preferred playing around in the snow?

In a traditional Japanese song, the lyrics say, "When snow falls, cats like to curl up under a kotatsu, while dogs like to play outside in the snow." –Editor

Yukiya Sakuragi

Not a snowman, but a snowdog!! Even the shape of the eyes is similar. She sits like a very smart dog. Although I hear there may be some rivalry with the snowdog next door?!

From Hashiguchi-san
in Saitama Prefecture

🐾 Pudding-chan (Chihuahua)

Pudding-chan loves the river. It was a hot day that day, so she looks so happy☆. It's like she's smiling. Surprisingly, she hates water that comes out of showers. Only Pudding knows the difference…

Yukiya Sakuragi

She really does look happy swimming!
Having the taste of swimming in a river, maybe she's not willing to downgrade to shower water? I wonder…

From Miyaoka-san in Kyoto

🐾 Sara-chan (Jack Russell terrier)

It had been five years since the dog her owner grew up with was lost to a car accident. Sara entered her life, and that all changed. It was love at first sight. I hope you live a powerfully long life for the other doggy that went up to Heaven, Sara-chan.

Yukiya Sakuragi

No matter how busy you get, your dog can always bring you some energy. I heard that the stamina of a Jack Russell terrier is incredible. I guess the best we can do is try to keep up with their energy level, right? (laugh)

From Ueda-san in Osaka

🐾 (Right) Bubu-kun (Left) Leo-kun
(Kishu and Pomeranian)

Bubu-kun's proud of his beautiful white coat. Plus, he's a big cat lover and will dash after one in the middle of a walk. But because he's so shy, when his little brother Leo-kun comes along to invite him to play, he shies away. But I'm sure eventually you'll play together a lot and cause all kinds of trouble for your owners, right, you two?

Yukiya Sakuragi

When I saw this picture, they looked like Lupin and Czerny-chan to me. (laugh) They seem to have a relationship like my Blanc and Jetta! At first my Blanc was completely powerless to his little brother Jetta. It worried me at first, but now they like to get into wrestling matches. I hope they stay close friends.

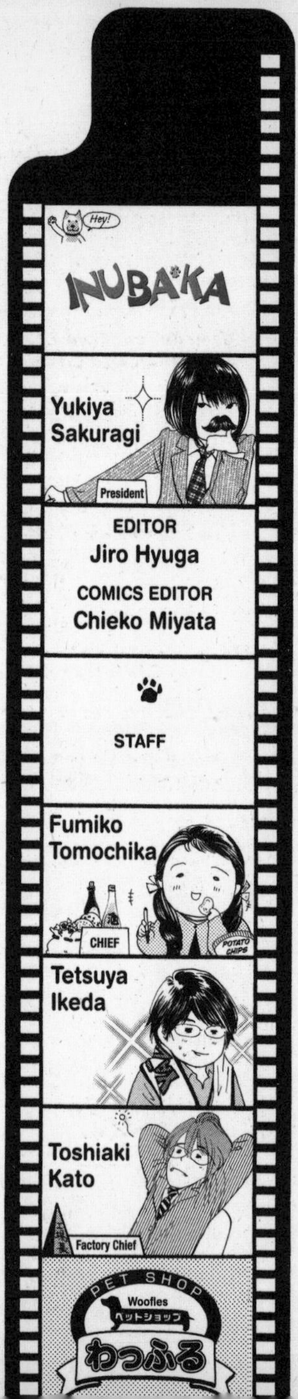
Hey!
INUBA*KA
Yukiya
Sakuragi
President
EDITOR
Jiro Hyuga
COMICS EDITOR
Chieko Miyata
STAFF
Fumiko
Tomochika
CHIEF
POTATO CHIPS
Tetsuya
Ikeda
Toshiaki
Kato
Factory Chief
PET SHOP
Woofles
ペットショップ
わっふる

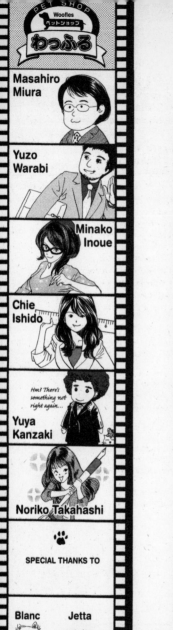

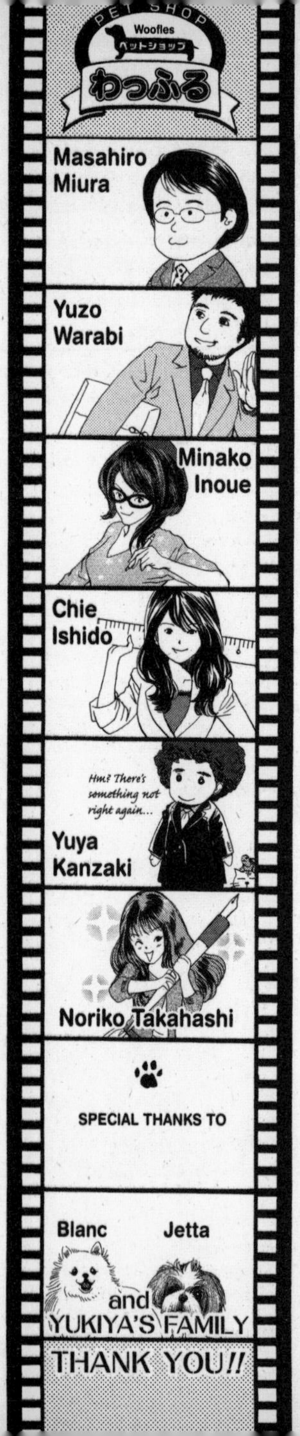
PET SHOP
Woofles
ペットショップ
わっふる
Masahiro
Miura
Yuzo
Warabi
Minako
Inoue
Chie
Ishido
Hm? There's something not right again...
Yuya
Kanzaki
Noriko Takahashi
SPECIAL THANKS TO
Blanc
Jetta
and
YUKIYA'S FAMILY
THANK YOU!!

Inubaka
Crazy for Dogs
Vol. #14
VIZ Media Edition

Story and Art by
Yukiya Sakuragi

Translation/Maya Robinson, HC Language Solutions, Inc.
English Adaptation/Ian Reid, HC Language Solutions, Inc.
Touch-up Art & Lettering/Kelle Hahn
Cover & Interior Design/Hidemi Dunn
Editor/Carrie Shepherd

VP, Production/Alvin Lu
VP, Publishing Licensing/Rika Inouye
VP, Sales & Product Marketing/Gonzalo Ferreyra
VP, Creative/Linda Espinosa
Publisher/Hyoe Narita

INUBAKA © 2004 by Yukiya Sakuragi.
All rights reserved. First published in Japan in 2004 by SHUEISHA Inc., Tokyo.
English translation rights arranged by SHUEISHA Inc.

Printed in the U.S.A.

Published by VIZ Media, LLC
P.O. Box 77010
San Francisco, CA 94107

10 9 8 7 6 5 4 3 2 1
First printing, October 2009

www.viz.com
store.viz.com

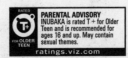

At Your Indentured Service

Hayate's parents are bad with money, so they sell his organs to pay their debts. Hayate doesn't like this plan, so he comes up with a new one—kidnap and ransom a girl from a wealthy family. Solid plan… so how did he end up as her butler?

Find out in *Hayate the Combat Butler*—
buy the manga at store.viz.com!

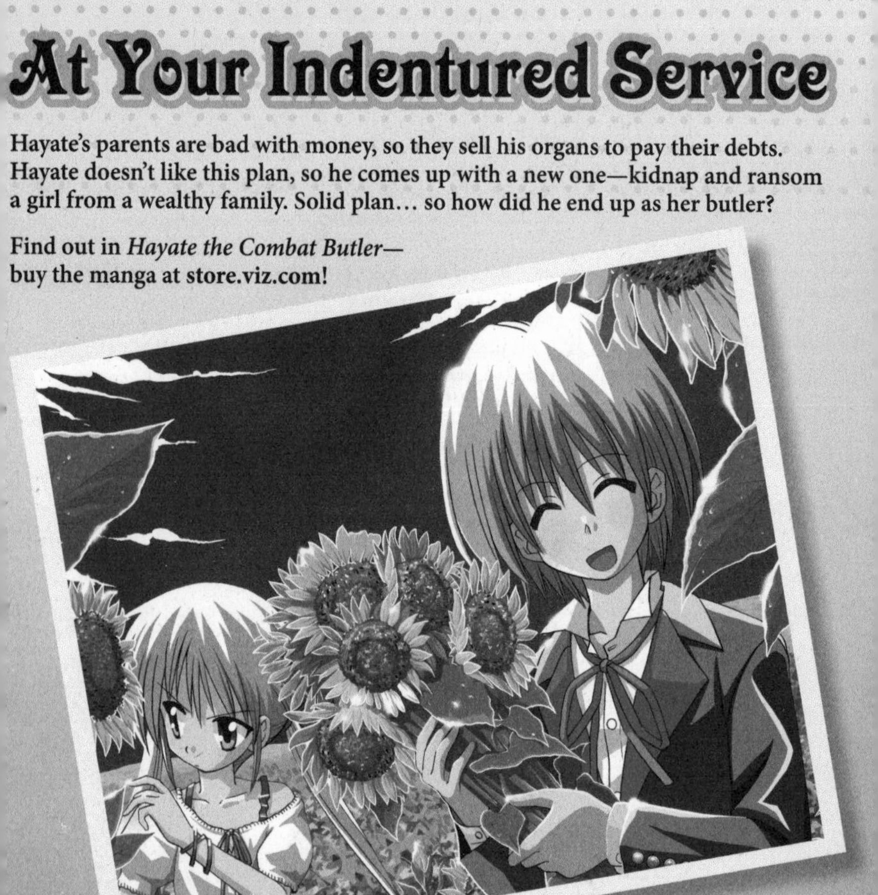

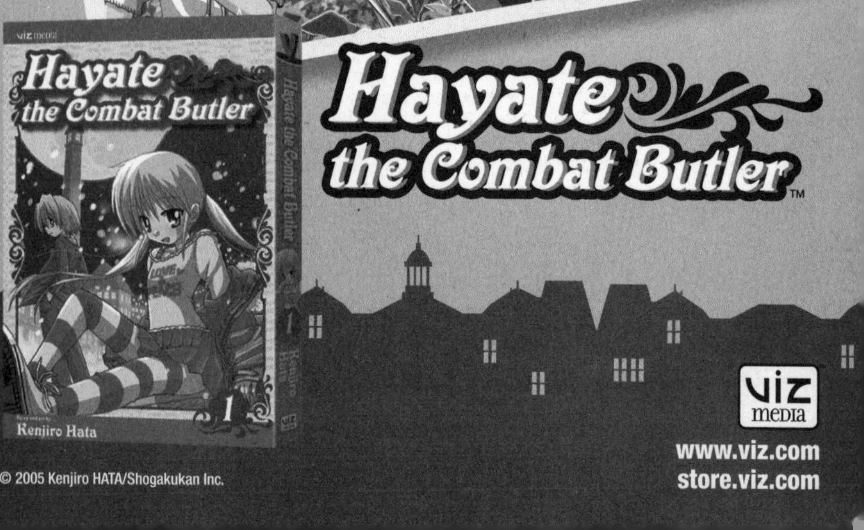
viz media
Hayate the Combat Butler
Hayate the Combat Butler
1
Kenjiro Hata

Hayate the Combat Butler™

viz media

www.viz.com
store.viz.com

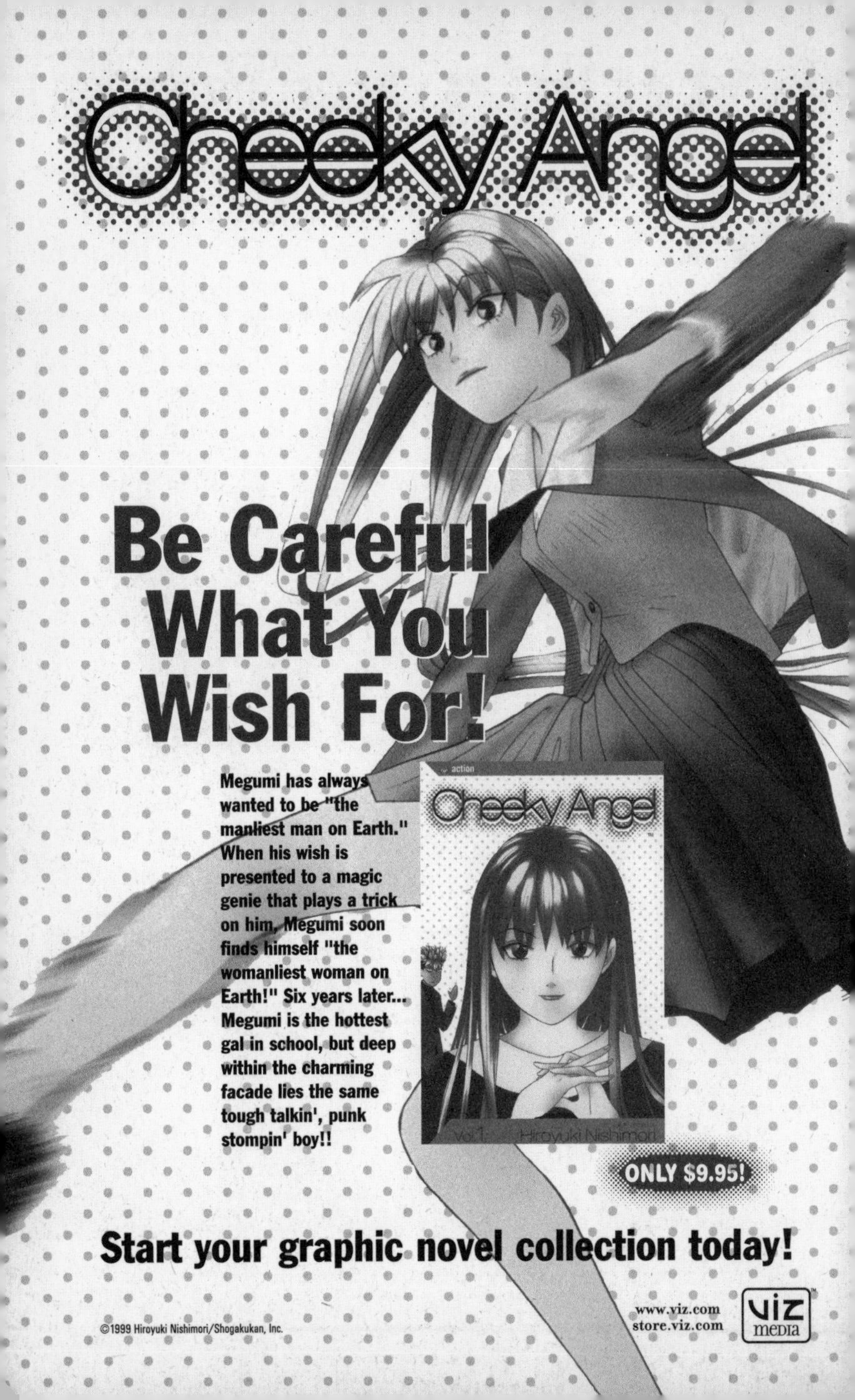
Cheeky Angel
Be Careful What You Wish For!
Megumi has always wanted to be "the manliest man on Earth." When his wish is presented to a magic genie that plays a trick on him, Megumi soon finds himself "the womanliest woman on Earth!" Six years later... Megumi is the hottest gal in school, but deep within the charming facade lies the same tough talkin', punk stompin' boy!!
action
Cheeky Angel
Vol.1 Hiroyuki Nishimori
ONLY $9.95!
Start your graphic novel collection today!
©1999 Hiroyuki Nishimori/Shogakukan, Inc.
www.viz.com
store.viz.com
VIZ MEDIA